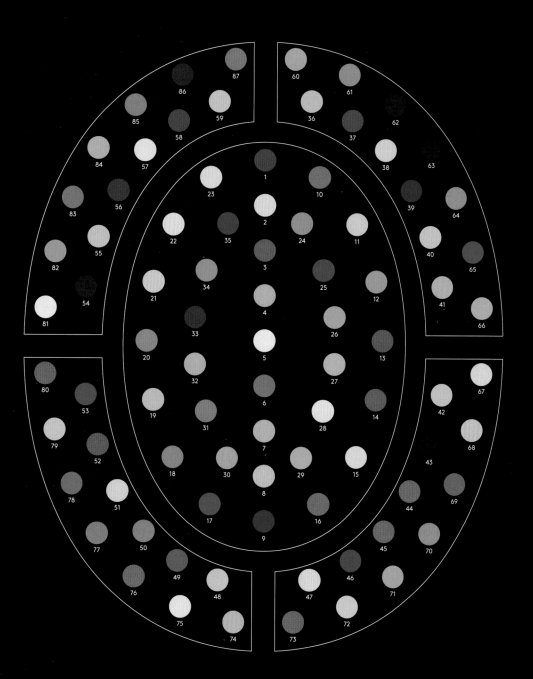

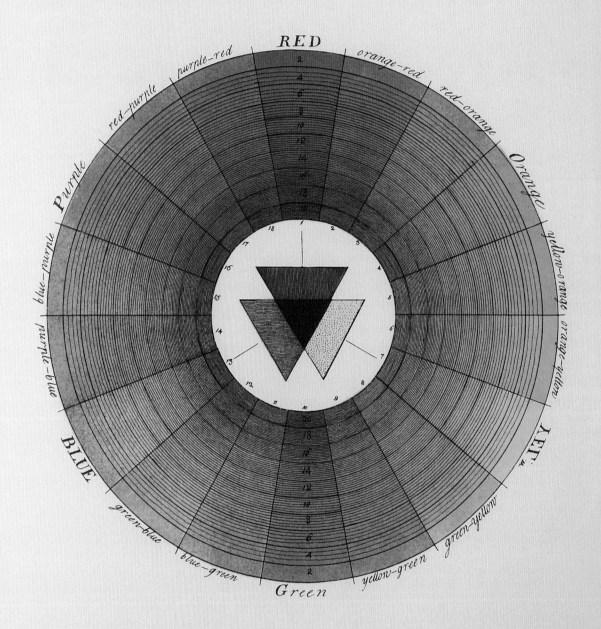

PATRICK BATY

THE ANATOMY OF COLOR

THE STORY OF HERITAGE PAINTS AND PIGMENTS

1,500+ IMAGES

FRONTISPIECE: EIGHTY-SEVEN COLORS DERIVED FROM *HISTORICAL COLOR GUIDE* (1938) BY ELIZABETH BURRIS-MEYER
OPPOSITE: COLOR WHEEL FROM *THE NATURAL SYSTEM OF COLOURS* (1766) BY MOSES HARRIS

1. IMPERIAL	19. CIEL	37. GERANIUM	55. LOTUS	73. FLAME
2. LIME	20. CANIS	38. COLONIAL YELLOW	56. GRIFFIN	74. JADE
3. INFANTA	21. INCA	39. JESSE	57. EVENING	75. BEIGE
4. GOLD	22. CHILCA	40. GOLD	58. ICE	76. MULBERRY
5. PEARL	23. PIZARRO	41. MALACHITE	59. MIST	77. MUMMY
6. LAUREL	24. FLAMINGO	42. TOPAZ	60. CELESTIAL	78. RESEDA
7. MARIE	25. PEACE	43. EBONY	61. MARIGOLD	79. MYRTLE
8. HOPE	26. CACTUS BLOOM	44. POMEGRANATE	62. SUNG	80. LE GREC
9. 1820	27. SUNSET	45. MONKEY	63. PRAYER	81. L'ARGENT
10. LIGHT	28. PEON	46. SAPPHIRE	64. IVY	82. SCARAB
11. TARTAR	29. ELECTRIC	47. BISQUE	65. COBALT	83. VIOLETTE
12. JOSEPH	30. FEAR	48. ALI BABA	66. WATTEAU	84. LEAF
13. WINE	31. POMPEY	49. BERYL	67. AVRIL	85. L'EGYPTIENNE
14. PASSION	32. JASPER	50. LAVENDER	68. L'AMOUR	86. OMBRE
15. AURORA	33. MADONNA	51. VESTA	69. COBRA	87. FIRE
16. SPRING GARDEN	34. WRATH	52. MARY	70. BREADFRUIT	
17. BEAU	35. PINE	53. CHANSON	71. PALMETTE	
18. MAYFAIR	36. FORGET-ME-NOT	54. PLUSH	72. DHAK	

[FRONT COVER] Color samples from *A Tint Book of Historical Colours* (1934), Thomas Parsons.
[BACK COVER] Color samples from "Cabot Tower" ready mixed paints (1930s).

Thames & Hudson

SULPHUR YELLOW

EQUIVALENT TO
BRITISH COLOUR COUNCIL — Sulphur B.C.C. 1/2, Lemon Yellow 33
RIDGWAY
REPERTOIRE
OSTWALD — XIV 1 pa

History:
Foreign Synonyms:
Horticultural Examples:

CANARY YELLOW

EQUIVALENT TO
BRITISH COLOUR COUNCIL — Barium Yellow B.C.C. 1/3
RIDGWAY
REPERTOIRE
OSTWALD — Jaune Primevere 19:4

History:
Foreign Synonyms:
Horticultural Examples:

AUREOLIN

EQUIVALENT TO
BRITISH COLOUR COUNCIL — Nil
RIDGWAY
REPERTOIRE
OSTWALD

History:
Foreign Synonyms:
Horticultural Examples:

LEMON YELLOW

EQUIVALENT TO
BRITISH COLOUR COUNCIL — Lemon B.C.C. 21
RIDGWAY
REPERTOIRE — Jaune d'Austalieu 22:4
OSTWALD — XIV 2 pa

History:
Foreign Synonyms:
Horticultural Examples:

BUTTERCUP YELLOW

EQUIVALENT TO
BRITISH COLOUR COUNCIL — Buttercup B.C.C. 53
RIDGWAY — Light Cadmium 19
REPERTOIRE
OSTWALD — Jaune de Cadmium 47:3

History:
Foreign Synonyms:
Horticultural Examples:

INDIAN YELLOW

EQUIVALENT TO
BRITISH COLOUR COUNCIL — Indian Yellow B.C.C. 6
RIDGWAY
REPERTOIRE
OSTWALD — Jaune indien 37:4

History:
Foreign Synonyms:
Horticultural Examples:

SAFFRON YELLOW
(Synonym: Cadmium Yellow)

EQUIVALENT TO
BRITISH COLOUR COUNCIL — Saffron B.C.C. 14
RIDGWAY — Cadmium Yellow 17
REPERTOIRE
OSTWALD — Jaune de Cadmium 45:4

History:
Foreign Synonyms:
Horticultural Examples:

FIRE RED

EQUIVALENT TO
BRITISH COLOUR COUNCIL — Nil
RIDGWAY — Nil
REPERTOIRE — Rouge Feu 78:3
OSTWALD

History:
Foreign Synonyms:
Horticultural Examples:

POPPY RED

EQUIVALENT TO
BRITISH COLOUR COUNCIL — Poppy B.C.C. 97
RIDGWAY — Scarlet 3
REPERTOIRE — Rouge Grenadier 82:1
OSTWALD — XIV 6 pa

History:
Foreign Synonyms:
Horticultural Examples:

MANDARIN RED

EQUIVALENT TO
BRITISH COLOUR COUNCIL — Nil
RIDGWAY
REPERTOIRE — Rouge nopaline 83:1 & 83:3
OSTWALD

History:
Foreign Synonyms:
Horticultural Examples:

VERMILION

EQUIVALENT TO
BRITISH COLOUR COUNCIL — Nil
RIDGWAY
REPERTOIRE — Rouge de Cinnabarre 88:4
OSTWALD

History:
Foreign Synonyms:
Horticultural Examples:

SCARLET

EQUIVALENT TO
BRITISH COLOUR COUNCIL — Nil
RIDGWAY — Starlex Red 3
REPERTOIRE — Rouge vermillon 87:2
OSTWALD

History:
Foreign Synonyms:
Horticultural Examples:

GERANIUM LAKE

EQUIVALENT TO
BRITISH COLOUR COUNCIL — Nil
RIDGWAY — Spectrum Red 1
REPERTOIRE — Rouge Cardinal 112:1, Laque Geranium 89:1
OSTWALD — XIV 7 pa

History:
Foreign Synonyms:
Horticultural Examples:

CARMINE

EQUIVALENT TO
BRITISH COLOUR COUNCIL — Nil
RIDGWAY
REPERTOIRE — Carmine de Cochenille 116:3
OSTWALD

History:
Foreign Synonyms:
Horticultural Examples:

RHODAMINE PURPLE

EQUIVALENT TO
BRITISH COLOUR COUNCIL — Nil
RIDGWAY — Rhodamine Purple 67
REPERTOIRE
OSTWALD

History:
Foreign Synonyms:
Horticultural Examples:

CYCLAMEN PURPLE

EQUIVALENT TO
BRITISH COLOUR COUNCIL — Nil
RIDGWAY
REPERTOIRE — Purple (Tyr) 63
OSTWALD — XIV 10 pa

History:
Foreign Synonyms:
Horticultural Examples:

ORCHID PURPLE

EQUIVALENT TO
BRITISH COLOUR COUNCIL — Nil
RIDGWAY
REPERTOIRE
OSTWALD

History:
Foreign Synonyms:
Horticultural Examples:

PETUNIA PURPLE

EQUIVALENT TO
BRITISH COLOUR COUNCIL — Petunia B.C.C. 108
RIDGWAY
REPERTOIRE
OSTWALD

History:
Foreign Synonyms:
Horticultural Examples:

IMPERIAL PURPLE

EQUIVALENT TO
BRITISH COLOUR COUNCIL — Imperial Purple B.C.C. 109
RIDGWAY — Violet Purple 63
REPERTOIRE
OSTWALD — XIV 11 pa

History:
Foreign Synonyms:
Horticultural Examples:

BISHOPS VIOLET

EQUIVALENT TO
BRITISH COLOUR COUNCIL — Nil
RIDGWAY
REPERTOIRE
OSTWALD

History:
Foreign Synonyms:
Horticultural Examples:

AMETHYST VIOLET

EQUIVALENT TO
BRITISH COLOUR COUNCIL — Nil
RIDGWAY — Amethyst Violet 61
REPERTOIRE — Nil
OSTWALD

History:
Foreign Synonyms:
Horticultural Examples:

FRENCH BLUE

EQUIVALENT TO
BRITISH COLOUR COUNCIL — Nil
RIDGWAY — Bradley's Blue 51
REPERTOIRE
OSTWALD

History:
Foreign Synonyms:
Horticultural Examples:

COBALT BLUE

EQUIVALENT TO
BRITISH COLOUR COUNCIL — Nil
RIDGWAY — Spectrum Blue 49
REPERTOIRE — Nil
OSTWALD — XIV 14 pa

History:
Foreign Synonyms:
Horticultural Examples:

SPECTRUM BLUE

EQUIVALENT TO
BRITISH COLOUR COUNCIL — Spectrum Blue B.C.C. 84
RIDGWAY — Nil
REPERTOIRE — Nil
OSTWALD

History:
Foreign Synonyms:
Horticultural Examples:

CERULEIN BLUE

EQUIVALENT TO
BRITISH COLOUR COUNCIL — Nil
RIDGWAY — Methyl Blue 47
REPERTOIRE
OSTWALD

History:
Foreign Synonyms:
Horticultural Examples:

ORIENTAL BLUE

EQUIVALENT TO
BRITISH COLOUR COUNCIL — Nil
RIDGWAY — Nil
REPERTOIRE
OSTWALD

History:
Foreign Synonyms:
Horticultural Examples:

ENAMEL BLUE

EQUIVALENT TO
BRITISH COLOUR COUNCIL — Nil
RIDGWAY — Cerulean Blue 45
REPERTOIRE
OSTWALD — XIV 15 pa

History:
Foreign Synonyms:
Horticultural Examples:

PORCELAIN BLUE

EQUIVALENT TO
BRITISH COLOUR COUNCIL — Nil
RIDGWAY
REPERTOIRE
OSTWALD

History:
Foreign Synonyms:
Horticultural Examples:

NICKEL GREEN

EQUIVALENT TO
BRITISH COLOUR COUNCIL — Nil
RIDGWAY — Nil
REPERTOIRE — Nil
OSTWALD

History:
Foreign Synonyms:
Horticultural Examples:

PARIS GREEN

EQUIVALENT TO
BRITISH COLOUR COUNCIL — Nil
RIDGWAY — Emerald Green 35
REPERTOIRE — Nil
OSTWALD — XIV 28 pa

History:
Foreign Synonyms:
Horticultural Examples:

CYPRUS GREEN

EQUIVALENT TO
BRITISH COLOUR COUNCIL — Nil
RIDGWAY
REPERTOIRE
OSTWALD

History:
Foreign Synonyms:
Horticultural Examples:

AGATHIA GREEN

EQUIVALENT TO
BRITISH COLOUR COUNCIL — Nil
RIDGWAY
REPERTOIRE
OSTWALD

History:
Foreign Synonyms:
Horticultural Examples:

PEA GREEN

EQUIVALENT TO
BRITISH COLOUR COUNCIL — Pea Green B.C.C. 172
RIDGWAY — Yellow Green 51
REPERTOIRE
OSTWALD

History:
Foreign Synonyms:
Horticultural Examples:

SAP GREEN

EQUIVALENT TO
BRITISH COLOUR COUNCIL — Nil
RIDGWAY — Bright Green Yellow 29
REPERTOIRE
OSTWALD — XIV 24 pa

History:
Foreign Synonyms:
Horticultural Examples:

URANIUM GREEN

EQUIVALENT TO
BRITISH COLOUR COUNCIL — Nil
RIDGWAY — Greenish Yellow 33
REPERTOIRE
OSTWALD

History:
Foreign Synonyms:
Horticultural Examples:

CARROT RED

EQUIVALENT TO
BRITISH COLOUR COUNCIL — Carrot B.C.C. 144
RIDGWAY — Nil
REPERTOIRE — Nil
OSTWALD

History:
Foreign Synonyms:
Horticultural Examples:

CHINESE CORAL

EQUIVALENT TO
BRITISH COLOUR COUNCIL — Nil
RIDGWAY — Nil
REPERTOIRE — Nil
OSTWALD

History:
Foreign Synonyms:
Horticultural Examples:

SHRIMP RED
(Synonym: Peter Red)

EQUIVALENT TO
BRITISH COLOUR COUNCIL — Nil
RIDGWAY — Nil
REPERTOIRE — Rouge Crevette 75:4
OSTWALD

History:
Foreign Synonyms:
Horticultural Examples:

AZALEA PINK

EQUIVALENT TO
BRITISH COLOUR COUNCIL — Nil
RIDGWAY — Nil
REPERTOIRE — Fraise écrasé 109:4, Rose Saumoné 124:4
OSTWALD — X 6 Ia

History:
Foreign Synonyms:
Horticultural Examples:

CARMINE ROSE

EQUIVALENT TO
BRITISH COLOUR COUNCIL — Nil
RIDGWAY — Nil
REPERTOIRE — Laque Geranium 112:1, Rose Pourpré 105:4
OSTWALD

History:
Foreign Synonyms:
Horticultural Examples:

NEYRON ROSE

EQUIVALENT TO
BRITISH COLOUR COUNCIL — Neyron Rose B.C.C. 34
RIDGWAY — Nil
REPERTOIRE — Nil
OSTWALD — X 8 Ia

History:
Foreign Synonyms:
Horticultural Examples:

PHLOX PINK

EQUIVALENT TO
BRITISH COLOUR COUNCIL — Nil
RIDGWAY — Rose Color 11:6
REPERTOIRE — Fuchsia 140:3
OSTWALD

History:
Foreign Synonyms:
Horticultural Examples:

CADMIUM ORANGE

TANGERINE ORANGE

ORPIMENT ORANGE

MARIGOLD ORANGE

ORANGE

SATURN RED

NASTURTIUM RED

CRIMSON

ROSE MADDER

TYRIAN ROSE

ROSE BENGAL

SOLFERINO PURPLE

MAGENTA

FUCHSIA PURPLE

VIOLET

CAMPANULA VIOLET

ASTER VIOLET

METHYL VIOLET

HYACINTH BLUE

LOBELIA BLUE

GENTIAN BLUE

KINGFISHER BLUE

INDIAN BLUE

CAPRI BLUE

LANGITE GREEN

JADE GREEN

VIRIDIAN GREEN

CHRYSOCOLLA GREEN

DRESDEN YELLOW

PRIMROSE YELLOW

EMPIRE YELLOW

STRAW YELLOW

CHINESE YELLOW

MAIZE YELLOW

APRICOT

FUCHSINE PINK

MALLOW PURPLE

MAUVE

COBALT VIOLET

HELIOTROPE

VERONICA VIOLET

FLAX BLUE

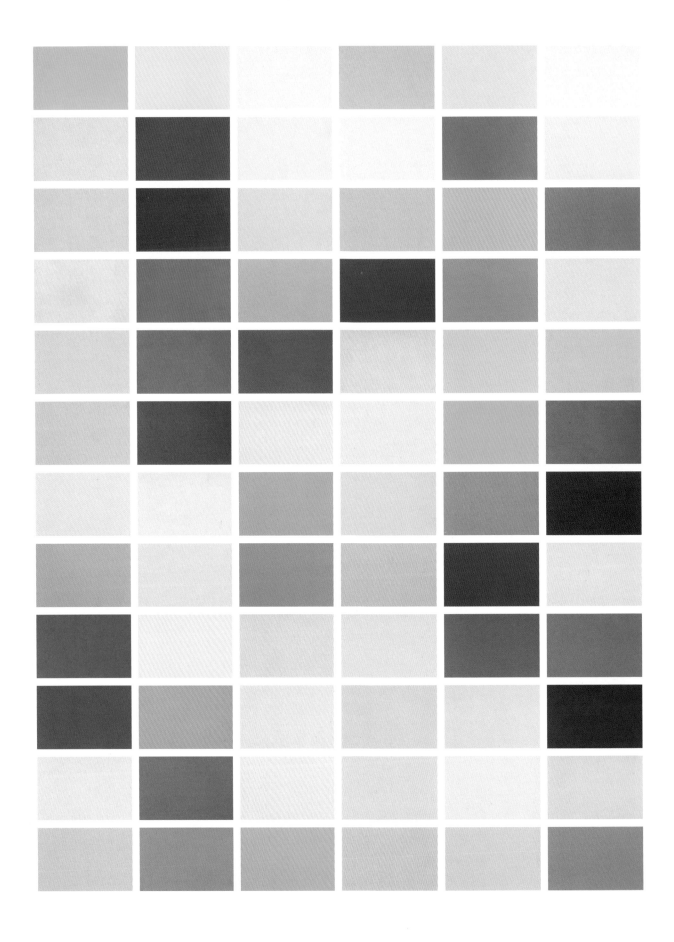

CONTENTS

[OPPOSITE] Seventy-two colours derived from British Standard Colour Cards, 1955 (see pp. 296–297).

INTRODUCTION

Decorative colour is important in our daily lives, yet it is often taken for granted or little understood. Whether in an urban or more rural environment, or perhaps when visiting a house open to the public, we are faced with colour that has been applied with differing degrees of skill and success. Employed with subtlety, colour can enhance a building and mask the unfortunate. If mishandled, the effect can be uncomfortable.

Few are taught about colour, but many seem to possess an innate sense of it and are aware when colours are used in a harmonious way. While working on the restoration of the 1740s picture gallery at Temple Newsam in Leeds, northern England, I was surprised to find that the first decorative colour scheme used there combined a pale pink ceiling and dark green walls. This classic example of the use of complementary colours was employed a full century before the first widely published work on colour theory appeared in the English language.

Colour can also be fun. It can lift the spirits, stimulate the senses and imbue a sense of serenity. An individual's selection of colours says something about their conformist nature, their aspirations and their aesthetic sensitivity. It is important to understand the language and historical associations of colour when decorating a house that was inhabited by an historical figure. Now it is possible to discover the paint colours originally used in historic houses, and to make interior restorations far more authentic.

Paint analysis is a forensic process that is one of the most useful tools for establishing what changes have taken place in a building and when that work was carried out. A branch of archaeology, it is undertaken not only to reveal the colour of a surface, but also to provide information about the structure and its development. Unfortunately, the knowledge and understanding of colour among those who work in historical buildings can be sketchy. Often the original subtlety of an earlier decorative scheme is lost when the information on it is mishandled. Even when, following analysis, hand-painted samples matched to the original scheme are produced, they are often given to someone with little historical colour experience. As a result, the original subtlety of a decorative scheme is lost in the attempt to recreate it. It might even be that a contractor is tasked to find the closest colour among the numerous proprietary paint ranges.

Sometimes, the result is reasonably convincing, but the chances are that the overall effect is somewhat two-dimensional and rather coarse.

Controversy can arise, especially when dealing with iconic landmarks, such as London's Tower Bridge: the change in 1976 from a uniform grey to red, white and blue did not pass without notice. Memory sometimes plays tricks. In the 1980s, the eighth Duke of Wellington was insistent that the railings in front of Apsley House at Hyde Park Corner had always been black, yet when, following analysis, the earlier green was reinstated, his childhood memories of the green railings came flooding back. The dust took a long time to settle after the elaborate 1986 scheme on Hammersmith Bridge was replaced by the original bronze green found during analysis. Some even suggested that an influential shop-owner had been behind the colour choice.

Authorities usually try to establish the decorative history of a significant structure before repainting it. Generally, the same questions will have been faced before and useful tips can be learnt from the past. In addition, the data can provide part of the ammunition to counter critics. For example, in the early 1900s it was discovered that a chocolate-coloured paint had lasted four times longer than a steel grey one on a particular railway bridge. Considering that some fifteen tons of paint were required, to say nothing of the labour and disruption to service, the importance of this nugget of information can be appreciated. Some colours simply perform better than others: reds and greens are still inclined to fade, for example, despite technological advances.

The focus of this book is the use of paint and colour within buildings during the past three hundred years. It does not set out to be a history of decoration or to provide a prescription of how to decorate. Instead, it provides readers with a greater understanding of what comprised early paints and how they were used. It also surveys many of the colours that were available, how they were specified and the conventions of their use. Of particular interest is the fine, convoluted thread that includes a small volume of colour references taken by Charles Darwin on his voyage on HMS *Beagle* and the British Standard colour range of the 1950s. The influence of one paradigm upon the other, and the subtle changes in between, is explored.

SOME TRADITIONAL PIGMENTS

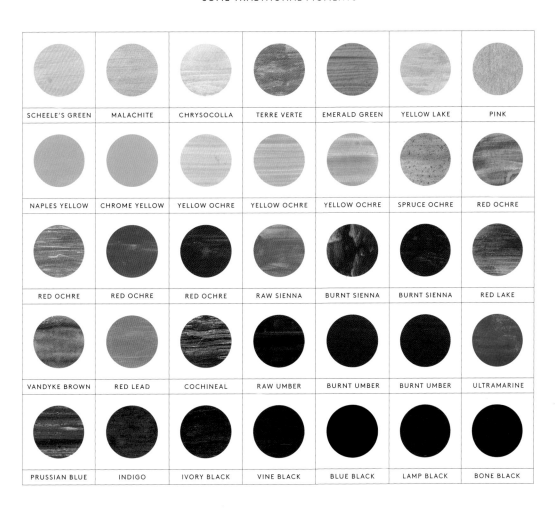

SCHEELE'S GREEN	MALACHITE	CHRYSOCOLLA	TERRE VERTE	EMERALD GREEN	YELLOW LAKE	PINK
NAPLES YELLOW	CHROME YELLOW	YELLOW OCHRE	YELLOW OCHRE	YELLOW OCHRE	SPRUCE OCHRE	RED OCHRE
RED OCHRE	RED OCHRE	RED OCHRE	RAW SIENNA	BURNT SIENNA	BURNT SIENNA	RED LAKE
VANDYKE BROWN	RED LEAD	COCHINEAL	RAW UMBER	BURNT UMBER	BURNT UMBER	ULTRAMARINE
PRUSSIAN BLUE	INDIGO	IVORY BLACK	VINE BLACK	BLUE BLACK	LAMP BLACK	BONE BLACK

SOME TRADITIONAL COMPOUND COLOURS

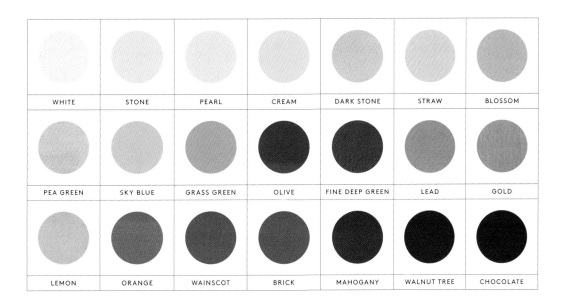

WHITE	STONE	PEARL	CREAM	DARK STONE	STRAW	BLOSSOM
PEA GREEN	SKY BLUE	GRASS GREEN	OLIVE	FINE DEEP GREEN	LEAD	GOLD
LEMON	ORANGE	WAINSCOT	BRICK	MAHOGANY	WALNUT TREE	CHOCOLATE

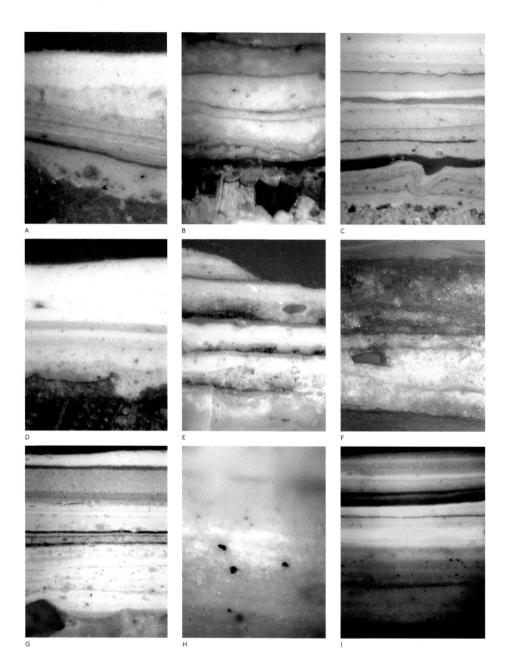

[A] A sample from a 1790s plaster addition to the 1740s library ceiling at Stowe. Surface primed with a paint based on lead white with added red lead. The first (fifth) scheme was off-white. This element was gilded for the sixth scheme. The subsequent schemes were all off-white, although French ultramarine was added on one occasion (see p. 54). [B] The lower layers of paint from the walls of a 1730s panelled room in Soho. The red primer is characteristic of those applied prior to c. 1740 (see pp. 34 and 63). The first scheme was black, which is exceptionally unusual. [C] An early nineteenth-century white primer. Graining, in imitation of oak, was employed in c. 1850. This was revarnished on two occasions. (see p. 160). [D] A 1950s 'pink' primer applied to semi-stripped 1730s panelling. The use of a pink primer, tinted with red lead, is characteristic of those applied in the second half of the twentieth century. Fragments of the 1730s red primer and overlying paint can be seen underneath it (see p. 63). [E] A sample showing that an egg and dart moulding of a 1740s cornice had been gilded as part of the third, fourth and sixth schemes. [F] Smalt applied to the iron balustrade of the Prince of Wales's staircase at Hampton Court Palace in c. 1700 (see p. 55). [G] The paint layers applied to the lower walls of the entrance hall of a late seventeenth-century house. Pale stone colours had been employed until the mid 1850s when graining, in imitation of oak, was applied (see p. 97). [H] The fifth scheme applied to the walls of the entrance hall of a late seventeenth-century house. It contained the pigments Prussian blue, vermilion and a little charcoal black. These are the constituents of the colour French grey, which is known to have been visible here in 1771 (see p. 100). [I] The paint layers on a late eighteenth-century skirting board seen under ultraviolet light. The layers containing zinc oxide display high fluorescence (see p. 47), while those containing lead white have low fluorescence, and those containing titanium dioxide hardly any.

Agreed standard names are fine for broad indications of colour, but a more sophisticated language is required for accurate reproduction. Over the years, various systems were developed to transmit this information. Today, clients can be reasonably sure that they will get what they ask for.

Many years ago, I was asked to review a book on historical paints that emphasized esoteric foodstuffs among the ingredients of the paints. It is true that, at a pinch, a few of them could have been eaten, but to claim that most traditional paint constituents came from 'environmentally friendly sources' is an overstatement. Ill-judged comments about the petrochemical industry and the use of phrases such as 'plastic paints' cast modern paints in an unfavourable light. Such negativity ignores the fact that these products have been developed continually and refined over time, solving problems such as high toxicity and the slow-drying nature of early formulations. It is not easy to manufacture a paint that can be used straight from the tin. To believe that a more efficient one can be produced on the kitchen table is unrealistic. Furthermore, it is not 'eco-friendly' to import paints from distant manufacturers or to paint more frequently than is necessary.

In reality, few of the ingredients found in early paints would have met with approval from today's Health and Safety Executive. Lead, arsenic, mercury, cobalt, copper, manganese and cadmium were all used, which perhaps explains why the house-painter was dreaded in the early nineteenth century as one who dispensed 'plagues and pestilence in every direction'. Such was the problem with lead-contaminated clothing that painters tended not to keep pets for fear of poisoning them.

The conviction that traditional paints were, by definition, durable and long-lasting is a new one. Early manufacturers of paint recommended that exterior woodwork be repainted once every three years, as it was inclined to dust off. In Anthony Trollope's *Barchester Towers* (1857), Mr Harding was informed that in the terms of the wardency of Hiram's Hospital 'he should paint inside every seven years, and outside every three years' – hardly acceptable today. Having examined countless samples from external surfaces, it can be determined all too clearly the frequency with which they were painted.

There are few reliable sources concerning historical paints and colours, and I have tried to set the record straight. I have also attempted to supply a basic grounding in the evolution of paints so that readers might feel equipped to question paint colours they see in the future.

Take nothing for granted. Some years ago, while preparing for a lecture on the influence of John Fowler on the decoration of the English country house, I sat down to re-read a chapter in a book that he had written with the eminent architectural historian John Cornforth. When I first discovered *English Decoration in the 18th Century* (1978), it became my 'bible'. Certainly, it is a good book and a convincing read, with many references to early sources. But as I scrutinized the chapter on paint line-by-line I saw that many of the older sources were misunderstood and in some cases misrepresented.

Dr Ian Bristow was the first modern author to produce hard evidence of how buildings were painted in the past, and his twin volumes, although out of print, are essential reading to students of historical decoration. I can make no claims to the same degree of scholarship, but hope that this work might reach an even broader audience. Anyone who develops an interest in the subject is advised to track down Bristow's many published articles.

Even with today's advanced printing processes, the accurate reproduction of colour is still very difficult. It would be best to regard the colour samples shown in this book as indicative. Paint matches to the majority of the colours can be obtained from Papers and Paints in London.

[PREVIOUS] [PP. 4–5] John Myland & Sons paint shop at 128 Stockwell Road, London SW9 in 1907. [PP. 6–7] *Klaer Lightende Spiegel der Verfkonst* (1692, 'A Clear Survey of the Art of Painting') is a painting manual produced by a Dutchman from Delft known only as A. Boogert. A huge work, with more than seven hundred pages, it describes how to produce a wide range of shades in watercolours. Although intended as a guide for artists, it seems that only one copy was made. [PP. 8–9] The Painted Room at Spencer House. Designed and painted in 'the antique manner' by the architect James 'Athenian' Stuart, it is one of the most famous eighteenth-century interiors in England. It is also the earliest complete neoclassical ensemble in Europe. It was begun in c. 1759 and finished in 1765. [PP. 10–11] Pages from *The Wilson Colour Chart* (1938) (see also pp. 262, 264–67). [PP. 12–13] Photographs from the stair hall and eating parlour of Headfort House in Ireland. Richard Ireland recently reinstated the Robert Adam scheme following extensive analysis. Note the treatment of the triglyphs to see how many samples are required to uncover all the details in rooms such as these. [PP. 14–15] A selection of colour wheels from colour systems developed between 1708 and 1921. [PP. 16–17] Interiors taken from a series of guides produced by the Walpamur Company in 1955 (see also pp. 322–25, 328–31).

The Art of Painting in Oyl (1676; this edition 1723), John Smith

L'art du peintre, doreur, vernisseur (1753; this edition 1778), Jean Félix Watin

The Handmaid to the Arts (1758; this edition 1796), Robert Dossie

The Natural System of Colours (1766), Moses Harris

Valuable Secrets Concerning Arts and Trades (1775; this edition 1780), Anon.

Tableaux détaillés des prix de tous les ouvrages de bâtiment (1804–06), M. R. J. Morisot

The Modern Painter (1842), T. Elliott

The Principles of Beauty in Colouring Systematized (1845), D. R. Hay

The Laws of Harmonious Colouring adapted to Interior Decorations (1847), D. R. Hay

Analogy of Sound & Colour (1869), John Denis Macdonald

Painting for the Million (1878; this edition 1890), W. H. Swingler

House Decoration (1897), Paul N. Hasluck

Practical Painters' Work (1909), Paul N. Hasluck

House Painting and Decoration (1912), Arthur Seymour Jennings

Color Standards and Color Nomenclature (1912), Ridgway

Painters' and Decorators' Work (1916), Henry Geo. Dowling

Red-Lead and How to Use It in Paint (1920), Alvah Horton Sabin

Painting and Decorating Working Methods (1922), F. N. Vanderwalker

Paints & Varnishes (c. 1935), Glidden

New Rooms for Old (1935), Pinchin Johnson & Co.

Historical Color Guide (1938), Elizabeth Burris-Meyer

The Wilson Colour Chart (1938), The British Colour Council

Laxton's Builders' Price Book (1940), Laxton Co. Ltd

Building Materials and Components (1944), British Standards Institution

Modern Home Painting and Decorating (undated, early 1950s), W. P. Matthew

Screetons Colour Range (c. 1953), Screeton Ltd

Building Bulletin (1953), Ministry of Education

Colour and Pattern in the Home (1954), Noel Carrington

Architects' Special Colour Range (1955) Joseph Mason & Co. Ltd

Colour in Buildings (1955), The Walpamur Co. Ltd

Smith's Art of House-Painting (1821), William Butcher

The Painter's and Varnisher's Pocket Manual (1825), Anon.

The Painter's, Gilder's and Varnisher's Manual (c. 1827), G. A. Smeaton

The Decorative Painters' and Glaziers' Guide (1827), Nathaniel Whittock

The Painter's & Colourman's Complete Guide (1830), P. F. Tingry

Outlines of Analogical Philosophy (1839), George Field

Practical Graining and Marbling (1902; this edition 1923), Paul N. Hasluck

Paint and Colour Mixing (1902; this edition 1907), Arthur Seymour Jennings

Répertoire de Couleurs (1905), Société française des chrysanthémistes

Three Hundred Shades (1907), A. Desaint

Ornamental Decoration (1908), Thos. Parsons & Sons

The Lead and Zinc Pigments (1909), Clifford Dyer Holley

The Decoration and Renovation of the Home (1924), A. S. Jennings

BS 381 Schedule of Colours, (1930), British Engineering Standards Association

The Ostwald Colour Album (1930), J. Scott Taylor

Parsons' Decorative Finishes (c. 1930), Thos. Parsons & Sons Ltd

Cashmore's Paint (c. 1932), Cashmore Co. Ltd

A Tint Book of Historical Colours (1934), Thos. Parsons & Sons Ltd

Colour Schemes and Modern Furnishing (1945), Derek Patmore

Colour and Lighting in Factories and Offices (1946; this edition 1964), British Colour Council

Orr's Zinc White 1898–1948 (1949), The Imperial Smelting Corporation Ltd

Maleriets Teknik (1950), Peder Hald

Modern Technique in Painting & Decorating (1950), John P. Parry

Decorators Materials (1950), Cotterell Brothers Ltd

Decorative Schemes No. 5 (1955), The Walpamur Co. Ltd

Walpamur Golden Jubilee 1906–1956 (1956), The Walpamur Co. Ltd

Practical Home Decorating and Repairs (1958), various contributors

An Exterior-Interior Heritage Colour Collection (c. 1975), Fuller O'Brien

Colours in Oil (c. 1985), Historic Paints Ltd

Authentic Colonial Colours (1986), The Martin-Senour Company

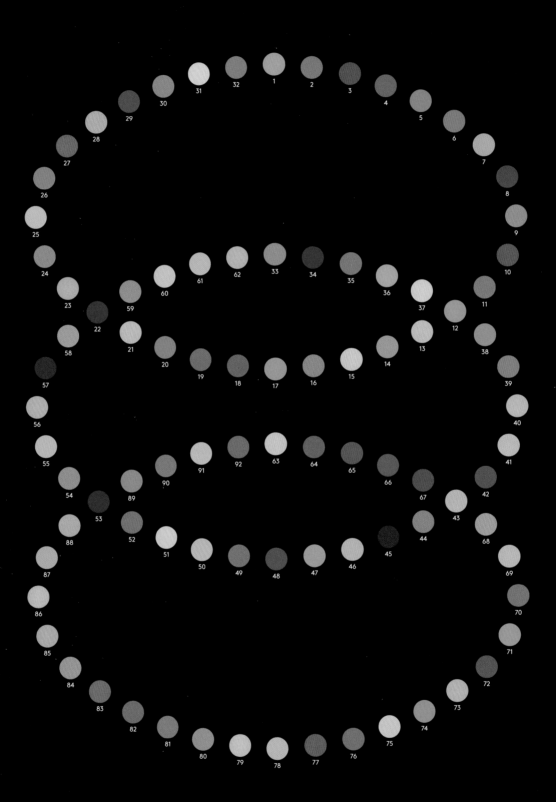

PAINTS, PIGMENTS AND INTERIORS

1650 – 1830

OPPOSITE: NINETY-TWO COLOURS DERIVED FROM
WIENER FARBENKABINET ODER VOLLSTÄNDIGES MUSTERBUCH ALLER NATUR-, GRUND-, UND ZUSAMMENSETZUNGFARBEN (1794)
(VIENNESE COLOUR COLLECTION OR COMPLETE BOOK OF SAMPLES OF ALL NATURAL, BASIC AND COMBINED COLOURS)

1. DARK LEMON YELLOW
2. DULL SCORIA BLUE
3. FULL CARMINE RED
4. SAXON GREEN
5. STRONG VERDIGRIS
6. STRONG LILY RED
7. PALE BLUE
8. DARK RADIANT GREEN
9. COMMON SPRING GREEN
10. STRONG APRICOT RED
11. LIGHT SCORIA BLUE
12. BRIGHT BROWNISH YELLOW
13. STRONG BLUISH GREEN
14. LIGHT BLOOD-RED PEACH
15. COMMON LEMON YELLOW
16. BRIGHT RADIANT GREEN
17. APRICOT RED
18. BLOOD-RED PEACH
19. LIGHT GREY GREEN
20. COMMON YELLOWY RED
21. INTENSE OCHRE
22. COMMON BLUE
23. INTENSE SAFFIAN YELLOW

24. STRONG BRUNSWICK GREEN
25. HIGHLY REFRESHING BLUE
26. COMMON APRICOT RED
27. LIGHT SUNRISE RED
28. DULL SPRING GREEN
29. NO. SCORIA BLUE
30. BRUNSWICK GREEN
31. PALE GREENISH YELLOW
32. DARK YELLOWY RED
33. BRIGHT GARNET GREEN
34. STRONG TURQUOISE BLUE
35. LIGHT MOUNTAIN GREEN
36. DULL APRICOT RED
37. PALE SAFFIAN YELLOW
38. OCHRE
39. STRONG YELLOWY RED
40. PALE RED
41. LIGHT BLUE
42. STRONG GARNET GREEN
43. INTENSE BLUISH GREEN
44. INTENSE SAXON GREEN
45. DARK PURPLE RED
46. INTENSE BLOOD-RED PEACH

47. ROSE RED
48. APPLE GREEN
49. DULL VIOLET RED
50. BRIGHT BRUNSWICK GREEN
51. SAFFIAN YELLOW
52. FULL PALE RED
53. INTENSE GREY GREEN
54. PALE HYACINTH BLUE
55. GREENISH YELLOW
56. FAINT YELLOWY RED
57. DARK SAXON GREEN
58. VERDIGRIS
59. BRIGHT LILAC
60. INTENSE VERDIGRIS
61. PALE VERDIGRIS
62. INTENSE BROWNISH YELLOW
63. INTENSE BLOOD RED
64. STRONG LILAC
65. DARK ASPARAGUS RED
66. BRIGHT TURQUOISE BLUE
67. BROWNISH RED
68. PALE RADIANT GREEN
69. PALE BLOOD-RED CHERRY

70. RADIANT TURQUOISE BLUE
71. PALE YELLOWY RED
72. PURPLE RED
73. INTENSE YELLOWY RED
74. LIGHT ATLAS RED
75. PALE BRUNSWICK GREEN
76. COMMON HYACINTH BLUE
77. BROWNISH YELLOW
78. SUBTLE VERDIGRIS
79. QUINCE YELLOW
80. WHITISH SCORIA BLUE
81. BLOOD RED
82. BLUISH GREEN
83. SUNRISE RED
84. INTENSE RADIANT GREEN
85. SUBTLE YELLOWY RED
86. STRONG QUINCE YELLOW
87. WHITISH BLUE
88. PALE LILAC
89. LILY RED
90. DULL SAXON GREEN
91. INTENSE BLOOD-RED CHERRY
92. STRONG OCHRE

In its simplest form, paint is a liquid that is applied to a surface and converts to a solid film. It is most commonly used to protect or decorate an object and is composed of the colouring matter known as pigment, a vehicle to carry it, known as the medium or binder, and the diluent or solvent, added to make it flow. Traditionally, the word 'paint' means an oil-based medium, but the term is commonly extended to include other coatings, too, such as water-based paint. This section details the composition and application of oil paint, distemper, limewash and milk paint in homes between 1650 and 1830.

OIL PAINT

Until the early years of the twentieth century, oil paint was prepared invariably with white lead as the main pigment, with perhaps another pigment to add colour, together with linseed oil and turpentine. The finish or degree of sheen was regulated by altering the ratio of oil and turpentine. The more oil that was added the shinier the finish, and the more turpentine the more matt the result.

The early house-painter tended to use oil-based paint on woodwork and some plaster surfaces. Water-based paint was almost totally restricted to plaster surfaces, especially ceilings. Resin-based varnishes were often applied on timber and as a protective coat over painted imitations of marble and woodgrain.

The principal oil used for making paint was linseed oil, which was obtained from the seed of the flax plant *Linum usitatissimum*. It was produced by bruising and then crushing the seed, from which the oil was extracted with the application of heat.

The main disadvantages of linseed oil were its amber colour and its slowness in drying, both of which could be remedied to a certain extent by letting the oil stand for many months. Oil that was heated for a few days in the absence of air and allowed to stand was generally known as stand oil. It tended to produce a paint with a more elastic, less brittle film than that made with raw linseed oil.

All the painting manuals of the early house-painting period included recipes for improving the drying properties of raw linseed oil. They usually contained a proportion of litharge (a form of lead oxide) or of white copperas (zinc sulphate), which was added to the oil and heated up. The mixture was then allowed to cool and clear before it was bottled; the result was generally termed 'boiled oil'. The improved drying properties of boiled linseed oil made it suitable for use in exterior paints and in primers, in which it was important that the paint did not remain sticky for more than a short time. The drawback of using boiled linseed oil was its deeper amber colour, which had the effect of muddying the final colour, whichever pigment was added.

The inherent yellowness of both forms of linseed oil meant that alternatives were used in work 'where any nicety [was] required in colouring' (G.A. Smeaton, *The Painter's and Vernisher's Pocket Manual*, 1825), and especially where a white paint was specified. In this case, nut oil or poppy oil was recommended, particularly in France. The former was obtained from the kernels of several sorts of nuts, mainly walnuts and hazelnuts, whereas the latter was derived from the seeds of the white poppy, *Papaver somniferum* (opium poppy).

Both these oils had the advantage of being almost colourless, but they were more expensive than linseed oil. Poppy oil also required mixing with litharge before it could be used, and great care was needed to avoid depriving it of its colourless property.

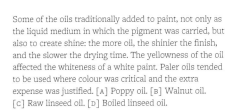

Some of the oils traditionally added to paint, not only as the liquid medium in which the pigment was carried, but also to create shine: the more oil, the shinier the finish, and the slower the drying time. The yellowness of the oil affected the whiteness of a white paint. Paler oils tended to be used where colour was critical and the extra expense was justified. [A] Poppy oil. [B] Walnut oil. [C] Raw linseed oil. [D] Boiled linseed oil.

A   B   C   D

[TOP LEFT] The seeds of the flax plant, *Linum usitatissimum*, provided the most common
and inexpensive oil – linseed – used in traditional paints, but its amber colour was undesirable
in paler formulations and, where budget allowed, less colourful oils gave preferable results.
[TOP RIGHT] The oil that is extracted from the nut of the walnut (*Juglans regia*) is pale yellow.
[BOTTOM LEFT] White poppy (*Papaver somniferum*) seeds produce a very fine, pale oil that
requires mixing with litharge and takes a long time to dry. [BOTTOM RIGHT] The oil that
is extracted from the nut of the hazelnut (*Corylus avellana*) is a pale greenish yellow.

USE OF TURPENTINE

Turpentine is a volatile fluid that dries by evaporation, leaving behind little or no resin, depending on its purity. It is mainly obtained from various species of pine tree, which are tapped for their oleoresin, which is, in turn, processed into spirits of turpentine. It was added to oil paint in order to help make it flow, and also employed in a process called flatting (when a dull or 'flat' paint finish was desired).

Early oil paints dried to a glossy finish that tended to dull down after only a short time. The linseed oil content in these paints caused them to turn yellow, especially in areas that were deprived of light. This effect was most obvious in white paint, but coloured paints would alter in appearance too, with blue shades taking on a greenish tinge, for example. The tendency to yellow could be corrected by adding either black or a little blue, and often the problem could be avoided on external surfaces by the deliberate use of a stone-coloured paint. This gave better coverage than white paint, and had 'a warm and finished look' that 'last[ed] clean longer than a white' (John Pincot. *Pincot's Treatise on the Practical Part of Coach & House Painting*, c. 1811). The standard method of preserving a brighter white in interiors was by flatting or by using a paler oil than linseed, such as walnut or poppy oil.

During the seventeenth and early eighteenth centuries, the finish tended to be much shinier than today. There are recipes that demonstrate that rosin (a solid form of resin obtained from the pine tree) was sometimes dissolved into the oil using a gentle heat. The very influential editions of a manual written by John Smith, *The Art of Painting in Oyl* (first edition 1676; the following from the fourth edition, 1705) recommended:

> Take notice, that all simple colours used in house painting, appear much more beautiful and lustrous, when they appear as if glazed over with a varnish to which both the drying oyl before-mentioned contributes very much.

Records from the 1730s indicate that turpentine oil was sold at 12d (5p/6¢) per quart. This was the same price as 'best drying oil' and 2d (1p/1¢) more than linseed oil.

The addition of turpentine was not recommended for exterior paints, in which a finish with a high sheen was considered best able to cope with the vagaries of the weather.

USE OF PIGMENTS

White lead, or lead carbonate, is the pigment that formed the basis of most oil paints used in the decoration of houses until relatively recently. When combined with linseed oil, it forms a lead soap that gives it excellent working properties – drying and covering well, it produces a slightly elastic film that enables it to expand and contract with changes in the temperature in unison with the surface to which it has been applied. Although white lead is a superb white pigment, the main drawback to using it in paint is its toxicity, which has been known from the earliest days. It was made by corroding sheets of metallic lead with vinegar.

When a colour was desired, coloured pigments were added to the oil paint. Pigments came from a wide range of sources: some were local, but a number of the more exotic and usually brighter ones were from overseas. These latter were, inevitably, more expensive and consequently tended to be used on smaller areas. Some, such as carmine produced from the cochineal insect or genuine ultramarine from the semi-precious stone lapis lazuli, were far beyond the means of most clients. Others, such as the local earth pigments, saw constant use. These were strongly coloured earths, sifted and washed before use, and chosen for their low cost, availability and covering power.

Pigments ground by hand affected the appearance of oil paint. Their non-uniform particle size caused an unevenness of colour and influenced the way in which light was reflected, making the surface look more lively than the modern, highly refined products. The process of grinding pigments was labour intensive, some types requiring a lot of work to ensure complete dispersion in oil.

In the early eighteenth century, the introduction of horse-mills enabled the colour shops to develop their businesses of supplying finely ground pigments at a reasonable cost and in a convenient form. The pigments were sold in paste form, which was placed either in bladders, which were pierced with a tack in order to squeeze out the colour, or in kegs. The paste could then be added to white lead by the house-painter until the desired shade was obtained. One of the effects of this labour-saving innovation was to take some of the business out of the hands of the trained painter and put it into those of the amateur. The selection of colour, and therefore fashion, was largely dictated by technological limitations.

	Pigment		Ca - - - - - ru - - - - - le -				Cy...
			Candidu Hispan.	**Montanum.**		**Cy...**	
			Niveus. Snow wh.	Glastinus. Watchet		○	
			Ca - - - - - ru - - - - le -				
	Cerussa	●	Lacteus. Γαλακτικός / Blanch comme du Lait. Milky wh.	Argenteus. Ἀργύρεε / Silver Co.		Turcoisinus. / Turcois C	○
			- - ces.	**Lutei mixti.**		Di - - - - ri	
Sim‑pli‑ci‑	**Masticot**	●	Limoneus / Limon C	Paleus. / Straw C		Cymatilis / Wavd C	○
	Gutta Gambæ	●	Aureus. Χρυσοειδής / Couleur d'or. Gold Colour.	Luteolus. Ὑπόχλωρε / Yellowish.		Psittaceus. / Poppinjay gr	●
Lu‑te‑i	**Ochra**	●	Luteus. Ὠχρός. / Co. d'œuf. Clay Col.	Electricus. Ἠλέκτρικε / Amber Co.			●
	Auripig‑mentum	●	Citrinus. Κίτρινος / Orange Co	Byssinus. Βύσσινε / Raw silke C			●
	Umbria	●	Fuscus. Φαιός. Brun. Browne.	Subfuscus. / Dun.			●
			- - - ces.	**Rubei mixti.**		Pur - - - - - pu	
Ru‑bri	**Minium**	●	Igneus. Πυρροειδής / C. du feu. Fire Col.	Gilvus. Κιρρός / Bricke C.			●
	Ochra usta	●	Russus. / Carret C.	Helvus / Sorrel.		Badius. Βάδιε Bay. Bay.	●
Sim‑...	**Cinnabaris**	●	Miniatus. Μιλτώδης / du Vermillon.	Carneus Σαρκοειδής / Carnation			●
	Carmin	●	Coccineus. Κόκκινος / C. d'Escarlate. Crimson.	Roseus Ῥοδόης / Rosey		Molochinus Μολόχινε / Mallow C	●
...be‑i	**Lacca**	●	Rubinus. / Ruby-red.	Caryophylleus / Pinke Col.		Persicus / Peach Col.	●
	Sanguis Draconis	●	Sanguineus. Αἱματώδης / C. du Sang. Blood-red.				●
Pu‑...	**Rubrica**	●	Ferrugineus Σιδηροειδής / Rust Co.			●	●
	Atramentu Fuliginosu	●	Piceus. Πίσσινος / C. de poix. Pitchy.	Griseus / Gray		Canus Πόλιος / Hoary	●

	Smalt.	Litmase.	Indicum.	Atramentu...
Κυανεο	Lazurius Co.d'azure Azure	Diolaceus. Ιανθινος Diolet C.	Indicus. Ινδικος.	Coracini

- - - - i   Mi - - - - - - - x - - - - - - ti.

| Ὑποκυανεος Skid Col | Hyacinthinus Υακινθινος Jacinth C. | | | Plumbeus Co.de plo... |

- - - - des   Mi - - - - - - x - - - - - - ti.

Οισυινος Willow gr	Chalassinus Sea gr	Lividus Black & blew		Nigellus
Grass green	Porraceus. Πρασινος. Leek Co.			
Ὑαλινος Glass Co.				
			Murinus Mouse C.	Castaneu...

- - - - re - - - - - - i   Mix - - - - - - ti.

				Pullus.
				Aethiopi...
		Lividopurpureus. Gris de lion.		Fuligine...
Purple Royal	Dibaphus. Purple in grain	Purpureus. Πορφυρ. C.de Pourpr. Purple.	Atrabapticus	
...is Amathist Co.	Paonaceus.			Furvus...
				Preslus.
Bronze			Hiberus Moré Murrey	Ater.
Τεφρωδης Ash-col.	Ferreus. Iron-gray	Elbidus. Dark-gray		Niger.

In spite of the availability of ready-ground pigments and white lead in paste form, the house-painter still required a grindstone and muller in order to ensure the complete combination of his ingredients. The grindstone was usually granite or rance marble, heavy enough to remain 'fast and steady, while the colour is grinding on it' (W. Butcher. *Smith's Art of House-Painting*, 1821). The muller was an egg-shaped pebble, with the larger end broken off and then ground as smooth as possible. On the slab, the constituents of the paint would be ground together and turned over with a palette knife made of thin tempered steel. Some pigments, especially king's yellow, Naples yellow and patent yellow, were blackened by contact with iron or steel, and the painter would use an ivory or horn tool to scrape these off his stone. It was important to ensure that sufficient paint was made to complete the job as the variation in hue between batches of pigments, especially the natural earths, could be quite considerable.

The contents of the pot were mixed with other ingredients depending on the nature of the paint required. The first coat, or primer, would be made considerably thinner than the paint designed for the second and third coats. Frequently, the faster-drying boiled linseed oil was used at this stage. Traditional oil paint tended to dry slowly, and driers in the form of litharge, or the more expensive sugar of lead (lead acetate), were sometimes added, perhaps with a little red lead pigment. Despite this, the primer still took between two and three days to dry. It was crucial that the surface was completely dry before the next coat was applied.

A cheap and fast-drying method of sealing a plaster surface was to brush on a coat of glue size, made from animal bones, horns or skin, as a primer. Although this prevented the absorption of the oil into the plaster and led to a better coverage of the paint, it also meant that after many years the accumulated layers of paint tended to fall off the wall.

New softwood, particularly pine, often contains knots that require careful treatment to prevent the resin that they exude from damaging the paintwork. Some house-painters recommended the application of a mixture of red lead and litharge, with a small quantity of turpentine over each knot. Occasionally, a lump of fresh slaked lime was laid on the knot to kill it before it was covered with a coating of 'size knotting'. This was a preparation of red lead,

white lead and whiting, made into a thin paste with size. It was not until the 1840s that the method used today – painting the knot with shellac (a natural resin) – was first documented.

The use of white lead in the priming coat on timber appears to date from the second quarter of the eighteenth century; prior to that, it was more usual to apply Spanish brown, a natural red earth pigment, 'well ground and mixed very thin with linseed oil' (John Smith. *The Art of Painting in Oyl*, 9th edn., 1788). The transition from red to white is a useful aid to dating a surface.

A second coat of paint was applied once the primer was dry. Provided that the first coat had dried with a slight gloss, rather than leaving a powdery residue, the next coat was mixed to be slightly thicker. For the best result, an abrasive was used between coats. In the early years this might have been the skin of a dogfish or a coarse plant such as Dutch rushes. An early form of glass paper was available in the seventeenth century, but it was not until the 1830s that it was mass-produced. If the second coat covered well, the third would form the ground for the finish coat, but once again the second coat had to be allowed to dry first. If the final colour was to be other than white, it was at this stage that pigment was added, the tint often being darker than that of the finish coat.

Traditional oil paints dried to a mid-gloss finish, and until the middle of the eighteenth century a glossy finish was considered desirable on panelled walls and woodwork. Thereafter, secondary rooms would usually be left with a gloss finish, but in the best rooms – parlours, drawing rooms and dining rooms – an extra flatted coat was often applied. Seventy years later, this was still 'to be preferred for all superior work' (Peter Nicholson. *An Architectural Dictionary*, 1819). However, to paint a large surface area in this manner was exceptionally difficult and painters charged extra for this task.

A cheaper method of decorating was to use clearcole, which was white lead ground in water and mixed with size glue. This was described by John Pincot as:

> a cheap mode of painting well calculated for servants' rooms, attics and kitchens, old houses, small tenements or ship's cabins, where dispatch is necessary, or where it is necessary to paint often.

The problem with clearcole was similar to the use of size in priming, because later layers of paint tended to chip off, thereby necessitating the complete removal of the old paint.

[PREVIOUS] Richard Waller's 'Tabula Colorum Physiologica', from 'A Catalogue of Simple and Mixt Colours with a Specimen of Each Colour Prefixt Its Properties,' in *Philosophical Transactions of the Royal Society of London*, vol. 6 for the years 1686 and 1687 (1688). This chart of 119 colours was probably the first one designed to describe the colours of nature that was published in English. [ABOVE] Frontispiece of the third edition of P. F. Tingry's *The Painter's and Colourman's Complete Guide* (1830). Note the round brushes held by each of the three painters, and in the foreground the earthen paint pots, flagons, aprons, caps and the 'builder's cripple'. Note also the softener in the hand of the kneeling painter as he grains a door in imitation of oak.

Fine decorative plasterwork of the 1750s in a house in Lower Dominick Street, Dublin.
The application of a soft distemper would ensure that the detail remained crisp.

DISTEMPER

A less expensive matt finish that was widely used on plaster walls and ceilings was known as distemper, or size colour. This was made with whiting or ground chalk, bound with a glue size and tinted with a suitable pigment. It had many advantages: it was cheap, achievable in a wide range of tints, easy to make and quick to apply. It was also used when the colour of the intended scheme could only be obtained using pigments that were liable to change in an oil medium. Loosely bound, distemper could be washed off for renewal, but it was not particularly durable and was not suitable for areas of heavy traffic.

Distemper had one great advantage over oil-based paint: its permeability to moisture. New brickwork has been estimated to contain about 180 litres (40 gal) of water per cubic metre, and lime plaster contains more than 2 litres (0.4 gal) in each of its three coats per square metre. Some of this is permanently bound chemically, but many tons would slowly evaporate from a new building during the first few years, and not all of the water vapour would travel outwards. If obstructed by an impermeable layer of paint, the pressure that built up underneath would cause the paint to be pushed off the wall.

It is therefore surprising that only one early author drew attention to this problem. Peter Nicholson, in *An Architectural Dictionary* (1812–19), suggested applying distemper as a stop-gap measure:

> Painting in distemper, or water-colours mixed with size, stucco, or plaster, which is intended to be painted in oil when finished; but not being sufficiently dry to receive the oil, may have a coating in water-colours, of any given tint required, in order to give a more finished appearance to that part of the building.

When the walls were dry enough to be painted with oil paint, the distemper was washed off.

Although it appears from a number of early texts that size-bound distemper was used on wooden panelling, there were warnings against employing it in this way because it could not cope with the movement of the timber and flaked. Swiss chemist and mineralogist Pierre-François Tingry simplified the processes that had been described by French colour merchant Jean-Félix Watin for a many-layered water-based treatment for panelling. One was called chipolin and it involved the application of ten or so coats of Bougival white, or Spanish white (see p. 50), mixed with glue size, each being allowed to dry. Two coats of lead white, to which was added a few particles of Prussian blue and black, mixed with parchment size, were applied and softened with a brush. This surface was then given two thin coats of carefully strained parchment size. Finally, two or three coats of spirit varnish – made from shellac dissolved in alcohol – were applied.

This process is not unlike the many layers of gesso that were applied prior to water-gilding, and it was at this stage that the mouldings might have been gilded. The application of Bougival white was a very expensive process but one that produced a porcelain-like surface that gave beautiful effects under candlelight. A variant of this, called *blanc de roi* or royal white, from its use in palaces, was left unvarnished. As a result, it soon became dirty and the lead white would first turn yellow and then black.

The application of a varnish over the distemper certainly improved its durability, but the same problems encountered with the use of size as a primer still existed. The similar refractive index of oil and chalk also presented a problem, turning the distemper semi-translucent if an oil-based varnish were applied to a conventional whiting and size distemper. One method of avoiding this was to ensure that an argillaceous (clay-like) white pigment was used as a basis for the distemper, but white lead would have been better.

Ceilings were generally treated with a water-based coating. In the earlier years, this tended to be a simple slurry of whiting and water, brushed on quickly before it dried, and commonly known as whitening. This presented an extremely matt surface that was very friable and easily replaced. One benefit of this, especially on the elaborate three-dimensional plasterwork of late seventeenth-century ceilings or highly ornate cornices of the 1790s, was that it did not clog up the detail. A repaint would entail the complete removal and washing down of the previous coat.

Certain pigments tended to be more suitable in a particular medium; blue verditer, for example, was generally reserved for use in distemper because it was liable to darken and go green in oil, whereas chalk worked well in water but would become semi-translucent, and rather grey, in oil.

LIMEWASH

Limewash has been used for many years and is one of the simplest coatings in existence. It is made by adding water to slaked lime until the consistency of milk is achieved. Somewhat translucent when first applied, it cures through a reaction with carbon dioxide in the atmosphere to form calcium carbonate and gradually becomes opaque. In the past, the coating tended to see most use on the walls of vernacular buildings and it would seldom be found in larger town or country houses. A variant, in the form of a translucent wash, was sometimes used on the exterior of early nineteenth-century buildings.

Although neither long-lasting nor durable, limewash, or whitewash, was applied commonly on outbuildings and farm buildings, which contain a variety of rough surfaces – stone, brick and timber – that are difficult to wash and keep clean. Left uncoated, these surfaces collect dust, insect debris and waste and can become very dirty. A coat of limewash helps with sanitation by covering and smoothing over the rough surfaces. Further applications of limewash form layers that eventually flake off and remove surface debris in the process. The coating also has antimicrobial properties that provide hygienic and sanitary benefits for buildings housing livestock.

Limewash should not be applied over previously painted surfaces or to cover wood, metal or plastic. Bare plaster, render or brick (in certain circumstances) are the typical substrates on which it works best, but only if regular maintenance is upheld. It should also be noted that a conventional paint system cannot be applied in the future. And limewash certainly should not be considered for drawing room walls, even if the desired outcome is the 'faded palazzo' look. A broken colour paint effect can be achieved successfully using glazes or washes of conventional emulsion. Limewash can be employed in an urban house but its uses are limited. Under very few circumstances should a brick facade be painted with this coating – unpainted brick ought to be left as it is and limewash will not 'stick' on any existing masonry paint.

In certain cases, where the light and conditions are exactly right, this cheap and relatively simple treatment can provide an efficient and attractive means of decoration.

A garden wall may well be given a coat or three of limewash, and it is often the best treatment to utilize on a wall that does not have a damp-proof course. The slightly damp walls of an unconverted basement can usefully be coated with limewash. And the brilliant white nature of its untinted form can help to brighten up a grim coal-hole very effectively, while allowing moisture to pass through. Similarly, the crumbly brick walls of an unconverted attic can be consolidated, and the space considerably brightened, with a couple of coats of white limewash.

There are several companies that sell ready-mixed limewash. However, it is more than 90 per cent water, consequently bulky and not easily transported, so it might be worth making it from scratch. The level of commitment required to mix it yourself is considerable. The dense clay-like lime putty from which it is made can be obtained from a few specialist suppliers. This will need to be mixed well with water to the consistency of milk. Naturally white, limewash can be tinted to provide a limited number of colours, the palette dictated by the few pigments that remain unaffected by its high alkalinity. Consequently, it might not be possible to achieve an exact shade and there is little point in trying to obtain a perfect match to a fabric or existing paint. Later reproduction can be difficult, too, so it is a good idea to make more than is needed.

Limewash should be stored in an area free from frost, stirred before use and reapplied when necessary. Furthermore, it is important to be aware of its caustic nature while wet, whether bought ready-made or mixed at home. It can burn unprotected skin and is dangerous to the eyes. Goggles and rubber gloves are essential while working with it. If you are not going to apply limewash yourself, it is important that the painter understands the health and safety implications. Do not simply hand over a tub of limewash without a clear briefing.

Although limewash does not offer the ease, convenience and durability of conventional paint, if you are prepared to put up with the challenges of its preparation and application, it is a truly remarkable coating of great character and beauty.

The limewashed walls of the cloister of Magdalen College, University of Oxford, built in 1474–80 by William Orchard, were colour-matched by Lisa Oestreicher to restore the traditional scheme.

The Milk Maid, painted by Winslow Homer in 1878. [OVERLEAF] *Wiener Farbenkabinet oder vollständiges Musterbuch aller Natur-, Grund-, und Zusammensetzungfarben*, 1794 (Viennese Colour Collection or Complete Book of Samples of all Natural, Basic and Combined Colours). This two-volume work contains 4,608 hand-painted specimens, organized by colour, individually numbered and named and arranged forty-eight per page. The author discusses the colouring of linen, cotton, wool, silk, leather, wood, ivory, bone, ceramics of all sorts, stone, papier mâché, sealing wax, glass, enamel work, vellum and feathers. There are also notes on printing inks and papers used by bookbinders.

MILK PAINT

Many myths have grown up around the subject of traditional paints and painting processes. One that regularly resurfaces is that of milk paint, which conjures an appealing image of contented cows and milkmaids.

The reality is rather different: milk paint is described by a French scientist during the French Revolution as an expedient measure introduced when more suitable materials were in short supply. The original recipe has appeared in translation in a dozen later works in the United Kingdom and United States, but below is that found in William Butcher's 1821 version of John Smith's *The Art of Painting in Oyl*, because it is likely to have been the one that was followed most often.

> Milk Paint – The very offensive and injurious smell of common paint to sickly persons, may be obviated by the following recipe; which, we have been assured, will answer for inside work, as panelling etc., nearly as well as oil-paint.
>
> Take of skimmed milk nearly two quarts; of fresh slaked lime, about six ounces and a half; of linseed oil, four ounces; of whiting, three pounds. Put the lime into a stone-vessel, and pour upon it a sufficient quantity of milk to form a mixture, resembling thin cream; then add the oil a little at a time, stirring it with a small spatula; the remaining part of the milk is then to be added; and lastly, the whiting. The milk must, on no account, be sour.
>
> Slake the lime, by dipping the pieces in water, out of which it is to be immediately taken, and left to slake in the air. For fine white paint, the oil of carraways is best, because colourless: but, with the ochres, the commonest oils may be used. The oil, when mixed with the milk and lime, entirely disappears, and is totally dissolved by the lime; forming a calcareous sope [sic].
>
> The whiting, or ochre, is to be gently crumbled on the surface of the fluid, which it gradually imibes, and at last sinks: at this period it must be well stirred in.
>
> This paint may be coloured like distemper, or size-colour, with levigated charcoal, yellow ochre, &c., and is used in the same manner. The quantity here prescribed is sufficient to cover twenty-seven square yards with the first coat, and will cost about three halfpence per yard.
>
> For out-door work, add to the proportions of slaked lime, linseed-oil and white Burgundy pitch, each two ounces: the pitch to be melted in a gentle heat with the oil, and then added to the smooth mixture of the milk and lime. In cold weather it must be warmed, to facilitate its mixture with the milk.

The components of Butcher's recipe reveal that milk paint was somewhere between a primitive emulsion and a variant of limewash. Butcher admits that he has not tried the product, but attests: 'We have been assured, [it] will answer for inside work, as panelling etc., nearly as well as oil-paint.' It has never been established how widespread was the use of milk as an ingredient of paint. If employed at all, it is likely to have been more common in vernacular buildings than townhouses.

It is not known how many of the other authors who quoted the recipe had actually worked with it. Certainly, the author of a letter to the editor of *The New England Farmer and Horticultural Journal* in September 1828 had done so and was not overly impressed:

> Mr Fessenden: I think your correspondent... has taken a too favorable view of milk paint... Having used these materials for several buildings, and carefully prepared it too, I was I must own disappointed. The effects were of short duration to encourage further experiment...If so cheap a substitute for oil painting could be had, it would be a great benefit extending a neatness of appearance through the county. But I fear, too partial a view of its durability is entertained by your ingenious correspondent.

Although it has been documented that milk paint was employed occasionally on furniture, its tendency to flake and rub off would have made it a very problematic coating for wood. American paint analyst Susan Buck has examined many pieces of Shaker furniture and writes:

> The physical evidence makes plain that the Shakers generally used traditional oil-based paints to paint wooden objects and architectural elements, and recipes containing milk are primarily lime-based whitewashes or exterior paints, not furniture or interior paints.

To believe that milk paint might in any way be more efficient than the more noxious conventional lead paint of the past is fantasy.

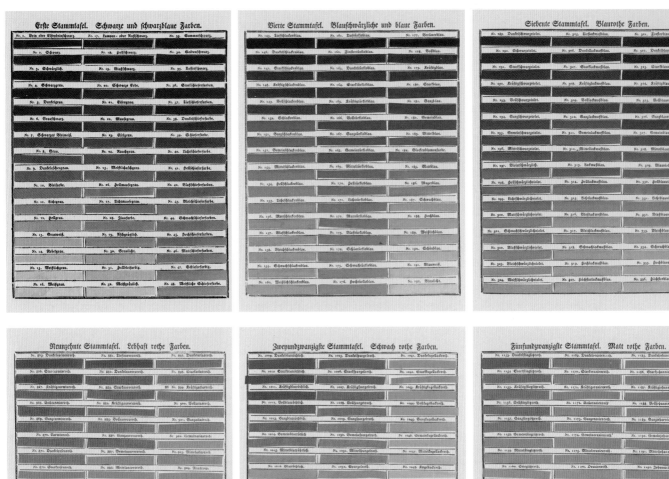

Erste Stammtafel. Schwarze und schwarzblaue Farben. — Vierte Stammtafel. Blauschwärzliche und blaue Farben. — Siebente Stammtafel. Blaurothe Farben.

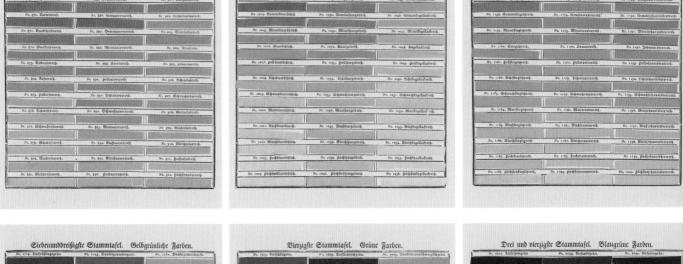

Neunzehnte Stammtafel. Lebhaft rothe Farben. — Zweyundzwanzigste Stammtafel. Schwach rothe Farben. — Fünfundzwanzigste Stammtafel. Matt rothe Farben.

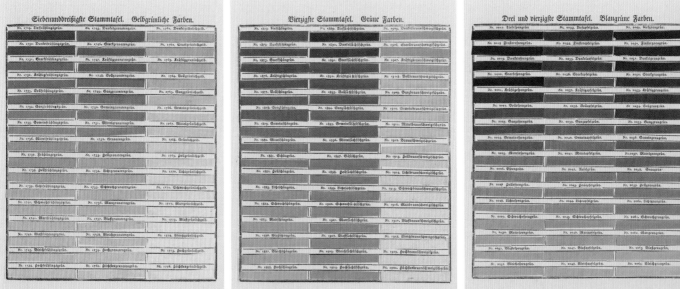

Siebenunddreißigste Stammtafel. Gelbgrünliche Farben. — Vierzigste Stammtafel. Grüne Farben. — Drei und vierzigste Stammtafel. Blaugrüne Farben.

Zehnte Stammtafel. Blaurothe Farben.

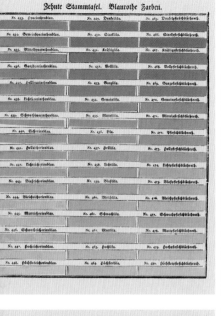

Dreizehnte Stammtafel. Rothblaue und röthliche Farben.

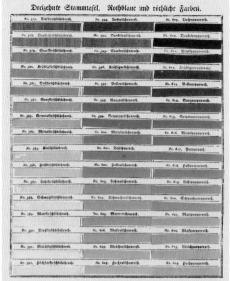

Sechzehnte Stammtafel. Rothe Farben.

Achtundzwanzigste Stammtafel. Rothgelbliche Farben.

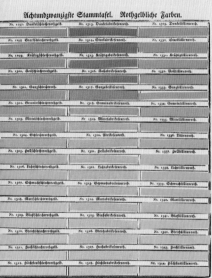

Einunddreißigste Stammtafel. Bräunlichgelbe Farben.

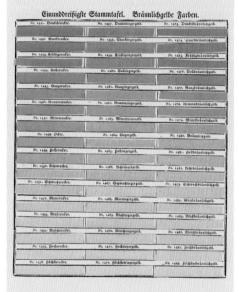

Vierunddreißigste Stammtafel. Lebhaft gelbe Farben.

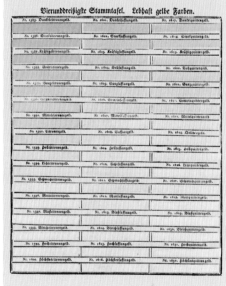

Sechsundvierzigste Stammtafel. Grüne Farben.

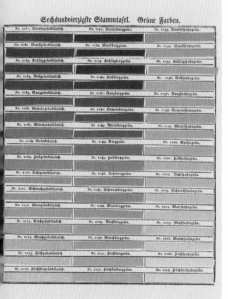

Zweyundfünfzigste Stammtafel. Blau und schwärzlich grüne Farben.

Neun und vierzigste Stammtafel. Vermischte grüne Farben.

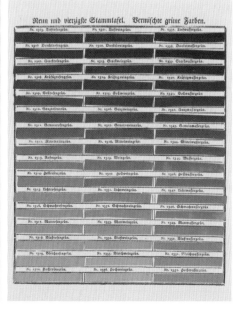

'When you come to grind Colours, let your Grinding-stone be placed about the height of your middle; let it stand firm and fast, so that it joggle not up and down; then take a small quantity of the Colour you intend to grind (two spoonfuls is enough) for the less you grind at a time, the easier and finer will your Colour be ground.'* This section presents the traditional pigments that formed the bulk of the house-painter's palette between 1650 and 1830, noting their places of origin, character and primary uses in interiors during that period.

*John Smith, *The Art of Painting in Oyl* (1676; this from the fourth edition, 1705)

[OPPOSITE] The range of traditional pigments available to the house-painter between 1650 and 1830 displayed according to colour group.

WHITES	BLACKS	BLUES	GREENS	BROWNS	REDS	YELLOWS
WHITE LEAD	LAMP BLACK	AZURITE	VERDIGRIS	RAW SIENNA	CARMINE	CHROME YELLOW
ZINC OXIDE	BLUE BLACK	BLUE VERDITER	GREEN VERDITER	BURNT SIENNA	ROSE PINK	DUTCH PINK
LITHOPONE	IVORY BLACK	ULTRAMARINE	VERONESE GREEN	RAW UMBER	BRAZILWOOD	WELD YELLOW
CHALK		INDIGO	CHRYSOCOLLA	BURNT UMBER	VERMILION	KING'S YELLOW
SPANISH WHITE		PRUSSIAN BLUE		VANDYKE BROWN	ENGLISH RED	NAPLES YELLOW
BOUGIVAL WHITE		SMALT			SPANISH BROWN	PATENT YELLOW
GYPSUM WHITE					VENETIAN RED	YELLOW OCHRE
					INDIAN RED	OXFORD OCHRE
					REALGAR	SPRUCE OCHRE
					RED LEAD	BROWN OCHRE

WHITE LEAD

A   B

In *The Painter's and Colourman's Complete Guide* (1830), P. F. Tingry described making white lead:

Sheets of lead about two feet long, five inches broad, and a quarter of an inch thick, are rolled up in loose coils, and placed in earthern (sic) pots, each capable of holding six pints of fluid, but into it as much vinegar only is poured as will rise so high as not to touch the lead, which rests on a ledge half way down. The pots are then buried in fresh stable litter, where they remain for about two months, during which time the vapours of the vinegar, elevated by the heat of the dung, oxidize the surface of the lead, and the oxide combines with the carbonic acid gas evolved from the fermenting materials of the bed. The carbonate appears as a white scaly brittle matter on the surface of the lead, and is separated by spreading the coils upon a perforated wooden floor, covered with water, and drawing them to and fro by rakes, which process detaches the white lead, and causes it to sink through the water and the holes of the floor to the bottom of a vessel placed below. It is afterwards ground in mills with water, and then dried in earthern pans, placed in stoves. It was formerly ground dry, by which method, from its deleterious nature, the workmen suffered severely.

DUTCH STACK METHOD

The process of making white lead known as the Dutch stack method was employed from the sixteenth to the late nineteenth century, with one small exception. A patent, obtained by Richard Fishwick in 1787, suggested the replacement of the horse manure with spent tan-bark (the bark of certain species of tree, usually oak and traditionally used for tanning hides). The aim was to transmit a higher and more uniform heat to the lead and vinegar, thereby ensuring a faster conversion to white lead.

The building of the stacks, which were usually about 7 metres (23 ft) high, was carried out by women, who worked barefoot carrying the tan-bark in baskets. In the United Kingdom, Newcastle-upon-Tyne was one of the principal sources of production, with other centres in London, Glasgow, Chester, Bristol and Sheffield.

The taking down of the stacks was performed by men only, who wore the regulation costume required by the Home Office for all workers in the white lead industry. The stacks were also dampened down to settle the dust, which was considered especially dangerous. At this stage, the white lead was scraped off before being ground in water and made into cakes.

The Factory and Workshop Act of 1883 introduced some safety measures, and further regulations in 1896 prohibited women from working in contact with white lead. The toxic nature of the pigment had been widely known for many years. Indeed, Pliny had warned of the various ways in which the pigment could cause harm. Alternatives to lead were considered, but it was not until the twentieth century that a satisfactory option, in the form of titanium dioxide, was introduced.

The corrosion of the lead coils took between three to four months. Inevitably, efforts were made to speed up the process, and in the late nineteenth century various modifications of the Dutch method were introduced.

CHAMBER PROCESS

The most successful variation of the Dutch stack method was known as the chamber process, in which heat and moisture – as steam – together with acetic acid and carbon dioxide were introduced into the building. The lead was hung in strips in the chamber, which was heated to a temperature of 60° Celsius (140° F). The time taken to produce lead carbonate was reduced to about four to six weeks.

Chamber lead is somewhat different in character to stack lead, being decidedly brighter in colour, probably owing to the absence of the tan-bark, which may slightly stain the stack lead and also cause discoloration due to by-products. It is also finer and more uniform in grain. Paint made with chamber lead works rather differently under the brush to that prepared by stack lead because of the difference in texture: it is smoother and has greater spreading power. For the same reason, the oil absorption of chamber lead is distinctly higher than that of stack. More recently, even quicker methods of production have been introduced and the precipitation method can now produce white lead in a matter of minutes. However, any paint made with modern lead will produce a very different effect to paint made from Dutch stack lead.

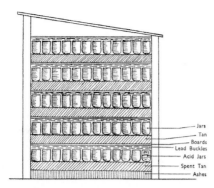

C

D

White lead in powder form was thought
to be particularly hazardous. One method of
reducing the risk to the house-painters and
colourmen who were forced to handle white lead
was to purchase the pigment from manufacturers
ready-ground in oil, as a thick paste, rather
than as a powder. Although there are numerous
references to the casks of ground white lead
that were kept ready for sale at the colourman's,
there is also the instruction to obtain the pigment
in dry cakes in order to ensure that it was free
from adulteration.

It would appear that there was as much
concern about the pigment being pure, as there
was about the 'deleterious' effects of using white
lead. Indeed, a number of later published works
provided quite sophisticated tests for the
detection of adulterants.

[A] Chamber white lead. [B] Stack white lead. [C] Traditional
stack lead, made from corroded lead coils exposed to vapours
of acetic acid in earthenware pots. [D] Chamber lead, in which
the lead corrosion process is sped up by the introduction of
steam at a temperature of 60°C (140°F). The grain produced
is finer and more uniform, and the white is brighter.

ZINC OXIDE

It has long been known that white lead was
a toxic pigment but it was not until 1782 that
a French chemist, Louis-Bernard Guyton de
Morveau, suggested zinc oxide as a satisfactory
alternative. It took another sixty-five years
before it came into commercial use. French
painter and contractor Edme Jean Leclaire
realized that 30 per cent of the painters who
were members of his Society of Providence and
Mutual Aid suffered from 'painter's colic', and so
began to experiment with paints made from zinc.
He used zinc oxide in place of the specified lead
white on many of his contracts. The results met
with great approval and, when he felt his position
sufficiently strong, he painted separate areas

with pure lead and zinc to convince his clients of
the superiority of zinc oxide. The lead inevitably
began to change colour and 'chalk', while the
zinc-painted surfaces retained their colour and
surface. Once his clients had been convinced
of the benefits, a new industry began to develop.

Before 1914 most zinc oxide used in the
United Kingdom was imported from France,
Belgium, Holland and the United States. British
architect Wyatt Papworth mentioned it in 1858,
and an early reference to its use in the United
Kingdom appeared in 1859. It was recommended
for rooms with gaslights where the 'clearness
and brilliancy' of the white was to be preserved.
(When carrying out paint analysis, it is useful
to know that zinc-based paint was not employed
before c. 1850.) It is quite distinctive, especially
when viewed under ultraviolet light, where it
fluoresces brightly. An early example of zinc
oxide paint was identified on a spiral staircase
installed in a Buckinghamshire country house
in 1853. The staircase was very dark and acted
like a chimney for the fumes of the gaslight at its
base, so zinc oxide would have seemed a good idea.

The chief disadvantage of zinc oxide is the
hardening effect it has on oil, which causes it
to produce a brittle paint film. This can lead to
premature breakdown of the paint on external
surfaces by cracking or chalking unless corrected.
As a result, zinc oxide was typically used in a
mixture with white lead in the first quarter of the
twentieth century. This blend made a very good
paint as the lead moderated any hardening action
of the zinc and so prevented brittleness.

[A] Women were employed to build the stacks of white lead. These were usually about 7 metres
(23 ft) high and consisted of alternating layers of spent tan-bark and earthenware pots containing
vinegar and lead coils. It is evident that no special workwear was provided routinely, despite lead
poisoning being widely acknowledged and its effects being cumulative. [B] Although protective clothing
and masks were provided for those dismantling lead stacks, these would have offered inadequate
protection against extended lead exposure. [C] A barefoot young woman prepares lead coils.
Unborn and young children are particularly at risk from lead poisoning.

[D] Men were employed in the highly toxic work of dismantling the stacks of corroded lead.
[E] The men in this photograph, lacking protective clothing or masks, are at great risk of chronic lead poisoning. Corroded lead coils in earthenware pots would have released large quantities of highly toxic dust. Symptoms of lead poisoning include serious and irreversible mental and behavioural defects, abdominal pain, infertility, anaemia, seizures, coma and death. Lead paint continues to be used in many countries, especially those with low and middle incomes. The Institute for Health Metrics and Evaluation (IHME) estimated in 2013 that lead exposure accounted for 853,000 deaths worldwide.

WHITE EARTHS

A   B   C

White pigments derived from the earth varied considerably in quality, depending on their origin and the method of preparation. Pure chalk was certainly not the only white earth pigment used for decorating in the eighteenth and nineteenth centuries. The naming of these pigments in the colour shops must have caused great confusion.

The Swiss chemist and mineralogist Pierre-François Tingry described white earth pigments as comprising two types: those that were largely clay, which were termed 'argillaceous', and those that contained large amounts of chalk, which were termed 'calcareous'.

Early writers on paint exhibit a strong European perspective in their texts. There are many references to fine grades of white pigments obtained in the Pays-de-Vaud in Switzerland, the Auvergne and Normandy, for example. With a few notable exceptions, it is unlikely that many of these would have been available in the United Kingdom or United States. On the other hand, the qualities exhibited by certain white earth pigments were undoubtedly identified among native sources, by employing a basic knowledge of science and a degree of common sense. As P. F. Tingry noted in *Painter's and Colourman's Complete Guide* (1804):

> Chalk is well known to every one; it abounds in the eastern and southern districts of this country. When levigated and washed, it is called whiting, which is found in the shops in powder, in lumps, and sometimes in balls.

The majority of the white earths would have found use in a water-based medium, such as distemper. When mixed with oil, the refractive index of chalk approaches that of the oil itself, resulting in a semi-translucent, dirty off-white.

Spanish white was perhaps the pigment that saw greatest use in the United Kingdom. Although it may have originated in Spain, hence the name, in the United Kingdom it was generally regarded as being whiting or finely powdered white chalk neutralized by the addition of water in which alum had been dissolved, and afterwards washed in several waters. In common with basic washed chalk,

it was used frequently for simple whitewashing. It was also employed to whiten plaster surfaces, especially ceilings, in the form of a simple slurry with water, when it was termed whitening.

The alkalinity of Spanish white, unless washed out of it, was liable to alter certain alkali-sensitive pigments, especially Prussian blue. When bound with a small amount of animal glue and pigment, it was known as colouring or soft distemper. Some authors suggested that it was sometimes used, for the sake of cheapness, in priming. However, it was not at all durable by itself and worked better with the addition of a proportion of white lead.

Bougival white was thought to have originated from a place called Marly, near Paris. It was described by Tingry in *The Painter and Varnisher's Guide* (1804) as being of a white 'much better for house-painting than any other white earth of a calcareous nature'. Commonly known as tobacco pipe clay, or pipe clay, it was used to make those objects. It was utilized by the potter Josiah Wedgwood, who obtained some from Normandy.

According to experiments made by Tingry, Bougival white contained nearly a third chalk, as a result of which it was considered inferior in oil painting to Spanish white and to white of Meudon. However, it was frequently used instead of white lead for priming in an effort to cut costs. Having been washed free of small stones and sand, it was sold in the shops in the form of oblong cakes, sometimes known as Rouen white.

Gypsum, or sulphate of lime (calcium sulphate) was described as a white for whitewashing apartments and for painting in distemper. It was employed by 'drowning' Plaster of Paris in a large quantity of water, so that it would not set hard, and was regarded as being very fine and providing a more delicate white than that of chalk. Gypsum perhaps saw more use in the extending of pigments, where a quantity could often be added without adverse effect.

[A] Spanish white. [B] Bougival white. [C] Gypsum. [D] For the production of lamp black, a conical canvas trapped soot from a fire. This could be lowered and shaken for the soot to be collected. From the *Encyclopédie*, edited by Diderot and d'Alembert, 1751–72. [OVERLEAF] The Stone Hall at Houghton Hall, Norfolk. Construction of the house began in 1722 and was completed in 1735 for Sir Robert Walpole. It is the work of architects Colen Campbell and James Gibbs with interiors by William Kent. The hall has stone walls and external architectural details and was designed to appear as a semi-external space.

THE BLACKS

LAMP BLACK

Lamp black was the soot that was collected after burning the resinous parts of fir trees. The burning process often led to incomplete combustion, which caused the pigment to have a slight shade of brown and to be somewhat greasy. It derived mostly from Sweden and Norway, although it was manufactured on a large scale in Germany, and even in Paris, at the beginning of the nineteenth century. In the late seventeenth century, John Smith referred to it, in one of the earliest house-painting manuals, as being made up in small boxes and barrels and exported to the United Kingdom.

Lamp black was the most commonly used of the blacks because it was cheap and plentiful. A very fine pigment, when ground with linseed oil its greasiness would delay the drying time, unless a drying agent was added. This might be the addition of either two parts of drying oil, or a drier such as white copperas (zinc sulphate). Smith recommended adding a small amount of verdigris for this purpose.

Both the colour and the natural fatness of lamp black could be improved by burning it in a crucible or iron ladle over a fire. This process tended to harden the pigment, which then required lengthier grinding. However, it also meant it commanded a higher price.

IVORY BLACK

Although mentioned in many early manuals, ivory black was always regarded as an expensive commodity not used in common work.

Traditionally, ivory black was made from the shavings and off-cuts of the comb-making industry, and from other waste fragments of ivory. These were burnt or charred to a black coal, ground very fine with water on a marble slab, and then dried. Ivory black worked well with oil and formed a beautiful pearl grey when mixed with white lead.

In the nineteenth century, the name 'ivory black' was often used to describe the pigment produced by burning animal bones, more properly called bone black, which was regarded as a 'very indifferent black, abounding in impurities, and suited only to the coarser kinds of painting' (P. F. Tingry. *Painter's and Colourman's Complete Guide*, 1830). It tended to produce a reddish hue, quite distinct from the richer effect derived from ivory. Genuine ivory is no longer used now that the animals that are its natural sources are endangered species.

BLUE BLACK

A black of a bluish hue was produced in Europe by the burning of vine twigs, which when ground carefully and mixed with white produced a silver white. Beech charcoal, used in the United Kingdom, was credited with a very similar tone. Frankfurt black, produced by burning wine lees and tartar, sometimes with the addition of ivory or peach stones, was manufactured in some parts of Germany.

In *The Mechanic's Companion* (1825), Peter Nicholson mentioned small amounts of blue black being used to brighten up the last two coats of a surface painted in white with oil. Others suggested Prussian blue or lamp black for the same purpose. In finer work, a charcoal black was likely to have been used, as seen in numerous historic decorative schemes.

D

THE BLUES

AZURITE

Azurite, or blue bice, was a natural mineral found in many parts of the world. Originally sourced in Armenia, extraction later moved to Germany. Caused by the weathering of copper ore deposits, it was a gritty pigment unless ground finely, which had the effect of making it very pale. Although it is found in early painted decoration, the introduction of Prussian blue in the early eighteenth century rendered it obsolete.

BLUE VERDITER

Blue verditer was an artificial form of azurite and much was produced as a by-product of the silver refining industry. Germany was the main source of the early pigment, but English verditer became highly prized. The blue variety was 'subject to change and turn greenish' (John Smith. *The Art of Painting in Oyl*, 1676). However, mixed with a yellow it produced a good green of a far brighter sort than was possible with any of the other available blues. The pigment worked best in a water-based medium, such as distemper, and was not generally considered fit for oil painting, as the oil rendered it very dark and transparent. However, if blue verditer was used in oil paint, it had to be mixed with a great deal of white, and it is in this form that it is generally found.

ULTRAMARINE

Produced from the semi-precious stone lapis lazuli since ancient times, ultramarine was prized for its beautiful blue colour. Although mentioned by name in the majority of the early house-painting texts, there is no evidence of it having been employed in anything other than specialized applications.

With the exception of its high price, ultramarine had several ideal properties of a pigment: it was suitable for use in both oil and water media, reasonably resistant to acids and alkalis, non-fading, and unaffected by moisture. It was also of a clean, slightly purple hue, unlike the darker greenish tints produced by the other blues used for house-painting. It is not surprising that a great effort was made to synthesize the pigment, and after a competition in the 1820s a method was invented by J. B. Guimet of Toulouse. Within a few years, factories in France, the United Kingdom, Germany, Belgium and the United States were manufacturing the pigment.

INDIGO

Derived from the plant of the genus *Indigofera*, indigo was grown in the East and West Indies, Brazil and Peru. A good account of its manufacture was given by 'Citizen' Brulley of the French colony of Hispaniola in the Caribbean.

The use of indigo, called a dangerous drug and described as the 'food of the devil', was prohibited by the British Parliament of Elizabeth I. Although this act was not repealed officially until the reign of Charles II, it appears that owing to the activities of the East India Company large quantities of indigo were imported throughout the early seventeenth century. Similar concerns were felt in Frankfurt, where a decree of the Diet, held in 1577, prohibited under the severest penalties 'the newly invented, pernicious, deceitful, eating and corrosive dye called the Devil's Dye'.

However, perhaps the greatest resistance to indigo came from the woad growers of Somerset, Lincolnshire and Cambridgeshire, who feared competition. Having described indigo as expensive and so usually mixed with white, John Smith went on to say that 'Vulgar Painters instead thereof use Blew Balls [woad], which they buy at the colour-Shops which nearly imitates it, but is not so good a Colour neither for Beauty nor lasting.'

Although found in early technical literature, indigo seldom presents in examination of any but the earliest paints.

Plate 35 from *Histoire générale des drogues,* 1694 (General History of Drugs) by the French apothecary to Louis xiv Pierre Pomet. The engraving shows slaves, under an overseer, cutting the anil or indigo plant, throwing it into water tanks, stirring it and then carrying it away to be dried.

Men extracting indigo dye from the *Indigofera tinctoria* plant. In large tanks, the indoxyl-rich mixture made from fermented indigo is stirred to mix it with air. This helps to oxidize the indigo into the pigment indigotin, which settles to the bottom of the tank and can then be filtered and dried.

PRUSSIAN BLUE

This blue pigment was named after it was invented in Berlin and it was also known as Berlin blue. In 1706 a colour maker, Johann Jacob Diesbach, was trying to make a cochineal red lake in the laboratory of the alchemist Johann Konrad Dippel when he accidentally produced a very effective blue colour. The process was kept secret until it was published in England in 1724, although there was some controversy as to whether it had been used in place of ultramarine in the decoration of the Cupola Room of Kensington Palace in May 1722.

A century later, Prussian blue was described by London colourman T. H. Vanherman in *The Painter's Cabinet, and Colourman's Repository* (1828) as 'the most general and useful blue we have, either for inside or out-door painting'. He went on to say that combined with some of the reds and most of the yellows, it 'produces purples and greens, of numberless tints and gradations, but does not harmonize with patent yellow'. This latter comment emphasizes how important it was for the painter to understand the exact nature of his materials. For example, Prussian blue was inclined to discolour when exposed to alkaline compounds. It was also one of the pigments that was used in small amounts to correct the yellowing tendency of white paint. In the 1730s, Prussian blue was regarded as an 'extraordinary colour' and was charged at twice the rate of the common colours.

SMALT

Smalt was a glass-like pigment of a rich blue colour verging on purple. It was coloured by cobalt obtained from the numerous mines of Saxony, which led to its name Saxon blue. As with azurite, or blue bice, the colour was always strongest when ground coarsely; however, in that form, it handled with difficulty.

One method of obtaining the best colour was to scatter the pigment on a coat of pale blue oil paint that had been allowed to stand for a short while after application. As a result, the particles adhered to the still-sticky surface and remained embedded in the paint film. The effect was best when viewed from a distance.

Although smalt was encountered in some early decorative schemes, the pigment seems largely to have been used for specific purposes. It has been found on sundials, clock-faces, sign-boards and also on fine ironwork. Smalt was perhaps most useful as a blue in the ceramics industry, and until the introduction of French ultramarine in the nineteenth century it was also used by laundresses to blue their linen.

A disadvantage of smalt was that it was gradually altered by moisture and by the carbon dioxide in the atmosphere, becoming paler and greyer; moreover, the finer the particle size, the more rapid the change. The blue could disappear completely within a few years. An example of smalt preserved in a cross-section of a paint sample can be seen on page 22, image F.

THE BROWNS

THE SIENNAS

A   B

THE UMBERS

C   D

One of the earliest references to the use of a native earth brought from Siena, Italy, for house-painting purposes, dates to 1823. The pigment became available at about the same time and was used chiefly in wood graining and marbling, where its translucency proved invaluable for the glazes used in overgraining. The raw variety was a deep warm yellow colour, used in the imitation of satin wood and, inevitably, in the representation of sienna marble. The burnt pigment was used as a glazing colour, especially in imitations of mahogany.

The earth pigment umber was described as being a kind of clay brought from Nocera Umbra, Italy. It was suggested that earth umber was an inaccurate translation of the French term *terre d'ombre*, which more literally translates as 'earth of the shadows'. P. F. Tingry mentioned two types of the pigment – Turkey umber and English umber – 'the best comes from Turkey, or rather from the island of Cyprus, where it occurs in beds'. Indeed, the north-west hills of that island still provide the best source today. The English umber was found primarily in Derbyshire and Somerset and was employed in low-priced work. Both types of umber were used in the production of different varieties of drab and stone colour, in oil and in distemper. Like the other earth pigments, when umber was roasted, its colour altered, becoming browner and approaching red. In this form, it was known as burnt umber.

VANDYKE BROWN

Known variously by names such as Vandyke brown, Cologne earth and Cassel earth, this type of pigment was a translucent bituminous brown that was very useful as a glazing colour in the imitation of woods. However, it was an expensive pigment and saw little use otherwise as a result.

[PREVIOUS] Drawing room, James Brice House, Annapolis, Maryland, with colour scheme based on that of 1766–73. [A] Raw sienna. [B] Burnt sienna. [C] Raw umber. [D] Burnt umber. [BELOW] 'The Invention of Oil Paint', engraving plate 15 from *Nova Reperta* (New Discoveries) engraved by Philip Galle in *c*. 1600. Note the apprentices grinding pigments. [OVERLEAF] The eating parlour at Headfort House, Ireland. The Adam scheme of the 1770s was recently reinstated.

THE GREENS

VERDIGRIS

Verdigris is basic copper acetate, produced by exposing sheets of copper to the acidic fumes of vinegar, usually made from wine, although cider tended to be used in the United Kingdom. The poisonous pigment has been used since ancient times, and the name means 'the green of Greece'. Verdigris made in Montpellier, in the south of France, was considered to be a superior product.

In the late seventeenth century, John Smith described verdigris as 'the best and most useful green of all others', although it inclined to blue and had rather a coarse texture. Its translucency drew recommendations of a green undercoat of Prussian blue and yellow, while its fast-drying nature sometimes led to it being mixed with the very slow-drying blacks.

A purer, brighter variety of verdigris is described by several authors as being obtainable from the colour shops. This was cleared of 'dross and filth' by being dissolved in distilled vinegar and filtered; the liquid was allowed to evaporate, and the resultant crystals were called distilled verdigris. Its high price prevented it from being employed in everyday work.

ARSENICAL GREEN

The arsenical greens appeared from the end of the eighteenth century and during the first quarter of the nineteenth century. It was well understood that they were poisonous but the colours were unlike any previously available greens. The best known, Scheele's green, was discovered by the Swede Carl Wilhelm Scheele in 1775. It was characterized variously as apple green and light sea green in colour. G. A. Smeaton commented in *The Painter's, Gilder's & Varnisher's Manual* (*c.* 1827) that it 'grinds well with oil, and is in much request for the painting of the cabins of ships'. Schweinfurt, or emerald green, was a later development, described by the colourman George Field as being a new copper green, the 'most vivid of this tribe of colours'. It was more opaque and more durable than the others, and was mainly used in distemper and in the manufacture of wallpaper.

Prussia had prohibited the sale of articles coloured with arsenical pigments by the 1830s and Bavaria followed suit in 1845. France was not long behind, but it was not until 1880 that William Morris stopped using arsenical greens in his wallpapers in the United Kingdom.

GREEN VERDITER

Green verditer had the same chemical composition as malachite. It was very closely related to blue verditer and can be synthesized in a similar way. As the name 'verditer', derived from the French *verd de terre*, suggests, the green variety was produced first and a further process turned it blue.

Green verditer is a gritty colour with poor covering power, which, in spite of 'all the grinding imaginable', would never work well in oil. As such, it was generally regarded as being unfit for oil painting and was better suited for distemper. A similar colour could be obtained in oil paint by mixing two or three parts of verdigris with one part of white lead.

GREEN EARTH

Green earth is a blue green earth pigment that was generally sourced from Hungary, although Saxony, Verona and many parts of France are also credited with fine green earths. In *Artists' Pigments* c. 1600–1835 (1982), Rosamond Harley gave three classifications for these natural copper greens: a) *terre verte*, b) chrysocolla or mountain green, and c) malachite or green bice. Good examples of malachite and green bice can be found in China, Germany and Siberia.

Natural copper earths saw limited application and they were used most commonly in distemper. If ground with oil, they were mixed with equal, or greater, parts of white lead.

THE REDS

RED LAKES

A red lake was a red pigment made by the lake process, that is, the extraction of a dye from a substance and the precipitation of it onto a base such as aluminium hydroxide. These substances could be either animal or vegetable in origin.

Indian lake was a rich crimson colour that was extracted from the crude shellac resin excreted by the lac insect, known as *Coccus lacca*, which infested various trees in Asia and India. It was imported by the East India Company.

A better quality lake was prepared from the cochineal insect *Coccus cacti*, which was found in Latin America. The dried insect bodies were boiled in water with a little cream of tartar and alum added while still on the fire, before allowing the solution to cool. The colouring matter settled to the bottom of the vessel, and the clear liquid was poured off carefully and kept. The product that remained was allowed to dry and was called carmine. The decanted liquid was then treated with a solution of tin (stannous chloride), which yielded more carmine 'little inferior to the first product' and generally known as cochineal lake.

It was not easy to distinguish between a lake prepared from cochineal and one from some other colouring substance. The hallmarks of a good lake were its resistance to the action of the atmosphere and of light, which would only become obvious with time.

The most common vegetable sources were the red-brown brazilwood, or pernambuco wood, obtained from trees of the genus *Caesalpinia*. Incidentally, the country Brazil took its name from the dyewood. Another source was the American *Haematoxylum campechianum*, which was more commonly known as logwood or campeachy.

As red lake was so difficult to manufacture, an early nineteenth-century author suggested that it might be obtained indirectly from the clippings of scarlet cloth. Lake, whatever its source, provided the house-painter with a range of red colours not adequately supplied by other substances. In spite of its cost and its tendency to fade, it remained a highly desirable range of pigments until the late nineteenth century.

ROSE PINK

A less expensive substitute for the various red lakes was a pigment called rose pink, which was prepared from chalk coloured with brazilwood. It was fugitive to light and inclined more to purple than scarlet. However, when used as a glazing colour and afterwards varnished, it appears to have lasted moderately well. As rose pink was relatively low in cost, it is highly likely that this pigment was utilized frequently in distemper.

VERMILION

Vermilion was a bright scarlet pigment produced by combining sulphur and mercury to form red mercuric sulphide. Cinnabar was the natural form, which was less common but often preferred because of the tendency of the colour shops to adulterate the artificial variety with red lead. In late eighteenth-century Germany, it was used as a sedative and an antispasmodic.

Early commentators reveal that vermilion was manufactured chiefly in Holland but that the best quality came from China. Such was the difficulty in obtaining it in a pure state that it was considered necessary to place the order directly with a Chinese manufacturer to ensure its freedom from adulteration.

Vermilion was a powerful colour and there was nothing quite like it on the house-painter's palette. However, concern was expressed occasionally about its durability, and it was often considered liable to turn black. This would seem to be associated more with its adulteration with red lead than with an inherent weakness in the pigment itself.

In 1847, vermilion cost about 4s 10d (24p/30¢) per pound in China, while its price in the United Kingdom varied from three shillings to six shillings (15p/19¢ to 30p/38¢) per pound (Hay, *Harmonious Colouring*, sixth edition, 1847, p. 139).

REALGAR

Realgar was usually mentioned in association with the yellow sulphide of arsenic known as orpiment, and was the red form of that mineral. Although found in nature, it could be made artificially by melting together arsenic and sulphur, and gave a good red, which was used in varnish. All the early writers who refer to it were aware of its highly toxic nature, and it is unlikely that it saw general use where alternative pigments were available.

RED OCHRES

Red ochres came in many different forms and provided a number of reds for the early house-painter. Spanish brown, Venetian red and Indian red, when in their natural states, were pigments used as they were found, whereas light red was made by roasting yellow ochre, and English red was one of a large number of artificial red oxides produced from the by-products of certain industrial processes. The eighteenth-century French colourman Jean-Félix Watin described a good variety coming from Deptford, London.

The natural red ochres were prepared by simple washing. As the sand and stones that they contained were heavier than the coloured earth, these sank to the bottom, thus allowing the ochre to be carried off into a lower container. When the ochre had subsided, the clear water was drawn off and the ochre taken out and dried.

Spanish brown, in spite of the name, was not brought from Spain. It was usually a low-grade red earth colour from a variety of locations, used principally in priming woodwork until the 1740s and for external purposes. Venetian red was a red ochre that came from a number of places, but the name was generally used to describe the redder variety. In the early days, some may have been brought via Venice, but it was also produced in France, Germany and other countries. In the

nineteenth century, like many of the red earth colours, it was prepared artificially from iron sulphate in the manufacture of sulphuric acid. Strictly speaking it was then regarded as a 'red oxide' rather than a 'red ochre'.

A more prized red earth was Indian red, which originally was brought in from the East Indies. However, once an artificial variety could be produced from the manufacture of sulphuric acid, it was no longer imported. It tended to have a bluish undertone. A variant was a red iron oxide called colcothar of vitriol (more prosaically known as purple brown). This was created in the same way but heated to a higher temperature. It produced the chocolate paint that was used commonly for the woodwork in basements and other secondary areas.

RED LEAD

Red lead was made by heating litharge, a yellow lead oxide. As a pigment it had a very mixed reputation and was often used more for its drying properties than for its orange-red colour, which was liable to turn black in oil.

Due to its quick-drying nature, it was somewhat difficult to work with, hardening into an unmanageable mass, and adhering '...so strong to the bottom of the paint-pot, that it proves a troublesome task to liberate it and bring it into a working condition again'. (Vanherman, 1829)

Yet this quality was of considerable use at a time when a coat of oil paint could take several days to dry, and the decoration of a room, perhaps, a week. The addition of red lead to an undercoat would ensure that it would be ready to receive the finish coat as soon as possible. The pigment is often found in nineteenth-century primers and it provided the pink colour seen in wood primers until the late twentieth century.

[A] Logwood. [B] Carmine. [C] Brazilwood. [D] Venetian red. [E] English red. [F] Indian red. [OVERLEAF] The gallery at Attingham Park, Shropshire. The red colour was based on John Nash's scheme of 1807 and was recently applied by the National Trust following investigations.

THE YELLOWS

CHROME YELLOW

Chrome yellow was discovered in the late 1790s by the eminent French chemist Nicolas-Louis Vauquelin, and was the first bright yellow that was reasonably durable and yet worked in both oil- and water-based media. It was the yellow pigment that the artist and the house-painter had been waiting for.

It began to appear in quantity in the second quarter of the nineteenth century and is a useful marker pigment when examining paint in cross section. Its immediate effect was on the production of dark greens, for when mixed with Prussian blue it enabled the brighter Brunswick greens (chrome greens) to be produced. Until the 1820s, dark greens tended to be dull and either termed as bronze greens or invisible greens. By the 1840s, chrome yellow was described as 'almost the only bright yellow now in use'.

PINKS

A   B

The use of the word 'pink' to indicate a light red colour appears to date from the early eighteenth century. Before then, 'pink' described a wide variety of yellows produced from plant sources, of which several recipes are given in early manuals. Latterly, pink was usually qualified by an adjective, such as brown pink, Dutch pink, English pink, Italian pink, light pink, pink yellow and yellow pink.

The main source was the woad plant *Isatis tinctoria*, a plant common in France and Spain, which was also used to produce a blue similar to indigo. Another source was the small or narrow-leaved buckthorn *Rhamnus infectoria*, the berries of which, when collected green, are called *graine d'Avignon*, yellow berries or more usually French berries. Whichever source was used, the method of production was similar. The plant was boiled in a solution of alum, then the coloured liquid mixed with chalk. In this form, the pigment worked best in distemper and was also commonly used in the production of wallpaper.

KING'S YELLOW / ORPIMENT

Orpiment, or yellow sulphide of arsenic, was found in deposits across Europe and Asia and had been used since early times. An artificial variant has nine parts arsenic and one of sulphur.

This pigment was extremely toxic. As the house-painter T. H. Vanherman advised:

> I think it necessary to caution the use of [King's yellow], unless any one has a wish to be driven out of house and home with his family; in that case, he has only to order one small apartment to be painted with King's yellow, and he will be gratified; for the smell cannot be confined, but sends its vile effluvia into every corner of the house, and instead of growing weaker, it gains strength every day, and the only remedy, should such a misfortune occur, is to bestow on it two coats of patent yellow, and then two coats of light carriage varnish. This pigment is a combination of sulphur and arsenic, and should be excluded, not only on account of the above annoying quality, but also its antipathysing with most other colours.

NAPLES YELLOW

In the 1770s, the Frenchman Auguste-Denis Fougeroux de Bondaroy identified Naples yellow as being a synthetic lead-based pigment. It covered reasonably well in oil and varnish, but in water-based media a coat of varnish was needed to prevent blackening. Naples yellow also reacted with iron and steel implements as well as iron-based pigments such as ochres and Prussian blue. The pigment was often used with blue to form green, as can be seen in several decorative schemes of the late eighteenth century.

Naples yellow and the later patent yellow superseded earlier lead pigments such as massicot. This term refers to either lead-tin yellow (lead stannate) or canary litharge (lead monoxide), made during the sixteenth century in Flanders or Germany.

MONTPELLIER YELLOW / TURNER'S PATENT YELLOW

Known as Turner's yellow after James Turner, who patented the process for its manufacture in 1781, this pigment was known in France as Montpellier yellow. It had a comparatively short life and was all but superseded, for house-painting purposes, in the first thirty years of the nineteenth century by the gradual introduction of chrome yellow. However, it seems to have found a place in coach-painting.

The pigment was made by mixing two parts of litharge and one part of salt with water, and allowing it to stand until the mixture had turned white. It was then washed and dried, before being heated in a crucible.

Patent yellow is perhaps best known for its use in the two first floor drawing rooms of Sir John Soane's Museum in about 1812. The existing scheme is based on this.

YELLOW OCHRES

C   D   E   F

Like the other family of earth pigments, the umbers, ochres saw constant use in house-painting from the earliest times. Readily obtained, they encompassed a large range of hues whether natural or calcined (roasted).

In 1676 John Smith mentioned the two basic types in what was perhaps the first manual on house-painting:

> Yellow Oaker, Is of two sorts; the one gotten in England, the other brought from beyond the Seas: the one is light Yellow, much like the colour of Wheat straw; the other is somewhat of a deeper colour.

Essentially, ochres were derived from sands and clays, the mixture of silica, alumina and hydrated iron oxide giving them their yellow colour. They were generally light- and lime-fast, and also inert. However, as a natural product ochres could vary in both colour and quality in the same underground seam. This inconsistency led to them being synthesized from an early date. Many methods were used, but the principal one consisted of the oxidation of iron sulphate (also known as green vitriol, or copperas), mixed with alum and precipitated by means of an alkali.

The Swiss chemist and mineralogist Pierre-François Tingry discovered:

> Many of the yellow ochres when burnt become of a red colour, and are then occasionally used for more delicate processes.

When calcined, the pigment was generally known as light red. If further heat was applied, the colour deepened to a dark purplish-brown. The darkest synthetic ochre to be produced in this way was known as colcothar of vitriol.

Oxford ochre displayed many of the best properties for a house-painting pigment. The earliest detailed account of it was given by Robert Plot, the first professor of chemistry at Oxford University. In his *Natural History of Oxfordshire* (1677), he described how difficult it was to find. The best sort came from Shotover, where the vein ran between 2 and 9 metres (7 and 30 ft) below the surface from east to west. The ochre was wrapped within ten folds of earth, rather like an onion skin, and came in two forms: 1) stone ochre, which needed crushing before use, and 2) clay ochre, which was soaked and washed for two or three days, then beaten into thin broad cakes with clubs that were cut into tiles and laid out to dry before being sold.

Oxford ochre was still being processed in the early twentieth century and it appears in paint ranges of the period. However, by 1928 supplies were described as being 'almost exhausted'.

A darker, second-best ochre is often encountered in early works, in which it is referred to as Dutch or spruce ochre. Another regional ochre came from Gorran Haven, Cornwall, and this pigment was exported to Germany for colouring bricks and paint.

[A] Weld. [B] Dutch pink. [C] Oxford ochre. [D] Spruce ochre. [E] Brown ochre. [F] French ochre. [OVERLEAF] Kirtlington Park Room, Metropolitan Museum, New York. This was originally the dining room at Kirtlington Park, Oxfordshire, designed by John Sanderson in c. 1745. The plasterwork was by Thomas Roberts and the chimneypiece by either John Cheere or his brother Sir Henry Cheere. The museum bought the room in the 1920s and it was erected in 1955. Paint analysis in 1995 revealed that it had been painted in a straw-coloured distemper. However, the museum colourwashed the walls, giving a very different effect.

House-painting, with regards to maintenance was carried out by property owners on an ad-hoc basis from the earliest days. However, for the purposes of decoration, it is more likely that it would have been undertaken by a professional. In the larger cities, craftsmen carrying out both decorative and necessary painting tended to form themselves into fraternities or guilds. In the City of London, these guilds exercised more or less effective control over their trade from the Tudor period. This section outlines the formation of the company of painter-stainers in 1581 and its role in training apprentices. It charts the subsequent rise of DIY painters and the role of the colourman in supplying ready-made paints and other tools of the trade.

A

B

C

D

[A] This trading card for oil and colourman T. Neave of Fleet Street, London, dates from 1815–16. [B] Nathan Drake, at the White Hart in Long Acre, London, was a leading artists' colourman from the 1750s to 1780s. [C] The card of Emerton & Manby of 720 Strand, London, shows a horse-powered mill for grinding colours. This card dates from the 1790s. [D] A nineteenth-century trade card for oil and colourman W. Fry, of Church Street, Greenwich, London, who mixed paints, melted tallow and made candles and brushes.

THE PAINTER-STAINER

The earliest surviving ordinances of the Painters' Company date from 1283 and show the existence of an organized body. At this time, the main occupation of the members was the painting of saddle bows (the arched upper front part of a saddle). The Stainers' Company produced stained or painted cloths, which were used instead of pictures on plaster walls because they were portable and less expensive than tapestries.

In 1502 the two companies presented a petition to the Lord Mayor for their union as 'Payntour Steynours'. A man could become a freeman of the company by 'patrimony' if his father had been a liveryman of the company; by 'servitude' if he had served the requisite number of years as an apprentice to a member of the company; or by 'redemption' upon paying a fee.

When its trade began to suffer at the hands of untrained painters, the company petitioned Queen Elizabeth. The result was the grant of a Charter of Incorporation in 1581. This was followed by the confirmation of a set of rules known as 'The Book of Ordinances', which spelt out the restrictions on the trade of painting. It decreed that every person practising painting within a four-mile compass of the City of London should pay quarterly dues to the company, and that, with the exception of gentlemen exercising the art 'for recreation or private pleasure', no one should use the art unless he had been apprenticed for seven years to a painter.

The quality of work was controlled carefully. Work that was intended to stand the weather was to be carried out only by expert workmen 'with oil colours and gilt of fine gold'. No one was to produce work 'wrought with stencil or otherwise as painted...upon cloth, silk, leather or other things...'; this was considered false and deceitful. The master and wardens had the power to enter, without force, any premises within four miles of the City and inspect all works relating to the art. They could fine the painter, owners or seller of a work that did not meet the required standards.

DISPUTE WITH THE PLASTERERS

Competition was largely unaffected by the Charter, but an Act of Parliament was brought against plasterers in 1606. The Act pointed out that they now practised the art of painting in oil as well as water-based distemper, to the great injury of the painter-stainers, who were thereby 'disabled to get any competent living for the relief of themselves and their poor wives and children'. As a result, it was decreed that no plasterer from then on should use the art of painting, unless previously apprenticed to a painter for seven years. It was accepted nonetheless that a plasterer might use certain pigments in distemper on plaster. Further such Acts were passed in 1612 and 1626, but in 1664 they were still seeking assistance in the dispute.

At about this time, the painter-stainers were divided into four main groups: arms painters, house-painters, leather gilders and picture makers. This seems to be the first reference to a house-painting element by name, and indicates how recent the use of oil paint on buildings was. Prior to this, interior walls would have been covered by tapestry or painted hangings, and latterly by oak wainscot. However, by the mid seventeenth century, the cutting down of oak trees for ship building, and the consequent growth in the importation of softwood for house building, had led to the expansion of the house-painting trade. The increased use of softwood in building meant that a protective coating to preserve it from the action of air and damp would be required. As the trade fragmented into different branches, many aspects of the earlier system ceased to be of relevance. This, together with various economic and social factors, and certain technical developments, led to the gradual decline in control of the trade by the livery company, and the consequent relaxation of the regulation of standards.

THE GREAT FIRE OF LONDON

The rebuilding necessitated by the Great Fire of London in 1666 drew attention to the restrictive practices of the livery companies and seriously weakened their authority. The Rebuilding Act of 1667 transferred the authority to regulate prices and wages from the companies to the government, and, although limited to seven years, it allowed all building workers the same right to work in London as freemen of their trades.

In spite of the fact that great numbers of buildings were erected in the City in the years after the Great Fire, many people who had fled the conflagration stayed in the suburbs. A report

[A/B] A house-painter painting a window, *c.* 1820. Note his typical paper cap, round brush and pot for holding paint. [C/D] An example of a portable, patented platform, *c.* 1830 – a major improvement on the builder's cripple shown on page 35.

of 1673 mentions that 3,423 houses and shops remained unoccupied, and measures were taken to encourage the repopulation of the Square Mile. All persons who took up permanent residence in the newly built houses were admitted into the freedom of the City without paying any joining fees. This concession led to an increase of more than 10,000 admissions in the period 1675–80. The effect on the painter-stainers must have been profound, especially as many house-painters would have been reluctant to submit to the control of the company. Furthermore, once a freeman, any man could lawfully relinquish the trade in which he had originally served his apprenticeship 'and exercise any other trade at his will and pleasure'.

THE RISE OF DO-IT-YOURSELF PAINTING

The late seventeenth century was a difficult period for the Painter-Stainers' Company as any kind of monopoly that it may have had over the activity of house-painting was being eroded. This is demonstrated by the increasing availability of semi-prepared painting materials and the number of publications explaining their use. This development eliminated the need to possess the 'chief secret' of house-painting: namely the mixing and compounding of the colours. John Smith, in *The Art of Painting in Oyl* (1676; this edition 1687), remarked:

> Those that [like] not to be at the trouble of grinding colours themselves, may have of any sort...ready ground, at the colour shops, at reasonable rates, either in smaller or larger quantities.

And in 1718, a patent was granted to Marshall Smith for a 'machine or engine for the grinding of colours, to be used in all kinds of paintings'.

In 1734, William Salmon in his *Palladio Londinensis, or The London Art of Building,* noted:

> It is well known and daily experienced since the Advertisement of Alexander Emerton, that several Noblemen and Gentlemen have by themselves and Servants painted whole houses without the Assistance or Direction of a Painter, which when examined by the best Judges could not be distinguished from the Work of a professed Painter.

The 1788 edition of John Smith's *The Art of Painting in Oyl* claimed:

> The whole Treatise being so complete, and so exactly fitted to the Meanest Capability, that all Persons may be able, by the Directions, to paint in Oil Colours, all Manner of Timber-Work; such as Posts, Pales, Palisadoes, Gates, Doors, or any Thing else that requires either Use, Beauty, or Preservation from the Violence or Injury of the Weather.

And John Pincot in his *Treatise on the Practical Part of Coach and House Painting* (*c.* 1811) explained:

> ...the easiest and cheapest method of painting according to the principles of the old school, by which gentlemen, builders and others may direct, and persons of moderate capacity may understand, and by attentively observing saving to themselves or their employers 50 per cent.

By 1827, Nathaniel Whittock had acknowledged both the decline of the apprenticeship system and its cause, when he referred to the lack of trained painters in his *The Decorative Painters' and Glaziers' Guide*:

> The facility with which ready prepared colours can be procured at the respectable colour shops in London and other large towns, has led to the great neglect of information on the first principles of painting; and it is not one house-painter in twenty who is acquainted with the pigments and vehicles necessary to his business.

APPRENTICESHIP AND TRAINING

In spite of its diminishing influence, the apprenticeship system continued in a reduced form for another two hundred years or so. It flourished in most of the major towns and cities in the United Kingdom, where parents went to some lengths to arrange apprenticeship for their sons. Applicants were required to find a suitable master, agree on the contract and pay the premium. Masters were limited in the number of apprentices that they could take on.

When training was completed, the apprentice's skills were tested by representatives of the livery company. Then, at three successive meetings, the apprentice was 'called', and if there were no objections to his election, he was sworn in as a member of the company.

In many trades, the seven-year apprenticeships were merely a way of providing masters with a significant amount of cheap labour. The basics of most skills could be learnt in a few months,

THE
Art of Painting
In OYL.

Wherein is included each particular Circumstance
relating to the beit and moft approved Rules
for preparing, mixing, and working of Oyl
Colours.

The whole Treatife being fo full Compleat, and
fo exactly fitted to the meaneft Capacity, that
all Perfons whatfoever, may be able by thefe
Directions, to Paint in Oyl Colours all manner of Timber work; that require either Ufe,
Beauty, or Prefervation, from the violence or
Injury of the Weather.

In which is alfo laid down all the feveral Cir-
cumftances required in Painting of Sun-Dials,
Printed Pictures, Shafh-Windows, &c. In Oyl-
Colours.

The Fifth Impreffion with fome Alterations, and
many Matters added, which are not to be
found in the former Editions.

To which is added, The whole Art and Myfte-
ry of Colouring Maps, and other Prints, with
Water-Colours.

By JOHN SMITH, C. M.

LICENSED,   Rob. Midgely.

LONDON:
Printed for A. Bettefworth, in Pater-Nofter-Row;
F. Clay, without Temple-Bar; and E. Syman,
in Cornhill, 1723.

A

THE
HANDMAID
TO
THE ARTS.
IN TWO VOLUMES,

TEACHING,

I. A perfect knowledge of the MATERIA
PICTORIA; or, the Nature, Ufe, Preparation, and Compofition of all the various Subftances employed in PAINTING,
as well Vehicles, Dryers, &c. as Colours;
including thofe peculiar to Enamel Painting on Glafs.
II. The Means of Delineation, or the feveral
DEVICES employed for the more eafily
and accurately making DESIGNS FROM
NATURE, or DEPICTED REPRESEN-
TATIONS; either by Off-tracing, Calk-
ing, Reduction, or other Means; with
the Methods of taking Cafts and Impref-
fions, from Figures, Bufts, Medals, Leaves,
&c.
III. The various manners of GILDING,
SILVERING, BRONZING, with the
preparation of the genuine GOLD and
SILVER Powders, and Imitations of them,
as alfo of the Fat Oil, Gold Sizes, and
other neceffary Compofitions;—the Art of
JAPANNING, as applicable not only to
the former Purpofes, but to Coaches,
Snuff-boxes, &c. in the Manner lately
introduced; and the method of STAINING
DIFFERENT KINDS OF SUBSTANCES,
with all the feveral Colours.

The whole being calculated, as well for conveying a more accurate
and extenfive Knowledge of the Matters treated of to profeffed
Artifts, as to initiate thofe who are defirous to attempt thefe Arts,
into the method of preparing and ufing all the Colours, and other
Subftances employed in Painting in Oil, Miniature, Crayons, En-
cauftic, Enamel, Varnifh, Diftemper, and Frefco; as alfo in Gilding, &c.

A NEW EDITION,
WITH CONSIDERABLE ADDITIONS AND IMPROVEMENTS.

VOL. I.

LONDON:
PRINTED FOR A. MILLAR, W. LAW, AND R. CATER;
AND FOR WILSON, SPENCE, AND MAWMAN, YORK.

Anno 1796.

B

L'ART
DU PEINTRE,
DOREUR,
VERNISSEUR,

*Ouvrage utile aux Artiftes & aux Amateurs
qui veulent entreprendre de Peindre, Dorer
& Vernir toutes fortes de fujets en Bâti-
timens, Meubles, Bijoux, Équipages, &c.*

Par le Sr. WATIN, Peintre, Doreur, Verniffeur,
& marchand de Couleurs, Dorures &
Vernis, à Paris.

NOUVELLE ÉDITION,

Revue, corrigée & confidérablement augmentée.

Artem experientia fecit.

A LIEGE,
Chez D. DE BOUBERS, Imprimeur-Libraire, près du Pont
des Arches, à la Vierge Marie.

M. DCC. LXXVIII.

C

VALUABLE
SECRETS
CONCERNING
ARTS AND TRADES:
OR, APPROVED
DIRECTIONS, from the beft ARTISTS,

FOR THE VARIOUS METHODS

Of engraving on Brafs, Copper,
or Steel.
Of the Compofition of Metals,
and Varnifhes.
Of Maftichs and Cements, Sea-
ling-wax, &c.
Of Colours and Painting, for
Carriage Painters.
Of Painting on Paper.
Of Compofitions for Limners.
Of Tranfparent Colours.
How to dye Skins or Gloves.
To colour or varnifh Copper-
plate Prints.
Of Painting on Glafs.
Of Colours of all Sorts, for Oil,
Water, and Crayons.
Of the Art of Gilding.
The Art of dying Woods,
Bones, &c.
The Art of Moulding.
The Art of making Wines.
Of the various Compofitions
of Vinegars.
Of Liquors and Effential Oils.
Of the Confectionary Art.
Of taking out all Sorts of
Spots and Stains.

Hæ tibi erunt Artes !   VIRG.

NORWICH:
PRINTED BY THOMAS HUBBARD.
1795.

D

Title pages of a number of important early works on paint and decoration. [A] John Smith, *The Art
of Painting in Oyl* (1676; this fifth edition, 1723). [B] Robert Dossie, *The Handmaid to the Arts* (1758;
this edition 1796). [C] Jean-Félix Watin, *L'art du peintre, doreur, vernisseur* (1753; this edition 1778).
[D] Anon, *Valuable Secrets Concerning Arts and Trades* (1775; this edition 1795).

according to critics. On the other hand, serving an apprenticeship was the most common way to become a full member of a livery company and to acquire the freedom of the City of London, which was an essential element of an ambitious young man's plans.

Apprentices were not officially paid. However, towards the end of their training they were likely to be as skilled as many of the journeymen (men who had completed an apprenticeship, but were not yet a master), and no doubt bargained with their masters to pay them wages. The taking of wages technically barred them from becoming a freeman of the City of London and therefore setting up on their own. But the majority had no hope of ever becoming a master. Indeed, many such apprentices never bothered to take up their freedom, as can be seen by the very great difference between the numbers who became apprentices and the numbers who became freemen.

Very little is known of the background of all but the most well-known apprentices. William Kent, the architect, was born the son of poor parents and is said to have been apprenticed to a coach-painter in Hull before being sponsored to make a tour of Italy, where his early interest was solely in painting.

Thomas Crace established a coach-making business in London in the early years of the eighteenth century. In 1741, at the age of fifteen, his son, Edward, was apprenticed to an artist, a member of the Painter-Stainers' Company, presumably because his talents lay in that direction. After serving his apprenticeship, he went on to found a firm of decorators that survived for 131 years and produced some of the best painted decoration in nineteenth-century England.

WORK CONDITIONS

Apprenticeships typically began at the age of sixteen. Work conditions varied but the average day began at 7.00 a.m. and lasted until 9.00 p.m., with a break of two hours for a midday meal. During the winter months, it would not have been possible to carry out much work on site after the late afternoon. Presumably the remainder of the day would have been spent carrying out the less pleasant, indeed more hazardous, tasks: the washing and preparation of pigments, the grinding of pigment with oil, and the cleaning of paint-encrusted kettles.

The grinding of pigment by hand, to produce particles small enough to be thoroughly wetted by the oil medium, took a considerable amount of time. It was, according to a nineteenth-century American painter, 'not a highly intellectual occupation, nor one calculated to lead the soul to longings after the ideal'. The painter working on the Earl of Leicester's new house at Holkham was paid for sixty-one days' work in 'mixing and grinding colours' alone.

It must be said, however, that the success of the industrious apprentice could not be guaranteed by hard work alone, as William Hogarth portrayed in his series of influential prints, *Industry and Idleness,* of 1747. A certain amount of 'studied sycophancy' and a calculated marriage were also required to ensure success.

There were surprisingly few innovations in the painter's trade in the two hundred years from the end of the seventeenth century. Apart from a number of bright new pigments that appeared in the 1820s, the medium and the methods remained largely similar. Robert Tressell's description of a painter's workshop in *The Ragged-Trousered Philanthropist* (1914) conveys quite vividly the early apprentice's conditions:

> This was the paint-shop. At one end was a fireplace...with an iron bar fixed across the blackened chimney for the purpose of suspending pails or pots over the fire... All round the walls of the shop – which had once been whitewashed, but were now covered with smears of paint of every colour where the men had 'rubbed out' their brushes – were rows of shelves with kegs of paint upon them...Scattered about the stone floor were a number of dirty pails, either empty or containing stale whitewash... The lower parts of the walls were discoloured with moisture. The atmosphere was cold and damp and foul with the sickening odours of the poisonous materials. It was in this place that Bert – the apprentice – spent most of his time, cleaning out pots and pails, during slack periods when there were no jobs going on outside.

With the declining influence of the livery company, there was less incentive to complete an apprenticeship. The restriction on the training of one apprentice at a time severely limited the possibility for a master to expand his business and to take on more clients. At a time when every branch of industry required greater capital to operate, this had the effect of virtually eliminating the traditional prospect of progression from apprentice to journeyman to master.

In 1747 William Hogarth made a series of twelve engravings to show the young that hard work would bring rewards. [A] The Fellow 'Prentices at their Looms. [B] The Industrious 'Prentice a Favourite, and entrusted by his Master. [C] The Industrious 'Prentice out of his Time and Married to his Master's Daughter. [D] The Industrious 'Prentice grown rich, and Sheriff of London. [E] The Industrious 'Prentice Alderman of London, the Idle one brought before him and impeach'd by his Accomplice.

TOOLS OF THE TRADE

The implements that were used to lay the paint on the surface played as important a part in the final result as the medium itself:

> Brushes were always made of hogs bristles. They are of several sizes and shapes, some round, and others flat. The round ones are of all sizes, from two inches diameter to a quarter of an inch; those of the largest size are for priming the work, and for laying such colours as are used in great quantities...The smaller sort of brushes are to use in such parts and places of any work in which larger ones cannot well come to work... Flat brushes are chiefly in use for drawings of lines, and in the imitation of olive and walnut work [i.e. graining].

The flat brushes that are used today were not known in the eighteenth century. They were described in 1898 as a 'recent innovation', when they were developed for 'coach and highly finished woodwork'. They were said to be of a 'far better form for leaving a highly finished surface than the oval or knot brush, but do not last so long in wear if used on ordinary general work'.

The round or oval brush, often known as a ground tool, was easier to produce in its simplest form because it was little more than a straight stick with bristles bound tightly around it. This brush has survived well; indeed, brushes of this type are still used widely in Europe for applying oil paint.

New brushes were usually broken in by being used as a dusting brush before being put into paint. The action of dusting away the debris after rubbing down removed any loose hairs and made the tips of the coarse bristles finer. Smaller brushes were used by the painter, too; these were known as sash tools because they were ideal for painting window frames and beading, and came in 'different sizes to suit the different sized bars of the windows, beads, &c'.

Not only did a painter need a dusting brush and a range of ground tools and sash tools, but the professional house-painter also kept duplicate sets of brushes: one for use with white and light coloured paints, the other for dark colours. The process of cleaning them was never considered entirely adequate.

The brushes used to apply distemper were of a different shape to those used to apply oil paints. The reason for this was that distemper needed to be laid on 'boldly, freely and equally, with a light free sweep of the brush', whereas oil paint had to be spread sparingly. As distemper was fast-drying, the larger an area covered with one sweep the better. Originally, distemper brushes were the two- or three-knot type; a flat double- or triple-pronged wooden fork with bristles bound around the prongs.

Pencils differed from brushes 'in the smallness of their size, and in being manufactured of a much finer and softer hair... The smallest are fitted into the barrel of quills, the larger sort into tin cases...'

THE HOUSE-PAINTER'S TOOLS (*HOUSE DECORATION*, 1897, CASSELL & SONS)

1.	HOUSE-PAINTER'S ORDINARY OVAL BRUSH	22.	HOG-HAIR LINING FITCH
2.	CHEAP STYLE OF BRUSH WITH COPPER BINDING	23.	LINING FITCH IN FLAT HANDLE
3.	ENGLISH SASH TOOL	24.	STENCIL TOOL
4.	SMALL SASH TOOL	25.	BEST FORM OF DISTEMPER BRUSH
5.	GERMAN PAINT TOOL	26.	WASHING OFF BRUSH
6.	LONG HAIRED SASH TOOL	27.	PADDLE DISTEMPER BRUSH ON NAILED STOCK
7.	QUILLED SASH TOOL	28.	PAINT STRAINING SIEVE
8.	SASH TOOL FOR GENERAL USE	29.	SCOTCH DISTEMPER BRUSH
9.	SASH PAINTING TOOL	30.	PASTING BRUSH
10.	HOG-HAIR FITCH IN ROUND TIN	31.	LIMER USED WITH LONG HANDLE
11.	HOG-HAIR IN FLAT TIN	32.	STIPPLER
12.	HOG-HAIR FLAT TOOL	33.	STIPPLER WITH REVERSIBLE HANDLE
13.	FRENCH ROUND TOOL	34.	STIPPLER WITH BRIDGE HANDLE
14.	OVAL BEVELLED VARNISH BRUSH	35.	HOW TO TIE A PAINT BRUSH
15.	FLAT VARNISH BRUSH IN TIN	36.	PRESERVING PAINT BRUSHES
16.	VARNISHING FITCH	37.	CHISEL OR BROAD KNIFE
17.	PALETTE KNIFE	38.	STOPPING KNIFE
18.	GLAZIER'S PUTTY KNIFE	39.	CHISEL-POINTED STOPPING KNIFE
19.	GLAZIER'S HACKING KNIFE	40.	PATCUT PAINT STRAINER
20.	ORDINARY HOUSE-PAINTER'S BRUSH	41.	PORTABLE BALCONY IN POSITION FOR USE
21.	HOUSE-PAINTERS' DUSTING BRUSH	42.	PERSPECTIVE SKETCH OF PORTABLE BALCONY

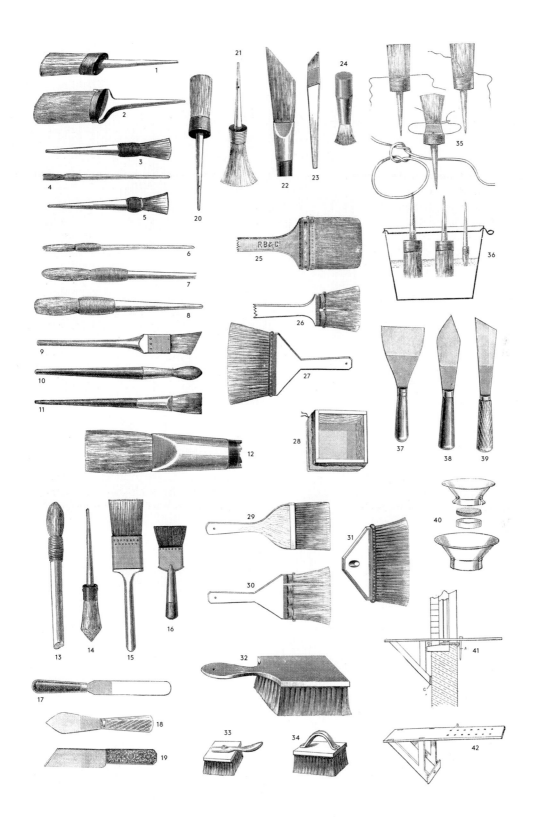

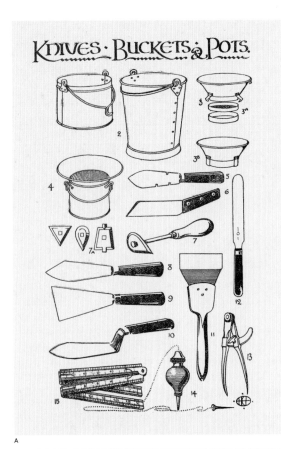

KNIVES · BUCKETS & POTS.

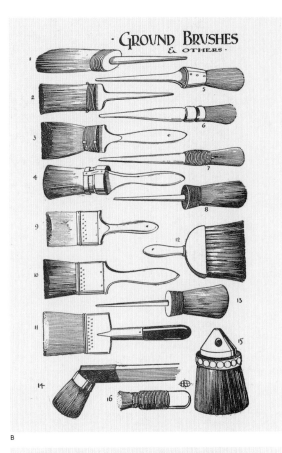

· GROUND BRUSHES
& OTHERS ·

A

B

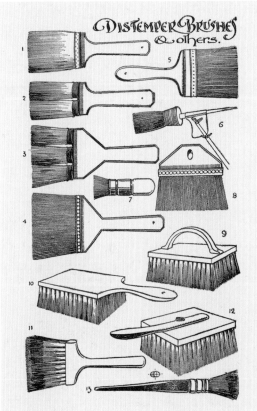

DISTEMPER BRUSHES
& others.

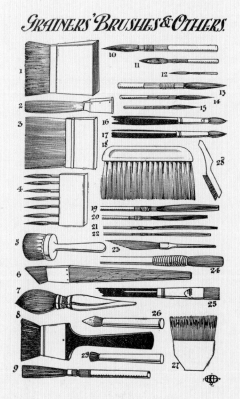

GRAINERS' BRUSHES & OTHERS.

C

D

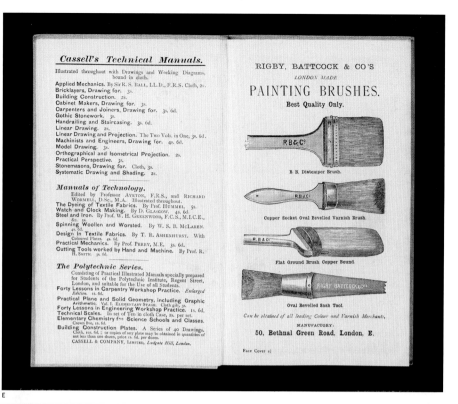

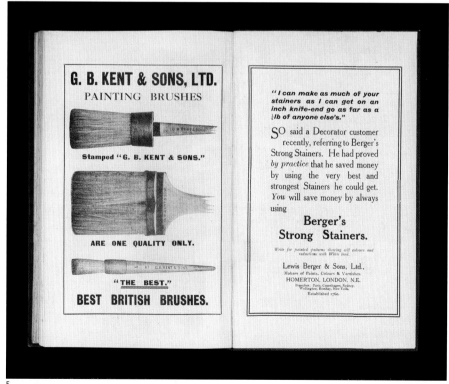

[OPPOSITE] Pages from Henry Geo. Dowling's *Painters' and Decorators' Work* (1916). [A] Knives, buckets and pots have changed little over the past century. [B] Ground brushes. Nowadays most paint brushes resemble No. 10, the flat varnish brush. [C] Distemper brushes. Most of these were still readily available in the 1980s. All bar the stencil, stippling and badger softener brushes are now obsolete. [D] Grainers' brushes. Very specialist brushes have changed little. [E] Advertisement for various painters' brushes from *House Decoration* (1897) by Paul N. Hasluck. [F] Advertisement for G. B. Kent's brushes and Berger's Strong Stainers from *Paint and Colour Mixing* (1915 edition) by Arthur Seymour Jennings.

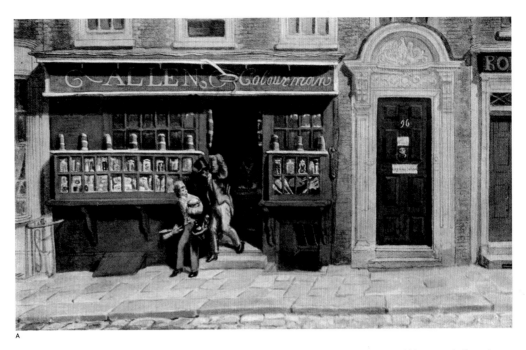

[A] Allen's shop in St Martin's Lane, London, by George Scharf (the elder), 1829. A house-painter and his apprentice leave the colourman's with fresh supplies. These seem to include at least four brushes, a jar of linseed oil, a small keg (25 kg/55 lb) of white lead on the painter's shoulder and a paint pot of ground paste. Presumably it is Mr Allen who is seen grinding pigment through the open doorway. [B] Trade card of the leading colourman and pencil-maker James Newman of 17 Gerrard Street, London.

THE COLOURMAN

The emergence and rapid growth of the colourman's trade was the result of two developments. By the mid seventeenth century, painting had ceased to be the sole province of the Church and it began to be regarded more as an art than a craft. The painting of watercolours and the colouring of maps became a genteel pastime and a desirable skill for persons with pretension to taste and a rounded education. A growing number of wealthy amateurs required a dependable source of high-quality paints and materials for this new activity. Not wanting to spend time on the dirty work of preparing pigments, they were all too eager to leave it to those who had the technical understanding and the facilities to produce their colours.

A ready supply of semi-prepared oil paint was also required by the recently emerged house-painting trade, which boomed in the years after the Great Fire of London, when large quantities of softwood were used in the construction of new houses. The following extract from William Salmon's *Palladio Londinensis or the London Art of Building* (1734) describes what would happen if the wood were not painted:

PAINTING, if not the chief, is as necessary a Part of Building as any other whatever, both for Use and Ornament, the doing of which well and often being the surest way of preserving all the rest, instances of which may be seen in several Buildings, about London, where the Misfortunes of the Builders have prevented them from finishing their Works, it may be observed that the Sash-Frames, Sashes, Window-Shutters, Doors and Door-Cases, for want of Painting, in a very few Years, are so much decayed, that were those Buildings to be made tenantable, most of the outside Timber-Work must be renewed; Iron-Work, tho' of a much stronger Nature than Timber, if not well secured by Painting, is likewise subject to the same misfortune: On the contrary, where Timber-Work is often painted it will endure many Ages, no Weather being able to penetrate thro' it...

Interior panelling tended to be left unpainted when it was constructed of oak, but 'knotty' pine was never acceptable. The reasons were not only aesthetic. A work of 1703 praised the innovation of 'painted Wainscot, now so much used' for its effect on 'Cleanliness and Health'. A great amount of paint must have been produced to cover all the newly panelled rooms being built at the time. In France, if not painted, oak panelling might have been varnished. This treatment was known as *boiserie à la capucine*, because it resembled the bareness of the walls of the cell of a Capuchin monk.

The same source also provides one of the first references to do-it-yourself:

> Painters Work being very expensive, and this being the only part in Building wherein a Gentleman can be assisting either by himself or Servants, it being almost impossible for any Gentleman to do either Masons, Bricklayers, Carpenters, or Smiths Works; whereas it is well known and daily experienced since the Advertisement of ALEXANDER EMERTON, that several Noblemen and Gentlemen have by themselves and Servants painted whole Houses without the Assistance or Direction of a Painter, which when examined by the best Judges could not be distinguished from the Work of a professed Painter.

Grinding by hand was slow, but the introduction of horse-mills in the first quarter of the eighteenth century transformed the market, and the colourman was able to sell pigment ground in oil as a paste that could be 'let down' by the addition of linseed oil. The bulk of the sales would have consisted of white lead paste, but ready-mixed colours were also offered and records survive of the colours available and the prices charged.

Current knowledge of the early eighteenth-century colourman is based largely on literature relating to the Emerton family. Alexander traded from premises 'At the Bell over against Arundel Street, Strand' in London until his death in 1737. His widow continued to run the business in direct competition with her brother in law, Joseph Emerton.

Initially, the colourman would have supplied both the house-painter and the artist alike. In the 1740s, Joseph Emerton was distributing a handbill giving directions for painting interiors, but also stating that he 'Sells to the Ladies all sorts of Water Colours and Varnish, with every thing necessary for the New Japanning'. A few years later, and primarily as a result of the horse-mills, a new trade had developed: the colour-maker. He bought the raw materials in large quantities and ground the pigments into fine powder. At some later stage, the colourman

decided to concentrate on either the house-painting trade or on supplying artists' materials.

In *The London Tradesman* (1747), Robert Campbell wrote:

> The Colour-Man buys all manner of Colours uncompounded: He is, in some shape, the Apothecary to the Painter; as he buys the simple Colours and compounds some of them: He grinds such as require grinding, and adds that Expence to the prime Cost. He ought to be a thorough Judge of Colours, to know all their Properties, and the common Tricks that are used in sophisticating Dyes of all sorts, not with an Intention of cheating his Customers, but to guard against the Imposition of those who would impose upon him in the Sale of Goods.

The colourman would purchase pigment from the colour-maker and grind it with oil into a paste using a hand-cranked colour mill, or a muller and slab. In the early days, the colourman sold the paste in a cleaned and prepared pig bladder. By the 1840s, bladders had been replaced by a collapsible metal paint tube. In the 1687 edition of *The Art of Painting in Oyl*, John Smith illustrated the efficiency of these bladders in the preservation of pigments, with an anecdote:

> I remember I had a parcel of Colours given me in the year 1661, by a Neighbouring Yeoman, that were as he said, left at his House by a Trooper, that quartered there in the time of the Wars, about the year 1644. This Man was by profession a Picture-Drawer, and his Colours were all tyed

B

A trade card of oil and colourman T. Reeves & Son at 80 Holborn Bridge, c. 1786. William Reeves began the business in Well Lane in 1766 and developed the moist watercolour cake in 1781. Reeves continues to trade art supplies today.

A trade card of John Rich, Oil & Colourman, Union Street, Bishopsgate Street, London, nineteenth century. Rich also sold a variety of household items such as soap, candles, starch, matches, waxes. hardware and ironmongery.

up in Bladders, according to the method before prescribed, and when I had opened them, I found them in a very good condition, and to my thinking as fit for use, when mixt with a little fresh Oyl, as if they had been but very lately ground, though they had remained in this condition about seventeen years.

Watercolours were first made in London in the late 1760s. Initially, the pigments were finely ground in water and blended into gum Arabic before being pressed into cleaned half shells. At a later date, semi-moist cakes were produced, however these were the province of the artist rather than the house-painter.

The occupation of colourman was clearly highly skilled, as Campbell noted:

No Man is fit to keep a Colour-Shop who has not served an Apprenticeship: The Articles they deal in are so many, and require such a nice Eye, and so great Practice to be a Judge of them, that even seven Years are too little to learn this Trade.

In eighteenth-century London, many colourmen were located on Long Acre, which also happened to be the centre of the coach-building trade. Related trades were often based near each other for obvious reasons. Campbell describes one such business in the area:

But the Colour-Man properly confines himself to what relates to Painting; of this Sort, I know but one in London, viz. Mr. Kateing, at the White-Hart in Long-Acre. This Gentleman deals in all Colours for the House-Painter; but his chief Business consists in furnishing the Liberal

Painters with their fine Colours: A Painter may go into his Shop and be furnished with every Article he uses, such as Pencils, Brushes, Cloths ready for drawing on, and all manner of Colours ready prepared, with which he cannot be supplied either in such Quality or Quantity in any or all the Shops in London. He is himself an excellent Judge of Colours, and has no mean Taste in Painting; and, all things considered, I know none in the Trade so fit as this Gentleman to propose as a Pattern for all Colour-Men.

By the early 1820s, paint was being supplied in a form that is recognizable today. Cheap oil paints for external purposes 'in a state ready to use' were being offered in casks of 28 pounds, 56 pounds and 112 pounds (13, 25 and 51 kg). Also offered was a range of green paints, either in a stiff state requiring thinning with oil or ready for use in containers as small as 2-pound (0.9 kg)and 7-pound (3 kg) jars. Three coats with a dark grey undercoat were recommended. It is interesting to note that the same size containers were still being used in the twentieth century.

The prices charged for paint were very stable throughout the eighteenth and nineteenth centuries. In the 1740s, Alexander Emerton was selling the common colours ready ground in oil at 4d (1.75p/2¢) or 5d (2p/2.5¢) per pound, and in the 1890s:

The oil and colour man mixes paint of any colour generally at 6d, and sometimes even at the low rate of 5d, per pound. He sends it to you ready for use in a tin can or an earthen paint-pot, and in addition to all this he will lend you a brush wherewith to apply it...

Peintre en bâtimens, échafaudage simple (House painter, simple scaffolding).
Plate 3, engraving, from *L'Encyclopédie de Diderot et d'Alembert* (1783),
fourth edition (Panckoucke edition). Eighteenth-century French house-painters
used platforms – an early form of scaffolding – to carry out their work.

'Every one must have observed that certain colours, when brought together, mutually set each other off to advantage, while others have altogether a different effect. This must be carefully attended to by every Painter who would study beauty or elegance in the appearance of his work.'* This section discusses the paint colours available between 1700 and 1830 and categorizes them by expense. It also examines the main decorative uses of the different colours in interiors during the period.

*G. A. Smeaton, *The Painter's, Gilder's and Varnisher's Manual* (c. 1827)

[OPPOSITE] The paint colours offered by London colourman Alexander Emerton in the first half of the eighteenth century. They were listed with their prices in William Salmon's *Palladio Londinensis* (1734).

SOME EIGHTEENTH-CENTURY PAINT COLOURS

COMMON	TIMBER	EXPENSIVE	MORE EXPENSIVE
CREAM	CHOCOLATE	GOLD	ORANGE
LEAD	WALNUT TREE	OLIVE	LEMON
PEARL	MAHOGANY	PEA GREEN	STRAW
STONE	CEDAR	SKY BLUE	PINK
WAINSCOT		VERDIGRIS	PEACH BLOSSOM
WHITE		BUFF	FINE DEEP GREEN

THE COMMON COLOURS

The cheapest colours were those that saw everyday use and, as a consequence, they were known as the common colours: cream colour, lead colour, pearl colour, stone colour, wainscot (or oak) colour and white.

The common colours were available, in paste form ground in oil, at 4d or 5d (1.75p/2¢ or 2p/2.5¢) per pound. The tinting components were inexpensive iron oxide pigments and black in a lead white base. It is possible that a tiny amount of Prussian blue was added to the pearl colour.

The colours were generally of a light or mid tone, and it was common practice to use a (mainly) single colour throughout a house in the early eighteenth century. Of these colours, one tends to be found more than any other. Indeed, in almost every house of this period, a colour that might be termed stone colour was used at some point. Perhaps this should be qualified as one family of colours, because as with many early colour names 'stone colour' was a generic term, encompassing pale through to dark and warm shades to cool tints.

THE TIMBER COLOURS

Slightly more expensive than the common colours were those referred to as the timber colours: chocolate colour, walnut colour, mahogany and cedar. They were available, ground in oil, at 6d (2.5p/3¢) per pound. These colours required greater amounts of pigments, consisting largely of red and yellow oxides and black.

In the early eighteenth century, John Smith suggested that a colour resembling new oak could be made with umber, and that spruce ochre and a little umber added to a white lead base made a light timber colour. It appears that in the early years the use of a colour name, such as mahogany colour, might have implied graining (the imitation of that wood), yet Alexander Emerton was selling a mahogany-coloured paint at 6d (2.5p/3¢) per pound in the 1730s.

No recipes for chestnut colour have been found, although we know that the wood was highly prized in its natural state, being described as 'one of the most sought after by the Joyner and carpenter' (Neve, 1726). It is likely that a paint of a similar tonality was mixed and applied.

THE EXPENSIVE COLOURS

The expensive colours were gold colour, olive colour, pea green, sky blue, verdigris and buff. They ranged in price from 8d to 12d (3.25p/4¢ to 5p/6¢) per pound, and were at least twice as costly as the common colours.

In order to produce these colours, pigments that required more elaborate processing were employed – possibly the lead pigment massicot in the gold colour and Prussian blue and yellow iron oxide in the olive colour. Pea green could have been made in a number of different ways, involving the use of verdigris or Prussian blue and either Naples yellow or massicot.

THE MORE EXPENSIVE COLOURS

At roughly three times the price of the cheapest colours were the very expensive colours: orange, lemon, straw colour, pink and blossom colour, all available at 12d (5p/6¢) per pound.

Orange may have been made with yellow iron oxide and red lead, whereas lemon might have been produced with Naples yellow or an organic yellow. The fact that straw colour cost 12d (5p/6¢) per pound suggests that it was not composed of yellow iron oxide as indicated by contemporary authors such as John Smith. It is more likely that it was a brighter colour, perhaps containing one of the lead-based yellows. Pink is a deceptive name, because it now means a light red or rose pink, whereas in the eighteenth century it referred to a yellow colour produced from a number of organic sources. Blossom seems likely to have been made with vermilion or red lake.

The final colour in this category, costing an incredible 2s 6d (12.5p/16¢) per pound, is fine deep green. At between six and seven times the price of the common colours, its use on the walls would certainly have made a statement of wealth.

[A] A freshly painted and gilded ceiling of a 1760s house in St James's, London.
[B, C] The 'ancient cedar parlour' is contrasted with the 'modern living room'. From
Humphry Repton's *Fragments on the Theory and Practice of Landscape Gardening,
including some Remarks on Grecian and Gothic Architecture* (1816).

APPLICATION OF TRADITIONAL PAINT COLOURS

B

C

The use of colour in the decoration of early eighteenth-century interiors was far more straightforward and austere than many people believe. Certainly, the relative complexity of the panelled wall surface was not an excuse for the elaborate 'picking out' beloved by so many modern interior designers. In a simplified form, the panelled wall was designed to suggest the classical order: the dado represented the pedestal, the wall indicated the column and the cornice the entablature.

Softwood panelling was meant to be painted, almost invariably in one colour from the base of the skirting to the top of the cornice. An exception might be the painting of the skirting fascia (the flat part) in a dark colour – often chocolate brown. Sometimes this dark colour would be extended across the base of doors and architraves, too. This makes absolute sense, especially when one considers that this element is known as the mopboard in the United States. The use of a practical dark colour was not restricted to skirtings; it was also found on window shutters and doors, which would have received frequent handling, as well as on door and window architraves.

In rooms of the 'middling sort', it is most unlikely that the mouldings would have been picked out. If the cheaper, or common colours, were being applied, the extra cost of the labour would have been disproportionate. Colour was used to tie together all the elements rather than subdivide them. The fussy picking-out of architectural detail that is seen on much panelling today betrays a lack of understanding and seems largely to be the influence of twentieth-century interior decorators such as John Fowler. One of his biggest legacies

has been the 'three shades of white' painted on doors and panelling.

In wealthier households, it was not unusual to encounter a room (or smaller closet) of greater elaboration, where more expensive colours, marbling, graining, japanning, gilding or gilded leather had been employed. However, the use of a single paint colour might also convey status.

The range of paint colours was very limited and it was restricted by a number of factors, including the compatibility of pigments, their availability and cost (several were imported from the East and West Indies, for example), and the conventions of the day – although these conventions were related to the other factors. Paint prices were noticeably stable throughout the eighteenth and nineteenth centuries. In the 1740s, Alexander Emerton was selling the common colours ready-ground in oil for 4d or 5d (1.75p/2¢ or 2p/2.5¢) per pound, while in the 1890s the same colours cost 6d and 5d (2.5p/3¢ and 2p/2.5¢) per pound (Young, *c.* 1890).

The nature of rooms changed dramatically between 1700 and 1820, and this development is best illustrated by two views from Humphry Repton's *Fragments* (1816), in which he contrasts the 'modern living room' with 'the ancient cedar parlour'. These illustrations and the accompanying verse provide perhaps the clearest commentary on changes in the use and the arrangement of rooms that had occurred by the latter date. The colours already described continued to be used, but in a different manner.

No more the Cedar Parlour's formal gloom with dulness chills, 'tis now the Living-Room; where guests, to whim, or taste, or fancy true. Scatter'd in groups, their different plans pursue.

THE USE OF THE COMMON COLOURS

Stone colour is a name that is encountered frequently in early documents and it seems that no matter the status of the building stone colour predominated in the early eighteenth century. Three very different interiors of the 1730s examined recently show its widespread use, from a small house in Soho to a larger one in Mayfair and a series of rooms in Hampton Court Palace.

Originally, the two smaller houses were decorated in a predictable manner, very simply with a single stone colour being applied to all surfaces apart from the doors and skirting fascias, which were generally a chocolate brown. However, it is slightly surprising to note that a similar simple scheme was employed in the Cumberland suite at Hampton Court, which was painted in variations of stone colour throughout the whole of the eighteenth and nineteenth centuries. One might have expected to see the use of something more expensive than one of the common colours in the private apartments of George II's favourite son, William Augustus, the Duke of Cumberland. These rooms had been designed by William Kent in the 1730s and they were later occupied by William V, Prince of Orange.

In 1771 Sir William Chambers proposed that most of the principal rooms in a newly built house be painted in 'a fine stone colour as usual'. The same architect, writing to his client John Colecroft in 1772, refers to 'our agreement for common stone colouring all over the house'. He added 'if you mean to have…dead white or party colours in your principal floor please to let me know and I will order it accordingly charging you with the difference'. 'Dead' in this case meant a matt or 'flatted' finish and 'party colours' meant more than one colour.

A seven-year lease signed on 19 December of the same year between Samuel Kirkham, the builder of the recently completed No. 14 Royal Crescent in Bath, and the new resident, Charles Hamilton, stated:

> The whole house is to be properly painted, the two best rooms in particular four times in oil of the best Dead white colour and the rest of the rooms in the house are to be painted four times in oil of a good stone colour or common white except the outward doors which are to be painted of a dark brown or chocolate colour as the said Charles Hamilton shall choose and the garret doors and ground floor doors are to be painted chocolate colour.

The taste for stone colour continued into the nineteenth century, as seen in a letter written in 1807 in which a house-painter advised his prospective client:

> The most fashionable colours for Plaster walls are The Stone and Gray Colours, for wood work and Cornices White, doors Mahogany and Wainscot Colour.

In fact, the convention continued even longer, for in 1841 the English architect and editor of *The Builder*, Alfred Bartholomew, gave instructions to the plasterer working on a Rectory House:

> To colour of a teint of stone colour as shall be directed all the plastered walls and sides of the interior of the building where the same are not papered.

The effect of being an external space was emphasized by the use of painted imitations of ashlar, with the wall surfaces lined out to suggest blocks of stone. A well-known example is the entrance hall and the staircase of the Sir John Soane's Museum in Lincoln's Inn Fields, London.

The grey known as lead colour was another of the family of inexpensive common colours employed by the eighteenth-century house-painter. These staples are encountered when investigating many eighteenth-century interiors, and the lead colour found in a house lived in by George Frederic Handel was reintroduced a few years ago following analysis. There, lead colour had been employed throughout the building, in combination with chocolate colour. Handel had lived in what is now the Handel House Museum in Mayfair, London, from the 1720s to his death in 1759. The next-door house, which was occupied by Jimi Hendrix in 1969, was found to have been painted in a single stone colour throughout.

Although the palette of the eighteenth-century house-painter was somewhat limited, he had three different blacks – lamp black, the most common and inexpensive; ivory black, 'not used in any common work'; and blue or charcoal black, frequently added to white oil paint to 'clear' the white – to work with before having to resort to the addition of other pigments.

Greys have remained popular and are among the most versatile of all families of colours. Some of the more interesting are those that Arthur Seymour Jennings, the author of a number of decorating books in the early twentieth century, would have labelled 'greys' – those produced by

A

B

The Handel House Museum. [A] From the 1730s onwards, in Handel's rehearsal room on the first floor at the front of the house, the walls were painted lead colour, as were the door architrave and skirting. [B] This room on the second floor at the front of the house was probably where Handel died in 1759. In this, more private, room, the door architrave and skirting were painted in chocolate colour, which would have been better at hiding the marks of a broom, foot or hand. This decoration has been established by paint analysis.

[LEFT] The staircase balustrade of the Georgian Group headquarters at 6 Fitzroy Square are painted in a lead colour that was found during paint analysis. This was the conventional colour for such surfaces during the eighteenth and early nineteenth centuries.

[OPPOSITE] The Tulip Stairs and lantern of the Queen's House, Greenwich. Dating from *c.* 1630, it is the first helical staircase constructed in England without a central support. The stairs are cantilevered from the walls and each tread rests on the one below. Recently, the balustrade was painted in a blue colour that was matched to smalt (see p. 55 and p. 22, image F).

[A] Drayton Hall, Charleston, South Carolina, early 1750s. This is the family dining room on the first floor. The Federal-style chimneypiece was installed in the early 1800s. This paint is from the mid twentieth century. The original colour scheme, ascertained by paint analysis, was a monochromatic yellow ochre. [B] The dining room of James Brice House, Annapolis, Maryland. Constructed between 1766 and 1773, when the house was redecorated in the 1980s, the panelling was painted in straw colour and the other elements were grained. This is probably a nineteenth-century scheme, but the tonality of the graining is like a timber colour. The decoration is currently being reappraised.

mixing black and white alone. However, each of the black pigments employed by the early house-painter had its own characteristics and great subtlety could be achieved by their careful use. Jennings suggested that 'grays' were the result of adding a colour to a black-and-white mix, but he seems to have been fighting a losing battle as the different spellings now usually indicate a British (grey) or an American (gray) writer.

Throughout much of the eighteenth century, the entrance hall (and to an extent, the staircase too) was regarded as being a semi-external space. This had a bearing on both the furnishing of the room and the colouring applied to the walls. In the larger houses, this external feel could be emphasized by the architectural treatment of the hall. The Stone Hall at Houghton in Norfolk (see pp. 52–53) is perhaps the best-known example, in which a full complement of external architectural details – stone walls, pedimented doorcases, sculptural reliefs, niches and false windows – is included. At Wolterton Hall, also in Norfolk, built by Thomas Ripley in the mid 1720s, the use of external features has been taken to such an extent that the stairwell looks as though the house has been turned inside out, with entablatured windows looking onto it. At the slightly smaller Davenport House in Shropshire, the walls are heavily rusticated giving a very strong feeling of stone.

A neutral stone colour was frequently employed on the walls, and the effect was very occasionally emphasized by the surfaces being sanded (that is, strewn with dry sand while the paint was still tacky) to suggest stone.

The transition from darker to lighter colours is often seen in the stratigraphy when analysing the paint of houses of the early eighteenth century. For example, evidence suggests that the South Hall at Wilbury (1710) and the entrance hall at Roehampton House (1712) both adopted paler stone colours in the 1730s having originally been painted in darker colours of different kinds. It is possible that the influence came from France.

At the beginning of the century, darker colours such as olive green and drab had been considered fashionable and finishes tended to have a high level of sheen, but within thirty or forty years there was a gradual introduction of a lighter palette, and often in a more matt finish. White (in reality, off-white) was a colour often used on external surfaces. The German novelist Sophie von La Roche was struck by the 'big well-kept windows whose panes are framed in fine white painted wood', when she visited London in the 1780s.

THE USE OF
THE TIMBER COLOURS

Timber-coloured paints have been found on the doors, architraves, skirtings and shutters in a number of early eighteenth-century houses. A dark colour would have had the advantage of not showing up dirt or fingermarks. Chocolate colour was also used for this reason. Frequently, whole rooms would have been painted in a colour resembling timber of various species (see p. 98), to protect the surface and evoke a natural effect, without going to the much greater expense and effort of imitative graining techniques.

THE USE OF
THE EXPENSIVE COLOURS

It is apparent that in the second half of the eighteenth century, pea green was considered a special colour. In 1759 Lady Caroline Fox had her dressing room painted pea green to match some china. In the early 1770s, Sir William Chambers advised a client for whom he was building a house in Berners Street, London:

If you have any Particular fancy about the Painting [of] your principal Rooms be pleased to let me know[.] my intention is to finish the whole of a fine stone Colour as us[u]al excepting the Eating Parlour which I purpose [sic] to finish pea Green with white mouldings & ornaments.

At much the same time, Mrs Philip Lybbe Powys noted that the breakfast parlour at Fawley Court in Buckinghamshire had pea green walls with a gilded border and a chimneypiece of green marble with gilt ornaments. The gallery at Osterley Park in Hounslow, London (see p. 101), was painted pea green by 1772. And in 1810 the German poet Goethe wrote of green:

The eye experiences a distinctly grateful impression from this colour...The beholder has neither the wish nor the power to imagine a state beyond it. Hence for rooms to live in constantly, the green colour is most generally selected.

The recipes for producing pea green vary, depending upon their date and also whether it was an oil paint or a soft distemper that was being made. Prior to the introduction of chrome yellow to the house-painter's palette in the late 1820s, pea green in an oil paint tended to include verdigris in the recipe. In the fascinating manuscript of recipes titled *Miscellanea Curiosa*,

A

[A] A timber colour applied to the panelling of the oak bedchamber on the first floor
of Peyton Randolph House, Colonial Williamsburg, built between 1715 and 1718, and
refitted with new panelling in *c.* 1752. Susan Buck found that the colour was mixed with
red iron oxide, burnt sienna and chalk, and this colour has been matched to the original.
[B] The stair hall at Drayton Hall, Charleston, South Carolina. Susan Buck found that
the mahogany lower wall and handrail were originally given a vermilion-based stain,
while the panelling was cream coloured. The current scheme dates from *c.* 1880,
by which time the family had recovered their fortune by phosphate mining.

or a Memorandum of Many Useful Receipts, which dates from 1795 to 1816, a pea green oil paint was made up of:

> 3oz Pale or washed Massicot
> 4oz Paris white [a fine grade of chalk]
> 2oz Distilled Verdigris [a purer form of the pigment]
> Ground in Linseed oil.

Although not mentioned by William Salmon in 1748, another reasonably expensive colour that had a long history of use in the later eighteenth century was one known as French grey. In 1771 Mrs Lybbe Powys described the hall at Fawley Court as being 'stucco'd of a French grey'. When the paint stratigraphy on the lower wall of the hall was examined, there was, as the fifth scheme, a pale bluish grey that was the only one that could be described as such. On microscopic examination, it could be seen that the colour was achieved by the addition of the pigments Prussian blue, vermilion and a little charcoal black to the lead white base of the oil paint. These ingredients formed the 'classic' recipe for French grey. This enabled the fifth scheme to be dated to *c.* 1770, and after a few other clues were unearthed, dates were established for most of the twenty schemes applied in that room. As a result, the later ornate plaster ceiling and cornice, the joinery and the sash windows could also be dated.

Indeed, French grey is quite distinctive when examined under the microscope as it invariably contains blue and red pigments, sometimes with black. An 1821 update of the original English house-painting manual (John Smith's *The Art of Painting in Oyl*) gave the following instructions:

> Take white lead and Prussian blue, or blue verditer;
> and, to make a more beautiful and pleasant
> colour, take a small quantity of Lake or Vermilion.

Artist and house-painter T. H. Vanherman noted in 1828 that 'French grey should neither be dark nor yet too light, but a middle tint.' Using a different red pigment and not mentioning the addition of black, the same early nineteenth-century recipe suggested adding:

> as much ground Prussian blue as shall make it to
> your mind, then add as much Lake, or Rose Pink,
> as will bestow on it a faint bloom.

French grey appears frequently as a name in accounts of the late eighteenth and early nineteenth centuries. For example, the bill for the painting of the hall at Osterley Park in the 1760s specifies that it was done in white and French grey with the trophy panels 'minutely pick'd in with three tints of grey'. This is a particularly useful document for its indication of the period when tints were applied. The bill also notes that picking out using tints was regarded as an extra expense rather than a standard treatment for painting doors.

In 1772 the walls of the dining room at Gordon Castle, Moray, Scotland, were painted French grey. A near-contemporary account of French grey in use was in the Venetian parlour of Mansion House in the City of London, where it was employed at 8d (3.25p/4¢) a yard in 1779. Sir John Soane specified French grey in 1792 at Letton Hall, Norfolk, his first country house:

> French grey in breakfast parlour, best
> staircase passages, attics, housekeeper's
> room and store room.

French grey was always a 'fancy' colour that would incur a small surcharge on the bill.

THE USE OF THE MORE EXPENSIVE COLOURS

Some years ago, paint analysis was carried out on a number of the interiors at Newhailes in East Lothian, Scotland. Surviving accounts reveal that in 1742 Sir James Dalrymple had bought fine green paint from Joseph Emerton (the brother of Alexander). The price charged was 4s (20p/25¢) per pound – some ten to twelve times the cost of the common colours. He would also have paid to ship the paint up to Scotland from the Strand, London, so he was clearly making a very bold statement. Analysis showed that the dining room retained its fine green until 1870, when the house was tidied up for letting.

William Hogarth used fine green to show the status of the new countess in his *Marriage à-la-mode* (1743–45) series. It is contrasted with the humble wainscot colour of her father's London home to which she returned to die.

CONVENTIONS OF USE

In the second half of the eighteenth century, a number of more exotic colours and schemes began to appear. Robert Adam played a significant part in this development following his return from Italy in 1758. He reintroduced the technique, adopted from the catacombs and subterranean vaults of Roman palaces, of using

A

B

[A] A verdigris glaze has recently been applied to the joinery in this room at Thomas Everard House, Colonial Williamsburg, Virginia. [B] The gallery at Osterley is painted pea green, which by the second half of the eighteenth century was considered a special colour. A complementary pink has been used below the dado rail. [OVERLEAF] [P. 102] The entrance hallway at Locko Park, looking through to the picture gallery. This is the sort of colour that might be achieved by combining blue verditer and a little vermilion. [P. 103] The Black and White Hall at Mount Stewart House, County Down, Northern Ireland, showing a sky blue colour achieved by the use of Prussian blue.

A

B

[A] The dining room at Newhailes, East Lothian. fine deep green had been used in 1742.
[B] The large library at Goodwood, Sussex, with classically inspired 'Etruscan red' cabinet doors.
[OVERLEAF] [p. 106] A peach blossom colour has been applied to the walls of the entrance hall
and stairs of Castle Coole, County Fermanagh, Northern Ireland. [p. 107] Horace Walpole's
Tribune at Strawberry Hill, Middlesex, was built to house his most valuable treasures. Miniatures
were displayed in a rosewood cabinet (now in the Victoria and Albert Museum). The walls of the
Tribune have been painted in a colour mid-way between fine green and stone colour.

an intricate profusion of small motifs – tendrils, arabesques, medallions and reliefs – in his painted and plaster decoration. Although happy to employ the motifs of the ancients, be they Greeks or Etruscans, it was a few years before architects began to use their colours on large expanses.

The first floor rooms at Spencer House in London were among the first to feature elements derived from classical Greece. The sequence culminates in the Painted Room, which was begun in about 1759. Designed and painted in 'the antique manner' by James 'Athenian' Stuart, it is perhaps one of the most famous eighteenth-century interiors in England. The main themes of the painted decoration were love, harmony and marriage, and in particular that of John Spencer, the first Earl Spencer, to Georgiana Poyntz. Theirs was regarded as one of the love matches of the day.

Spencer House's Painted Room was the forerunner of the many classically inspired Pompeian and Etruscan rooms that followed, and the Adam brothers in their *Works in Architecture* (1778) gave credit to Stuart as having 'contributed greatly toward introducing the true style of antique decoration'. At the same time, they acknowledged William Kent as having been the first to introduce fashionable grotesque paintings. Analysis of the painted surfaces some years ago showed that the walls had originally been painted fine green.

The large library at Goodwood in Sussex, England, shows James Wyatt, in the closing years of the eighteenth century, adopting small areas of Etruscan red in the panels of the dado cupboards, whose designs were influenced directly by Greek vase decoration. The walls, incidentally, appear from paint analysis to have been painted a complementary pale green.

The earliest recreation of a Pompeian scheme using the strong colours reminiscent of the excavated ruins seems to have been at Packington Hall, Warwickshire, England, where Joseph Bonomi decorated a room for the fourth Earl of Aylesford between 1785 and 1788. Such a heavy effect was an acquired taste, and Nathaniel Whittock (author of *The Decorative Painters' and Glaziers' Guide*) commented in 1827 that 'this style of decoration is not much used at present'.

When creating imitative effects of wood graining or marbling, a matt finish was neither possible nor desirable. A specification for marbling a rectory (Bartholomew, 1841) made the suggestion:

> To paint the walls of the principal stair-case and of the entrance-hall and of the lobbies adjoining thereto, in the most artistlike manner in imitation of Sienna marble, lined out with masonry-jointing, and varnished twice with the best copal.

Copal was a natural resin and the main constituent of the varnishes used by nineteenth-century house- and coach-painters. Lower coats would have been rubbed down with finely powdered limestone (tripoli or rottenstone). The result would have been smooth and very shiny.

TOWARDS A LIGHTER AESTHETIC

At the beginning of the nineteenth century, there had been little development in materials and pigments since the early days of the house-painting trade in the mid seventeenth century. The most important new pigment, Prussian blue, had replaced most of the earlier blues and there were a number of not altogether successful yellows and greens, but the basic palette remained the same. However, the tonality of the room lightened considerably and wall treatments underwent a radical change.

The full panelling of the earlier period became unfashionable and was gradually reduced. The easiest way to do this was to remove the panel mouldings on the upper wall surfaces and to stretch hessian over the upper wall. This was then covered with lining paper and either painted or hung with wallpaper. There is evidence of this being carried out in the more fashionable households from *c.* 1750. This 'smoothing out' was invariably accompanied by the adoption of much lighter colours and, if the context allowed, by the addition of such decorative elements as papier mâché swags or pendants. In effect, the walls were simplified and were made to look like plaster. Such an addition was found at Wilbury House in Wiltshire. Paint analysis has shown that full panelling frequently survived another fifty years in some cases, and very many examples of unaltered early eighteenth-century panelling can still be seen today.

The panelling on lower walls was usually next to go, and it is not uncommon to find original paint on the skirtings, chair rails and shutters (which were frequently nailed closed), as well as a later sequence of coatings on the lower and upper walls in samples from a room in an early eighteenth-century house. Plaster cornices were often substituted for original timber ones, and a 'stepped' skirting, with an extra fascia, was common in the early nineteenth century.

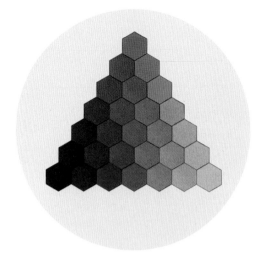

BOUTET (1708)

MAYER (1758)

Claude Boutet published his *Traité de la peinture en mignature* (Treaty of Painting in Miniature) in 1708. In it he illustrated two colour circles: one of seven colours and one of twelve. Above is the former, which contains yellow, orange, scarlet, crimson, violet, blue and green.

The circles are thought to have been the first to have been based on the seven colours in Isaac Newton's optical spectrum (red, orange, yellow, green, blue, indigo and violet). However, Boutet was unable to represent a true red with any pigment, so he employed two reds – fire red and crimson – and disregarded Newton's indigo.

Some editions of this work have a faulty seven colour circle, in that the violet and orange were transposed (as above), and the result makes no sense.

This circular diagram became the model for many colour systems of the eighteenth and nineteenth centuries.

Tobias Mayer (1723–62) was a German mathematician and astronomer. In a lecture given to the Göttingen Academy of Sciences in 1758, he set out to identify the exact number of colours that the human eye is capable of perceiving. His colour triangle was based on the painters' three primaries of red, yellow and blue, and he used vermilion, massicot and azurite to represent them. Mayer held that the human eye was not able to recognize small variations in colour so in his triangle he adopted gradients of twelve, using the three primary colours. Each colour mix therefore contained a notation that added up to twelve, together with the first letter of each colour: 'b' for *blau* (blue), 'g' for *gelb* (yellow) and 'r' for *rot* (red). Thus, 'b11g1' represents eleven parts blue and one part yellow.

The centre of the triangle was filled with colours produced by mixing all three pigments, resulting in a more complicated notation, for example, b5g3r4: the parts again adding up to twelve. This resulted in a triangle of ninety-one different colours. Mayer then added up to four parts of black or white to the triangle, which resulted in a three-dimensional array of colour hexagons containing 910 different colours that he claimed could be distinguished by the eye. The colour diagram above is a simplified version devised by physicist Georg Lichtenberg in 1775.

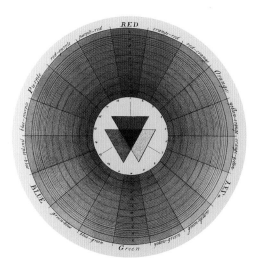

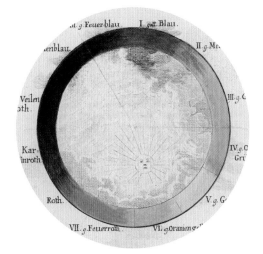

HARRIS (1766)

SCHIFFERMÜLLER (1772)

Moses Harris (1730–c. 1788) was an English entomologist and engraver. He wrote several reference books on British insects, which he illustrated with detailed hand-coloured engravings. In his short treatise on colour, *The Natural System of Colours* (1766), he tried to show the enormous range of colours that could be mixed from the three primaries of red, blue and yellow, which he rendered with vermilion, ultramarine and king's yellow. He related these three 'primitives' to the wild poppy, the cornbottle flower and the butter flower, or meadow ranunculus.

By mixing these colours, he created three 'mediates': orange, green and purple. Harris then mixed each adjacent colour so that one of the two components predominated. This resulted in eighteen colours. He then subdivided each of the colours into twenty concentric circles of different saturation levels, to simulate the addition of black, to create a total of 360 hues in what he termed the prismatic circle (see above).

He also illustrated the results of mixing the three mediates: orange, green and purple. These three colours relate to the garden marigold, the leaves of the lime tree and the flower of the common Judas tree. This compound circle represented the final mixing.

Ignaz Schiffermüller (1727–1806) was an Austrian entomologist, whose main speciality was butterflies. In order to more accurately describe the insects he studied, he set out to identify the colours encountered in nature in *Versuch eines Farbensystems* (Experimental Colour System) published in 1772.

To begin with, he provided a model comprising a table of thirty-six different blues laid out in a three-by-twelve matrix. Names of the colours were provided in German, Latin and French in a similar fashion to later systems of the early twentieth century.

The work also contained a full-page engraving with a colour circle, hand-tinted with twelve colours shading, almost imperceptibly, one to another (see above). This colour circle appears to have been inspired by the theories of the Jesuit priest Father Louis-Bertrand Castel (1688–1757), who wrote a treatise on the melody of colours and whose 'ocular organ' can be seen on page 152.

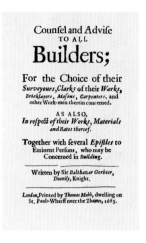   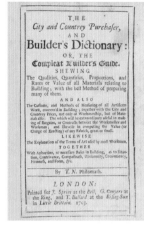

COUNSEL AND ADVISE
TO ALL BUILDERS (1663)
BALTHAZAR GERBIER

The first useful work in the study of house-painting, Balthazar Gerbier's descriptions of building materials and their prices are among the earliest to be published in the United Kingdom. Gerbier (1592–1663) was an Anglo-Dutch diplomat, artist and architectural designer who was knighted by Charles I. Unfortunately, the king's execution and Samuel Pepys's rudeness about the book put paid to his career.

In spite of this, Gerbier's remarks concerning contemporary building practices shed useful light on this early period. For example, in late seventeenth-century practice, ceilings were whitened (by brushing over with a slurry of whiting, or chalk, in water), panelling could be painted in 'wall-nut red colour' in distemper, and the fairest green distemper might be varnished. He also reveals that a 'fair stone colour in oyl upon windowes and doores' was priced at 12d (5p/6¢) a yard and that the same price was charged for 'laying over a wall white in oyl'.

THE ART OF PAINTING
IN OYL (1676)
JOHN SMITH

The early work of clockmaker and writer John Smith (c. 1647–1727) was the first to explain in detail how to prepare pigments for painting, what colours work best with others, and how to make and apply paint. In the early editions, several of the chapters focus on the painting of sundials; however, by the fifth edition of 1723 the emphasis was more on what Smith termed:

Vulgar Painting on...all Manner of Wainscot, Doors, Windows, Posts, Rails, Pails, Gates, Border-Boards for Gardens, or any other Material that requires either Beauty, or Preservation from the Violence of Rain, or Injury of Weather.

The Art of Painting in Oyl was published in several editions until the 1780s (the page shown above is from the 1723 edition), but it makes little mention of developments in materials or taste; for example, nothing is said of the pigment Prussian blue, nor of the taste for flat finishes. It is more of a reflection on late seventeenth-century painting practices. It also formed the basis of a much later edition that made a few concessions to technical developments but was still hopelessly archaic – William Butcher's *Smith's Art of House-Painting* (1821).

A TREATISE OF JAPANING
AND VARNISHING (1688)
JOHN STALKER AND GEORGE PARKER

This is one of the best known of the early manuals, although it deals purely with one particular aspect of decoration. It describes the application of layers of highly polished lacquer rather than conventional paint, but is well worth reading for the prose alone:

What can be more surprizing, then to have our Chambers overlaid with Varnish more glossy and reflecting than polish't Marble? No amorous Nymph need entertain a Dialogue with her Glass, or Narcissus retire to a fountain, to survey his charming countenance, when the whole house is one entire Speculum.

He also urges the decorator to make sure there is no grit on his polishing cloth:

Circumspectly examin your Tripolee and clout, least some miscievous, unwelcome gravel, grittiness, or grating part, unawares steal in, and rase or scratch your work: it will prove no easie matter to hide the flaw and damage.

THE CITY AND COUNTREY
PURCHASER, AND BUILDER'S
DICTIONARY (1703)
RICHARD NEVE

This work describes very well the treatments and colours that were being used in the late seventeenth and early eighteenth centuries. During this period, exterior wood was primed with a dark red brown primer consisting of 'Spanish-brown, Spanish-white, and Red-lead' before a paler undercoat and a white top coat were applied.

On panelling, darker colours such as wainscot colour and walnut tree colour are listed along with 'Plain Japan, either black or white', although how often the latter process was employed is not clear.

It is interesting to note that Japan was charged at 3s 6d or 4s (17.5p/22¢ or 20p/25¢) per yard, while white paint was 10d or 1s (4p/5¢ or 5p/6¢) per yard.

PALLADIO LONDINENSIS: OR, THE LONDON ART OF BUILDING (1734)
WILLIAM SALMON

This three-part book by William Salmon (1703–79) is one of the first really useful works for builders and decorators. In addition to providing such useful advice as geometrical solutions for describing a number of different shapes, including polygons, arches and groins, it lists the cost of labour and materials of most of the trades involved in the building process.

The section on painting is especially interesting for its list of semi-prepared colours available from the colourman Alexander Emerton. These are shown by price, and immediately it can be seen that the tonality of rooms had changed by this date. The colours are lighter than at the beginning of the century, and a clear hierarchy is evident, with fine deep green, for example, being charged at seven times the rate of everyday stone colour. Although not named as such, the cheaper common colours are grouped for the first time.

L'ART DU PEINTRE, DOREUR ET VERNISSEUR (1753)
JEAN-FÉLIX WATIN

After first appearing in Paris in 1753, this work was published in revised editions in different cities in French up to 1823, with German translations released in 1784 and 1834 (the page shown above is from the 1778 edition). Jean-Félix Watin (b. 1728) was a painter of carriages, furniture and ironwork, and he sold his varnish from his shop at the carré de la Porte Saint-Martin in Paris.

This book is a highly influential work, which not only contains many examples of European practices, such as the multi-coated distemper systems of *blanc de roi* and chipolin, but also describes colour mixtures that reflect some of those employed by contemporary British house-painters. Watin describes in some detail the treatment of ironwork and the colours used. He also deals with the painting of trelliswork and garden furniture, neither of which receive much attention in books of this date.

THE HANDMAID TO THE ARTS (1758)
ROBERT DOSSIE

This work by Robert Dossie (1717–77) first appeared in 1758 and was published in later editions throughout the century (the page shown above is from the 1796 edition). It is extremely useful for its lengthy account of the pigments and materials used in painting. Inevitably, as with many other works, *The Handmaid to the Arts* deals primarily with artists' use, but many of the entries are equally applicable to the house-painting trade of the period.

Amongst other things he tells his readers that:

> Spanish brown, or brown red, is a native earth found in the state, and of the colour in which it is used; it is nearly of the same colour with the Venetian red, but fouler. It was probably from its name brought originally from abroad, and was then most of a finer kind, but what is now used in the produce of our own country, being dug up in several parts of England.

The book is also interesting for its information on wallpapers, gilding and such things as a transcript of Dr Woodward's account of the manufacture of the pigment Prussian blue.

VALUABLE SECRETS CONCERNING ARTS AND TRADES (1775)
ANON

In this compendium (the page shown above is from the 1780 edition), recipes and directions are given for making many pigments, such as indigo, verdigris and brown pink. It also advises on the imitation of porphyry and serpentine marble, and gives an account of the painstaking process required to achieve a highly polished surface:

> To Paint in Varnish on Wood
> [1] The preparation of the wood, previous to the laying of colours, and the general process observed in laying them on it.
> [2] You must first lay on the wood two coats of Troyes-white, diluted with size water. Next, lay over these a third coat of ceruse. Then having mixed the colour you want with turpentine oil, add the varnish to it, and lay it on the wood, previously prepared as follows.
> [3] Polish the wood, first, with shavegrass or horsetail, and then with pounce-stone. Lay afterwards six or seven coats of colour mixed with varnish, allowing after each coat a sufficient time to dry, before laying on the next; then polish over the last coat with pounce-stone grinded on marble into a subtile powder. When this is done, lay two or three coats of pure white varnish. As soon as this dry, rub it over with a soft rag dipped into fine olive oil, then rub it with tripoly reduced into subtile powder; and having wiped it with a clean piece of linen, pass a piece of wash-leather all over it.

INTERIOR DECORATION 1800–1830

Among the papers relating to a ruined Scottish country house, a very rare, perhaps unique, discovery was made: a collection of hand-painted cards produced by a house-painter for a prospective client – Mr Robert Vans Agnew of Barnbarroch House in Wigtownshire. In effect, these were like a set of modern proprietary colour cards, in that they give insight into the sorts of paint colours that were on offer at a particular time. The remarkable thing about these cards is that they were made in 1807 and are, therefore, the most accurate indication of genuine 'historical colours' – certainly those of the late Georgian and early Regency periods. As the colours were applied in a distemper medium and stored in an envelope, they are still remarkably fresh.

The painted colour cards are also important for the accompanying information that survives with them. It reveals that two house-painters were consulted – Andrew Clason from Glasgow and M. Ross from Edinburgh. Letters from both tradesmen, outlining costs and recommendations for finishes and colours, indicate, for example:

> The most fashionable colours for Plaster walls are The Stone and Gray Colours. Oil Colours are at present used on the wood & plaster walls of Lobbies, stair cases, Passages, Dining Rooms, Parlours, Billiard Rooms & Libraries.

These colours would have formed part of the staple house-painting palette of the Regency period. Most of them had been available for at least eighty years, and many would have still formed the bulk of those on offer for everyday purposes until the early years of the twentieth century.

The year 1807 was also the date that designer Thomas Hope published sketches of the furniture and interiors of his house in Duchess Street, London, in a folio volume titled *Household Furniture and Interior Decoration*. This was to have considerable influence and brought about a change in the upholstery and interior decoration of houses. The line engravings, with their use of sparse outline, recall the Greek red- and black-painted vases, and also the drawings of the sculptor John Flaxman. They fail, however, to convey the vividness of the colour schemes. In the Indian drawing room, for example, the upholstery was in deep crimson, the walls sky blue, and the ceiling pale yellow intermixed with azure and sea green. Ornaments of gold in various shades relieved and harmonized these colours. Although Hope had travelled in the East, there was nothing remotely Indian about the shape or proportions of the room, which retained a strong neoclassical air. Sadly, Hope's style was too uncompromising to attract a large following.

In 1821 a partially updated reprint of the classic, indeed probably original, work on house-painting – John Smith's *Art of Painting in Oyl*, which first appeared in 1676 – was published. This was William Butcher's *Smith's Art of House-Painting* and it must have met with reasonable success because it was reprinted four years later in 1825. This relaunch of a somewhat dated trade manual was obviously an early attempt to cash in on the growing interest in interior decoration. For, with the increased wealth among the upper and middle classes – caused largely by the Industrial Revolution and the conclusion of the war with the French – not only was more attention being paid to existing housing, but also new buildings were being constructed in large numbers.

Useful sources of information on early nineteenth-century colours include a small American handbook published in New Haven in 1812, by Hezekiah Reynolds, titled *Directions for House and Ship Building*. In this, Reynolds suggests mixing 1 pound (454 g) of verdigris with 10 pounds (4.5 kg) of white lead to make pea green for exterior purposes. There is little evidence of a similar use in the United Kingdom.

Another work of interest is Peter Nicholson's *The Mechanic's Companion* (1825), in which he gives the pigment mineral green as the main component of pea green. However, this is a very imprecise name and could mean one of several pigments – variously Scheele's green or a number of copper chloride or copper sulphate pigments.

Most of these colours, especially the more expensive pigments, would have related to what is called 'polite architecture'. For more everyday usage, there are examples, such as the recipe in John Bennett's *The Artificer's Complete Lexicon* (1833) for producing 'a cheap colouring for the walls of rooms in dwelling houses', that would certainly raise the eyebrows of the Health and Safety Executive:

Take four pounds of Roman Vitriol, and pour it in a gallon of boiling water; when dissolved, add two pounds of Pearl Ash and stir the mixture well with a stick, until the effervescence ceases, then add a quarter of a pound of pulverized yellow arsenic, and stir the whole together; let it be laid on with a paint or white wash brush, and if the wall has not been painted before, two, or even three coats will be requisite. If a pea-green is required, put in less; and if an apple-green, more of the yellow arsenic.

T. H. Vanherman, an early nineteenth-century London house-painter, illustrated how colour names were very imprecise and that there was a degree of flexibility in the way that colours were produced:

Pea-Green, Sage-Green, and Drab-Green. Are formed with Spruce Ochre and Prussian blue, and then lowered with white; or, if black is substituted for the blue, you will have a variety of different greens; and substituting Raw Umber, instead of the Ochre, you will obtain another distinct set of greens. All these tints are chosen, and likewise all the middle-tint drabs, on account of their repose to the sight, and their solid and quiet tone.

The last sentence has echoes of Goethe's thoughts on restful greens (see p. 97).

Green verditer was a common component of pea green. For example, in an early edition of Laxton's book of builders' prices of 1818 it was listed as being among the most expensive colours applied by a plasterer: 1 shilling and 2 pence (6p/7¢) to 'wash, stop and apply pea green', compared to 4d (1.75p/2¢) to do the same with a common colour. The costs per yard of various colours being, in shillings and pence:

Wash, stop, and common colour	0–4
Wash, stop, and Buff colour	0–5
Wash, stop, and Lemon colour	0–6
Wash, stop, and Grey colour	0–7
Wash, stop, and Blue colour	1–2
Wash, stop, and Pea Green, with verditer	1–2

Furthermore, Laxton described pea green as a 'tender tint along with blue verditer, lilacs, pinks etc.' Later recipes usually include chrome yellow and Prussian blue in their ingredients.

Pea green appeared in two important nomenclatures of colour and, inevitably, there was a difference of opinion. In his *Nomenclature of Colours* (1845), David Ramsay Hay described his pea green:

In the popular nomenclature of colours, the tints of green have a greater number of appellations than those of any other colour, as will be observed in the sequel. But the only one of these that can be applied to a pure tint of this colour, with the exception of light or pale green, is the well-known one of pea-green, all the others being modified either by the predominance of one of their constituent parts, or by their being gently neutralized with red.

Robert Ridgway, a North American ornithologist and author of *Color Standards and Color Nomenclature* (1912), shows a much bluer version.

Advances in the field of colour theory, the painted imitation of woods and marbles and the discovery of a few breakthrough pigments made the first quarter of the nineteenth century a key period in the development of the house-painting trade. Three very important pigments were to appear in the space of fourteen years.

The first of the bright near-primary colours, emerald green, was made in Germany in 1814. It was a bright, slightly blue and highly toxic green, which tended to be used to best effect in the printing of wallpaper.

French ultramarine, a bright blue that did not incline towards green, and yet was cheaper and easier to use than the natural ultramarine obtained from the semi-precious stone lapis lazuli, was introduced in 1828. It does not seem to have been taken up with quite the same speed as Prussian blue one hundred years before. However, by the middle of the century it saw great use, particularly in distemper, whose alkaline nature tended to discolour its predecessor. Wallpaper manufacturers and laundresses alike also benefited from this discovery – a commercial version, sold as Reckitt's blue, could be added to the rinse water to brighten dingy 'whites'.

The new pigment that was to have the most profound effect upon the palette of the house-painter of the early nineteenth century was chrome yellow, which was introduced in *c.* 1818. Not only was a bright yellow that kept its colour now possible, but so also was a range of clearer greens. When mixed with Prussian blue, chrome yellow produced a colour that was termed Brunswick green in the United Kingdom and chrome green in the United States. This combination is in evidence on external surfaces throughout the century that followed and beyond.

Coach-painters were certainly quick to exploit this new bright yellow, replacing the rather disappointing patent yellow that had been their

A

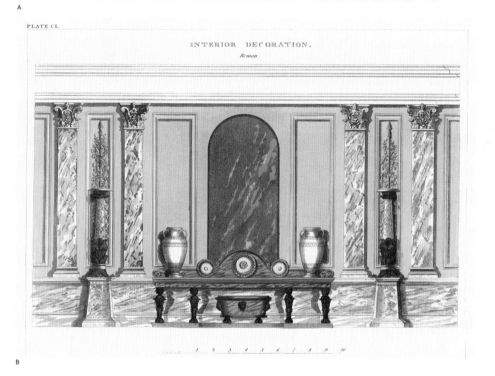

PLATE CL

INTERIOR DECORATION.

Roman.

1 2 3 4 5 6 7 8 9 10

B

[PREVIOUS] [P. 112] Samples of 1807 distemper colours. [A] *The Flemish Picture Gallery, the Mansion of Thomas Hope, Duchess Street, Portland Place* by Robert William Billings. [B] A plate from George Smith's *Cabinet Maker's and Upholsterer's Guide* (1826), a strong influence on decoration in the Regency period. [OVERLEAF] [P. 116] Plate from William Gell's *Pompeiana* (1817–19), drawn when Pompeii had only recently been excavated. [P. 117] Plates from Thomas Hope's *Household Furniture & Interior Decoration* (1807), showing his designs for historically inspired interiors. The black and white illustrations fail to convey just how colourful some of these rooms were.

Plate XIV

Drawn by Sir W. Gell.

Engraved by H. Moses.

POMPEII.

WALL OF THE PANTHEON.

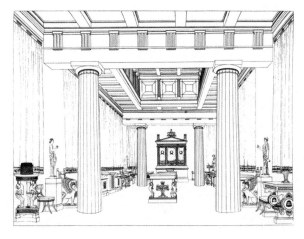

only option until this time. A pure yellow was a difficult colour to use in decoration, but notable examples of its use do exist. Best known are the south and north drawing rooms at the Sir John Soane's Museum, which still makes a great impact on visitors. However, it took a man with Soane's genius to employ such a scheme.

While in Rome between 1778 and 1780, Soane had bought a set of the coloured etchings of Angelo Campanella of the Villa Negroni, which had been discovered in July 1777. These were used as sources for the decoration of his house at Pitzhanger Manor, Ealing – in particular his breakfast room, which was designed in 1802.

Analysis carried out a number of years ago by Dr Ian Bristow revealed the full extent of the decorative effects and has shown that the surviving drawings prepared by Soane did not accurately reflect what had been executed. This is a point that makes the study of early interiors particularly difficult. On a number of occasions, coloured drawings marked 'as executed' have been shown by paint analysis not to have been followed exactly.

At Pitzhanger Manor, much use had been made of painted imitations, with marbling applied in dark green and a grey blue, together with large areas of porphyry. The caryatids and flying figures in the spandrels of the pendentive ceiling had also been dusted with powdered silver to look like tarnished metal, and the central oculus of the ceiling had been painted to resemble a sky. Elsewhere on the ceiling, Soane had, in a very abstract way, converted elements of flat-painted Pompeian decoration into shallow incised motifs.

It would be unrealistic to regard Soane's designs as indicative of the general trend in interior decoration, but aspects of his translations from the antique were to find their way into wider circles. In 1792, twelve years after returning from Rome, Soane bought No. 12 Lincoln's Inn Fields. One of the many things that he brought back from his travels was a fragment of red-painted wall plaster from Herculaneum, and this was to influence some of the colour schemes employed in his house in 1812.

According to paint analysis by Bristow, it was in the dining room of No. 12 that Soane showed himself to be one of the early users of Pompeian red as the main colour for the walls of a room. The colour alone, independent of designs or motifs, was Pompeian red. Below this, on the dado area, he used satinwood graining. Soane

went on to use a 'picture gallery red' at Dulwich Picture Gallery, London, in 1811. This recalls John Nash's use of the same colour in the picture gallery at Attingham in 1807.

It is very hard to get away from Soane. Not only was he using a strong red colour as an overall wall treatment, but he was also among the earliest exponents of wood graining – in its nineteenth-century highly imitative guise. Previously, until its decline in popularity in the early eighteenth century, graining had been more impressionistic, barely acting as a mirror to nature.

The early imitation of light woods, such as satinwood, has been encountered on a pair of doors that were originally made for Carlton House, the Prince Regent's residence in Pall Mall. It is recorded that French grainers were working there in 1782, and although the house was demolished in 1827 many elements were salvaged and reused. It took time for innovations such as graining to be recognized, but paint analysis of some of the stucco-fronted buildings of the 1820s in Brighton and Hove reveal its use in certain rooms, as does a recently discovered specification of 1818 for No. 22 Charlotte Square in Edinburgh. Wood graining was used on surfaces inside and out. In both cases, it was varnished and presented a glossy, long-lasting surface. Provided that the surface was wiped down and revarnished occasionally, it would last for many years.

When Soane rebuilt No. 13 Lincoln's Inn Fields as his home in 1812, in addition to using a Pompeian red colour in his new dining room, he used it in his library. In subsequent repaints, the red has departed from the original colour and become less earthy. In combination with the red, Soane also applied a bronzed green paint finish. Again, he was an early user of the bronzed effects that were to continue in one form or another for the remainder of the century.

Bronze powders had been introduced from Germany in the previous century and were often used to highlight surfaces. The effect of bronze could either be implied by using a green or a brown green paint, in which case it was known as 'bronze green', or bronze metallic powder could be dusted on an appropriately coloured surface to give a metallic glint.

At Lancaster House, close to Buckingham Palace, the plaster surface of the atlantes in the staircase was treated to resemble tarnished metal. A recent cross section taken from it indicates that the surface was painted only twice.

A

[PREVIOUS] [P. 118] *Pitture antiche della Villa Negroni*, 1778, by Angelo Campanella. Adonis setting out on a hunt. From a series of prints, etched by Campanella and printed by Pietro Marco Vitali. They record antique frescoes that were discovered in 1777 in the grounds of the Villa Negroni in Rome. [P. 119] Pompeian red in Sir John Soane's library-dining room at No. 13 Lincoln's Inn Fields. This colour is believed to be based on a piece of red plaster that Soane brought back from Pompeii. [A] The recently decorated New Room at George Washington's Mount Vernon. A green verditer colour was applied on the walls.

B

C

[B] This yellow in the north drawing room at the Sir John Soane Museum in London's
Lincoln's Inn Fields is based on the patent yellow found in analysis by Dr Ian Bristow.
[C] The original dull red on the walls of the Dulwich Picture Gallery was restored following
work undertaken by Bristow. [OVERLEAF] Aquatint plate from an elephant folio bound for the
Prince Regent's guests' perusal at John Nash's Royal Pavilion, Brighton (1815–22). The interiors
of the Royal Pavilion are a colourful mix of neoclassical, Chinese, Indian and gothic themes.

The first scheme of 1838 shows a dark green paint, heavily speckled with bronze powder, while the existing scheme of about 1870 can be seen to be much darker and less bronzed.

Stair balusters were frequently bronzed. The sixth Duke of Devonshire's house in Kemp Town, Brighton, has examples from the 1820s and 1830s. The use of bronze powder to help give the appearance of metal can also be seen on balustrades in buildings of the same date on the south side of Charlotte Square in Edinburgh.

Johann Goethe, the German polymath, had a significant, if indirect, influence on the colours used in interior decoration towards the end of the Regency period. In his book on colour theory, *Zur Farbenlehre* (1810), Goethe developed the idea that the eye sought a complementary colour next to every hue used. These 'harmonious contrasts' were, he believed, immediately applicable to aesthetic purposes. Although this book was not published in English until 1840, Goethe's ideas seem to have influenced a number of English artists by the early 1800s, and there was certainly a Goethe circle established in Edinburgh to discuss his work. The Edinburgh painter and writer David Ramsay Hay expands

on many of the themes introduced by Goethe in *The Laws of Harmonious Colouring* (1828).

By the end of the Regency period, a series of rules specifically for the use of colour in interior decoration had been established, and their influence may still be seen in diagrams that appeared in some of the house-painting manuals towards the end of the nineteenth century. These clearly illustrate how sophisticated harmonies could be achieved. Some are a simple harmony of two colours: for example, complementary salmon buff and moss green placed side by side with their tints. More complex harmonies include warm green, greeny blue, terracotta, salmon and their tints placed in a carefully arranged sequence. The following is a list of recommendations for specific sorts of rooms that appeared in T. H. Vanherman's *The Painter's Cabinet, and Colourman's Repository* in 1828:

> For libraries, crimson is recommended, ...being a colour that agrees with books and their bindings. Another author agreed, saying that 'scarlet and crimson will ever hold preference' in libraries and eating rooms. The characteristic colouring of the latter should be warm, rich, and substantial;

and where contrasts are introduced, they should not be vivid.

In David Hay's *The Laws of Harmonious Colouring adapted to Interior Decorations* (6th edn., 1847), the following advice is given:

> The most appropriate style of colouring for libraries is rich and grave, and no higher colouring should be employed than is necessary to give the effect of grandeur, and unite the painting with the richness produced by the bookbinder's art.

An elegant tint for a drawing room in the early nineteenth century would have been lavender colour, which was a variant of peach blossom colour. And, it was on the first floor that Vanherman stressed that:

> ...the skill and taste of the painter must be exerted, and the contents of his pallet consulted, and applied to give due effect without affectation, or overloading; but by a just combination, the eye may be pleasingly surprised, yet not dazzled by too many glaring lights. This...should be the most splendid, but of a mellow and calm tone, brilliant,

but not gaudy; magnificent, but not heavy. As we advance higher we should adopt the aerial tint; this gives a feeling of lightness that beguiles the labour as we mount – just as a traveller, rising a hill, is not sensible of the toil, being surrounded by enlivening objects.

Indications of what colour to use in the bedroom are scarce; however, in 1836, south-facing bedrooms in 'summer residences' were considered pleasing in white or blue, whereas those with a northerly aspect were warmed with buff, pink or red tones – this was particularly true of wallpapers, where floral designs were preferred for north-facing rooms. Paintwork was generally coloured to match the grounds of the paper. David Hay suggests that in bedrooms:

> a light, clearly, and cheerful style of colouring is the most appropriate. A greater degree of contrast may be here admitted between the room and its furniture than in any other apartment, as the bed and window-curtains form a sufficient mass to balance a tint of equal intensity upon the walls. There may also, for the same reason, be admitted gayer and brighter colours upon the carpet.

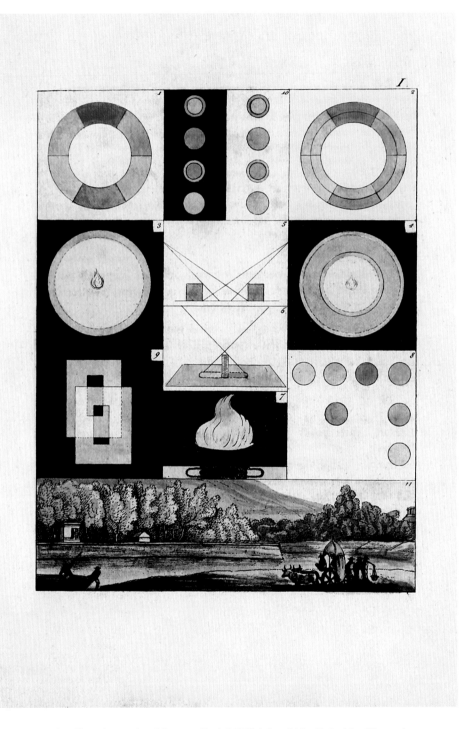

These illustrations are from Johann von Goethe's highly influential *Zur Farbenlehre* (Theory of Colours) of 1810. He shows (above) what a person suffering from acyanopsia (the inability to recognize blue tints) is likely to see: for example, in colour wheel No. 2, the outer circle shows the colours seen in normal vision and the inner one those equivalents seen by an acyanopsic. Goethe provided a number of diagrams that illustrated his experiments with light and prisms (opposite). He showed that there were two ways of producing a spectrum with a prism - one with a light beam in a dark room and the other with a dark beam (a shadow) in a light room. He recorded the sequence of colours at various distances from the prism in both circumstances and found that the yellow and blue edges remain closest to the side that is light, and the red and violet edges remain closest to the side that is dark.

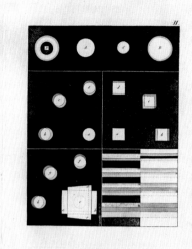

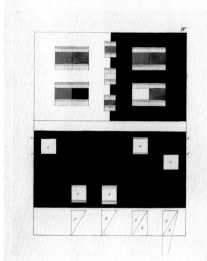

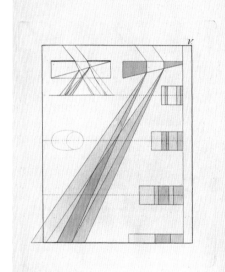

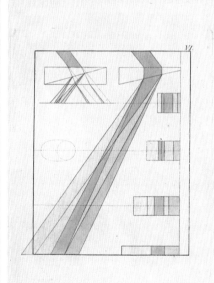

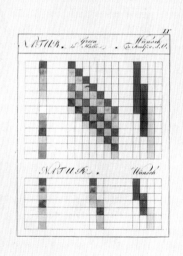

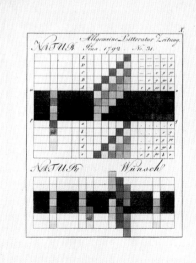

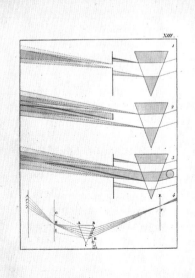

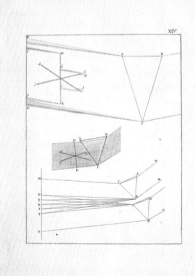

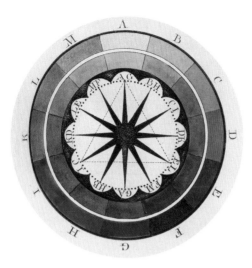

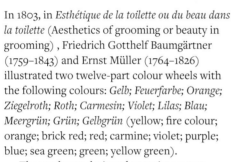

MÜLLER (1803)

SOWERBY (1809)

In 1803, in *Esthétique de la toilette ou du beau dans la toilette* (Aesthetics of grooming or beauty in grooming) , Friedrich Gotthelf Baumgärtner (1759–1843) and Ernst Müller (1764–1826) illustrated two twelve-part colour wheels with the following colours: *Gelb; Feuerfarbe; Orange; Ziegelroth; Roth; Carmesin; Violet; Lilas; Blau; Meergrün; Grün; Gelbgrün* (yellow; fire colour; orange; brick red; red; carmine; violet; purple; blue; sea green; green; yellow green).

The work was designed to assist women with their choice of hairstyle, clothing and make-up. The last section of the book is dedicated to colour – principally the colour of clothing – and it shows which colours work best with particular skin and hair tones. It included two hand-tinted colour wheels that explained the laws of harmony and showed complementary colours.

James Sowerby (1757–1822) was a distinguished author of books on botany and natural history. In 1809 he published *A New Elucidation of Colours, Original Prismatic and Material: Showing Their Concordance in the Three Primitives, Yellow, Red and Blue: and the Means of Producing, Measuring and Mixing Them: with some Observations on the Accuracy of Sir Isaac Newton.*

To display the 'three primitives', Sowerby employed gamboge, carmine and Prussian blue and these are displayed at three saturation levels as 'full tints', 'middle tints' and 'light tints' on the sides of the main triangle (above). Secondary mixes are shown in the corners of this triangle and ternary (three-part) mixes can be seen in the three rhombi at the bottom of the figure. A total of sixty-four colours are shown, including white, and in a separate diagram he identified each of them by a number and letter code.

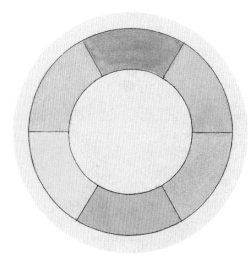

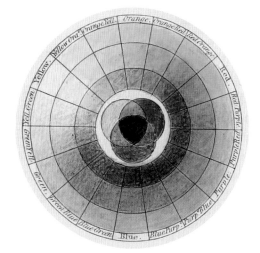

GOETHE (1810)

HAYTER (1813)

Zur Farbenlehre (Theory of Colours, 1810) by Johann Wolfgang von Goethe (1748–1832) contained the poet's views on the nature of colours and how they are perceived by man. As Wittgenstein was to later point out, it was not so much a theory as a series of examples by which the reader could experience a number of different colour-related phenomena. He offered no real explanation of the nature of colour.

This simple colour wheel (above) appeared in Goethe's first diagram (see p. 124). He explained that yellow, blue and red are placed triadically with their derived intermediates. Hence, the three primaries of red, yellow and blue, with the secondaries of green, orange and purple. The secondaries are placed opposite their complementary primaries – red opposite green, blue opposite orange and purple opposite yellow – or, as he wrote, '...for the colours diametrically opposed to each other...are those that reciprocally evoke each other in the eye'.

This colour wheel anticipated Ewald Hering's opponent colour theory by more than fifty years.

In a variation of this wheel, Goethe included various aesthetic qualities. He also associated red with the 'beautiful', orange with the 'noble', yellow with the 'good', green to the 'useful', blue to the 'common' and violet to the 'unnecessary'.

Charles Hayter (1761–1835) displayed three colour wheels under the heading 'The Painter's Compass', in his book: *An introduction to perspective, dialogues between the author's children* (1813). He added a compendium of genuine instruction in the art of drawing and painting (titled *Letters on drawing and painting*).

Hayter's basic triangle, comprising the three primary colours yellow, red and blue, was well established by this time and the black centre was probably derived from the prismatic circle of Moses Harris (1766). He came to the conclusion that 'all transient or prismatic effects can be imitated with the Three Primitive Colors...but only in the same degree of comparison as white bears to LIGHT'. Once again, the colours are laid out triadically, with the complementary colours opposite each other on the wheel (above).

'MEMOIR ON A METHOD OF PAINTING WITH MILK' (1801)
ANTOINE ALEXIS CADET-DE-VAUX

'Memoir on a Method of Painting with Milk' by French chemist Antoine Alexis Cadet-de-Vaux (1743–1828) was published in English in *The Repertory of Arts & Manufactures* in 1801 and on many subsequent occasions.

Although Cadet-de-Vaux is universally named as the originator of this recipe, a manuscript of 1774 in the National Archives of Scotland includes a very similar recipe among a list of pigments and prices. It is possible that the recipe is much older and had been copied through the generations. The last time that it appears in a painting manual seems to be in Ernest Spon's 'Workshop Receipts' of 1873.

In 1968 Richard M. Candee, in the journal of the Society for the Preservation of New England Antiquities, set out to dispel the myth of the widespread use of milk-based paints in colonial America. He traced the source to the translation of Alexis Cadet-de-Vaux's 'Memoir'.

In 1995 Susan Buck, the eminent American paint analyst wrote:

> the physical evidence makes plain that the Shakers generally used traditional oil-based paints to paint wooden objects and architectural elements, and recipes containing milk are primarily lime-based whitewashes or exterior paints, not furniture or interior paints.

TABLEAUX DETAILLES DES PRIX DE TOUS LES OUVRAGES DE BÂTIMENT (1804–06)
M. R. J. MORISOT

Joseph Morisot (1767–1821) was an architect and quantity surveyor working for Louis XVIII: he was well placed to produce a work of such impressive detail. The third volume deals with the work of the painter and the locksmith. Morisot describes the pigments used, their cost, and that of all the materials employed by the house-painter. He also imparts much detail about the fashions of the early nineteenth century. The washing down and filling of surfaces prior to painting is described in as much detail as the marbles and woods that were imitated.

Morisot also details such information as hourly rates; the quantity of oil or water and the time required to convert different pigments into a pound of paint; recipes; the prices of different pigments; and useful details on bronzing and gilding.

Some years ago, this work proved especially useful in restoring the early eighteenth-century Privy garden at Hampton Court Palace. The details on the different recipes for verdigris paint, for example, ensured that the appropriate depth of colour was achieved on the border boards. There is no work quite like it in English.

AN ARCHITECTURAL DICTIONARY (1819)
PETER NICHOLSON

Peter Nicholson (1765–1844) was a Scottish architect, mathematician and engineer who was also a prolific writer, contributing practical information on a wide range of technical subjects. The chapter on 'Painting' gives a very clear, brief account of the process of house-painting. It is particularly interesting for the description of having to let new plaster dry out naturally over two to three years before applying oil paints. This fact is rarely mentioned in texts and has implications for restoration work that is often at variance with modern programming. An early form of stain block is described as follows:

> When old plastering has become discoloured by stains, and it be desired to have it painted in distemper; it is then advisable to give the old plaster, when properly cleaned off and prepared, one coat at least of white-lead ground in oil, and used with spirits of turpentine, which will generally fix all old stains; and when quite dry, will take the waterl-colours very kindly.

In this publication and in his later *The Mechanic's Companion* of 1825, Nicholson provides useful recipes for colours.

SMITH'S ART OF HOUSE-PAINTING (1821)
WILLIAM BUTCHER

This rare booklet, we are told, contains the:

> best and most approved rules for preparing, mixing, and working of oil-colours, oil-cloth varnish and colour, milk-paint etc...so as to enable any person to paint and grain, in oil-colours, all sorts of timber or iron-work, in houses and ships; as gates, doors, posts, pales, palisad(o)es, and every thing that requires paint, whether for beauty or for preservation from the influence of the weather.

It was based heavily on John Smith's *Art of Painting in Oyl*, which came out in many editions between 1676 and 1788, and thereby lies its weakness. Although useful for what it reveals about eighteenth-century practices, it says little about early nineteenth-century painting. Tellingly, it makes no allowances for the developments in technology or the introduction of new pigments over the previous 120 years or so.

THE PAINTER'S & VARNISHER'S POCKET MANUAL (1825), ANON.

The Painter's & Varnisher's Pocket Manual of 1825 was among the earliest of the nineteenth-century house-painters' manuals that were not entirely derivative. However, the American book dealer Charles B. Wood states it is 'a work which probably has no real "author"; it was created by the publisher from other previously printed sources'. The working practices and materials that were to remain largely unchanged for another century are explained in a very clear and straightforward manner.

This publication not only contains numerous recipes for colours but also provides tests for the detection of adulteration in oils and pigments. It also draws attention to the hazardous nature of several of the materials of the trade. The recipe for milk paint that it includes has been taken directly from Antoine Alexis Cadet-de-Vaux's 'Memoir on a Method of Painting with Milk'.

THE PAINTER'S, GILDER'S AND VARNISHER'S MANUAL (c. 1827) G. A. SMEATON

This manual appears to be a development of a previous work and, although not widely acknowledged, it gives a clear idea of the working practices and materials of early nineteenth-century house-painters, which with few exceptions remained largely unchanged from the previous century. A number of recipes for cheap paints for external surfaces are supplied, and one of the common constituents is described as 'road dirt finely sifted'.

This work appeared in several editions and forms during the 1820s and 1830s, and was reprinted more than twenty-five times in the United States, with many alterations.

THE DECORATIVE PAINTERS' AND GLAZIERS' GUIDE (1827) NATHANIEL WHITTOCK

Nathaniel Whittock's guide is one of the three works mentioned by the architect, garden designer and author John Claudius Loudon as being important for the information it gives on house-painting. After a brief account of the pigments used, Whittock describes and illustrates numerous examples of graining and marbling. The chapters on interior and architectural decoration are very revealing for their views on contemporary practice and prejudice. Of graining, we learn of the:

very great improvement that has been made within the last ten years in the art of imitating the grain and colour of various fancy woods and marbles, and the facility and consequent cheapness of this formerly expensive work, has brought it into general use; and there are few respectable houses erected, where the talent of the decorative painter is not called into action, in graining doors, shutters, wainscots, etc.

THE PAINTER'S CABINET, AND COLOURMAN'S REPOSITORY (1828) T. H. VANHERMAN

T. H. Vanherman was an artist and house-painter who traded from 51 King Street, in Soho, London. This work was written with the knowledge '...acquired by half a century's practical experience'. It was republished with the rather snappier title *Every Man his Own House-Painter and Colourman* in the following year.

Vanherman's manual is a very thorough work dealing with all aspects of house-painting and it is often quoted. There are chapters describing the manufacture and tinting of 'anti-corrosive' and 'aromatic' paints; zinc – the non-toxic alternative to lead paint; the imitation of wood and marbles; oils; varnishes; and house paints.

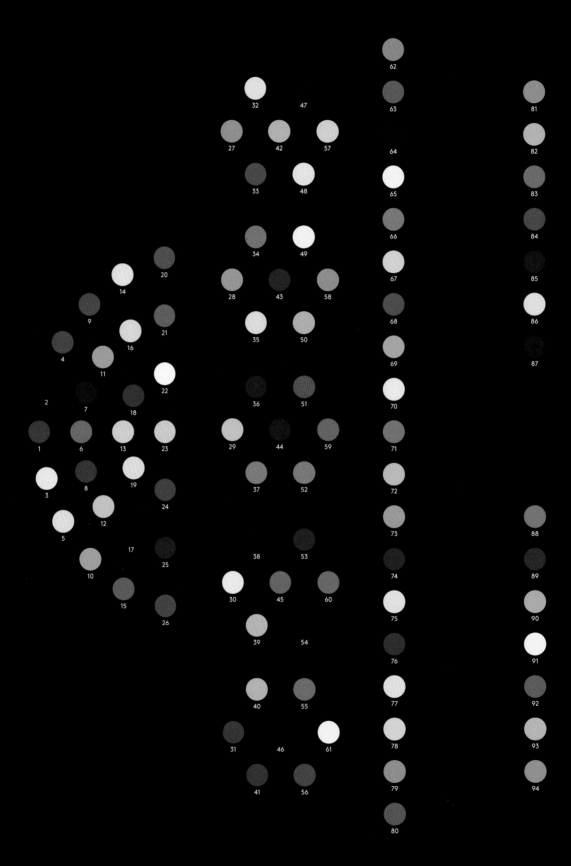

II.

PAINTS, COLOUR SYSTEMS AND INTERIORS

1830 – 1900

OPPOSITE: NINETY-FOUR COLOURS DERIVED FROM
WERNER'S NOMENCLATURE (1814) BY PATRICK SYME (SEE PP. 134–137)

1. CLOVE BROWN
2. PANSY PURPLE
3. PEACH BLOSSOM RED
4. CARMINE RED
5. KINGS YELLOW
6. ORPIMENT ORANGE
7. CHESTNUT BROWN
8. AZURE BLUE
9. BLACKISH GREY
10. GREENISH BLUE
11. EMERALD GREEN
12. AURORA RED
13. BUFF ORANGE
14. LEMON YELLOW
15. YELLOWISH BROWN
16. YELLOWISH GREY
17. PRUSSIAN BLUE
18. FLAX FLOWER BLUE
19. ASPARAGUS GREEN
20. VERMILION RED
21. BLUISH LILAC PURPLE
22. PRIMROSE YELLOW
23. OCHRE YELLOW
24. DEEP ORANGE BROWN

25. PALE BLACKISH PURPLE
26. HAIR BROWN
27. REDDISH ORANGE
28. VERDIGRIS GREEN
29. FRENCH GREY
30. SIENNA YELLOW
31. PURPLISH RED
32. FLESH RED
33. BERLIN BLUE
34. BROCCOLI BROWN
35. GAMBOGE YELLOW
36. PLUM PURPLE
37. SAP GREEN
38. UMBER BROWN
39. APPLE GREEN
40. BLUISH GREY
41. BROWNISH ORANGE
42. MOUNTAIN GREEN
43. INDIGO BLUE
44. BROWNISH RED
45. HYACINTH RED
46. LIVER BROWN
47. VIOLET PURPLE
48. SNOW WHITE

49. STRAW YELLOW
50. BLUISH GREEN
51. LAKE RED
52. TILE RED
53. CHINA BLUE
54. CHOCOLATE RED
55. OLIVE GREEN
56. CAMPANULA PURPLE
57. SULPHUR YELLOW
58. DUTCH ORANGE
59. HONEY YELLOW
60. LAVENDER PURPLE
61. CREAM YELLOW
62. GRASS GREEN
63. DEEP REDDISH ORANGE
64. SCOTCH BLUE
65. ASH GREY
66. WAX YELLOW
67. CELANDINE GREEN
68. COCHINEAL RED
69. PISTACHIO GREEN
70. WINE YELLOW
71. ULTRAMARINE BLUE
72. OIL GREEN

73. BROWNISH PURPLE RED
74. BLACKISH GREEN
75. PEARL GREY
76. BLUISH PURPLE
77. SISKIN GREEN
78. GREYISH WHITE
79. CRIMSON RED
80. ARTERIAL BLOOD RED
81. LEEK GREEN
82. GREYISH BLUE
83. GALLSTONE YELLOW
84. RED LILAC PURPLE
85. IMPERIAL PURPLE
86. SMOKE GREY
87. BLACKISH BROWN
88. SCARLET RED
89. AURICULA PURPLE
90. GREENISH GREY
91. ROSE RED
92. DUCK GREEN
93. VERDITER BLUE
94. SAFFRON YELLOW

Colour charts for use in taxonomic descriptions of plants and animals were published from the last years of the seventeenth century. Perhaps the best known of these is A. G. Werner's *Von den äusserlichen Kennzeichen der Fossilien,* 1814 (On the External Characteristics of Minerals). This section introduces the first colour standards and also the first colour systems with a practical application to achieve worldwide acceptance.

[OPPOSITE] Greys, blacks, blues and purples from *Werner's Nomenclature* (1814).
[OVERLEAF] Greens and yellows from *Werner's Nomenclature.* [PP. 136–137] Pages from *Werner's Nomenclature* and ornithological plates by John Gould. [A] Orange: 77 buff orange corresponds to the streak from the eye of the kingfisher. [B] *Alcedo ispida*, kingfisher. [C] Red: 87 arterial blood red, head of the cock goldfinch. [D] *Carduelis elegans*, goldfinch. [E] Red: 98 chocolate red, breast of bird of paradise. [F] *Seleucides nigricans*, wired bird of paradise. [G] Browns: 104: yellowish brown: light brown spots on guinea-pig, breast of hoopoe. [H] *Upupa epops*, hoopoe.

GREYS.

Nº	Names.	Colours.	ANIMAL.	VEGETABLE.	MINERAL.
9	Ash Grey.		Breast of long tailed Hen Titmouse.	Fresh Wood ashes	Flint.
10	Smoke Grey.		Breast of the Robin round the Red.		Flint.
11	French Grey.		Breast of Pied Wag tail.		
12	Pearl Grey.		Backs of black headed and Kittiwake Gulls.	Back of Petals of Purple Hepatica.	Porcelain Jasper.
13	Yellowish Grey.		Vent coverts of White Rump.	Stems of the Barberry.	Common Calcedony.
14	Bluish Grey.		Back and tail Coverts Wood Pigeon.		Limestone
15	Greenish Grey.		Quill feathers of the Robin.	Bark of Ash Tree.	Clay Slate. Wacke.
16	Blackish Grey.		Back of Nut-hatch.	Old Stems of Hawthorn.	Flint.

BLACKS

No	Names	Colours	ANIMAL	VEGETABLE	MINERAL
17	Greyish Black		Water Ousel. Breast and upper Part of Back of Water Hen.		Basalt.
18	Bluish Black		Largest Black Slug	Crowberry.	Black Cobalt Ochre.
19	Greenish Black		Breast of Lapwing		Hornblende
20	Pitch or Brownish Black		Guillemot. Wing Coverts & Black Cock.		Yenite Mica
21	Reddish Black		Spots on Large Wings of Tyger Moth. Breast of Pochard Duck.	Berry of Fuchsia Coccinea	Oliven Ore
22	Ink Black			Berry of Deadly Night Shade	Oliven Ore
23	Velvet Black		Mole. Tail Feathers of Black Cock.	Black of Red and Black West-Indian Peas.	Obsidian

BLUES

No.	Names	Colours	ANIMAL	VEGETABLE	MINERAL
24	Scotch Blue		Throat of Blue Titmouse.	Stamina of Single Purple Anemone.	Blue Copper Ore.
25	Prussian Blue		Beauty Spot on Wing of Mallard Drake.	Stamina of Bluish Purple Anemone.	Blue Copper Ore.
26	Indigo Blue				Blue Copper Ore.
27	China Blue		Rhynchites Nitens	Back Parts of Gentian Flower.	Blue Copper Ore from Chessy.
28	Azure Blue.		Breast of Emerald crested Manakin	Grape Hyacinth. Gentian.	Blue Copper Ore.
29	Ultra marine Blue.		Upper Side of the Wings of small blue Heath Butterfly.	Borrage.	Azure Stone or Lapis Lazuli.
30	Flax-flower Blue.		Light Parts of the Margin of the Wings of Devils Butterfly.	Flax flower	Blue Copper Ore
31	Berlin Blue.		Wing Feathers of Jay.	Hepatica.	Blue Sapphire.
32	Verditter Blue				Lenticular Ore.
33	Greenish Blue			Great Fennel Flower.	Turquois. Fluor Spar.
34	Greyish Blue		Back of blue Titmouse	Small Fennel Flower.	Iron Earth.

PURPLES.

Nº	Names	Colours	ANIMAL	VEGETABLE	MINERAL
35	Bluish Lilac Purple.		Male of the Lebellula Depressa.	Blue Lilac.	Lepidolite.
36	Bluish Purple		Papilio Argeolus. Azure Blue Butterfly.	Parts of White and Purple Crocus.	
37	Violet Purple.			Purple Aster.	Amethyst.
38	Pansy Purple.		Chrysomela Goettingensis.	Sweet-scented Violet.	Derbyshire Spar.
39	Campa-nula Purple.			Canterbury Bell. Campanula Persicifolia.	Fluor Spar.
40	Imperial Purple.			Deep Parts of Flower of Saffron Crocus.	Fluor Spar.
41	Auricula Purple.		Egg of largest Blue-bottle. or Flesh Fly.	Largest Purple Auricula.	Fluor Spar.
42	Plum Purple.			Plum.	Fluor Spar.
43	Red Lilac Purple.		Light Spots of the upper Wings of Peacock Butterfly.	Red Lilac. Pale Purple Primrose.	Lepidolite.
44	Lavender Purple.		Light Parts of Spots on the under Wings of Peacock Butterfly.	Dried Lavender Flowers.	Porcelain Jasper.
45	Pale Blackish Purple.				Porcelain Jasper.

GREENS.

Nº.	Names	Colours	ANIMAL	VEGITABLE	MINERAL
46	Celandine Green.		Phalæna Margaritaria.	Back of Tussilago Leaves.	Beryl.
47	Mountain Green.		Phalæna Viridaria.	Thick-leaved Cudweed, Silver-leaved Almond.	Actynolite Beryl.
48	Leek Green.			Sea Kale, Leaves of Leeks in Winter.	Actynolite Prase.
49	Blackish Green.		Elytra of Meloe Violaceus.	Dark Streaks on Leaves of Cayenne Pepper.	Serpentine.
50	Verdigris Green.		Tail of small Long-tailed Green Parrot.		Copper Green.
51	Bluish Green.		Egg of Thrush.	Under Disk of Wild Rose Leaves.	Beryl.
52	Apple Green.		Under Side of Wings of Green Broom Moth.		Crysoprase.
53	Emerald Green.		Beauty Spot on Wing of Teal Drake.		Emerald.

GREENS.

No.	Names	Colours	ANIMAL	VEGETABLE	MINERAL
54	Grass Green		Scarabæus Nobilis.	General Appearance of Grass Fields, Sweet Sugar Pear	Uran Mica.
55	Duck Green		Neck of Mallard	Upper Disk of Yew Leaves.	Ceylanite.
56	Sap Green.		Under Side of lower Wings of Orange tip Butterfly.	Upper Disk of Leaves of woolly Night Shade.	
57	Pistachio Green.		Neck of Eider Drake.	Ripe Pound Pear, Hypnum like Saxifrage.	Crysolite.
58	Asparagus Green.		Brimstone Butterfly.	Variegated Horse-Shoe Geranium.	Beryl.
59	Olive Green.			Foliage of Lignum vitæ.	Epidote Olvene Ore.
60	Oil Green.		Animal and Shell of common Water Snail.	Nonpareil Apple from the Wall.	Beryl
61	Siskin Green.		Siskin.	Ripe Coalmar Pear, Irish Pitcher Apple.	Uran Mica.

YELLOWS.

Nº.	Names	Colours	ANIMAL	VEGETABLE	MINERAL
62	Sulphur Yellow.		Yellow Parts of large Dragon Fly.	Various Coloured Snap dragon.	Sulphur
63	Primrose Yellow.		Pale Canary Bird.	Wild Primrose.	Pale coloured Sulphur.
64	Wax Yellow.		Larva of large Water Beetle.	Greenish Parts of Nonpareil Apple.	Semi Opal.
65	Lemon Yellow.		Large Wasp or Hornet.	Shrubby Goldilocks.	Yellow Orpiment.
66	Gamboge Yellow.		Wings of Goldfinch, Canary Bird.	Yellow Jasmine.	High coloured Sulphur.
67	Kings Yellow.		Head of Golden Pheasant.	Yellow Tulip, Cinque foil.	
68	Saffron Yellow.		Tail Coverts of Golden Pheasant.	Anthers of Saffron Crocus.	

YELLOWS.

Nº.	Names	Colours	ANIMAL.	VEGITABLE.	MINERAL.
69	Gallstone Yellow.		Gallstones.	Marigold Apple.	
70	Honey Yellow.		Lower Parts of Neck of Bird of Paradise.		Fluor Spar.
71	Straw Yellow.		Polar Bear.	Oat Straw.	Schorlite Calamine.
72	Wine Yellow.		Body of Silk Moth.	White Currants.	Saxon Topaz.
73	Sienna Yellow.		Vent Parts of Tail of Bird of Paradise.	Stamina of Honey-suckle.	Pale Brazilian Topaz.
74	Ochre Yellow.		Vent Coverts of Red Start.		Porcelain Jasper.
75	Cream Yellow.		Breast of Teal Drake.		Porcelain Jasper.

WERNER'S CLASSIFICATION OF COLOUR

Abraham Gottlob Werner was an eminent German mineralogist and geologist, who was Bergmeister at the mining school in Freiberg, Saxony. In his book *On the External Characteristics of Minerals* (1774), he put forward a system for the classification of colour in order to describe and classify all characteristics of 'fossils' – rocks and minerals dug out of the earth. Werner's system was known to natural philosophers – other than geologists – and was considered a valuable aid for the organization of colour despite a number of recognized drawbacks.

Patrick Syme's book titled *Werner's Nomenclature* first appeared in 1814; a second edition was published seven years later. Syme was an Edinburgh flower painter and teacher of art. He was introduced to Werner's work through another resident of the city, Robert Jameson, one of Werner's favourite pupils. Jameson reconstructed Werner's colours from his list using actual minerals, and these formed the basis for Syme's colour samples. Given the artist's attention to detail, it is unlikely that the hand-colouring was assigned to anyone but himself.

Syme extended Werner's seventy-nine colours to 110, identifying each by its familiar name, as well as providing an animal, vegetable and mineral equivalent – for example: tile red – breast of the cock bullfinch – shrubby pimpernel – porcelain jasper.

A copy of *Werner's Nomenclature* was carried by the naturalist Charles Darwin on his voyage on HMS *Beagle*. In January 1833, he recorded his first sighting in a small field notebook:

> Many glaciers beryl blue most beautiful contrasted with snow.

This was presumably a term that he would have taken from the page of greens, where two (bluish) colours are described as 'Beryl' under the heading 'Mineral'. A snake that Darwin recorded in his field notebook in 1835 was described as 'primrose yellow', No. 63 on one of the pages of yellows.

When the Reverend Leonard Jenyns wrote up the description and classification of the fishes that Darwin had seen and brought back (preserved in spirits of wine), he used Darwin's notes and his own copy of (Syme's

revision of) *Werner's Nomenclature*. The book was invaluable as the fish specimens were, in Jenyns' words, 'much altered by the action of the spirits'. The strong solution of ethanol in water had a bleaching effect, and today these specimens are a ghostly white.

It is important to be cautious in treating the colours as they are labelled. Syme made no bones about this. He pointed out, for example, that 'Prussian blue, is Berlin blue, with a considerable portion of velvet black, and a small quantity of indigo'. To confuse matters further, 'Indigo blue is composed of Berlin blue, a little black, and a small portion of apple green'. In this case, 'Berlin blue' is Prussian blue and it is thought that 'velvet black' is bone black (probably made from the feet of sheep) and 'apple green' probably a green earth pigment.

The colours have been measured using a spectrophotometer and it is possible to reproduce them in modern house-paint. However, it must be said that not all the colours are immediately relevant for the decoration of houses – arterial blood red is unlikely to have universal appeal, although its 'animal' name 'head of the cock gold-finch' might hold greater promise.

However, there are some wonderfully subtle colours – brownish purple red found on the flower of the deadly nightshade; pistachio green found on the neck of the eider drake; and orpiment orange found on the belly of the warty newt.

Finally, in *Darwin: A Life in Poems* (2009), Darwin's great-great-granddaughter, the poet Ruth Padel, draws his 'voice' from direct but carefully adjusted quotations from letters, journals and notebooks and shows how invaluable *Werner's Nomenclature* would have been to the naturalist as he observed the exotic wildlife on the Galapagos Islands:

> Pure volcano. A mantle of hot bare rock. 'Nothing could be less inviting. A broken field of black basaltic lava thrown into most rugged waves and crossed by fissures.' Lava tubes, tuff cones and bright, red-orange crabs. A land iguana! One saffron leathery elbow, powdery as lichen, sticking out. Ruth Padel: 'On Not Thinking About Variation in Tortoise Shell.'

ORANGE.

Nº	Names	Colours	ANIMAL	VEGITABLE	MINERAL
76	Dutch Orange		Crest of Golden crested Wren	Common Marigold, Seedpod of Spindle-tree	Streak of Red Orpiment
77	Buff Orange		Streak from the Eye of the King Fisher	Stamina of the large White Cistus	Natrolite
78	Orpiment Orange		The Neck Ruff of the Golden Pheasant, Belly of the Warty Newt	Indian Cress	
79	Brownish Orange		Eyes of the largest Flesh-Fly	Style of the Orange Lily	Dark Brazilian Topaz
80	Reddish Orange		Lower Wings of Tyger-Moth	Hemimeris, Buff Hibiscus	
81	Deep Reddish Orange		Gold Fish lustre abstracted	Scarlet Leadington Apple	

RED.

Nº	Names	Colours	ANIMAL	VEGETABLE	MINERAL
82	Tile Red		Breast of the Cock Bullfinch	Shrubby Pimpernel	Porcelain Jasper
83	Hyacinth Red		Red Spots of the Lygaeus Apterus Fly	Red on the golden Rennette Apple	Hyacinth
84	Scarlet Red		Scarlet Ibis or Curlew, Mark on Head of Red Grouse	Large red Oriental Poppy, Red Parts of red and black Indian Pea	Light red Cinnaber
85	Vermillion Red		Red Coral	Love Apple	Cinnaber
86	Aurora Red		Vent coverts of Pied Wood-Pecker	Red on the Naked Apple	Red Orpiment
87	Arterial Blood Red		Head of the Cock Gold-finch	Corn Poppy, Cherry	
88	Flesh Red		Human Skin	Larkspur	Heavy Spar, Limestone
89	Rose Red			Common Garden Rose	Figure Stone
90	Peach Blossom Red			Peach Blossom	Red Cobalt Ore

A

B

C

D

RED.

Nº	Names	Colours	ANIMAL	VEGETABLE	MINERAL
91	Carmine Red			Raspberry, Cocks Comb, Carnation Pink	Oriental Ruby
92	Lake Red			Red Tulip, Rose Officinalis	Spinel
93	Crimson Red				Precious Garnet
94	Purplish Red		Outside of Quills of Tercio	Dark Crimson Officinal Garden Rose	Precious Garnet
95	Cochineal Red			Under Disk of decayed Leaves of None-so-pretty	Dark Cinnaber
96	Veinous Blood Red		Veinous Blood	Mask Flower, or dark Purple Scabious	Pyrope
97	Brownish Purple Red			Flower of deadly Nightshade	Red Antimony Ore
98	Chocolate Red		Breast of Bird of Paradise	Brown Disk of common Marigold	
99	Brownish Red		Mark on Throat of Red-throated Diver		Iron Flint

E

F

BROWNS.

Nº	Names	Colours	ANIMAL	VEGETABLE	MINERAL
100	Deep Orange-coloured Brown		Head of Pochard, Wing coverts of Sheldrake	Female Spike of Cakstail Reed	
101	Deep Reddish Brown		Breast of Pochard, and Neck of Teal Drake	Dead Leaves of green Panic Grass	Brown Blende
102	Umber Brown		Moor Buzzard	Disk of Rudbeckia	
103	Chesnut Brown		Neck and Breast of Red Grouse	Chesnuts	Egyptian Jasper
104	Yellowish Brown		Light Brown Spots on Guinea-Pig, Breast of Hoopoe		Iron Flint, and common Jasper
105	Wood Brown		Common Weasel, Light parts of Feathers on the Back of the Snipe	Hazel Nuts	Mountain Wood
106	Liver Brown		Middle Parts of Feathers of Hen Pheasant, and Wing coverts of Corn-bunk		Semi Opal
107	Hair Brown		Head of Pintail Duck		Wood Tin
108	Broccoli Brown		Head of Black-headed Gull		Zircon
109	Clove Brown		Head and Neck of Male Kestril	Stems of Black Currant Bush	Axinite, Rock Crystal
110	Blackish Brown		Storng Beard, Wing Coverts of Black Cock, Forehead of Pennart		Mineral Pitch

G

H

PLATE 1.

Lizars sc.

Plate 1 shows the three primary colours above the three secondaries. [OVERLEAF] [pp. 140–145]
In plate 2, the three tertiaries are placed above the three secondaries. The remaining plates
show the effect of further more complex mixes of colours and by the addition of white and
black. Plate 5 illustrates the effect of adding white and black in varying proportions to two
of the primary colours – white to red to produce tints and black to green to produce shades.

HAY'S COLOUR THEORY

David Ramsay Hay was a decorative painter and writer on art and design. Taking the advice of Sir Walter Scott to study house-painting, rather than risk obscurity and penury as an artist, he set out to master the art. In April 1820 he commenced work at Abbotsford for Sir Walter.

By the late 1820s, Hay was established at 89 and afterwards at 90 George Street, Edinburgh. He carried out many important commissions – Holyrood Palace, the National Gallery of Scotland in Edinburgh, and the hall of the Royal Society of Arts, London, among them. In the early 1840s, he was appointed 'decorative painter to Her Majesty, Edinburgh'.

Hay published the first of a number of books, *The Laws of Harmonious Colouring,* in 1828. This work ran to six editions in nineteen years, each edition increasing in scope. It is the last of these, *The Laws of Harmonious Colouring adapted to Interior Decorations, with observations on the practice of house painting* (1847), that is the most useful for anyone studying the use of paint and colour in nineteenth-century decoration.

The success of his first book encouraged Hay to produce a series of other highly theoretical volumes, which investigated such subjects as the harmony of form, the principles of colouring, and the role of symmetry and proportion in defining beauty. Among these works, the most successful was *A Nomenclature of Colours, Hues, Tints, and Shades, Applicable to the Arts and Natural Sciences; to Manufactures, and other Purposes of General Utility* (1845). As one of the most attractive works on colour of the mid nineteenth century, it earned him much acclaim from the British press, as well as the acceptance of scientific authorities as respected as James David Forbes and James Clerk Maxwell, both of whom made use of Hay's numerical system of colour relationships based on the primary, secondary and tertiary colours.

Hay was influenced by George Field's *Chromatography; or, a Treatise on Colours and Pigments*, Johann Goethe's *Theory of Colours* and Patrick Syme's edition of *Werner's Nomenclature of Colours*. The *Nomenclature* is one of Hay's scarcest books and also one of the most important. It is an early and rare collection of numbered colour samples, many of which are named. Therein lies its significance as a reference source today. Instead of relying on twenty-first century interpretations of colour names, with Hay's *Nomenclature* one can see examples of what was felt to be 'drab colour', 'sage green', 'olive' etc. in the 1840s. As in some of Hay's other books, the plates are made up of multi-coloured triangles of coloured paper pasted on engraved card stock. There are forty plates with a total of 240 mounted and identified chips (228 different).

Hay's *Nomenclature* is very complex. Below are descriptions of the primary, secondary and tertiary colours as defined by Hay.

OF PRIMARY COLOURS

RED | It unites with the other two primaries in the production of the secondary colours, orange and purple, which are its melodizing tones, and the union of the other two primaries in green forms its contrasting colour. The tertiary colour or hue in which red predominates is a reddish-brown called russet.

The first decided change that occurs in its admixture with yellow is intense scarlet; and in its progress on the other side towards blue, the first change that takes place upon it, is the production of that beautiful species of red called crimson.

In art, the purest red that can be produced is carmine, a pigment that is made from the cochineal beetle.

YELLOW | Combines with red in the production of orange colour and with blue in that of green, which colours are its melodizing tones. Its contrasting colour is purple, resulting from the combination of the other two primaries.

The hue in which yellow predominates is called citrine, a compound of orange colour and green.

The pigments used in art are for the most part the product of minerals, among which the chromate of lead, called chrome yellow, is the purest.

BLUE | It imparts to every hue of which it forms a constituent a cooling and retiring quality, and enters into combination with yellow in the production of green, and with red in that of purple, which are consequently its melodizing colours. The contrasting colour to blue is orange, and the tertiary in which it predominates is olive – a composition of green and purple. Among minerals, lapis lazuli presents the purest blue that can be conceived, and is converted by a very simple process into an equally beautiful pigment.

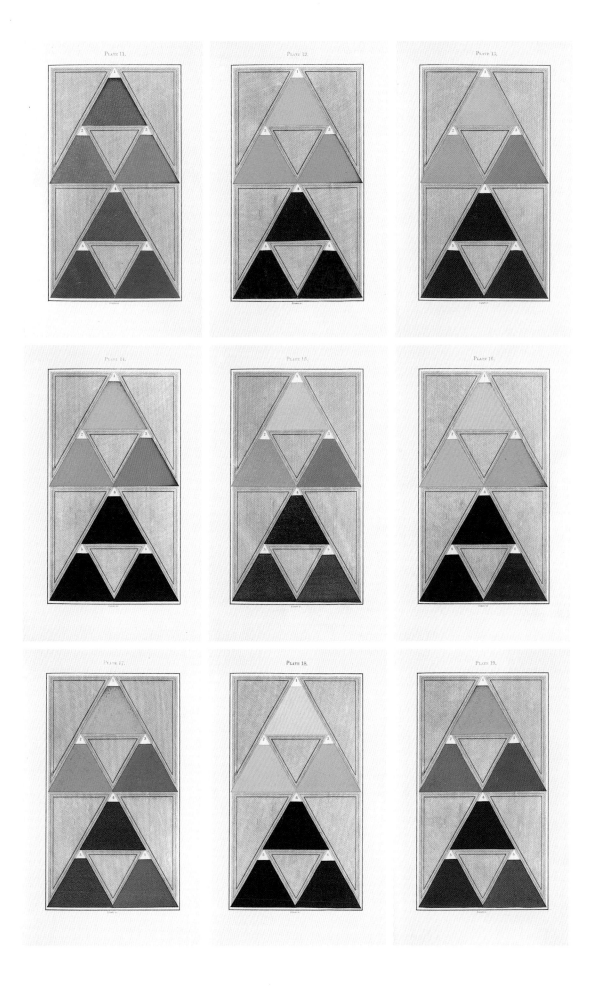

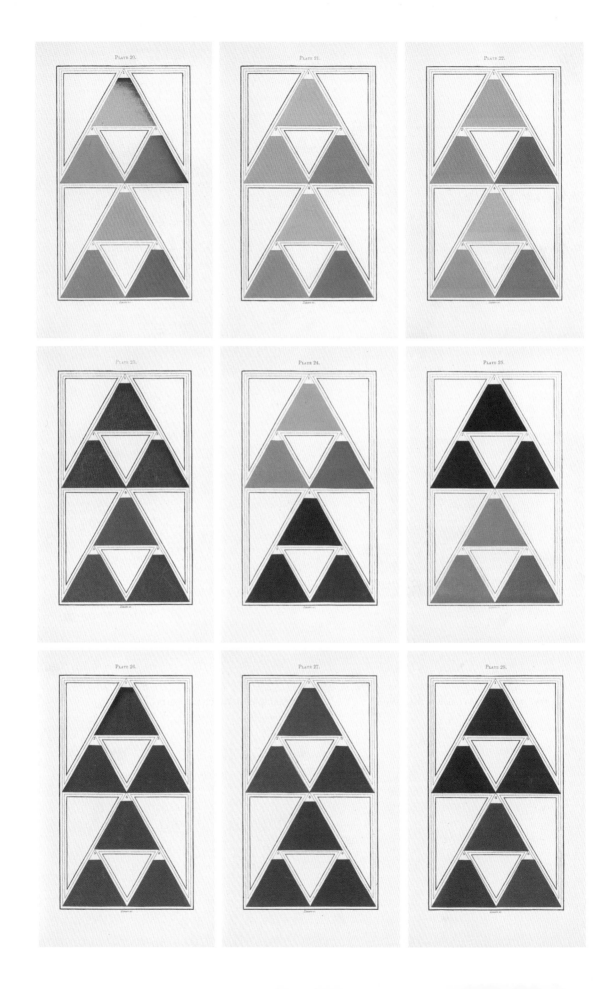

ORANGE | Orange colour is the most powerful of the secondaries, and is a compound of yellow and red. Between these two colours, it appears in the prismatic spectrum, rainbow and other natural phenomena. They are, therefore, its melodizing colours, and its contrasting colour is the primary blue. From its combination with green arises the hue citrine, and with purple that of russet.

GREEN | Green is the medial colour of the secondaries, and is a compound of yellow and blue; its melodizing tones being these two primaries, and its contrasting colour red.From the union of green with orange arises the lightest of the hues, citrine; and from that with purple the deepest, olive colour – to which it is particularly allied.

PURPLE | Purple arises from the union of red and blue, and forms the proper contrast to pure yellow. The two colours of which it is compounded are its melodizing tones. In combination with green, it produces that soft and useful hue, olive; and with orange the most powerful of this class, russet.

OF TERTIARY COLOURS, OR PRIMARY AND SECONDARY HUES

Hues are those combinations in which the three elements occur in their full intensity and in such proportions as give them a distinct character. The three primary hues are those which arise from the combination of the secondary colours with one another. That arising from the combination of orange and green is called citrine – that from orange and purple, russet – and that from purple and green, olive. Their distinctions arise from a double occurrence of yellow in the first, of red in the second, and of blue in the third.

There is a second class of hues, or semi-neutrals, formed by the union of the first class. Thus, the mixture of citrine and russet produces a hue having the same relation to orange that citrine has to yellow. That of citrine and olive produces one having the same relation to green that olive has to blue; and that of russet with olive, another having the same relation to purple that russet has to red.

RUSSET | The tertiary colour russet was produced by mixing the secondary colours orange and purple.

CITRINE | The tertiary colour citrine was produced by mixing the secondary colours orange and green.

OLIVE | The tertiary colour olive was produced by mixing the secondary colours purple and green.

Having demonstrated the basics, Hay then went on to show the effect of intermixing the colours in all possible permutations and by adding white or black. He did not regard white and black as being colours themselves, but:

simply the modifiers of colours, in reducing them, and the hues arising from them, by their attenuating and neutralizing effects, to tints and shades respectively.

CREATING TINTS AND SHADES

In plate 5 (see p. 140), Hay illustrates the effect of adding white and black in varying proportions to two of the primary colours: white to red to produce tints and black to green to produce shades. In plate 11 (see p. 141), he alters two primaries by adding a proportion of two secondaries – in this case red and blue are altered by the addition of orange and green. He adds orange to red in the ratio of five parts of orange to fifteen of red; equal parts of both colours to make red orange and then fifteen parts of orange to five parts of red. These are contrasted with examples in which five parts of blue have been added to fifteen of green; then equal parts of both colours to make blue green and fifteen parts of blue added to five parts of green. Hay progresses through the many options, adding white and black. Plate 15 (see p. 141) shows the results of adding these modifiers to the red orange and the blue green referred to above. He adds five parts of blue green to fifteen of white; equal parts of blue green and white and then fifteen parts of blue green to five parts of white. He contrasts these with examples in which five parts of red orange have been added to fifteen of black; then equal parts of both colours and then fifteen parts of red orange added to five parts of black.

Hay carries out the same exercise with the tertiary colours, and up to this point the permutations have been predictable. However, he complicates things by illustrating the 'neutral greys' produced by adding primary colours such as yellow with secondaries such as purple, or by adding secondaries such as green with tertiaries such as russet.

'Hues' are formed by adding tertiaries such as citrine and olive to make green hue, or olive and russet to make purple hue. Plate 26 (see p. 142) shows the results of adding grey to the tertiary russet and to green hue. The format is the same, being fifteen parts of russet added to five parts of grey; equal parts of russet and grey and then five parts of russet added to fifteen parts of grey. Similarly, fifteen parts of green hue are added to five parts of grey; equal parts of both colours are added together and five parts of green hue are added to fifteen parts of grey. The book continues, with white being added to the results of many of the previous complex mixes. Hay wrote:

> The contrasts produced by these tempered colours are of a soft and pleasing character, and the colours themselves seem to possess, by this process, that intrinsically mellow tone so much admired in the works of the best colourists of antiquity. Among these tints, that of the rose, the primrose, and the lilac, are the most decided of those that arise from the reduction of the positive colours.

Subsequent volumes dealt with Hay's ideas on beauty and proportion to the human head, the human figure, and architecture, culminating in his treatise of 1856, *The Science of Beauty*. This work was largely premised on Pythagorean notions of harmonic numbers and ratios.

THE INFLUENCE OF HAY AND FIELD

Hay's theories reflect a curious mix of influences, ranging from Scottish Common Sense Realism to phrenology, and demonstrating a close proximity to the ideas of George Field (Oxford DNB), probably the most widely read authority on colour in nineteenth-century Britain. Field was also the author of the theory of chromatic equivalents, which established specific mathematical proportions for defining colours.

Both Field's and Hay's theories were adopted in the 1850s by the Science and Art Department at South Kensington, which was a government body that functioned from 1853 to 1899, promoting education in art, science, technology and design in the United Kingdom and Ireland. Their theories continued to be taught in the government-supported schools of art and gained currency through their incorporation into the works of art-education authorities such as Richard Redgrave and Owen Jones. Although most of Hay's ideas are completely discredited today, his influence in his own time was extensive (ibid).

PRACTICAL RESOURCE

Where Hay's *Nomenclature* was used to guide the decoration of a room, it was as much for its wide collection of colours as for its theories. Indeed, in one copy was found a small piece of paper written in pencil, while painters were at work at 13 Moray Place, Edinburgh, in 1871. It appears that the owner, John Fraser, wanted the dado in one room to be painted in one of the reds on either plate 14 (see p. 141) or plate 20 (see p. 142). The walls in the large bedroom a colour from plate 30 (opposite) and the dado in a colour from either plate 17 (see p. 141) or plate 4 (see p. 140).

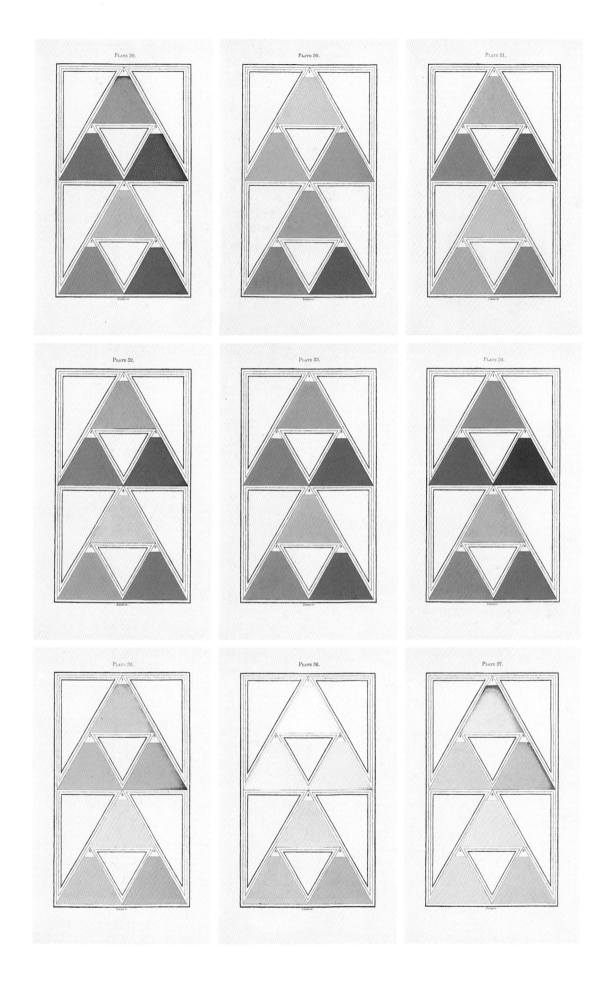

This plate from David Ramsay Hay's *The Laws of Harmonious Colouring adapted to Interior Decorations* (sixth edition, 1847) shows a central white triangle surrounded by three triangles, displaying the primary colours of yellow, red and blue. Adjacent to each primary colour are the relevant secondary colours of orange (a compound of equal parts yellow and red), purple (a compound of equal parts red and blue) and green (a compound of equal parts yellow and blue). The tertiaries of citron (a compound of green and orange), russet (a compound of orange and purple) and olive (a compound of purple and green) are situated at the outermost triangles within the whole and adjacent to their components.

EXAMPLE 1.

THE PRIMARY AND SECONDARY
COLOURS.

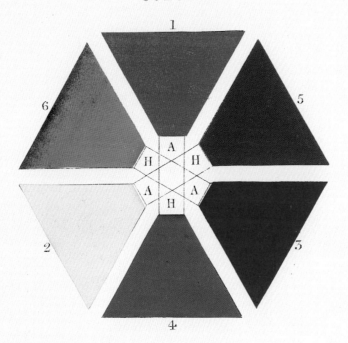

D.R.Hay Inv.ᵗ

Lizare Sc.

This plate from David Ramsay Hay's *The Principles of Beauty in Colouring Systematized*
(1845) displays the primary colours of red, blue and yellow interspersed with the secondary
colours of green, orange (this has discoloured as the red lead has blackened with time)
and purple to create a hexagon. [OVERLEAF] Hay shows that between any primary
and secondary colour there is a series of harmonies of contrast.

EXAMPLE II.

THE SECONDARY COLOURS CONTRASTED
WITH
THE PRIMARY HUES.

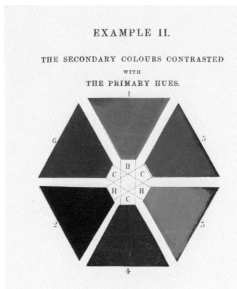

EXAMPLE III.

THE PRIMARY AND SECONDARY
HUES CONTRASTED.

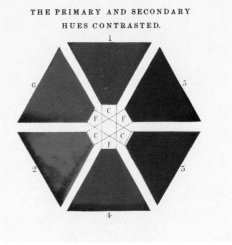

EXAMPLE IV.

BINARY MODIFICATIONS
OF
THE SECONDARY COLOURS.

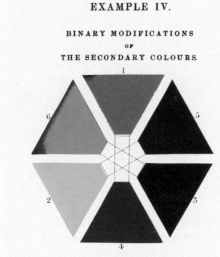

EXAMPLE V.

THE PRIMARY AND SECONDARY COLOURS
TEMPERED.

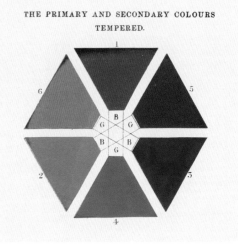

EXAMPLE VI.

THE PRIMARY COLOURS CONTRASTED
WITH
THE TEMPERED SECONDARIES.

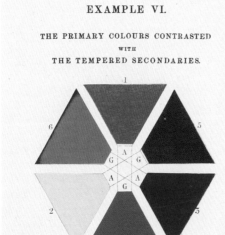

EXAMPLE VII.

THE SECONDARY COLOURS CONTRASTED
WITH
THE TEMPERED PRIMARIES.

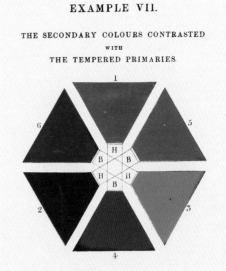

EXAMPLE IX.

HARMONY OF THE PRIMARY
RED.

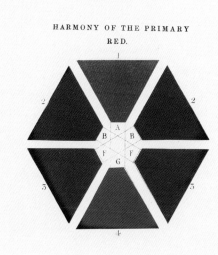

EXAMPLE X.

HARMONY OF THE SECONDARY
GREEN.

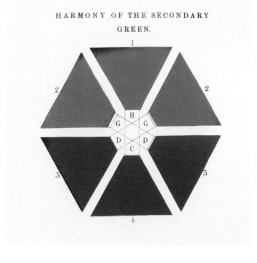

EXAMPLE XI.

HARMONY OF THE PRIMARY
YELLOW.

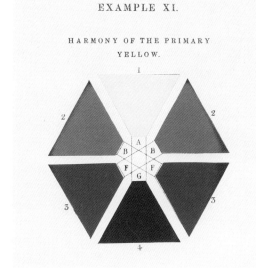

EXAMPLE XII.

HARMONY OF THE SECONDARY
PURPLE.

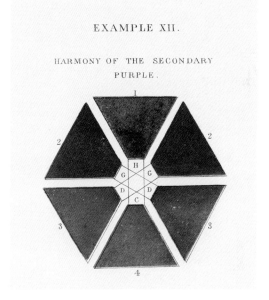

EXAMPLE XIII.

HARMONY OF THE PRIMARY
BLUE.

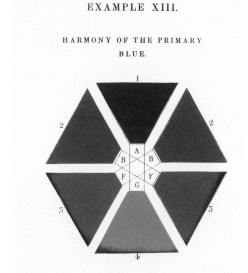

EXAMPLE XIV.

HARMONY OF THE SECONDARY
ORANGE.

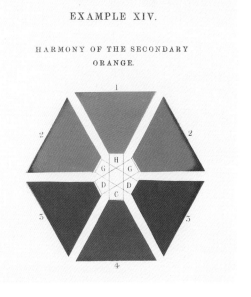

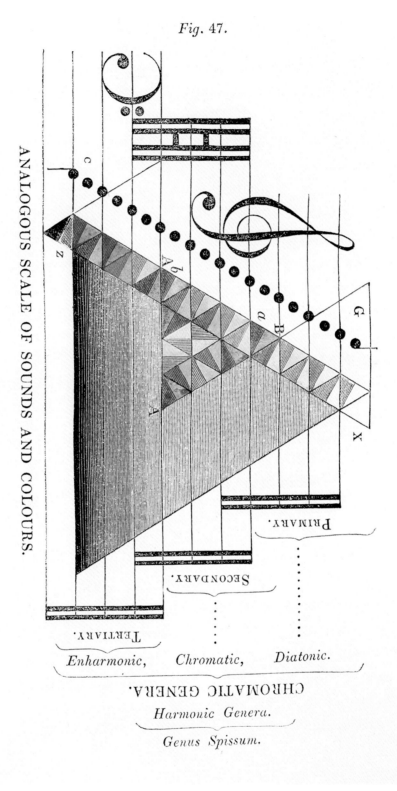

Fig. 47.

ANALOGOUS SCALE OF SOUNDS AND COLOURS.

PRIMARY.

SECONDARY.

TERTIARY.

Enharmonic,   *Chromatic,*   *Diatonic.*

CHROMATIC GENERA.

Harmonic Genera.

Genus Spissum.

A plate from George Field's *Outlines of Analogical Philosophy* (1839). Field saw the three primary colours of blue, red and yellow as being symbolic of the Holy Trinity. He also felt that they had a harmonic and melodic significance. Here he has allocated to them the musical notes of C, E and G with the secondaries of purple and orange being D and F. Light and dark shades represent high and low pitches, respectively.

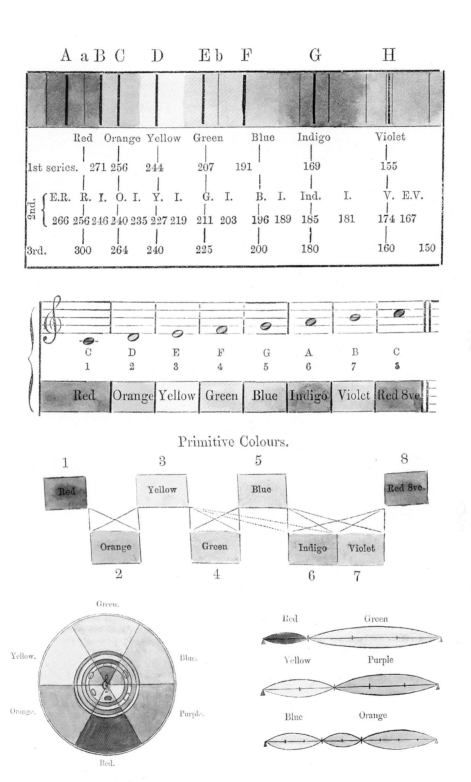

A plate from John Denis Macdonald's *Analogy of Sound & Colour* (1869). This is a very complex work; Macdonald based his sound and colour system in a different arrangement to Field. Here he allocated the musical notes of C, E and G to red, yellow and blue. Among Macdonald's many observations he describes various paintings in national collections and indicates any apparent musical discord that they exhibit.

Que n'ont ils tous Employés leur tems à la même Machine.
Le Pere Castel. raport des Sons et des Couleurs.

A caricature of the Jesuit priest Father Louis-Bertrand Castel playing his ocular harpsichord, by Charles Germain
de Saint Aubin. In the 1720s, Castel wrote of the analogy between sound and light and between tones and colours.
In the following decade, he produced a series of prototype instruments on which he continued to work for
the rest of his life. In January 1755, he gave a performance in front of 200 people: the instrument was
described as having coloured glass windows illuminated from within by a hundred wax candles.

A series of chords ranging from that of the dominant seventh to an imperfect common chord
of the sub-tonic taken from John Denis Macdonald's *Analogy of Sound & Colour* (1869).

'The house-painter should start with the principle so apparent in the colouring of nature..., namely, that bright and intense colours should be used with a sparing hand, especially in situations where they receive a direct light; and that such colours should only be employed to heighten the general effect, and to add splendour to rich and full-toned arrangements by their sparkling qualities.'* This section describes the evolving decorative tastes of the period and reflects on the impact of increased mechanization and scientific advances in the composition of paints.

*David Ramsay Hay, *The Laws of Harmonious Colouring adapted to Interior Decorations* (sixth edition, 1847)

[OPPOSITE] Colour plates from W. J. Pearce's *Painting and Decorating* (1898), illustrating: [A] A polychromatic colour scheme. [B] A complementary colour scheme. [C] A monochromatic colour scheme. [D] An analogous colour scheme.

A

B

C

D

DECORATING WITH WALLPAPER

One of the most significant changes that took place in interior decoration in the early nineteenth century was in the development and increasing use of wallpaper. Early wallpapers had been block-printed onto sheets of paper until the invention of continuous roll paper in the early nineteenth century. The printer coloured the carved pear or cherry wood block by lowering it down onto the colour tray, and once it was sufficiently inked it was lifted and manoeuvred over to the paper before being pressed down to create the print. This was a long, slow process and each colour required a separate block.

The first machine-printed wallpapers were produced in the 1840s, but by the time of the Great Exhibition in 1851 the mechanization of the industry was seen by many commentators to be the main cause of the decline in standards of design. The engraved rollers allowed illusionistic designs with fine detail and shading to be printed in a wide range of colours. However, this was not appreciated by everyone, for, in his official report on the wallpapers shown at the exhibition, Richard Redgrave suggested that excellence was being reckoned by the number of colours rather than by any other quality.

It was hard to disagree that mass production was responsible for a lowering of aesthetic standards. However, as Eric Entwistle noted in *The Book of Wallpaper* (1954), 'The benefits which lower prices brought to the great majority of ordinary people should not be underestimated.'

To some critics, the flat forms and blocks of unmodulated colour that characterize block printing were considered more 'honest' and 'appropriate' as decorations for flat surfaces such as walls. However, to put it into context, this slightly exaggerated description of the eponymous hero of Wilkie Collins' *Basil* (1852) visiting the home of the nouveau riche linen draper illustrates the direction in which design was heading:

> On my arrival at North Villa, I was shown into what I presumed was the drawing-room. Everything was oppressively new. The brilliantly-varnished door cracked with a report like a pistol when it was opened; the paper on the walls, with its gaudy pattern of birds, trellis-work, and flowers, in gold, red, and green on a white ground, looked hardly dry yet; the showy window-curtains of white and sky-blue, and the still showier carpet of red and yellow, seemed as if they had come out of the shop yesterday; the round rosewood table was in a painfully high state of polish; the morocco-bound picture books that lay on it, looked as if they had never been moved or opened since they had been bought; not one leaf even of the music on the piano was dogs-eared or worn. Never was a richly furnished room more thoroughly comfortless than this — the eye ached at looking round it. There was no repose anywhere.

The reference to the varnished door reveals that the joinery had been grained, probably in imitation of oak. Whereas the late seventeenth-century representations of woodgrain had been almost theatrical in their handling, in that they only read as wood from a distance, the early nineteenth-century grainer was encouraged to observe nature for the 'foundation of his future proficiency' and to produce realistic specimens.

Where wallpapers were used, they tended to be hung in a way that is very different to today's convention. In *Hints on Household Taste* (1868), Charles Locke Eastlake noted:

> Paper-hangings should in no case be allowed to cover the whole space of a wall from skirting to ceiling. A 'dado,' or plinth space of plain color, either in paper or distemper, should be left to a height of two or three feet from the floor. This may be separated from the diapered paper above by a light wood moulding stained or gilded. A second space, of frieze, left just below the ceiling, and filled with arabesque ornament painted on a distemper-ground, is always effective, but of course involves some additional expense. The most dreary method of decorating the wall of a sitting-room is to cover it all over with an unrelieved pattern of monotonous design.

Sometimes the upper wall was not wallpapered but was decorated with a polychromatic stencilled or painted design, and gilding might also have been applied. A good surviving (albeit restored) example is the Locarno Suite in the Foreign and Commonwealth Office, Whitehall. The pattern is reminiscent of the 'Empire Star' wallpaper seen in early 1860s photographs by Clementina, Lady Hawarden, of her daughters in their house at 5 Princes Gardens, South Kensington, London.

A

B

[A] The dining room of the Locarno Suite in the Foreign Office, Whitehall, London. George Gilbert
Scott's mid nineteenth-century room was restored in the 1980s. [B] Table setting in the Morris Room
at the cafe at the Victoria and Albert Museum, London, by Philip Webb. [OVERLEAF] Mid to late
nineteenth-century wallpaper samples with derived colours, from the National Archive at Kew, London.

GRAINING AND MARBLING

The imitation in paint of materials usually more expensive, or exotic, is thought to have been carried out since ancient times. However, as a means of decoration in interiors, graining seems to have originated in the mid sixteenth century.

By the following century, the effects of years of cutting down native oak trees for ship- and house-building were being felt. In addition, the Great Fire of London in 1666 led to an increased demand for softwood for the building and internal cladding of houses. This softwood needed protection in the form of paint, and sometimes painted imitations were employed to make it resemble hardwood.

At about the same time, John Smith referred to the imitation of 'olive wood' and 'walnut tree', and described them being veined over with a darker pigment. In his commentary on the seventeenth-century decoration at Dyrham Park, Gloucestershire, Dr Ian Bristow listed a number of painted woods, referred to in the accounts for the house. Among these were cedar colour, walnut colour, wainscot colour and princes-wood colour. Such names might imply merely the colour and tone of these woods, but at this early time, the imitation of a wood could also be indicated. It is only the context or the recorded price that makes clear what had been carried out.

No mention of graining is found in the 1804 edition of Swiss chemist and mineralogist Pierre-François Tingry's manual, probably reflecting its continental origins and the fact that the process had not yet become fashionable again. In England, a rekindled interest in imitating woods in paint developed in the 1810s. The art of graining and marbling probably reached its zenith in the mid nineteenth century. At the Paris Exposition Universelle of 1855, Thomas Kershaw, the Bolton grainer, won a gold medal, but felt obliged to carry out practical demonstrations after accusations that he was cheating were levelled at him.

However, not everyone was impressed by this skill as the art critic John Ruskin made clear in his *Stones of Venice* (1851):

> There is not a meaner occupation for the human mind than the imitation of the stains and striae of marble and wood.

This reaction to wood graining and marbling bubbled away for some years. The very influential Eastlake, whose *Hints on Household Taste* (1868) made his own feelings very clear:

> The practice of graining wood has not, however, been so long in vogue in this country as to command a traditional respect. It is an objectionable and pretentious deceit, which cannot be excused even on the ground of economy.

Walter Pearce, in his excellent manual *Painting and Decorating* (1898), gave a far more reasoned response, pointing out:

> Twenty years ago the authoritative answer was given that it was an admissible sham; but again its utility has thrust it to the front.

Pearce provided a few guidelines, suggesting that to grain rain-water pipes or the outside of a cast-iron bath when the inside was marbled was to overdo the decorative element in the same way as it made no sense to grain a skirting when the wall above was marbled. There was little doubt that a grained scheme was generally far more durable and, as a result, more economic than a plain painted one (Hasluck, 1902):

> From a practical standpoint, graining can be recommended; in some situations where paint is subject to unusual wear and tear, graining will be found not to show marks, to stand handling, being protected by varnish, and to clean down well; it can be touched up and re-varnished every two or three years, and it will look well to the last.

For many years, such economic and practical considerations still outweighed the accusations of graining merely being a sham, and the above passage was still appearing in reprints of the same book in the early 1920s.

By the 1930s, imitative graining was still found on front doors, and this tradition survives in Scotland, where first quality oak graining can be seen, especially in New Town, Edinburgh. Elsewhere, brush graining was employed, and examples can be found in many paint catalogues of the time (see p. 218).

The decline of the technique was caused by a number of factors, not least the 'members of the trade who decry graining because they prefer to rush over a job more cheaply and quickly, and do not want it to last too long' (Pearce, 1868).

A

B

[A] The Johnston-Felton-Hay House in Macon, Georgia. The house was built in the Italian Renaissance Revival style between 1855 and 1859. The grained lower wall on the stairs leading up to the second floor was discovered underneath painted canvas from 1912. [B] Holly Hill in Friendship, Maryland, was built in three stages between 1698 and 1733 by Richard Harrison and his son Samuel. It is one of the largest and best preserved of its period in Maryland. The bed chamber shows rare surviving marbling from the early period. [OVERLEAF] Imitation graining and marbling paint effects from Nathaniel Whittock's *The Decorative Painters' and Glaziers' Guide* (1827).

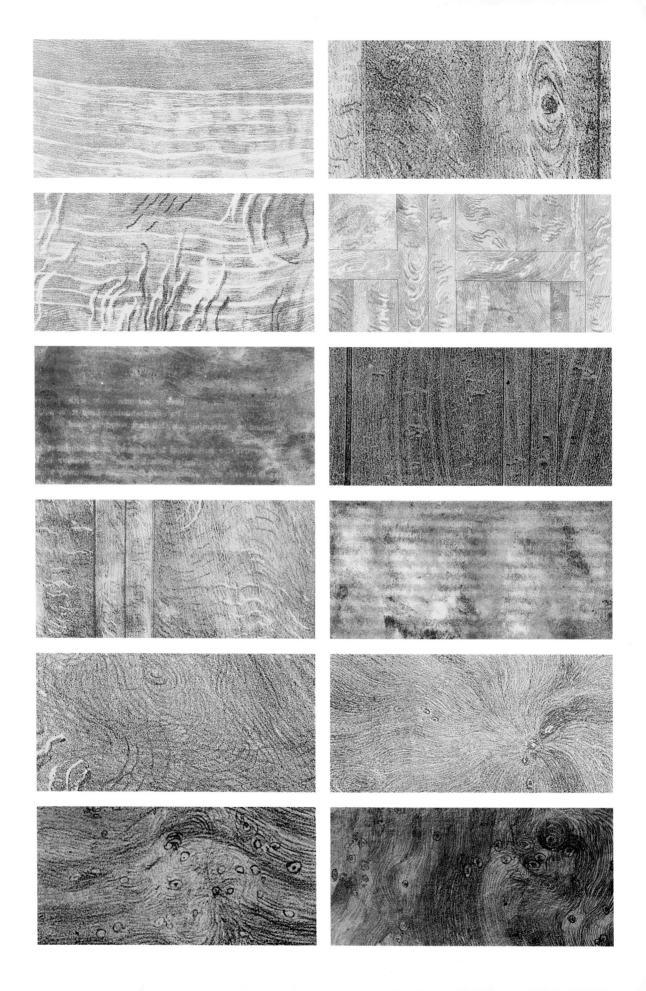

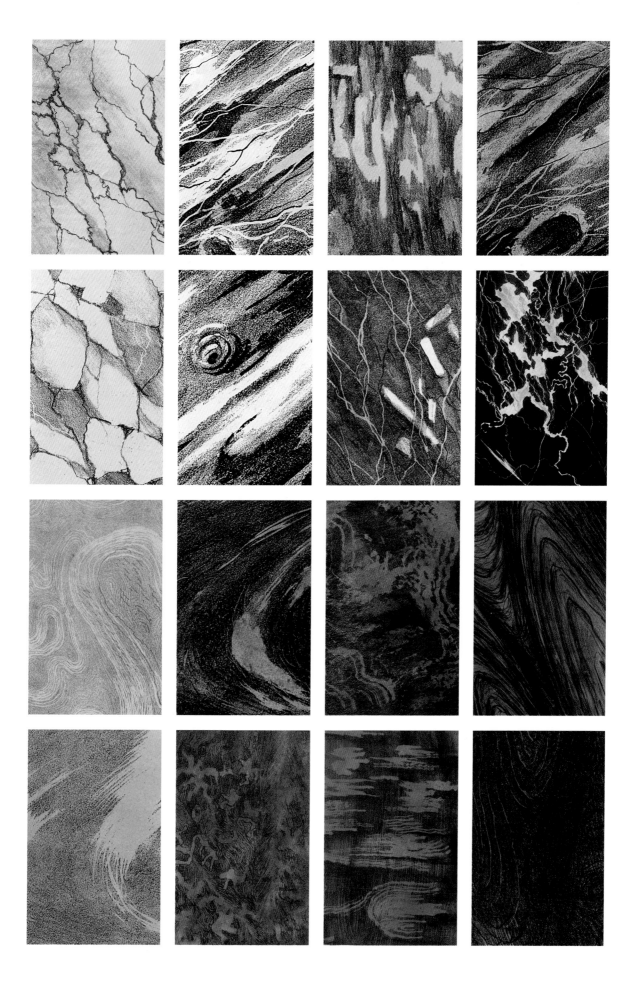

DECORATIVE SCHEMES AND FINISHES

Eastlake also provided some advice on paint colours and finishes, suggesting that doors might be painted a 'good flat tint of dark green or chocolate colour'. He admitted that a flatted finish was more liable to be soiled than oil paint, but held that it was 'far pleasanter in effect'. In a well-lit entrance hall, he suggested that a dull Pompeian red would be an excellent colour, although if there was only a small fanlight above the door a 'delicate green or warm grey'.

Traditional oil paints, made by grinding lead carbonate in linseed oil, with pigment added to give colour, typically dried to a mid-gloss finish. From the early nineteenth century, descriptions began to appear in the technical works on painting that refer to the process of flatting, which imparted a matt finish to an oil-painted surface. An oily undercoat (which should have completed the obliteration of the surface) was applied on the day before the application of the flatting. The flatting coat was made from pigments ground in turpentine (or a very low percentage of oil, for example white lead in paste form, containing only 8 per cent oil). After the flatting had been applied, the turpentine evaporated leaving behind the pigment, which firmly adhered to the tacky undercoat. To paint a large surface, such as a wall, was exceptionally difficult and painters would charge extra for this work, effectively doubling the cost of applying two coats of paint. The following account from *Painting and Graining* (1830) by W. and J. T. Towers shows the effort involved:

> It should be observed that the flatting must be made one shade lighter (than the undercoat) as the ground colour will not be so apt to show through; and it will thereby, give the work a more solid appearance...it is also necessary to observe that good soft spreading brushes must be used, otherwise it will be impossible to make good work. If the wall be from eight to ten feet high it will require two men to flat it. Fix a scaffold from one end of the wall to the other a proper depth from the ceiling in order to reach with ease the top of the work... Be careful to have everything provided as you cannot leave off work till one flank is finished. The bottom of the wall must be commenced first, painting not more than twelve or eighteen inches wide at a time. Move the brush in a perpendicular direction, and when you have painted as far as you can conveniently reach, carefully cross the work with a light hand in order to give the colour a uniform extension. When this is done, finish the work by laying it off very lightly beginning at the bottom and striking the brush up about a foot, then from the top, lightly draw the brush to the bottom. When this is done, the man on the plank must begin where the other left off and finish the top. In the meantime, the man standing on the floor must begin another width: and so proceed till one side of the wall is finished.

In a smaller house, all the walls and woodwork on the ground floor were painted and flatted (except for the kitchen, office passage, pantry, china closet, store closet and the insides of the other closets). The dining room and the drawing room were given special treatment, being 'finished in three teints' (the panels and mouldings of doors would have been picked out).

In a larger house, the walls of the principal staircase, the entrance hall and the lobbies were marbled in imitation of Siena marble, lined out with masonry jointing and given two coats of varnish. Both sides of all the doors on the ground floor were grained in imitation of oak and varnished twice. The remaining walls and woodwork on that floor were flatted in stone colour, while the joiners' work in the best three rooms was 'finished in three teints'.

Not everyone approved of busy detailing. In 1883 Robert Edis, an architect who published two books on furniture and decoration, noted:

> The fashion of 'picking out' the cornice enrichments with gold and many colours is not only offensive to the eye but eminently costly and artistically objectionable...the general tone of the colouring of the upper portion of the wall surface... should be used in the cornice and gradually lightened off to meet the mass of white or slightly relieved surface of the ceiling.

By the end of the century, sanitary distempers or washable water paints, such as Duresco, were being marketed, and these took over from the more expensive flatted finish. On the other hand, the varnishing of woodwork was increasingly recommended, because the shiny surface prolonged the woodwork's life and allowed it to be cleaned easily. Such was the desire for a shiny, non-toxic and bright surface towards the end of the century that a major development took place

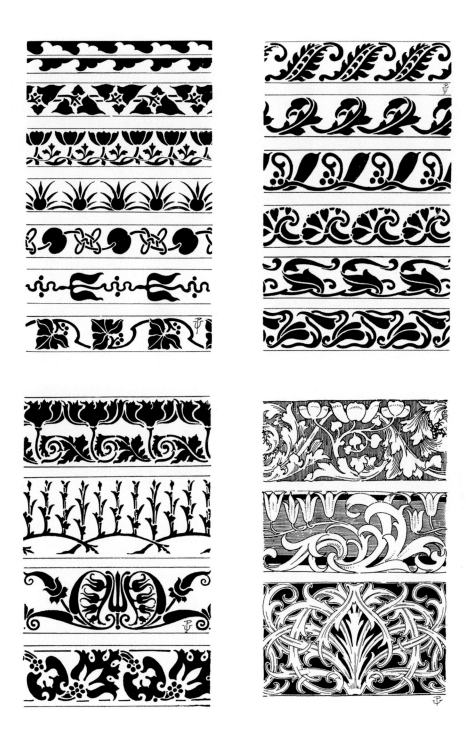

Ornamental motifs from Walter Pearce's *Painting and Decorating* (1898). [OVERLEAF] [P. 166] The
Durbar Room at Osborne House, built in 1891 and decorated by Lockwood Kipling (father of Rudyard
and director of the Lahore School of Art) and carved by Bhai Ram Singh, shows the range of influences
that were current at the time. [P. 167] Construction of the Arab Hall at the home of Frederic, Lord
Leighton in Kensington, London, began in 1877 under architect George Aitchison. It is modelled on
an interior from a twelfth-century Sicilio-Norman palace, Il Castello della Zisa, in Palermo. The tiles,
mostly from fifteenth- and sixteenth-century Damascus, are of international importance.

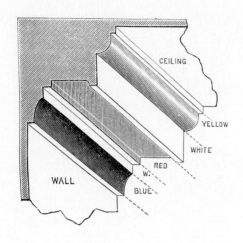

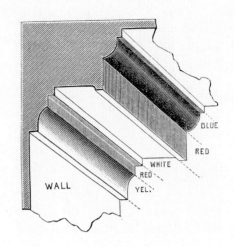

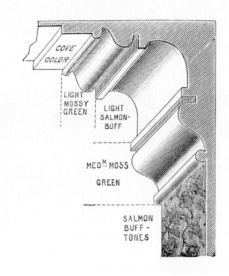

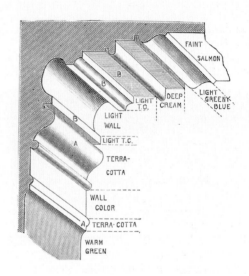

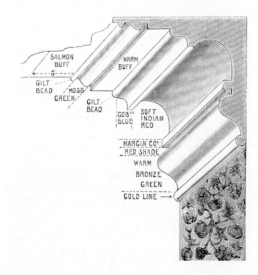

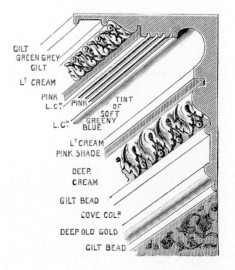

A

in the range of paints. This was the introduction of zinc oxide as an alternative base for oil paint. Zinc oxide was a pigment that had been known since the 1780s and it had been experimented with in the early years of the nineteenth century. However, in 1850 it was still regarded as a curiosity. One of its earliest uses was in a scheme of 1853 in the house of a well-known railway engineer, whose knowledge of technical matters was clearly up-to-date.

Zinc oxide was employed as the basis for many of the ranges of proprietary enamel paints that promised to be everything that lead paint was not, and that could be wiped clean on a daily basis with no loss of colour. The preoccupation with wipeable surfaces becomes clearer when one considers that for much of the nineteenth century houses were lit by both oil and gas lamps. The smoking of an untrimmed wick can be well-imagined by anyone who has lit a storm lamp, but the drawbacks to using gas are less apparent. Edis brings home the extent of the problem with the following words:

> It is hopeless to discuss the manifold evils and discomforts which arise from the filthy gas which is supplied by gas companies for lighting our rooms; we can only trust that electric lighting may ere long take its place in our houses and in our streets, and thus once and for all get rid of the terrible effects arising from the present system of lighting.

Another way of providing a 'healthier' surface was to employ a soft distemper, a reversible coating that could be washed off. It was used commonly on ceilings and on other surfaces that required frequent redecoration. In particular, it was recommended for bedrooms and nurseries, where the wall covering was changed perhaps once every two years, or after bouts of sickness. Similarly, soft distemper was deemed appropriate for the walls of the kitchen and other rooms in the basement, where the washing off of the tainted coating and its replacement with a brand new one would have undoubtedly freshened up the area.

Decorative techniques and styles did not cease with the death of one sovereign and start afresh with another. There was little noticeable difference in the use of paint colour as the nineteenth century passed into the twentieth. A colour card produced for HM Office of Works by the Edinburgh paint manufacturers Craig & Rose in the 1900s illustrates this well, and the sharp-eyed will spot the similarity with the window display of John Myland's shop in 1907.

B

[A] Colour combinations considered suitable for late nineteenth-century cornices, from Paul Nooncree Hasluck's *House Decoration* (1897). [B] Stencil designs for dado decoration also from Hasluck's manual.

These curious images come from *Intérieures Modernes* (*c.* 1895), a work produced by the French decorator George Rémon. Rémon specialized in the decoration of the great ocean liners, such as *La France*, with its magnificent Moorish Lounge; *the Paris*; *Île-de-France* and the majestic *Normandie* with its art deco and streamline moderne interiors. He also contributed articles to many magazines and wrote *Les jardins de l'antiquité à nos jours* (1943).

When Rémon's background is understood, these interiors make more sense. They feature saturated colours and eclectic historical influences. Their exaggerated nature would have precluded wide-scale copying, but elements cane be seen in some early twentieth-century interiors. [OVERLEAF] Ornamental motifs from Walter Pearce's *Painting and Decorating* (1898).

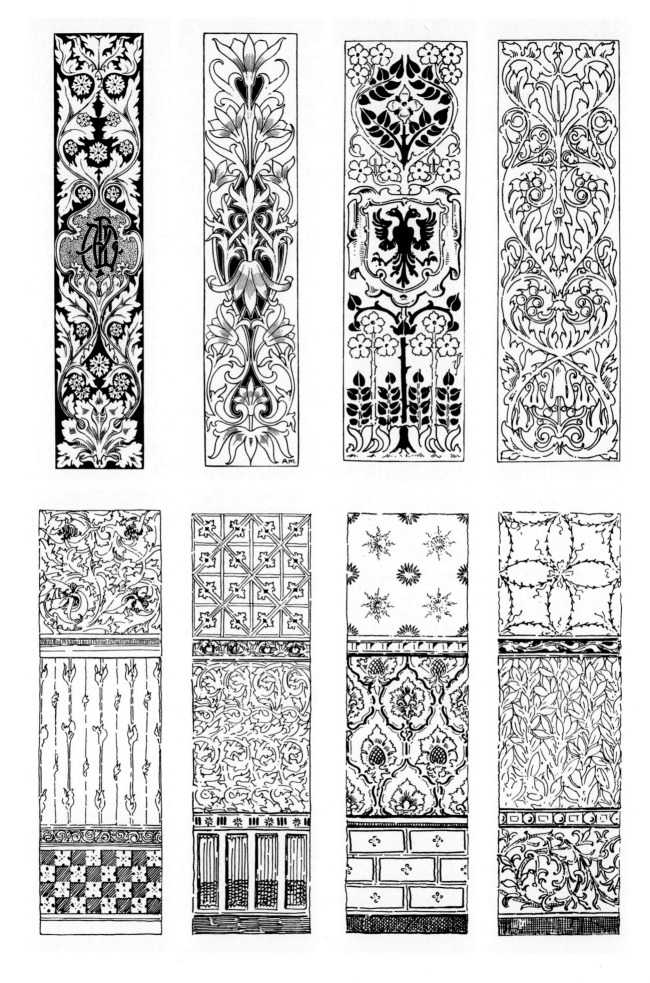

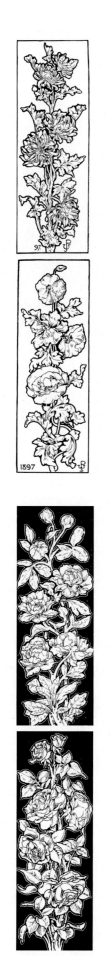

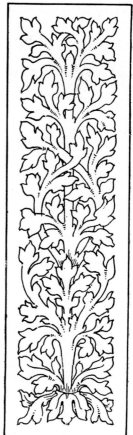

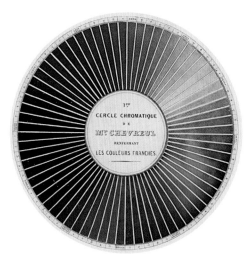

CHEVREUL (1839)

SCHREIBER (1868)

Michel-Eugène Chevreul (1786–1889) was a French chemist and director of the Gobelins tapestry works, where he carried out his research on colour contrasts. His work *De la loi du contraste simultané des couleurs et de l'assortiment des objets colorés* was published in France in 1839. It was translated into English in 1854 by Charles Martel as *The principles of harmony and contrast of colours.*

Chevreul's interest in colour theory started with a complaint from his weavers, who reported that the black thread from the dye works looked different when used alongside blue thread. He determined that the appearance of a colour was influenced by those surrounding it, a concept later known as 'simultaneous contrast'. Chevreul observed that the effect was more noticeable when shared by complementary colours.

Chevreul's work influenced painters, including Georges Seurat and Paul Signac, who developed the technique of pointillism or divisionism, in which dots of colour are applied to form an image. As author and colour consultant Faber Birren said:

> The British received it with great enthusiasm
> and later so did America. No other book on color
> except Newton's Optics went into so many
> editions over so long a period of time...it was
> kept in print for over twenty-five years.

Guido Schreiber (1799–1871) was a professor of geometry at the Karlsruhe Institute of Technology. His main focus was on descriptive geometry, but he also wrote on perspective and colour in *Die Farbenlehre. Für Architekten, Maler, Techniker und Bauhandwerker, insbesondere für Bau- und polytechnische, höhere Gewerb- und Realschulen,* (Colour Theory for Architects; Painters; Technicians and Builders) published in 1868.

Schreiber was greatly influenced by Goethe and he covered many of the same topics. He took Goethe's colour triangle with the primary, secondary and tertiary colours, and displayed it in a manner that is reminiscent of David Hay, although whether he was aware of Hay is not known. His interest in geometry can clearly be seen in his examination of diffraction theory and the phenomena of coloured margins.

Like Goethe he wrote at leangth about the aesthetic effect of colour and included a very interesting section on colour combinations. This diagram is an unusual one, in that the colours are arranged like the segments of an orange and it is hemispherical.

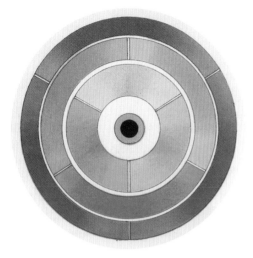

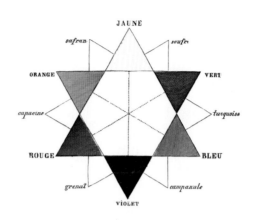

BACON (1872)

The diagram of colour, from *The theory of colouring: being an analysis of the principles of contrast and harmony in the arrangement of colours: with their application to the study of nature, and hints on the composition of pictures, etc.* (1872) was devised by John Bacon to show, at a glance, 'all the theoretical principles of combination, harmony and contrast'. He stated: 'Many are averse to use theoretical principles in the study of art: *science*, it is said, may be learned by *theories*, but art only by *practice*. Truly, mere "theoretical principles" will never make an artist without *practice*, which they are intended to direct, not to supplant. They are to guide the student in his work, not to do his work for him.'

In the centre, Bacon showed the primaries of yellow, blue and red. When these were mixed they formed the secondaries of green, purple and orange, which occupied the middle ring. When the secondaries were mixed they produced the tertiaries of broken green or citron, grey or olive and brown or russet.

Other illustrations featured throughout this small book show combinations of these colours in the context of landscapes and still lifes.

BLANC (1876)

Charles Blanc (1813–82) was the director of the Department for the Visual Arts at the Ministry of the Interior, France. He also served as director of the École des Beaux-Arts for a number of years.

Blanc further developed the laws of simultaneous contrast originally established by Michel-Eugène Chevreul and practised by Eugène Delacroix. Of his many books, two were especially important for the development of colour theory. His *Grammaire des Arts du Dessin* (Grammar of Painting and Engraving) and the *Grammaire des Arts Décoratifs* (Grammar of Decorative Arts) had a significant influence on several of the artists of the time, especially on the neo-impressionists, or divisionists. They believed that by following scientific rules and colour theory they could maximize the amount of light in their works rather than the more traditional approach of relying on instinct and intuition to create colour.

In this star-shaped diagram made up of two interlocking triangles, the primaries are placed on the three points of the first triangle with the secondaries between each making up the second inverted triangle. The tertiaries have names not given elsewhere. Between yellow and green is sulphur, between green and blue is turquoise, between blue and violet is campanula, between violet and red is garnet, between red and orange is nasturtium and between orange and yellow is saffron.

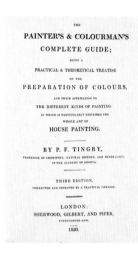

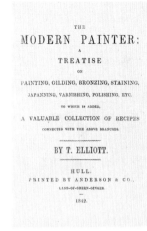

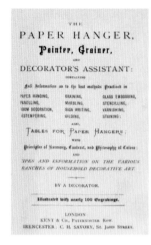

THE PAINTER'S & COLOURMAN'S COMPLETE GUIDE (1830)
P. F. TINGRY

Pierre-François Tingry (1743–1821) was a Swiss chemist and mineralogist from Geneva, who had first published a work on paint and varnish in 1803. This was translated into English the following year and further revised some years later. *The Painter's & Colourman's Complete Guide* of 1830 is the third revision, which had been 'corrected and improved by a practical chemist'. Although this edition is far less continental in outlook than the previous editions, many of the pigments described are from European sources. One wonders how much white of Moudon, Rouen white or white of Troyes would have found its way into the hands of British colourmen.

It is one of the three works regarded by Scottish writer John Claudius Loudon as being the most useful. In addition to being good on pigments, it reveals that oak graining was particularly recommended for use on street doors and shutters, for example.

THE MODERN PAINTER (1842)
T. ELLIOTT

Nothing is known of the author and this work is exceptionally rare. It is an excellent manual apparently based on experience rather than cribbing from others. The conclusion is revealing and utterly charming:

To families who from a well-placed economical design may wish to become their own house-painters, this work will doubtless prove a useful companion, as it contains the best methods for the most important part of the process – that is, mixing up the colours. It will also, I have no doubt, fully answer the wishes of persons who are desirous of gaining information on the nature and properties of colours. The methods of laying them on are, I am fully satisfied, the best extant. In short, I have, as far as my ability would allow, made this work a complete vade mecum to the amateur and practitioner. I have nothing further to say than to thank the reader for following me through the different branches, and I hope the time spent in the perusal of them will not be considered time wasted. I must now take my farewell, and I sincerely wish, that HE who rules and governs the universe may bestow on the dear reader a life of unchequered bliss.

RUDIMENTS OF THE PAINTER'S ART (1850)
GEORGE FIELD

George Field (*c.* 1777–1854) was a chemist and manufacturer of artists' colours who also wrote about colour. His publications include *Chromatics; or, an Essay on the analogy and harmony of colours* (1817) and *Chromatography, or, A treatise on colours and pigments, and of their powers in painting* (1835). However, *Rudiments of the Painter's Art* is the most useful for giving an understanding of pigments, colour theory and harmony from the house-painter's perspective.

In this work Field warns the house-painter regarding which pigments tend not to work with others. For example, he asserts that chrome yellow destroys Prussian blue. Perhaps Field was referring to the tendency of the blue to 'float' to the surface when used on exteriors.

The book forms the basis of Ellis Davidson's revision, which appeared in many editions in the late nineteenth century, and is the larger part of the latter's *House-Painting, Graining, Marbling, and Sign-Writing*.

THE PAPER HANGER, PAINTER, GRAINER AND DECORATOR'S ASSISTANT (1876)
ANON

In common with several other titles that appeared at the end of the nineteenth century, *The Paper Hanger, Painter, Grainer and Decorator's Assistant* is particularly helpful for its detailed instructions on the making and application of distemper and oil paint, the mixing of colours, and the imitation of wood and marble, as well as the processes of varnishing and gilding.

Although much attention is given to late Victorian decoration, this work is nonetheless very relevant to the study of eighteenth-century house-painting. With a few exceptions, the recipes for mixing the various paint colours are identical to those provided one hundred years earlier. In addition, there are recipes not often discovered in earlier handbooks, including recipes for chestnut, freestone and snuff, for example.

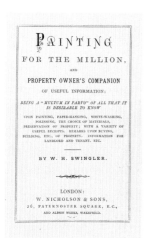

PAINTING FOR THE MILLION (1878)
W. H. SWINGLER

The full title of this short work well describes the range of topics covered: *Painting for the million, and property owner's companion of useful information: being a* multum in parvo [*much in little*] *of all that is desirable to know upon painting, paper-hanging, white-washing, polishing, the choice of materials, preservation of property; with a variety of useful receipts. Remarks upon buying, building, etc., of property. Information for landlord and tenant, etc.*

Echoing T. H. Vanherman's title of fifty years before – *Every Man his Own House-Painter and Colourman* (1829) – Swingler's work 'was designed alike for the Artisan and Aristocrat, the Cottager and Property owner, the Landlord and Tenant, as well as the Tradesman'. Among other things, the recipe for 'self-oak' confirms that wood was still being imitated by a flat paint rather than by graining.

PIGMENTS, PAINT AND PAINTING (1893)
GEORGE TERRY

According to the introduction, the book is aimed at providing the house-painter with all the technical knowledge he might need concerning the manufacture of pigments. However, few painters will have read it from cover to cover. It is a very detailed work that gives recipes for the preparation of a considerable number of pigments for use by both artists and house-painters on an industrial scale. Vehicles and driers are also examined, and there is a chapter on the application of paint. It is perhaps of most use to anyone wanting to make batches of obsolete pigments for testing purposes. One of the better works on pigments, it is invaluable to the serious student and paint analyst.

Such is the detail contained in this book that there is nothing similar to be found elsewhere. Terry's description of visiting a Chinese vermilion factory is superb.

HOUSE DECORATION: COMPRISING WHITEWASHING, PAPERHANGING, PAINTING, ETC. (1897)
PAUL N. HASLUCK

Paul Nooncree Hasluck (1854–1931) wrote a large number of books at the end of the nineteenth century, with subjects ranging from lathe work to knotting and splicing ropes and cordage. However, *House Decoration: Comprising Whitewashing, Paperhanging, Painting, Etc.* is the one that is of most interest to the student of paint and colour.

This work, which appeared in several slightly different editions, meets its professed aim of being 'a standard authority for the professional painter and decorator'. He gives one very good piece of advice, which in modified form is still applicable today:

To guard against damp injuring the paint upon a plaster wall, it is safer to distemper the walls for the first two years, and then to wash it off and paint, taking care that the walls are perfectly dry. If the distemper is not greasy or dirty, it is better merely to brush it well down with a dry brush, and paint over it, without any washing.

Many of the techniques and materials mentioned would have been used in the eighteenth century.

PAINTING AND DECORATING (1898)
WALTER J. PEARCE

This work is one of the best for giving a feel for the materials in use by the eighteenth-century house-painter. Everything from wooden scaffolding poles to colour mixing is covered, and there are numerous illustrations. It was written shortly before great changes began to be seen in the trade.

As Albert Hurst wrote in the preface to the seventh edition, in 1949:

The original book *Painting and Decorating* by the late W. J. Pearce has been regarded during the last half century as the standard textbook for the practical painter and the student apprentice. That it served its day well is proved by the consistent demand for it over such an extended period.

This is one of the first handbooks to provide advice on how to stay healthy while working with traditional paints, which were not free from risk. Tips ranged from not using tools and brushes with unclean handles; not using bare hands when applying white lead putty and not inhaling the dust when rubbing down white lead paint and stopping.

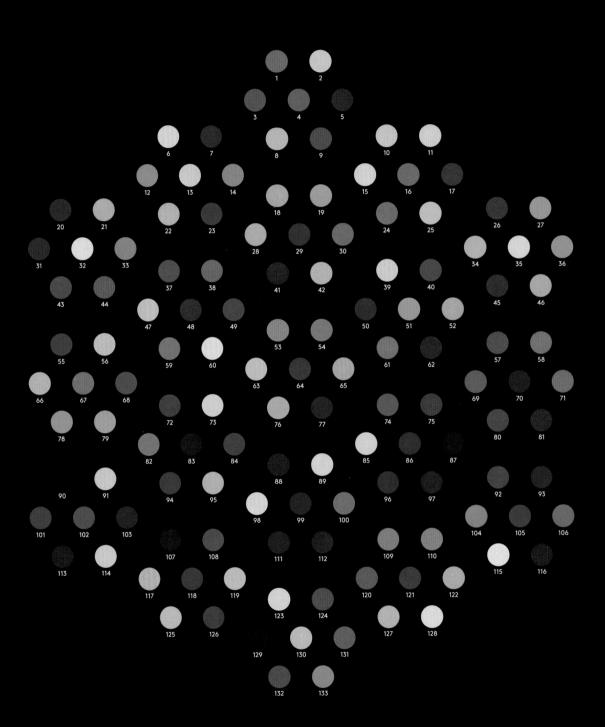

III.

PAINTS, COLOUR STANDARDS AND INTERIORS

1900 – 1945

133 COLOURS DERIVED FROM
COLOR STANDARDS AND COLOR NOMENCLATURE (1912) BY RIDGWAY
(SEE PP. 244 – 249)

1. DAPHNE PINK	35. PEARL BLUE	69. BLANC'S BLUE	103. INDULIN BLUE
2. PALE LEMON YELLOW	36. ZINC ORANGE	70. DIAMIN-AZO BLUE	104. OLD GOLD
3. AGERATUM VIOLET	37. DEEP MEDICI BLUE	71. GRENADINE RED	105. SPECTRUM VIOLET
4. PRUSSIAN GREEN	38. CORINTHIAN RED	72. VIOLET-SLATE	106. PORCELAIN GREEN
5. NEUTRAL RED	39. RIVAGE GREEN	73. YELLOW-GREEN	107. NAPHTHALENE VIOLET
6. NIGHT GREEN	40. SAILOR BLUE	74. BLUE-VIOLET	108. AMETHYST VIOLET
7. DUSKY GREEN-BLUE	41. MADDER BROWN	75. WALNUT BROWN	109. MOTMOT GREEN
8. LIGHT SULPHATE GREEN	42. LIGHT PHLOX PURPLE	76. JAPAN ROSE	110. FLAME SCARLET
9. RHODAMINE PURPLE	43. PHENYL BLUE	77. DUSKY VIOLET	111. DARK MINERAL RED
10. FLESH COLOUR	44. SCARLET	78. BENZOL GREEN	112. ANTIQUE GREEN
11. VENETIAN PINK	45. HYACINTH VIOLET	79. VERDIGRIS GREEN	113. CHOCOLATE
12. MALLOW PURPLE	46. GLAUCOUS-BLUE	80. VIOLET-PURPLE	114. APRICOT YELLOW
13. MUSTARD YELLOW	47. CENDRE GREEN	81. LIVID VIOLET	115. SEAFOAM GREEN
14. DEEP MALACHITE GREEN	48. MEDAL BRONZE	82. ULTRAMARINE ASH	116. MARS BROWN
15. LUMIERE GREEN	49. HELVETIA BLUE	83. LIVER BROWN	117. TURTLE GREEN
16. DULL VIOLET-BLUE	50. AZURITE BLUE	84. ANTHRACENE GREEN	118. BRAZIL RED
17. OLIVE-GREEN	51. VIVID GREEN	85. CALAMINE BLUE	119. VENICE GREEN
18. WISTARIA VIOLET	52. SALMON-ORANGE	86. POMEGRANATE PURPLE	120. PURPLE (TRUE)
19. GLAUCOUS-GREY	53. TYRIAN PINK	87. GREEN-BLUE SLATE	121. DUSKY GREENISH BLUE
20. DUSKY BLUE	54. CORNFLOWER BLUE	88. GARNET BROWN	122. LIGHT METHYL BLUE
21. JAVEL GREEN	55. TYRIAN ROSE	89. PALE BLUE-VIOLET	123. LIVID PINK
22. GERANIUM PINK	56. APPLE GREEN	90. BURNT LAKE	124. POMPEIAN RED
23. DARK SOFT BLUE-VIOLET	57. CALLA GREEN	91. CHRYSOLITE GREEN	125. DEEP ROSE-PINK
24. VARLEY'S GREY	58. TERRA COTTA	92. PLUMBAGO SLATE	126. ELM GREEN
25. WAX YELLOW	59. CAPRI BLUE	93. ROSLYN BLUE	127. VINACEOUS-GRAY
26. ALIZARINE BLUE	60. CHARTREUSE YELLOW	94. CYANINE BLUE	128. BRIGHT GREEN-YELLOW
27. MONTPELLIER GREEN	61. JASPER RED	95. ABSINTHE GREEN	129. BLUISH BLACK
28. COSSE GREEN	62. ANILINE BLACK	96. BERLIN BLUE	130. BREMEN BLUE
29. MYRTLE GREEN	63. MINERAL GREEN	97. DUCK GREEN	131. LIGHT DANUBE GREEN
30. PEACOCK BLUE	64. INDIGO BLUE	98. CITRON YELLOW	132. DAUPHIN'S VIOLET
31. INDIAN RED	65. FLUORITE GREEN	99. NIGROSIN BLUE	133. LETTUCE GREEN
32. SEASHELL PINK	66. DEEP CHROME	100. PARROT GREEN	
33. METHYL GREEN	67. RAW SIENNA	101. HAZEL	
34. ONION-SKIN PINK	68. ANTWERP BLUE	102. MEADOW GREEN	

'The English painter almost invariably employs a certain portion of red lead in his priming coat because it dries quickly and gives a firm, hard surface. The red lead, however, is not essential, and may be dispensed with. It ought never to be used beneath enamel, as it is likely to work through.'* This section charts the arrival of new white pigments to replace lead white, new washable water paints to replace distemper, and new flat oil and enamel paints for a durable smooth sheen, all available ready-prepared in containers.

* *The Modern Painter and Decorator* (3 volumes, 1921) by Arthur Seymour Jennings and Guy Cadogan Rothery

[OPPOSITE] Some of the colours offered by Thomas Parsons & Sons in 1908.

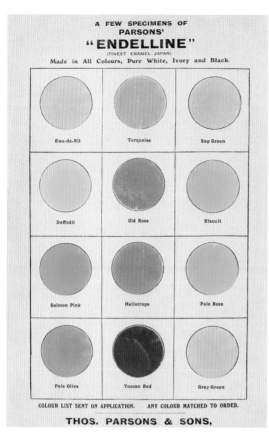

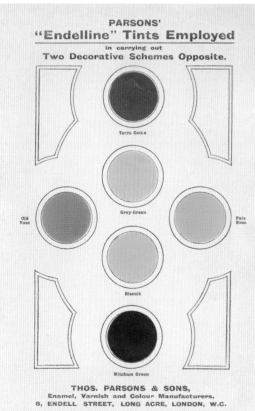

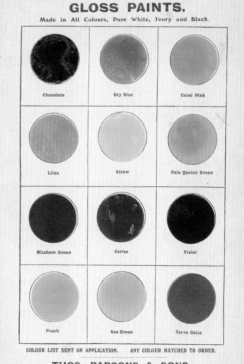

NEW WHITE PIGMENT PRODUCTION

In the early days of the trade, the house-painter would buy his raw materials and mix them together himself to produce his own paint. Pigments ground in oil to make a paste then became available from the colour shops, and these required only the addition of more oil until a workable consistency was achieved, together with some driers or thinners directly before application.

In the second half of the nineteenth century, ready-mixed paint was sold in tin cans, but it was often so badly formulated that the contents would settle into a hard mass at the bottom of the container. As a result of these early problems, the trade tended to be sceptical of the products, as documented by Irish author Robert Tressell in *The Ragged-Trousered Philanthopists* (1914):

> Crass's work as colourman was simplified, to a certain extent, by the great number of specially prepared paints and distempers in all colours, supplied by the manufacturers ready for use. Most of these new-fangled concoctions were regarded with an eye of suspicion and dislike by the hands, and Philpot voiced the general opinion about them one day during a dinner-hour discussion when he said they might appear to be all right for a time, but they would probably not last, because they was mostly made of kimicles.

A century later, similar comments can still occasionally be heard.

LITHOPONE

From 1860 to 1861, John Bryson Orr devoted himself to the search for a satisfactory white pigment and a sound practical method of producing it commercially.

Lithopone is a chemical combination of zinc sulphide and barium sulphate. However, the method of preparing the pigment is complicated, involving both precipitation and calcination processes. Orr carried out experiments on mixed zinc and barium pigment and seven years later began to produce the pigment in bulk. In 1872 he set up a factory in Glasgow for its manufacture. Although the Frenchman G. F. de Douhet is considered to be the pioneer of the lithopone industry, it was Orr who perfected the technique and who developed a viable method

of production. In 1874 he patented the process for making Orr's Zinc White (lithopone).

In 1880, shortly after his factory had burnt down, Orr formed the Silicate Paint Company in Charlton, on the outskirts of London. There, he manufactured lithopone (sold under the name Charlton White) and the first washable distemper, known as Duresco. To many people Duresco was at one time synonymous with washable distemper, although other versions became well known. It is no exaggeration to say that the washable distempers (or oil emulsion water paints, as they were called originally) were made possible by lithopone because no other white pigment was satisfactory as an ingredient in such paints.

In order to produce Orr's Zinc White, large-scale industrial processes were required. Zinc ore was roasted to zinc oxide and then dissolved in sulphuric acid and the solution purified. Barytes, the insoluble mineral sulphate of barium, was roasted with coal to make a water-soluble sulphide and extracted to a clear solution. The two solutions were mixed and the resulting white precipitate of zinc sulphide and barium sulphate roasted. The 'calcine' from this operation was dumped into water, dried in an oven and eventually packed as the finished product.

Around 1896, Orr realized the advantages of Widnes in north-west England as a centre for the large-scale production of his new pigment and arranged for Thomas Kenyon to deal with the manufacturing, while he looked after the commercial development in London. Presumably, the partnership did not work out. On 21 July 1898 Orr's Zinc White Ltd was incorporated as a limited company.

For every ton of zinc sulphide, an equal amount of barytes ore was required and so the company developed barytes mines, first at the Wrentall Mine, Minsterley, in Shropshire, then at the Gasswater Mine at Old Cumnock, in East Ayrshire, and later at the Cow Green Mine, South Durham, near Middleton-in-Teesdale. In this way, continuity of supplies was assured.

The paint and colour manufacturing activities of Orr's Zinc White Ltd continued until 1923, when they ceased because the sales of the pigment lithopone had grown to such an extent that it then seemed desirable to concentrate entirely on this aspect. In order to develop Orr's Zinc White for purposes other than paint, in

The Silicate Paint Company at Charlton, Kent, featured in *The Architect*, 12 April 1879. The factory occupied a 2-acre site on the banks of the Thames. The chief products were Griffith's patent white paint and Griffith's white (zinc sulphide). Dry pigment was processed and packed for sale as were mixed paints and enamels. The emphasis was on the non-toxic product that outperformed lead for coverage and for heat and gas resistance.

A

B

'Peaceful Harmony – Smooth Efficiency': illustrations of a sitting room [A] and a kitchen
[B] from a 1950s Walpamur guide, showing lithopone used in the home.

1902 James Ferguson of Glasgow had been given the sole selling agency in the United Kingdom for the linoleum, India rubber, cable and asbestos trades, and thanks very largely to his efforts the new pigment soon became as well established in those industries as it was in the paint industry.

Until the gradual introduction of titanium dioxide in the 1930s, lithopone was one of the most effective white pigments available. It covered better than either white lead or zinc oxide and was more flexible than the latter. It was inert in the presence of sulphur gases, which tended to discolour white lead paint. However, it had the drawback of blackening when exposed to the sun and of chalking; consequently, it was not suitable for exterior work. When mixed with white lead or colours containing a copper or lead base, it would also blacken due to the formation of sulphide of lead. This was liable to happen when a drier containing lead salts was used in the oil paint.

By the late 1940s, lithopone was still the sole white pigment specified by British Standard 1053 for water paint. An example of the established position of water paint at that time is that the Factory Act of 1937, which prescribed whitewashing for factory premises every fourteen months, allowed this period to be extended to three years if an oil emulsion water paint based on lithopone was used.

Lithopone was employed extensively in top quality interior paints, undercoats, flat oil paints and water paints. For some years, it continued to be the prime ingredient of Walpamur, and a very small proportion was used in some later emulsion paints. It has now ceased to be of any importance in the paint industry.

TITANIUM DIOXIDE

In spite of earlier experiments, white pigments produced from titanium dioxide are products of twentieth-century industrial development. Initially, it was found in combination with either barium sulphate or zinc, and it was in this form that it was introduced into the United Kingdom in 1921.

The paint industry was quick to realize its potential and there is some evidence for its early use. For example, titanium dioxide is known to have been employed in the decoration of the Mansfield Street house of the architect Sir Edwin Lutyens, who moved there in 1919. It has also been found in the analysis of the Civil Service Rifles' war memorial, which he designed in 1924. This had been erected originally in the central courtyard at Somerset House, but was later moved. The memorial is in the form of a column surmounted by an urn, with the Union flag on one side and the standard of the Civil Service Rifles on the other. All the white elements were painted with the newly developed titanium white.

Some of the early combinations had an ivory hue, but towards the end of 1927, as a result of extensive research, the difficulties of preparing a satisfactory pigment from the pure oxide were finally overcome, and a pigment of brilliant whiteness and intense opacity was introduced, containing approximately 98 per cent titanium dioxide.

The good obliterating power of some enamel paints of the 1930s suggests that their main pigment was the newly introduced titanium dioxide rather than the customary zinc oxide. Thomas Parson's half-time enamel may well have been one of these.

When looking at paint under the microscope, it is rare to find pure titanium dioxide in decorative schemes of the first half of the twentieth century. Far more common is the sort of combination described below in *Paint and its Part in Architecture*, published by Jenson & Nicholson Ltd in 1930:

FOR A FLAT PAINT FINISH

The third coat to consist of titanium dioxide and zinc oxide in equal parts with a vehicle of 95 per cent American turpentine and 5 per cent white oil varnish, to which must be added such additional pigment as will produce a colour to approved pattern. The pigments to be ground in American turpentine.

Development was curtailed by World War II, and the appearance of a scheme with titanium dioxide as the main constituent invariably marks the 1960s. In cross section, it does not fluoresce when examined under ultraviolet light.

Titanium dioxide has been the prime white pigment in house paints for the past fifty years. It also sees use as a pigment to provide whiteness and opacity to products ranging from plastics, papers, inks, foods and medicines (pills and tablets) to most toothpastes.

THE NEW WATER PAINTS

Soft distemper was fairly inexpensive and relatively easy to make and apply, but it was not durable. Throughout the nineteenth century, there were attempts made to produce a more robust water-based coating for plasterwork. One of the most common sorts of 'improved' distempers was the family of primitive emulsions known as oil-bound distemper, casein-bound distemper or more properly water paint. Note the use of the word 'emulsion' to indicate a mixture of liquids that normally cannot be combined, such as oil and water.

The two most successful water paints (this term is preferred in order to avoid confusion by using the word 'distemper') were Duresco and Walpamur. These two brands of the same type of paint were household names for a period of seventy to eighty years, yet nowhere is their history recorded. Any student of paint and colour will encounter these products in early twentieth-century literature and will need to know what they were. However, it is appropriate to quash any myths that they were in some way super paints, of a type that the world is poorer without. They were good, in their day, but both were eventually superseded by other paints with improved properties.

DURESCO

'Duresco on your walls will bring dignity, freshness and beauty to your home', promised the trade brochure. And Duresco, it seems, had good reason to call itself the 'king of water paints'. Apart from its fragility, the main problem with conventional distemper was that it could not be washed down:

> The objection to distempers that they cannot be washed down, led some thirty years ago [c. 1894], to the production of sanitary distempers or washable water paints. The author believes that the invention was due to Mr J. B. Orr, who founded the Silicate Paint Co., at Charlton, and who produced 'Duresco', which has ever since proved very popular, and there are a very large number of water paints which may be described as being somewhat similar on the market to-day. As a rule, they are not made from whiting, but from lithopone, a dense white, which is the base of most undercoats used under enamels and paints, and for inside work possesses many advantages.

By the very beginning of the twentieth century, it was announced that:

> The Guildhall, London was regularly treated with Duresco;
> The Foreign Department Buildings, Oslo was recently decorated outside with Duresco;
> The Bank of Brussels, The Old Palace of Flanders was recently decorated inside with Duresco;
> The Gleneagles Hotel had been treated *inside* and *outside* with Duresco.

Incredibly, for a product that was one of the first and better known of its kind, the only published record of Duresco is found in an obscure work that was written to celebrate the first fifty years of its main component, lithopone. Duresco was marketed and used widely with little modification. The colour range remained remarkably constant, seemingly little affected by the vagaries of fashion.

The colours shown in a colour card from *c.* 1901 were still listed thirty years later, and in that document the prices were also given. This is helpful as it reveals how the colours would have been used hierarchically – in much the same way as they were in the eighteenth century.

HOW IT WAS USED

Duresco came as a paste, known as body colour, and a liquid medium, known as petrifying liquid, was added to the paste in order to dilute it to a workable consistency.

The following extract from Paul N. Hasluck's *A Practical Guide to Painters' and Decorators' Work* (1913) describes a typical job in which Duresco was used as a 'washable' distemper:

> The walls being bare and clean, no washing or other preparation will be required, except that damaged places must be made good with pure plaster of Paris mixed with equal portions of water and Duresco thinners. Plaster thus mixed will set slowly – in about an hour – but when thoroughly set will be nearly suctionless. All patching of plaster throughout the job should be done as early as possible, in order that it may have an opportunity of drying before the colour wash is applied.
> The ceilings will require two coats, and they should be finished before the walls are begun. The first coat for the ceilings may be white, and should

An advertisement for Hall's Sanitary Washable Distemper of 1907, boasting seventy tints to choose from.
In the days of limited colour ranges, it would have just been possible to display such large samples of colour
in a showroom. [OVERLEAF] Suggested colour scheme for the dining room (left) and the nursery (right), from an
advertising booklet for Duresco paints. The emphasis here is on the paint's light, bright and easily washable surfaces.

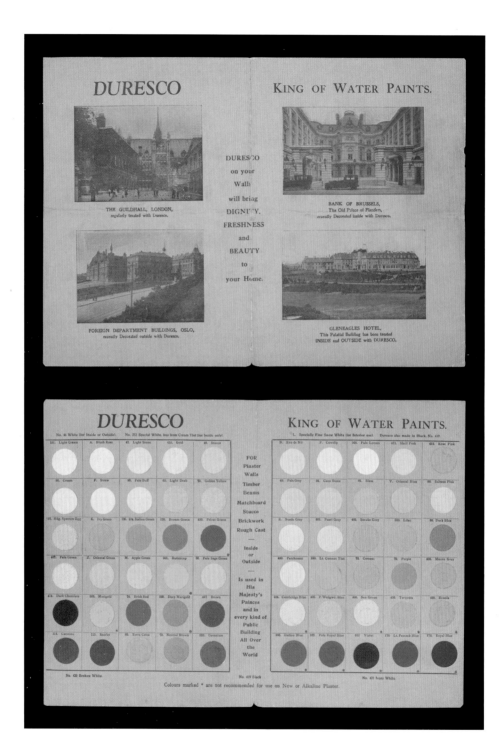

A Duresco colour card of about 1901.

be made of about one-third of the liquid thinners to two-thirds of the body, Duresco distemper, which is generally sold in the form of a stiff paste. It is not practicable, however, to lay down a hard and fast rule in this matter; everything depends on whether the plaster to be coated has much suction. If, on trial, a sample brushful works out to thin or too stiff, more body colour or more thinners can be added.

These distempers required to be used rounder than ordinary colour wash. A good general rule is to keep them as stiff as they can be worked comfortably. The more quickly these distempers can be made to dry the better. It is therefore advisable, in cold and damp weather, to have a fire in the room when they are being used; and at the finish a good draught of air should be allowed to circulate by opening the window or by some other means. In fine, warm weather, two or even three coats can be applied in one day, if it is necessary to get the work finished quickly. The ordinary procedure, however, is to allow a day for each coat. The second coat for the ceilings may be white or cream, and must be mixed rounder than the first, using water only, in place of the special liquid – for thinning the body colour – one part water to three parts body colour will generally be about the right proportions for finishing two coat ceiling work. Any splashes made on other parts of the room should be wiped up before they dry, as afterwards they are very difficult to remove.

The walls may require either two or three coats, according to the condition of the plaster. A little practice with these distempers will enable a man to make a first class job on fair plaster, with two coats and a touch up between. On such a wall a good round first coat can be applied. This first coat, when dry, will not be of a uniform colour; some places will have dried lighter or chalky. These light spots generally occur near angle beads, round fireplaces and door casings, and where the plaster has been patched. All such places should be touched up with a bit of stiff colour of the same tint as that used for first coating, before applying the second coat. When the work is dry, rub it down with glass paper. The second and finishing coat for the walls, as for the ceilings, should be mixed with water only, and applied as round as it can be comfortably worked. Some prefer the finishing coat stippled. This finish is in some cases desirable, but it is not absolutely necessary.

BENEFITS

The following is taken from the wonderful *Our Homes and How to Make Them Healthy* (1883) edited by Shirley F. Murphy:

The Silicate Paint Company manufacture a series of paints, into the composition of which is stated that no injurious ingredients enter. Lead, arsenic, copper and antimony salts are used in different ways to give brilliancy to many colours. To abolish these poisonous substances, and to substitute for them ingredients of perfectly neutral character, is without doubt a very valuable improvement on the score of health. These silicate paints are prepared from a pure silica obtained from the West of England. This is levigated, calcined and mixed with resinous substances. Besides their non-poisonous qualities, these paints are said to stand 200° heat without blistering, to have no chemical action on metals, and to cover, weight for weight, double the surface of ordinary paint.

The same company have patented a form of distemper which is called 'Duresco'. It is prepared from the 'Charlton white' described above, and when applied to brick, stone or plaster it hardens in such a manner as to indurate the surface. It is further claimed for this process that it is washable, that it is absolutely non-poisonous and that it prevents the percolation of moisture. It also has the great advantage of being so easy of application that a labourer can apply it in a similar manner to whitewash.

WALPAMUR

The river flowing through Darwen, near Blackburn in Lancashire, in the early nineteenth century was of particular use to the calico printing and bleaching industries, and it was here in 1818 that Richard Hilton established the paper-making industry that his sons were to develop into the largest paper-making works in the world.

In 1844 Hilton's was taken over by Charles and Harold Potter who already owned a calico printing business in the area. Wallpaper manufacturing (known as paper staining) was added to their repertoire, and the wallpapers that they produced were of such high quality that they soon become world famous.

The Potters were friendly with a designer named James Huntington, who was invited to become a partner in the firm and was joined by his two brothers ten years later. One of their sons, Major A. W. Huntington, became a partner in 1892, having returned from the Boer War. After the formation of a combine known as the Wall Paper Manufacturers Limited in 1899, he became a director. He set up a laboratory at the Hollins Paper Mill and experimented with making a reliable water paint. A satisfactory formula was discovered, and in August 1906 production commenced with a few hands borrowed from the mill. By 1908 the staff consisted of eight men and three boys. Initially, the water paint was sold under the name Hollins Distemper, but it was rebranded with the name WalPaMur, taken from the Wall Paper Manufacturers' title.

Drums at this time were made in three sizes – 28 pounds (12.5 kg), 56 pounds (25 kg) and 112 pounds (50 kg) – and they were returnable by clients. When they were sent back, they were washed out in vats with caustic soda and a number was stamped on them to show how many times they had been used. This practice continued until 1926. The early tins were decorated in green, black and white and these came in three sizes – 4 pounds (1.8 kg), 7 pounds (3 kg) and 14 pounds (6 kg).

THE PRODUCTS

A visit to the dry colour store would reveal piles of sacks, drums, barrels and boxes brought from places as far afield as Australia, Burma, Bolivia, West Africa and the Persian Gulf. The quantities used were considerable and as many as one hundred tons of pigment might be unloaded into the store in a single day. The media or binding agents were classified under three main headings: oil paints, water paints and nitro-cellulose paints.

Varnish was the most important binding agent for oil paints and comprised two main constituents: resin, chiefly from the Belgian Congo, and linseed oil from Argentina and Canada. At one time, Walpamur's varnish house was the largest plant of its kind in Europe. In the enamel paint department, the varnish was combined with pigment in pug-mills to form a paste. This was then ground in ball-mills to ensure more complete dispersion. The next stage saw the paste being fed through vertical steel roller-mills. One of the most colourful sights of the factory was provided by the paste as it was collected from the rollers by the scraper and flowed down to accumulate in rich folds. After further processes, the end result would be Duradio enamel paint.

The renowned Walpamur water paint was manufactured in a separate building. There, oil varnish was made and emulsified in water to produce the binding agent (in essence it was an early emulsion paint). This and the required pigments were ground together in a machine known as an edge-runner. As a company, Walpamur was very strong on research and development and it carried out a great deal of experimental work. One of its projects led to the production of water-based gloss and satin paints – the sort of paints that are in increasing demand today.

WALPAMUR WATER PAINT

Walpamur, or 'Wallop' as it was often referred to by the decorator, was an oil-bound, non-poisonous flat paint for walls. It was supplied in paste form and made ready for use by thinning with Walpamur petrifying liquid or water. It could be applied by brush or spray and it dried to a smooth matt finish.

For porous or loosely bound surfaces, it was recommended that a coat of Walpamur primer should be applied first to provide a sound foundation for the water paint. The primer was supplied in either a transparent or a suitably tinted form.

One hundredweight (50 kg) of Walpamur, when thinned to proper working consistency, covered approximately 292 square metres (350 sq yd) with two coats on smooth non-porous surfaces. Under normal conditions, two coats would produce a solid finish, but where Walpamur tinted primer of a suitable shade had been used, the second coat of water paint was not always necessary.

THE DEMISE OF WATER PAINT

With the introduction of the more stable and much more durable emulsion paints in the late 1950s, the age of water paint came to an end. In addition to being easy to apply, the new emulsions were free of the nightmarish property of failing when over-coated a couple of times. However, a combination of time, ignorance and marketing has led to a recent revival of these more primitive paints. The problems with water paint were comprehensively described by J. G. E. Holloway in his three-volume *The Modern Painter and Decorator* (1961):

> The strength of the bond of water paint is less than that of oil paint and, although the coating has some resistance to water, it is absorbent nonetheless. The liquid in a new coat of paint applied on top will soften it to some extent and cause it to swell. Water paint, moreover, is applied in thicker and heavier coats than oil paint. In drying, the paint contracts strongly and, in doing so, exerts a considerable pull on the underlying film, weakening the grip of any parts which are not firmly attached to the surface. Further coats add to the problem.

The edge-runners in Peel Mill, home of Walpamur's famous water paint, 1950s. A large vertical steel roller steadily revolves and grinds the paint in a circular trough. [OVERLEAF] [PP. 194-197] A number of colour samples in distemper that appear in a work of 1907 – *Three Hundred Shades and How to Mix Them. For Architects, Painters and Decorators* by A. Desaint, artistic interior decorator of Paris. [PP. 198-199] Pages from *Ornamental Decoration* (1908) by Thomas Parsons & Sons. [PP. 200-01] A series of plates demonstrating domestic interior colour schemes from *Your Home and its Decoration* (1910), published by the Sherwin-Williams Company Decorative Department.

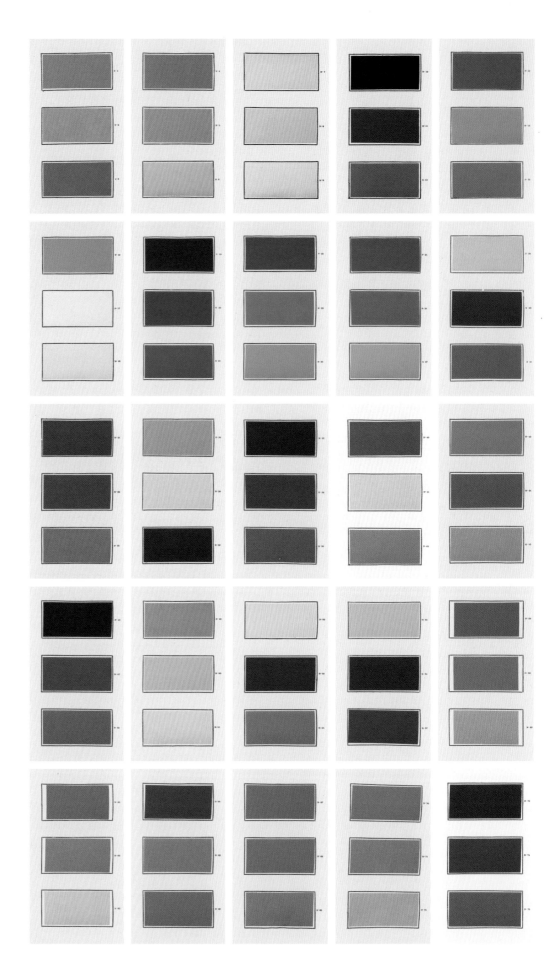

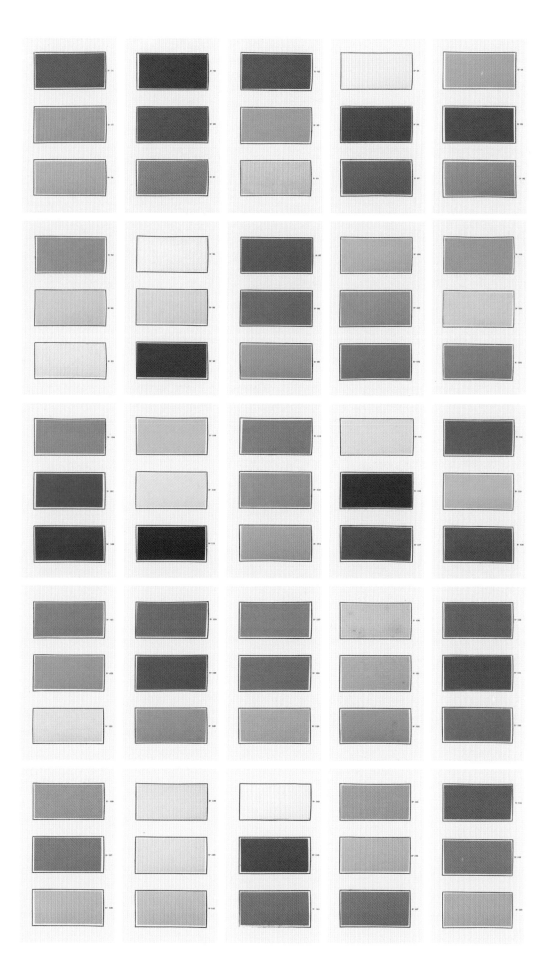

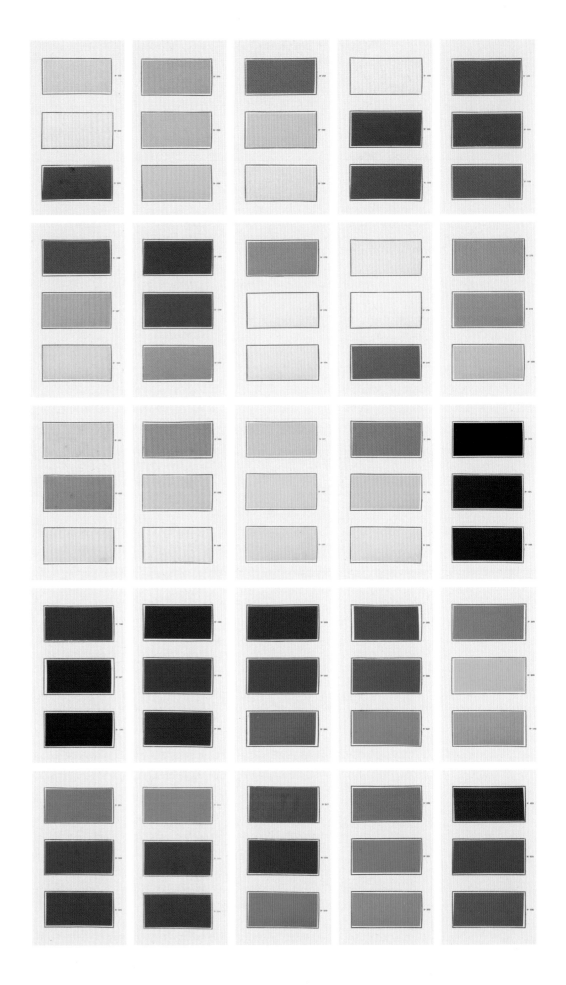

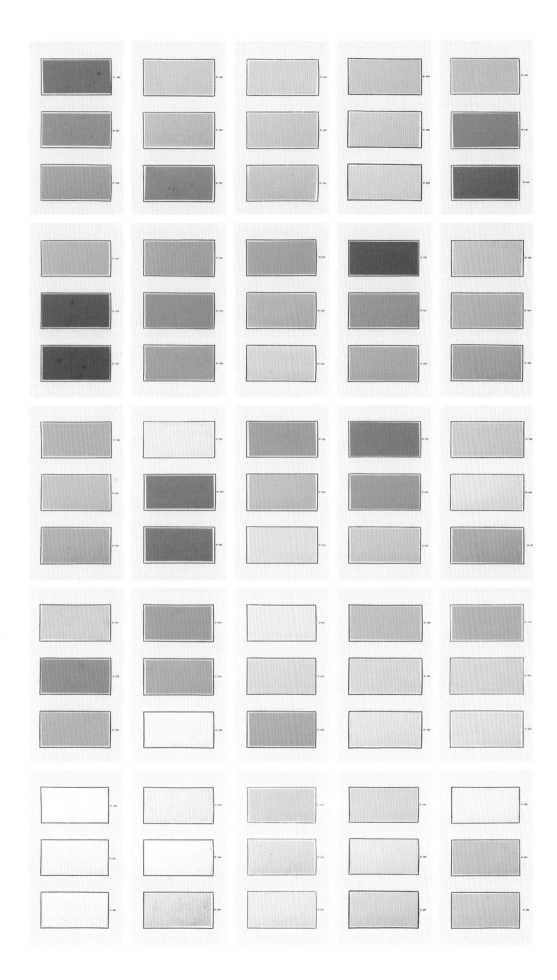

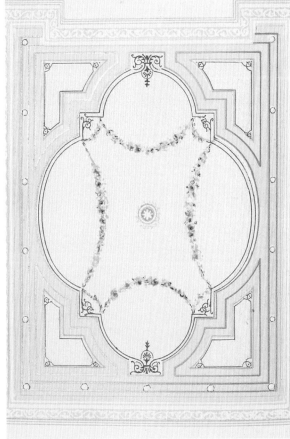

FLAT OIL AND ENAMEL PAINTS

Although the very popular water paint Duresco was available from the 1890s, ready-mixed oil paint took a little longer to perfect, only becoming widespread from the late 1920s. Once many of the teething problems had been ironed out, the ready-mixed paint could be used by the house-owner and amateur with no particular skill or knowledge required.

Several developments took place over the next decade and the paints produced by large companies, such as Thomas Parsons & Sons of London, were supplied in a wide range of colours and in finishes for most applications. However, supplies and further progress were limited during World War II, when the emphasis was on finding sources of regional pigments and supplying paints for protective and camouflage purposes. Consequently, this placed great restrictions on the paints available for household use at that time.

FLAT OIL PAINTS

In the 1930s, there were a number of different types of flat oil-based paints on the market, but most of them have now vanished from the house-painter's repertoire. Flat enamels were usually based on a linseed stand oil medium, sometimes with added resin. Flat oil wall paints (now known as flat oils), on the other hand, were a development of the old-fashioned flatting process employed by the early house-painter. They were tricky to use but effective in skilled hands.

These flat oil wall paints were made possible by the developments in pigment manufacture and by the increased use of tung oil in the production of paint. Lithopone and titanium white were employed together with extenders such as whiting, china clay and asbestine, introduced to help control consistency, brushing, sheen and flow. Matting agents, such as amorphous silica, magnesium carbonate, talc and diatomaceous earths, were used to control the level of sheen.

It was important that the paint was applied as part of a system, using a specially formulated primer and undercoat before the application of the flat oil. These paints had to be applied rapidly, but they covered well and produced a wonderful almost velvet-like finish and a hard matt surface with some resistance to washing.

However, unless care and consistency were employed, they tended to show flash marks.

UNICOTE FLAT OIL

This was a special type of flat oil paint produced by Thomas Parsons & Sons. It provided a flat provided a flat finish upon wood, plaster, wallpaper, metal and glass. It was much finer and more durable than a water paint and could even be scrubbed clean, thereby making it more hygienic. Unicote flat oil wall finish could also be applied over alkaline surfaces, such as concrete and cement, although it was advisable to write for special specifications before doing this. The covering capacity was approximately 75 square metres per 5 litres (90 sq yd per gallon).

ENAMEL PAINTS

Originally the word 'enamel' meant the fusing of powdered glass to a metal, glass or ceramic substrate. This was done by firing at high temperature, usually between 750 and 850° Celsius (1380–1560° F). The powder melts, flows and then hardens to a smooth, durable and glossy coating. The word is now used rather loosely in the painting and decorating trade, although in the early twentieth century its meaning was more precise. It was applied specifically to paint made with a small amount of finely ground pigment in a medium of linseed stand oil, with or without the addition of resins. This type of paint had poor opacity and was quite slow drying; however, it produced a durable film of considerable smoothness and lustre. Such a paint was often labelled Dutch enamel.

Enamels were not easy to apply and as they set slowly, every effort had to be made to avoid dust. It was recommended that the floor of the room to be painted was washed first. A bucket of water placed in the corner of the room also seemed to help attract dust away from the surface being painted. If the room temperature was low, the tin of enamel might be placed in a larger container of warm water in order to keep it free-flowing. These paints were designed to be used over a recommended undercoat, and if skilfully applied enamels would produce a perfectly smooth surface free from brush marks. A superior finish could be obtained if, after the enamel was dry, the surface was cut down with

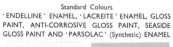

Standard Colours
'ENDELLINE' ENAMEL, 'LACREITE' ENAMEL, GLOSS PAINT, ANTI-CORROSIVE GLOSS PAINT, SEASIDE GLOSS PAINT AND 'PARSOLAC' (Synthetic) ENAMEL

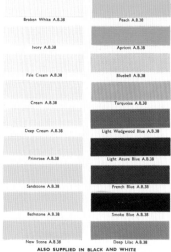

Broken White A.B.38	Peach A.B.38
Ivory A.B.38	Apricot A.B.38
Pale Cream A.B.38	Bluebell A.B.38
Cream A.B.38	Turquoise A.B.38
Deep Cream A.B.38	Light Wedgwood Blue A.B.38
Primrose A.B.38	Light Azure Blue A.B.38
Sandstone A.B.38	French Blue A.B.38
Bathstone A.B.38	Smoke Blue A.B.38
New Stone A.B.38	Deep Lilac A.B.38

ALSO SUPPLIED IN BLACK AND WHITE
Special colours matched on request.
24

Standard Colours
'ENDELLINE' ENAMEL, 'LACREITE' ENAMEL, GLOSS PAINT, ANTI-CORROSIVE GLOSS PAINT, SEASIDE GLOSS PAINT AND 'PARSOLAC' (Synthetic) ENAMEL

Pale Cerise A.B.38	Chestnut Brown A.B.38
Geranium A.B.38	Deep Endelbrown A.B.38
Parsons' Red A.B.38	Halford Brown No. 1 A.B.38
Tuscan Red A.B.38	Permanent Brown No. 1 A.B.38
French Grey A.B.38	Permanent Brown No. 2 A.B.38
Neutral Grey A.B.38	Permanent Brown No. 3 A.B.38
Light Drab A.B.38	Permanent Brown No. 4 A.B.38
Deep Nut Brown A.B.38	Permanent Brown No. 5 A.B.38
Tobac Brown A.B.38	Permanent Brown No. 6 A.B.38

ALSO SUPPLIED IN BLACK AND WHITE
Special colours matched on request.
25

Standard Colours
'ENDELLINE' ENAMEL, 'LACREITE' ENAMEL, GLOSS PAINT, ANTI-CORROSIVE GLOSS PAINT, SEASIDE GLOSS PAINT AND 'PARSOLAC' (Synthetic) ENAMEL

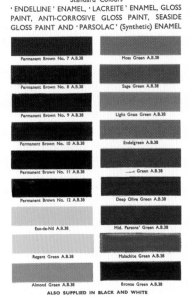

Permanent Brown No. 7 A.B.38	Moss Green A.B.38
Permanent Brown No. 8 A.B.38	Sage Green A.B.38
Permanent Brown No. 9 A.B.38	Light Grass Green A.B.38
Permanent Brown No. 10 A.B.38	Endelgreen A.B.38
Permanent Brown No. 11 A.B.38	... Green A.B.38
Permanent Brown No. 12 A.B.38	Deep Olive Green A.B.38
Eau-de-Nil A.B.38	Mid. Parsons' Green A.B.38
Regent Green A.B.38	Malachite Green A.B.38
Almond Green A.B.38	Bronze Green A.B.38

ALSO SUPPLIED IN BLACK AND WHITE
Special colours matched on request.
26

Standard Colours
PARSONS' 'HALF-TIME' ENAMEL

Ivory A.B.38	Oxford Grey A.B.38
Cream A.B.38	Tangerine A.B.38
Deep Cream A.B.38	Almond Green A.B.38
New Stone A.B.38	French Grey A.B.38
Primrose A.B.38	Mitcham Green A.B.38
Light Nut Brown A.B.38	Mid. Endelbrown A.B.38
Pale Cerise A.B.38	Mid. Blue A.B.38
Deep Nut Brown A.B.38	Deep Olive Green A.B.38
Parsons' Red A.B.38	Smoke Blue A.B.38
Chestnut Brown A.B.38	Deep Endelbrown A.B.38

ALSO IN BLACK, WHITE, AND BROKEN WHITE.
28

These four pages show a series of gloss colours that could be produced in a range of different paints, depending on the application. Thomas Parsons & Sons, 1930s.

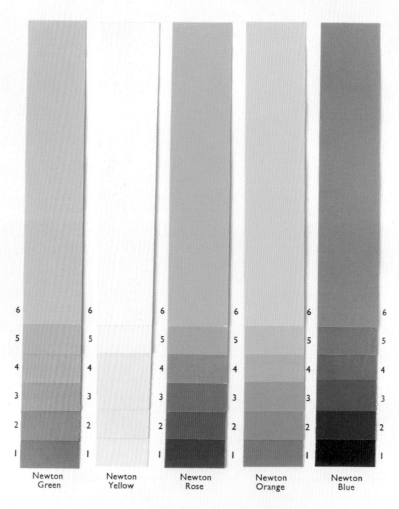

Newton Colour Series supplied in

PARSONS' 'ENDELFLAT' ENAMEL

THESE COLOURS ARE FOR INSIDE USE ONLY

Newton
Green

Newton
Yellow

Newton
Rose

Newton
Orange

Newton
Blue

*The NEWTON COLOUR SERIES can
also be supplied in Parsons' 'Endelline' and
'Lacreite' Enamels for inside work.*

38

Some examples of the bright, flat enamel paints offered by Thomas Parsons & Sons in the 1930s. This
particular series of graduated colours was designed for decorators wishing to colour-mix. [OVERLEAF]
Two colour cards produced by the Scottish paint company Craig & Rose. They probably date from
about 1910, and at that time they had premises in London, on the site of the present Globe Theatre.

pumice powder and then hand-polished with rottenstone (sometimes known as tripoli) and olive oil. The last traces of oil were removed, after wiping with a soft rag, by the application of pea flour. This gave a finish equal to any polished surface; it was very durable and would withstand considerable hard wear for many years.

A distinction was drawn between these enamels and those paints with greater covering power that were made with a higher proportion of pigment in a varnish medium. The latter were given such names as hard gloss paint, varnish paint or full gloss paint. Although there were several ways of achieving a glossy finish, the quality of the different methods was quite apparent on examination. An enamel would give a more porcelain-like finish rather than the brilliant lustre of a good varnish. For that reason, it was preferred for high-quality work.

In order to understand the properties of the enamel paints of the 1930s, it is worth looking at those offered by Thomas Parsons & Sons at that time. The exact composition of these paints is not known and the company has since ceased trading. However, an examination of a number of technical publications of the 1930s, plus a bit of guesswork, sometimes gives a clue as to how these enamels were produced.

ENDELLINE ENAMEL

This was the 'highest known quality of enamel for producing a porcelain-like finish' that could be repeatedly washed 'without deterioration'. Endelline enamel was recommended for the highest class of decoration, was extremely durable and suitable for interior and exterior use. Under normal conditions, it dried in about twelve to fourteen hours. The covering capacity was approximately 93 square metres per 5 litres (111 sq yd per gallon).

LACREITE ENAMEL

This was recommended when work would not bear the expense of Endelline. It could also be used for outside and inside work and covered approximately 83 square metres per 5 litres (99 sq yd per gallon). Lacreite enamel was also available in an egg-shell finish.

HALF-TIME ENAMEL

This product dried in half the time of ordinary enamel, was easily applied and had exceptional powers of obliteration (such that

an undercoating was not always essential). Both coats could be put on in a day and it had a covering capacity of approximately 83 square metres per 5 litres (99 sq yd per gallon). Half-time enamel was recommended principally for repainting business premises, cinemas, theatres and ships, where quick work was necessary to avoid interference with the ordinary routine.

These quick-drying enamels were based on medium oil length varnishes and in order to obtain the fast drying, the bulk of the oil was tung oil. The resin employed was either limed rosin or more usually a modified phenolic resin, which gives greater water resistance and durability. The good obliterating power of this enamel suggests that the main pigment employed was the newly introduced titanium dioxide rather than the zinc oxide that was generally used in enamels.

By the 1980s, flat enamels were seldom seen in everyday painting practice, but they were still called on for high-class work. They were especially useful where a matt finish was required on surfaces that were subject to frequent handling and where a flat oil wall paint would rapidly have become marked. A flat enamel possessed similar properties of flow to a gloss enamel, which meant that it dried with a smooth satin-like surface. Whereas most flat finishes were applied over a semi-gloss ground, that for a flat enamel had to be flat or eggshell (low sheen). By the time that the flat enamels disappeared from use, they were normally based on a tung oil and alkyd resin medium, with flatting agents and aluminium stereate added to increase the wet-edge time.

PARSOLAC

This paint was designed for interior and exterior use, and was very resistant to ultraviolet rays. As a consequence, it was suitable for shop fronts and dwelling houses, especially in industrial districts where its hard smooth properties shed dirt and kept the surface cleaner and fresher longer than any other finish. It had a brilliant gloss and excellent obliterating power; 5 litres would cover approximately 75 square metres (90 sq yd per gallon).

The reference to it having been 'very resistant to ultraviolet rays' and the suggestion that the paint film retained its condition on exposure to weather, even in towns or industrial atmospheres, imply that the pigment was titanium dioxide.

CRAIG & ROSE, L^TD

PAINT, VARNISH & ENAMEL
MANUFACTURERS,

CALEDONIAN OIL & COLOUR WORKS,

172 LEITH WALK,
LEITH, EDINBURGH.

Telegrams - - - "ROSE, LEITH."
Telephones - - 423 & 599 LEITH.

85 CADOGAN STREET,
GLASGOW, C. 2.

Telegrams - - - "ROSE, GLASGOW."
Telephone - - 1357 CENTRAL, GLASGOW.

BRITISH LION WHARF,
47-48 Bankside, LONDON, S.E.1.

Telegrams - "CRAIGROSE, BOROH, LONDON."
Telephone - - - 0547 HOP LONDON.

CONTRACTORS TO
H.M. GOVERNMENT,
ADMIRALTY,
WAR OFFICE,
AIR MINISTRY.

ESTABLISHED 1829.

DECORATOR'S PROTECTIVE PAINT

GLOSS FINISH

A PREPARED PAINT WHICH LIGHTENS WORK AND MAKES FOR ECONOMY

1. THE D.P.P. GLOSS FINISH is of special value to the trade in these days of higher working expenses.

2. It does away with the mixing of small quantities, an advantage of great importance during the rush of business in Summer and the short days of Winter.

3. Further, it dries with a lasting finish, thus doing away with the need of varnishing, and effecting a considerable saving of expensive material and highly paid labour.

4. Waste of material is entirely eliminated, and on account of its high-grade quality, the Paint can be used with absolute confidence for both outside and inside work.

5. It is eminently suitable for Firms doing a busy, high-class trade.

THIS PAINT IS GUARANTEED A SUPERFINE QUALITY FOR BEST DECORATIVE WORK.

Craig & Rose, Ltd.,
:: EDINBURGH ::
GLASGOW & LONDON

ESTABLISHED 1829.
CRAIG & ROSE LIMITED

THIS·PAINT·IS GUARANTEED·A SUPERFINE·QUALITY FOR·BEST DECORATIVE·WORK.

GLOSS FINISH

SUITABLE FOR INSIDE & OUTSIDE

DECORATOR'S PROTECTIVE PAINT

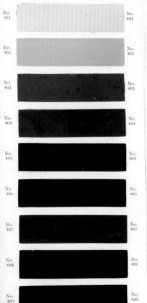

CRAIG & ROSE, Ltd.
London, Edinburgh, Glasgow.

No. 401 — No. 401
No. 402 — No. 402
No. 403 — No. 403
No. 404 — No. 404
No. 405 — No. 405
No. 406 — No. 406
No. 407 — No. 407
No. 408 — No. 408
No. 409 — No. 409

D. P. PAINT
GLOSS FINISH.

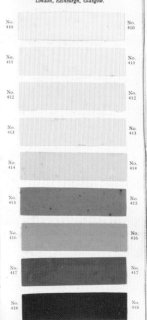

CRAIG & ROSE, Ltd.
London, Edinburgh, Glasgow.

No. 410 — No. 410
No. 411 — No. 411
No. 412 — No. 412
No. 413 — No. 413
No. 414 — No. 414
No. 415 — No. 415
No. 416 — No. 416
No. 417 — No. 417
No. 418 — No. 418

SUPPLIED IN DECORATED TINS,
½, ¼ and 1 Gallon.

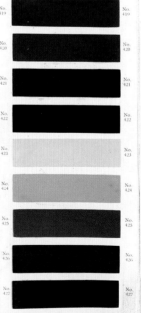

CRAIG & ROSE, Ltd.
London, Edinburgh, Glasgow.

No. 419 — No. 419
No. 420 — No. 420
No. 421 — No. 421
No. 422 — No. 422
No. 423 — No. 423
No. 424 — No. 424
No. 425 — No. 425
No. 426 — No. 426
No. 427 — No. 427

D. P. PAINT
GLOSS FINISH.

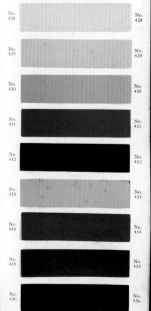

CRAIG & ROSE, Ltd.
London, Edinburgh, Glasgow.

No. 428 — No. 428
No. 429 — No. 429
No. 430 — No. 430
No. 431 — No. 431
No. 432 — No. 432
No. 433 — No. 433
No. 434 — No. 434
No. 435 — No. 435
No. 436 — No. 436

SUPPLIED IN DECORATED TINS,
½, ¼ and 1 Gallon.

ROSALIN

THE DECORATORS' IDEAL OF PERFECTION

PRE-EMINENT IN ENAMEL PAINTS

FOR **BRILLIANCY** AND **DURABILITY** STANDS UNRIVALLED

RESISTS ATMOSPHERIC INFLUENCES

Can be washed with Antiseptics without losing its porcelain-like gloss

INVALUABLE FOR

HOSPITALS	ASYLUMS
THEATRES	HOTELS
LIBRARIES	STEAMERS
COLD STORAGES	BREWERIES

OPLUS

STANDARD FOR HIGH-CLASS DECORATIVE ENAMEL PAINTS

FLOWS WELL AND WORKS EASILY

HAS GREAT **BODY** AND **COVERING POWER**

Dries well, giving a HARD, LUSTROUS and SOLID —— SURFACE ——

DURABLE, BOTH **INSIDE** AND **OUTSIDE**

Economical and always gives
- - SATISFACTION - -

CRAIG & ROSE · LTD

PAINT, COLOUR AND VARNISH MANUFACTURERS

LONDON
BRITISH LION WHARF
47 & 48 BANKSIDE, S.E

EDINBURGH
172 LEITH WALK &
85 CADOGAN STREET

GLASGOW

Specimens of Fine Enamels Gloss & Flat ROSALIN and OPLUS	Telegraphic ADDRESSES Craig Rose Borch LONDON Rose --- LEITH Rose-GLASGOW

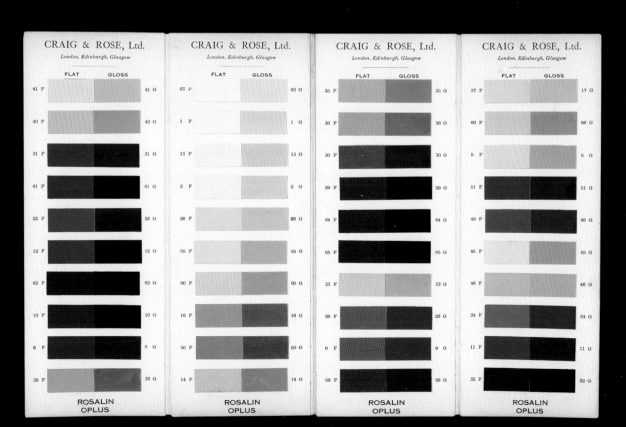

Plate II.

WALNUT	SIENNA
MAPLE	DOVE
MAHOGANY AND ROSEWOOD	ROUGE ROYAL
SATINWOOD	VEIN OR WHITE
BIRCH	ORIENTAL VERDANTIQUE
WAINSCOT AND DARK OAK	EGYPTIAN OR VERT DE MER
POLLARD OAK	ROUGE GROTTE
KNOTTED OR ROOT OF OAK	GRANITE

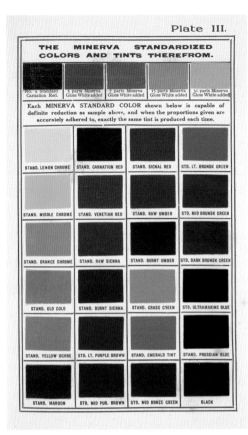

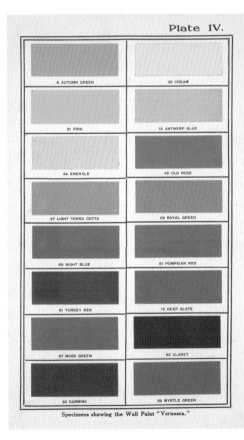

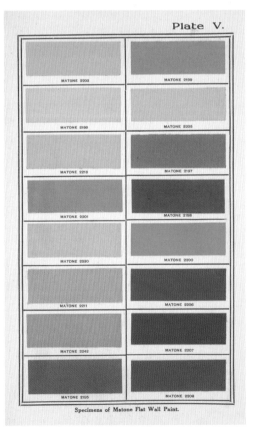

[ABOVE/OPPOSITE] Colours from the 1915 edition of *Paint and Colour Mixing* by Arthur Seymour Jennings.

Plate VI.

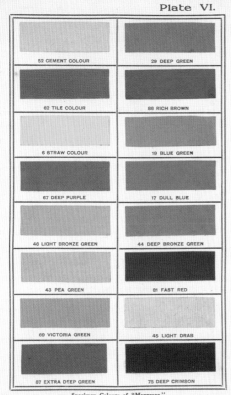

52 CEMENT COLOUR	29 DEEP GREEN
62 TILE COLOUR	88 RICH BROWN
6 STRAW COLOUR	19 BLUE GREEN
67 DEEP PURPLE	17 DULL BLUE
46 LIGHT BRONZE GREEN	44 DEEP BRONZE GREEN
43 PEA GREEN	81 FAST RED
69 VICTORIA GREEN	45 LIGHT DRAB
87 EXTRA DEEP GREEN	75 DEEP CRIMSON

Specimen Colours of "Mayresco."

PLATE VII

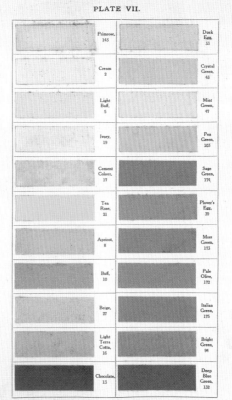

Primrose, 145	Duck Egg, 33
Cream, 2	Crystal Green, 43
Light Buff, 5	Mint Green, 47
Ivory, 19	Pea Green, 103
Cement Colour, 17	Sage Green, 179
Tea Rose, 21	Plover's Egg, 39
Apricot, 8	Moss Green, 173
Buff, 10	Pale Olive, 172
Beige, 27	Italian Green, 175
Light Terra Cotta, 16	Bright Green, 94
Chocolate, 13	Deep Blue Green, 138

Specimen Colours of SYNOLEO—The Oil-Bound Distemper.

PLATE VIII.

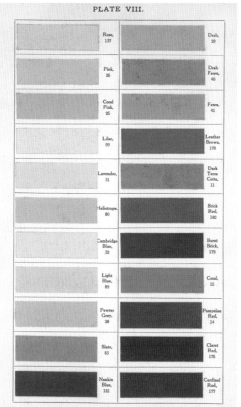

Rose, 137	Drab, 29
Pink, 26	Drab Fawn, 40
Coral Pink, 25	Fawn, 41
Lilac, 59	Leather Brown, 178
Lavender, 31	Dark Terra Cotta, 11
Heliotrope, 80	Brick Red, 180
Cambridge Blue, 32	Burnt Brick, 179
Light Blue, 89	Coral, 15
Pewter Grey, 28	Pompeian Red, 14
Slate, 83	Claret Red, 176
Nankin Blue, 181	Cardinal Red, 177

Specimen Colours of SYNOLEO—The Oil-Bound Distemper.

Plate ix.

Plate showing how 40 Tints may be produced by the intermixture of Blue (A), Yellow (B), Red (31), with White.

The Rule for obtaining these 40 Tints will be found within.

62		80	
63		81	
64		82	
65		83	
66		84	
67		85	
68		31	
69		86	
70		87	
71		88	
A		89	
72		90	
73		91	
74		92	
75		93	
76		94	
77		95	
B		96	
78		97	
79		98	

These Alabastine Tints have been stippled, the primaries will be seen on the back of this sheet, brushed plain.

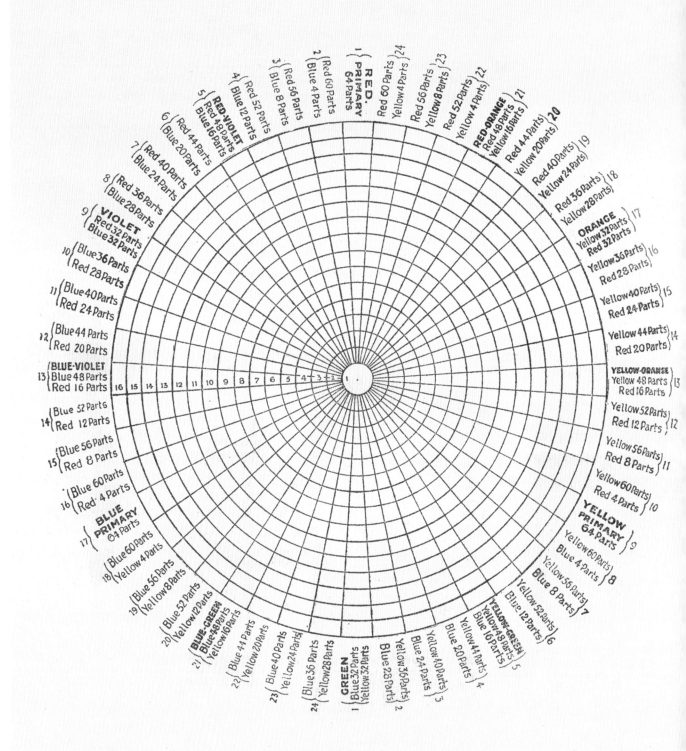

A blank colour wheel designed for the keen student to complete. From *The Decoration and Renovation of the Home* (1924) by Arthur Seymour Jennings. [OPPOSITE] Some suggestions for painting the frieze, wall and skirting and [OVERLEAF] walls from *The Decoration and Renovation of the Home* (1924) by Arthur Seymour Jennings.

AN EAST ROOM IN MATROIL
Frieze—White, *Stencil No.* 28/12. *Wall*—Pale Corn
Yellow. *Woodwork*—SCRUMBLE Antique Oak.

A SOUTH ROOM IN MATROIL
Frieze—White, *Stencil No.* 10/43. *Wall*—Porcelain.
Woodwork—EXILAC White Enamel.

A NORTH ROOM IN MATROIL
Frieze—White, *Stencil No.* 9/30. *Wall*—Pale
Venetian. *Woodwork*—SCRUMBLE Mahogany.

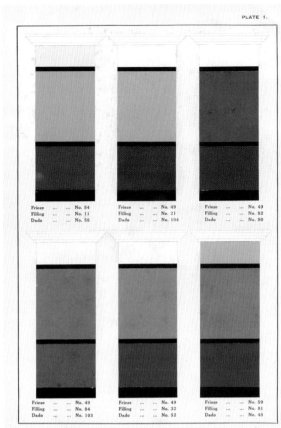

PLATE 1.

Frieze	...	No. 54	Frieze	...	No. 49	Frieze	...	No. 49
Filling	...	No. 11	Filling	...	No. 21	Filling	...	No. 82
Dado	...	No. 58	Dado	...	No. 104	Dado	...	No. 90

Frieze	...	No. 49	Frieze	...	No. 49	Frieze	...	No. 59
Filling	...	No. 84	Filling	...	No. 32	Filling	...	No. 81
Dado	...	No. 103	Dado	...	No. 52	Dado	...	No. 48

Sample Colours of AQUALINE WATER PAINTS.
By courtesy of Messrs. MANDER BROTHERS, WOLVERHAMPTON
(172)

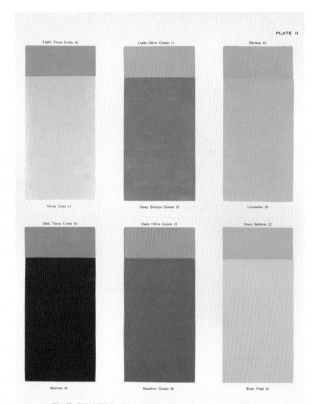

PLATE II

FLAT ENAMELS.—Wm. HARLAND & SON, MERTON, S.W.

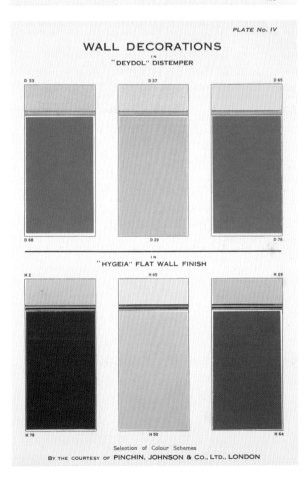

PLATE No. IV

WALL DECORATIONS
IN
"DEYDOL" DISTEMPER

IN
"HYGEIA" FLAT WALL FINISH

Selection of Colour Schemes
BY THE COURTESY OF PINCHIN, JOHNSON & Co., LTD., LONDON

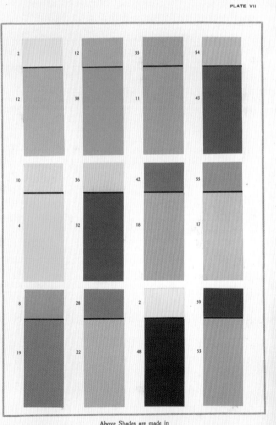

PLATE VII

Above Shades are made in
"COVERAL," "DECORAL," and "MORLEY'S RUBBER DISTEMPER."
By courtesy of Messrs. POSTANS & MORLEY BROTHERS, LTD., Nechells, BIRMINGHAM.

CHURCH'S "ALABASTINE" DISTEMPER.

Selection of Colour Schemes by the courtesy of
ALABASTINE CO. (BRITISH) LTD., CHURCH STREET, SOUTH LAMBETH, LONDON, S.W. 8.

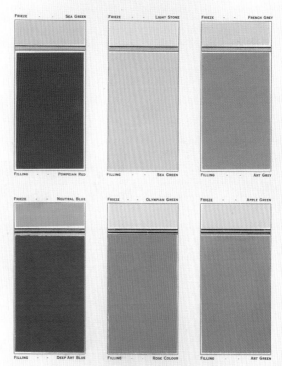

MURAL DECORATIONS
IN
"COMBINOL" FLAT-OIL PAINT

Colour Schemes in actual paint samples
BY THE COURTESY OF MESSRS. GOODLASS, WALL & CO., LTD., LIVERPOOL

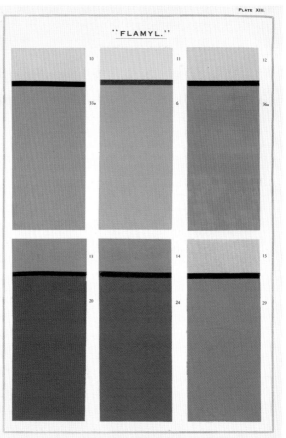

A number of advertisements for paints and varnishes from the 1920s. Many painting manuals of the time had such advertisements at the front and back. (Incidentally, one wonders how 'breathable' Morley's Rubber Distemper would have been.) [OVERLEAF] [P. 216] Some examples of gloss and flat enamels offered by Thomas Parsons & Sons during the 1930s. [P. 217] Some examples of water paints, tinted glazes applied over coloured base coats and metallic paints offered by Thomas Parsons & Sons during the 1930s. [P. 218] Some examples of tinted glaze and coloured base coats designed for graining; with textured paints for 'plastic painting' and stone effects. These were offered by Thomas Parsons & Sons during the 1930s. [P. 219] Some suggestions for painting the walls of hospitals, schools and public buildings, also offered by Thomas Parsons & Sons during the 1930s. [P. 220] From a catalogue of the different paints offered by the American company Glidden in the 1930s. Here are examples of flat enamels and Kalsomine (a distemper that was supplied as a dry powder to which water was added). [P. 221] Also from a catalogue of the different paints offered by Glidden in the 1930s. Here are examples of Jap-a-Lac gloss paint and Ripolin enamel. Ripolin was the first commercially available brand of enamel paint. It had been developed in the Netherlands originally but became a French company at the beginning of the twentieth century. [PP. 222–223] A colour card of quick-drying varnish paints, hard enamels and tinted glazes being offered by a Bristol-based company in the 1930s.

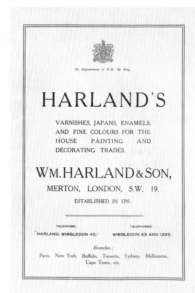

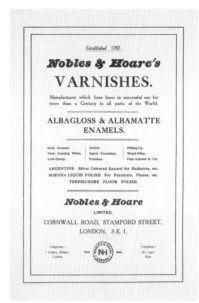

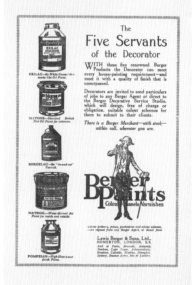

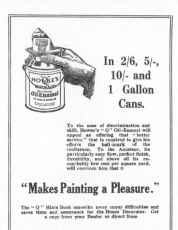

Standard Colours
'ENDELLINE' ENAMEL, 'LACREITE' ENAMEL, GLOSS PAINT, ANTI-CORROSIVE GLOSS PAINT, SEASIDE GLOSS PAINT AND 'PARSOLAC' (Synthetic) ENAMEL

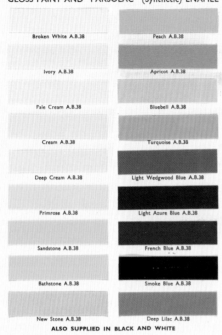

Broken White A.B.38	Peach A.B.38
Ivory A.B.38	Apricot A.B.38
Pale Cream A.B.38	Bluebell A.B.38
Cream A.B.38	Turquoise A.B.38
Deep Cream A.B.38	Light Wedgwood Blue A.B.38
Primrose A.B.38	Light Azure Blue A.B.38
Sandstone A.B.38	French Blue A.B.38
Bathstone A.B.38	Smoke Blue A.B.38
New Stone A.B.38	Deep Lilac A.B.38

ALSO SUPPLIED IN BLACK AND WHITE
Special colours matched on request.

24

Standard Colours
PARSONS' 'HALF-TIME' ENAMEL

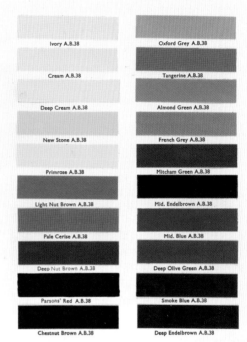

Ivory A.B.38	Oxford Grey A.B.38
Cream A.B.38	Tangerine A.B.38
Deep Cream A.B.38	Almond Green A.B.38
New Stone A.B.38	French Grey A.B.38
Primrose A.B.38	Mitcham Green A.B.38
Light Nut Brown A.B.38	Mid. Endelbrown A.B.38
Pale Cerise A.B.38	Mid. Blue A.B.38
Deep Nut Brown A.B.38	Deep Olive Green A.B.38
Parsons' Red A.B.38	Smoke Blue A.B.38
Chestnut Brown A.B.38	Deep Endelbrown A.B.38

ALSO IN BLACK, WHITE, AND BROKEN WHITE.

28

Standard Colours
'ENDELFLAT' ENAMEL, 'LACREITE' FLAT (and Egg-Shell) ENAMEL AND 'UNICOTE' FLAT WALL FINISH

Ivory A.B.38	Yellow Grey A.B.38	Pink Mauve A.B.38
Cream A.B.38	Smoke Grey A.B.38	Terra Cotta A.B.38
Sunshine Yellow A.B.38	French Grey A.B.38	Café-au-Lait A.B.38
Bath Stone A.B.38	Plumbago A.B.38	Deep Lilac A.B.38
Ecru A.B.38	Wedgwood Green No. 1, A.B.38	Deep Tuscan Red A.B.38
Chamois A.B.38	Pale Art Green A.B.38	*Turquoise Blue A.B.38
Mid. Stone A.B.38	Wedgwood Green No. 2, A.B.38	Wedgwood Blue A.B.38
Golden Brown A.B.38	Pale Sage Green A.B.38	Italian Blue A.B.38

ALSO IN BLACK AND WHITE
Turquoise Blue not recommended for use upon new plaster.

36

Standard Colours
'ENDELFLAT' ENAMEL, 'LACREITE' FLAT (and Egg-Shell) ENAMEL AND 'UNICOTE' FLAT WALL FINISH

Broken White A.B.38	Pink Carnation A.B.38	Louis Seize Grey A.B.38
Pale Cream A.B.38	Cambridge Blue A.B.38	Mist Grey A.B.38
Parchment A.B.38	Lilac A.B.38	Lavender Grey A.B.38
Primrose A.B.38	Pastel Blue A.B.38	Extra Lt. Wedgwood Blue A.B.38
Fawn A.B.38	Cornflower Blue A.B.38	Sky Blue A.B.38
Biscuit A.B.38	Venetian Blue A.B.38	Pale Grey Green A.B.38
Golden Yellow A.B.38	New Pompeian Red A.B.38	Adams Green A.B.38
Salmon Pink A.B.38	William and Mary Green A.B.38	Verona Green A.B.38

ALSO IN BLACK AND WHITE
For NEWTON SERIES OF BRIGHT COLOURS, see next page

37

Standard Colours
PARSONS' 'PARLYTE' WATER PAINT

X.2 Broken White A.B.38	X.43 Deep Fawn A.B.38	X.13 Brilliant Yellow A.B.38
X.3 Ivory A.B.38	X.44 Primrose A.B.38	X.14 Cavendish Grey A.B.38
X.4 Cream A.B.38	X.45 Biscuit A.B.38	X.15 Louis Seize Grey No.1 A.B.38
X.5 Bath Stone A.B.38	X.9 Golden Brown A.B.38	X.16 Yellow Grey A.B.38
X.6 Beige A.B.38	X.10 Deep Drab A.B.38	X.17 Autumn Gold A.B.38
X.7 Light Drab A.B.38	X.11 Oak A.B.38	X.18 Pink Carnation A.B.38
X.8 Fawn A.B.38	X.46 Caen Stone	X.19 Terra Cotta A.B.38

The above Colours are all fast to Lime, Light and Water.

(Continued on next page.)

41

Standard Colours
PARSONS' 'PARLYTE' WATER PAINT

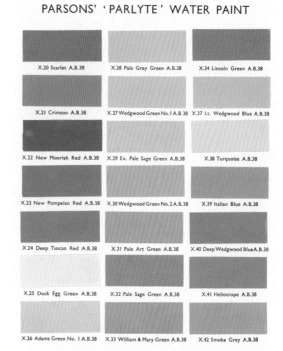

X.20 Scarlet A.B.38	X.28 Pale Grey Green A.B.38	X.34 Lincoln Green A.B.38
X.21 Crimson A.B.38	X.27 Wedgwood Green No.1 A.B.38	X.37 Lt. Wedgwood Blue A.B.38
X.22 New Moorish Red A.B.38	X.29 Ex. Pale Sage Green A.B.38	X.38 Turquoise A.B.38
X.23 New Pompeian Red A.B.38	X.30 Wedgwood Green No.2 A.B.38	X.39 Italian Blue A.B.38
X.24 Deep Tuscan Red A.B.38	X.31 Pale Art Green A.B.38	X.40 Deep Wedgwood Blue A.B.38
X.25 Duck Egg Green A.B.38	X.32 Pale Sage Green A.B.38	X.41 Heliotrope A.B.38
X.26 Adams Green No.1 A.B.38	X.33 William & Mary Green A.B.38	X.42 Smoke Grey A.B.38

The above Colours are all fast to Lime, Light and Water.

42

A Selection of Standard Colours
PARSONS' 'PARSO-GLAZE'
HAIR STIPPLED

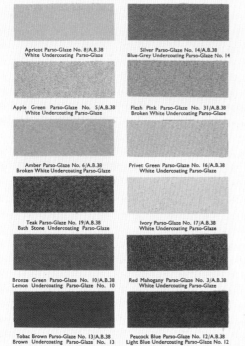

Apricot Parso-Glaze No. 8/A.B.38 White Undercoating Parso-Glaze	Silver Parso-Glaze No. 14/A.B.38 Blue-Grey Undercoating Parso-Glaze No. 14
Apple Green Parso-Glaze No. 5/A.B.38 White Undercoating Parso-Glaze	Flesh Pink Parso-Glaze No. 31/A.B.38 Broken White Undercoating Parso-Glaze
Amber Parso-Glaze No. 6/A.B.38 Broken White Undercoating Parso-Glaze	Privet Green Parso-Glaze No. 16/A.B.38 White Undercoating Parso-Glaze
Teak Parso-Glaze No. 19/A.B.38 Bath Stone Undercoating Parso-Glaze	Ivory Parso-Glaze No. 17/A.B.38 White Undercoating Parso-Glaze
Bronze Green Parso-Glaze No. 10/A.B.38 Lemon Undercoating Parso-Glaze No. 10	Red Mahogany Parso-Glaze No. 3/A.B.38 White Undercoating Parso-Glaze
Tobac Brown Parso-Glaze No. 13/A.B.38 Brown Undercoating Parso-Glaze No. 13	Peacock Blue Parso-Glaze No. 12/A.B.38 Light Blue Undercoating Parso-Glaze No. 12

Special colours made on request.

45

Standard Colours
PARSONS' 'MOSAICO' METALLIC PAINT

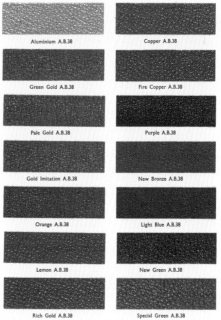

Aluminium A.B.38	Copper A.B.38
Green Gold A.B.38	Fire Copper A.B.38
Pale Gold A.B.38	Purple A.B.38
Gold Imitation A.B.38	New Bronze A.B.38
Orange A.B.38	Light Blue A.B.38
Lemon A.B.38	New Green A.B.38
Rich Gold A.B.38	Special Green A.B.38

69

A Selection of Standard Colours
PARSONS' 'PARSO-GLAZE'
BRUSH GRAINED

Satin Wood Parso-Glaze No. 1/A.B.38
Light Yellow Undercoating Parso-Glaze No.1

Teak Parso-Glaze No. 19/A.B.38
Putty Col. Undercoating Parso-Glaze No. 19

Oak Parso-Glaze No. 2/A.B.38
Dark Yellow Undercoating Parso-Glaze No.2

Brown Mahogany Parso-Glaze No. 23/A.B.38
Brown Undercoating Parso-Glaze No. 23

Mahogany Parso-Glaze No. 3/A.B.38
Tuscan Orange U'coating Parso-Glaze No. 3

Fumed Oak Parso-Glaze No. 25/A.B.38
Lt. Brown Undercoating Parso-Glaze No. 25

Pitch Pine Parso-Glaze No. 18/A.B.38
Dark Yellow Undercoating Parso-Glaze No.2

Walnut Parso-Glaze, No. 20/A.B.38
Light Buff Undercoating Parso-Glaze No. 20

Dark Oak Parso-Glaze No. 4/A.B.38
Light Brown Undercoating Parso-Glaze No. 4

Grey Parso-Glaze No. 22/A.B.38
White Undercoating Parso-Glaze

Blue Green Parso-Glaze No. 21/A.B.38
Pale Green Undercoating Parso-Glaze No. 21

Jacobean Oak Parso-Glaze No. 24/A.B.38
Dark Stone Undercoating Parso-Glaze No.24

47

Examples of Graining
PARSONS' GRAINING COLOURS
ON UNDERCOATING PAINT & VARNISHED

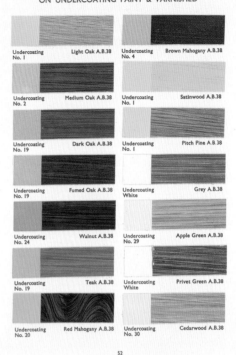

Undercoating No. 1   Light Oak A.B.38

Undercoating No. 4   Brown Mahogany A.B.38

Undercoating No. 2   Medium Oak A.B.38

Undercoating No. 1   Satinwood A.B.38

Undercoating No. 19   Dark Oak A.B.38

Undercoating No. 1   Pitch Pine A.B.38

Undercoating No. 19   Fumed Oak A.B.38

Undercoating White   Grey A.B.38

Undercoating No. 24   Walnut A.B.38

Undercoating No. 29   Apple Green A.B.38

Undercoating No. 19   Teak A.B.38

Undercoating White   Privet Green A.B.38

Undercoating No. 20   Red Mahogany A.B.38

Undercoating No. 30   Cedarwood A.B.38

52

Examples of Effects obtainable with
'PARSO-GLAZE'

Effect No. 1/A.B.38
Ivory Parso-Glaze and Untinted Parso-Glaze shaded on White Undercoating Parso-Glaze.

Effect No. 2/A.B.38
Beige Parso-Glaze stippled and rag rolled on White Undercoating Parso-Glaze.

Effect No. 3/A.B.38
Flesh Pink Parso-Glaze and Untinted Parso-Glaze clouded on Broken White Undercoating Parso-Glaze.

Effect No. 4/A.B.38
Celestial Blue Parso-Glaze No. 26 on Aluminium Undercoating Parso-Glaze. Hair stippled and rag rolled effect.

Effect No. 5/A.B.38
Lutyen's Green Parso-Glaze and Untinted Parso-Glaze shaded and rag rolled on White Undercoating Parso-Glaze.

Effect No. 6/A.B.38
Amber Parso-Glaze and Untinted Parso-Glaze shaded on Primrose Undercoating Parso-Glaze.

50

Examples of Actual effects
Parsons' 'PARSO-STONE' Paint

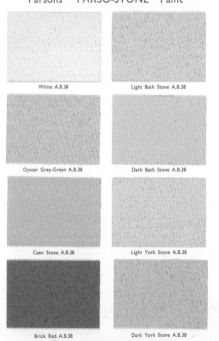

White A.B.38

Light Bath Stone A.B.38

Oyster Grey-Green A.B.38

Dark Bath Stone A.B.38

Caen Stone A.B.38

Light York Stone A.B.38

Brick Red. A.B.38

Dark York Stone A.B.38

Also supplied in WHITE which may be tinted.

77

Examples of Parsons' SELECTED SCHEMES
For HOSPITALS and PUBLIC INSTITUTIONS

Filling : No. 1/A.B.38 Cream Hospital Lacreite Enamel and Undercoating.

Dado : No. 1/A.B.38 Blue Hospital Lacreite Enamel and Undercoating.

Filling : No. 2/A.B.38 Cream Hospital Lacreite Enamel and Undercoating.

Dado : No. 2/A.B.38 Brown Hospital Lacreite Enamel and Undercoating.

A special folder containing a complete range of L.C.C. Colour Schemes for Hospitals will be sent on request.

90

Examples of Parsons' SELECTED SCHEMES
For HOSPITALS and PUBLIC INSTITUTIONS

Filling : No. 5/A.B.38 Pale Primrose Hospital Lacreite Enamel and Undercoating.

Dado : No. 5/A.B.38 Green Hospital Lacreite Enamel and Undercoating.

Filling : No. 7/A.B.38 Deep Primrose Hospital Lacreite Enamel and Undercoating.

Skirting : No. 7/A.B.38 Grey Hospital Lacreite Enamel and Undercoating.

A special folder containing a complete range of L.C.C. Colour Schemes for Hospitals will be sent on request.

91

Examples of Parsons' SELECTED SCHEMES
For SCHOOLS and PUBLIC BUILDINGS

Filling : Unicote Flat Wall Finish
No. F1/A.B.38

Line : Parsons' Gloss Paint
No. L1/A.B.38

Dado : Parsons' Gloss Paint
No. D1/A.B.38

Filling : Unicote Flat Wall Finish
No. F5/A.B.38

Line : Parsons' Gloss Paint
No. L5/A.B.38

Dado : Parsons' Gloss Paint
No. D5/A.B.38

A special folder containing a complete range of L.C.C. Colour Schemes for Schools will be sent on request.

92

Examples of Parsons' SELECTED SCHEMES
For SCHOOLS and PUBLIC BUILDINGS

Filling : Unicote Flat Wall Finish
No. F4/A.B.38

Line : Parsons' Gloss Paint
No. L4/A.B.38

Dado : Parsons' Gloss Paint
No. D4/A.B.38

Filling : Unicote Flat Wall Finish
No. F6/A.B.38

Line : Parsons' Gloss Paint
No. L6/A.B.38

Dado : Parsons' Gloss Paint
No. D6/A.B.38

A special folder containing a complete range of L.C.C. Colour Schemes for Schools will be sent on request.

93

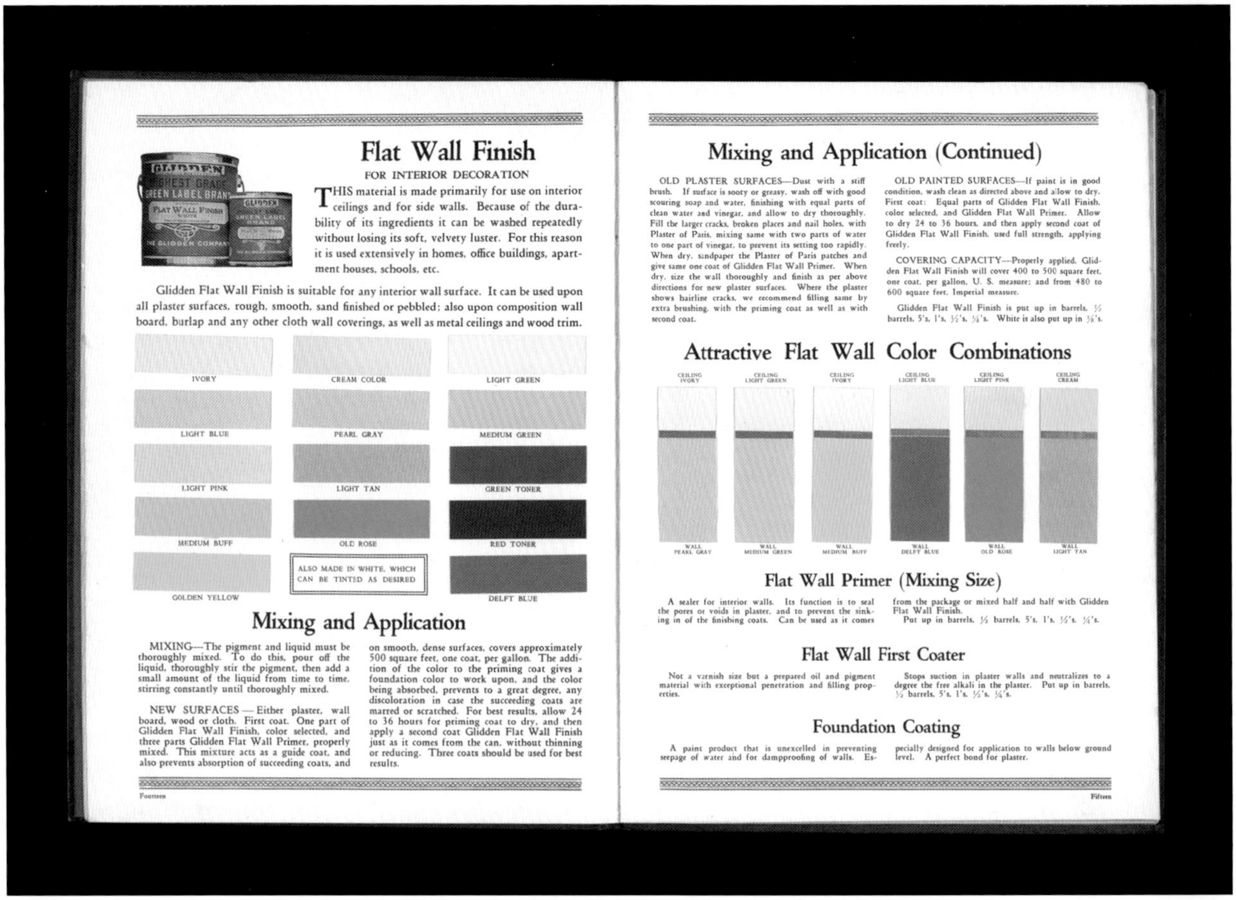

Flat Wall Finish

FOR INTERIOR DECORATION

THIS material is made primarily for use on interior ceilings and for side walls. Because of the durability of its ingredients it can be washed repeatedly without losing its soft, velvety luster. For this reason it is used extensively in homes, office buildings, apartment houses, schools, etc.

Glidden Flat Wall Finish is suitable for any interior wall surface. It can be used upon all plaster surfaces, rough, smooth, sand finished or pebbled; also upon composition wall board, burlap and any other cloth wall coverings, as well as metal ceilings and wood trim.

IVORY · CREAM COLOR · LIGHT GREEN · LIGHT BLUE · PEARL GRAY · MEDIUM GREEN · LIGHT PINK · LIGHT TAN · GREEN TONER · MEDIUM BUFF · ALSO MADE IN WHITE, WHICH CAN BE TINTED AS DESIRED · RED TONER · GOLDEN YELLOW · DELFT BLUE

Mixing and Application

MIXING—The pigment and liquid must be thoroughly mixed. To do this, pour off the liquid, thoroughly stir the pigment, then add a small amount of the liquid from time to time, stirring constantly until thoroughly mixed.

NEW SURFACES — Either plaster, wall board, wood or cloth. First coat. One part of Glidden Flat Wall Finish, color selected, and three parts Glidden Flat Wall Primer, properly mixed. This mixture acts as a guide coat, and also prevents absorption of succeeding coats, and

on smooth, dense surfaces, covers approximately 500 square feet, one coat, per gallon. The addition of the color to the priming coat gives a foundation color to work upon, and the color being absorbed, prevents to a great degree, any discoloration in case the succeeding coats are marred or scratched. For best results, allow 24 to 36 hours for priming coat to dry, and then apply a second coat Glidden Flat Wall Finish just as it comes from the can, without thinning or reducing. Three coats should be used for best results.

Mixing and Application (Continued)

OLD PLASTER SURFACES—Dust with a stiff brush. If surface is sooty or greasy, wash off with good scouring soap and water, finishing with equal parts of clean water and vinegar, and allow to dry thoroughly. Fill the larger cracks, broken places and nail holes, with Plaster of Paris, mixing same with two parts of water to one part of vinegar, to prevent its setting too rapidly. When dry, sandpaper the Plaster of Paris patches and give same one coat of Glidden Flat Wall Finish. When dry, size the wall thoroughly and finish as per above directions for new plaster surfaces. Where the plaster shows hairline cracks, we recommend filling same by extra brushing, with the priming coat as well as with second coat.

OLD PAINTED SURFACES—If paint is in good condition, wash clean as directed above and allow to dry. First coat: Equal parts of Glidden Flat Wall Finish, color selected, and Glidden Flat Wall Primer. Allow to dry 24 to 36 hours, and then apply second coat of Glidden Flat Wall Finish, used full strength, applying freely.

COVERING CAPACITY—Properly applied, Glidden Flat Wall Finish will cover 400 to 500 square feet, one coat, per gallon, U. S. measure; and from 480 to 600 square feet, Imperial measure.

Glidden Flat Wall Finish is put up in barrels, ½ barrels, 5's, 1's, ½'s, ¼'s. White is also put up in ½'s.

Attractive Flat Wall Color Combinations

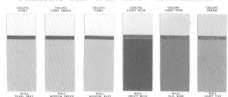

CEILING IVORY / WALL PEARL GRAY · CEILING LIGHT GREEN / WALL MEDIUM GREEN · CEILING IVORY / WALL MEDIUM BUFF · CEILING LIGHT BLUE / WALL DELFT BLUE · CEILING LIGHT PINK / WALL OLD ROSE · CEILING CREAM / WALL LIGHT TAN

Flat Wall Primer (Mixing Size)

A sealer for interior walls. Its function is to seal the pores or voids in plaster, and to prevent the sinking in of the finishing coats. Can be used as it comes from the package or mixed half and half with Glidden Flat Wall Finish.

Put up in barrels, ½ barrels, 5's, 1's, ½'s, ¼'s.

Flat Wall First Coater

Not a varnish size but a prepared oil and pigment material with exceptional penetration and filling properties.

Stops suction in plaster walls and neutralizes to a degree the free alkali in the plaster. Put up in barrels, ½ barrels, 5's, 1's, ½'s, ¼'s.

Foundation Coating

A paint product that is unexcelled in preventing seepage of water and for dampproofing of walls. Especially designed for application to walls below ground level. A perfect bond for plaster.

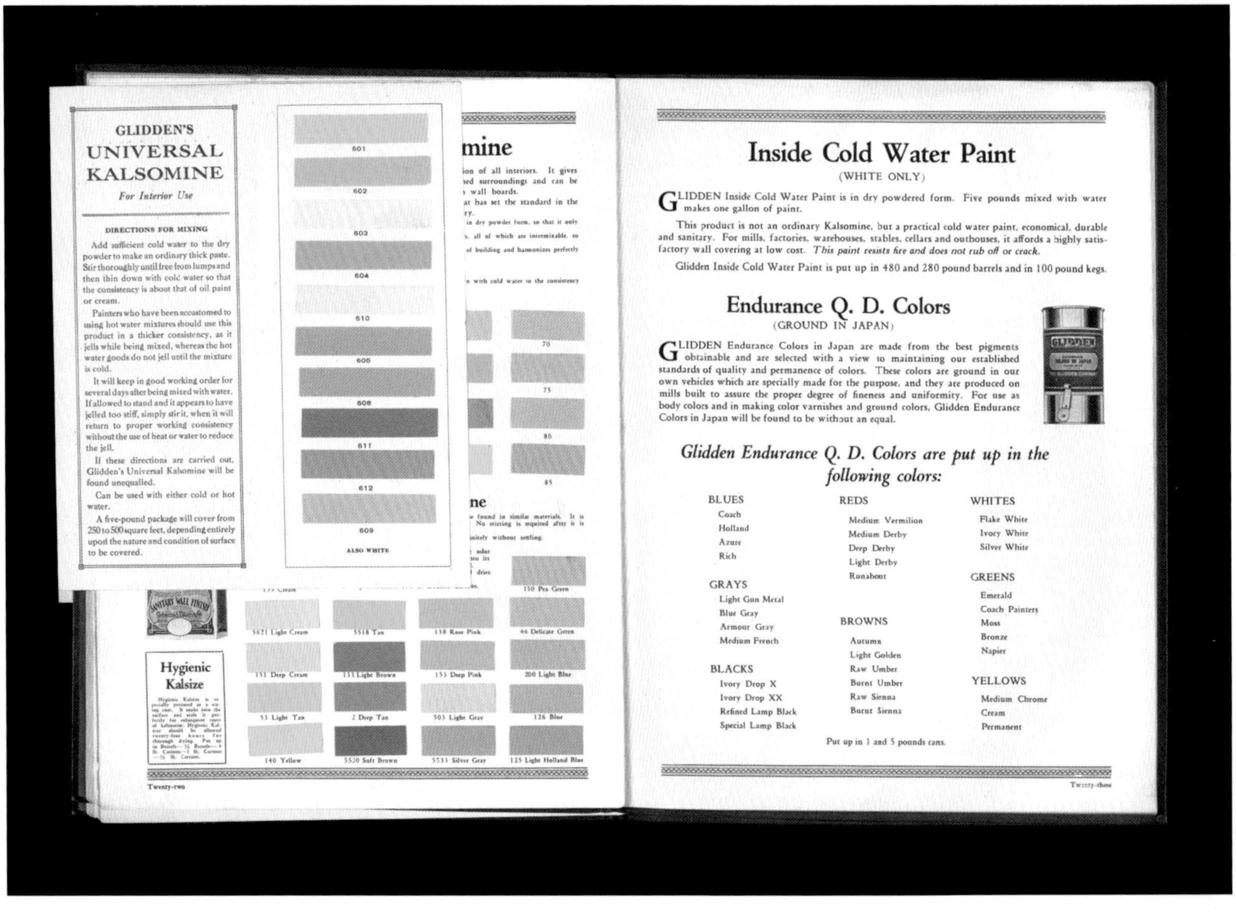

GLIDDEN'S UNIVERSAL KALSOMINE

For Interior Use

DIRECTIONS FOR MIXING

Add sufficient cold water to the dry powder to make an ordinary thick paste. Stir thoroughly until free from lumps and then thin down with cold water so that the consistency is about that of oil paint or cream.

Painters who have been accustomed to using hot water mixtures should use this product in a thicker consistency, as it jells while being mixed, whereas the hot water goods do not jell until the mixture is cold.

It will keep in good working order for several days after being mixed with water. If allowed to stand and it appears to have jelled too stiff, simply stir it, when it will return to proper working consistency without the use of heat or water to reduce the jell.

If these directions are carried out, Glidden's Universal Kalsomine will be found unequalled.

Can be used with either cold or hot water.

A five-pound package will cover from 250 to 500 square feet, depending entirely upon the nature and condition of surface to be covered.

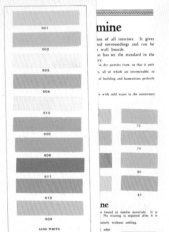

601 · 602 · 603 · 604 · 610 · 605 · 608 · 611 · 612 · 609 · ALSO WHITE · 70 · 75 · 80 · 85

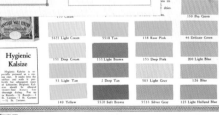

177 Chino · 150 Pea Green · 5621 Light Cream · 5518 Tan · 138 Rose Pink · 46 Delicate Green · 151 Deep Cream · 153 Light Brown · 155 Deep Pink · 200 Light Blue · 53 Light Tan · 1 Deep Tan · 503 Light Gray · 126 Blue · 140 Yellow · 5520 Soft Brown · 5533 Silver Gray · 125 Light Holland Blue

Hygienic Kalsize

Hygienic Kalsize is especially prepared as a top coat. It makes even the surface and adds to perfectly last subsequent coats of kalsomine. Hygienic Kalsize should be allowed thorough drying. Put up in Barrels—½ Barrels—5 lb. Cartons—1 lb. Cartons—½ lb. Cartons.

Inside Cold Water Paint

(WHITE ONLY)

GLIDDEN Inside Cold Water Paint is in dry powdered form. Five pounds mixed with water makes one gallon of paint.

This product is not an ordinary Kalsomine, but a practical cold water paint, economical, durable and sanitary. For mills, factories, warehouses, stables, cellars and outhouses, it affords a highly satisfactory wall covering at low cost. This paint resists fire and does not rub off or crack.

Glidden Inside Cold Water Paint is put up in 480 and 280 pound barrels and in 100 pound kegs.

Endurance Q. D. Colors

(GROUND IN JAPAN)

GLIDDEN Endurance Colors in Japan are made from the best pigments obtainable and are selected with a view to maintaining our established standards of quality and permanence of colors. These colors are ground in our own vehicles which are specially made for the purpose, and they are produced on mills built to assure the proper degree of fineness and uniformity. For use as body colors and in making color varnishes and ground colors, Glidden Endurance Colors in Japan will be found to be without an equal.

Glidden Endurance Q. D. Colors are put up in the following colors:

BLUES	REDS	WHITES
Coach	Medium Vermilion	Flake White
Holland	Medium Derby	Ivory White
Azure	Deep Derby	Silver White
Rich	Light Derby	
	Runabout	GREENS
GRAYS		Emerald
Light Gun Metal		Coach Painters
Blue Gray		Moss
Armour Gray	BROWNS	Bronze
Medium French	Autumn	Napier
	Light Golden	
BLACKS	Raw Umber	YELLOWS
Ivory Drop X	Burnt Umber	Medium Chrome
Ivory Drop XX	Raw Sienna	Cream
Refined Lamp Black	Burnt Sienna	Permanent
Special Lamp Black		

Put up in 1 and 5 pounds cans.

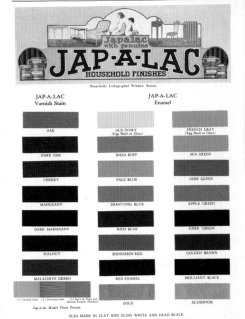

"CABOT TOWER

VARNISH PAINTS [Quick Drying]

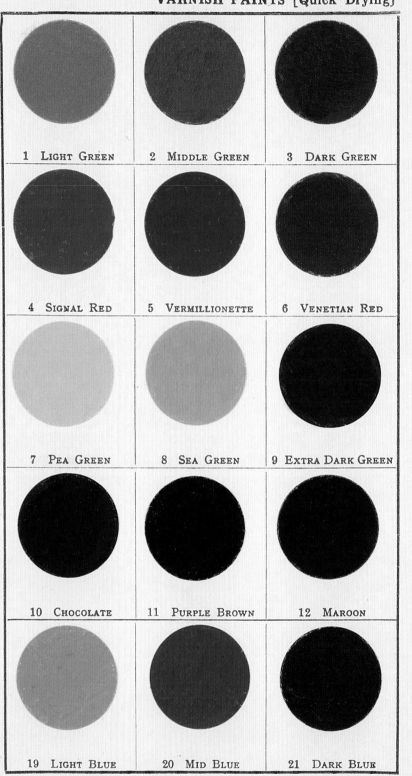

1 LIGHT GREEN	2 MIDDLE GREEN	3 DARK GREEN
4 SIGNAL RED	5 VERMILLIONETTE	6 VENETIAN RED
7 PEA GREEN	8 SEA GREEN	9 EXTRA DARK GREEN
10 CHOCOLATE	11 PURPLE BROWN	12 MAROON
19 LIGHT BLUE	20 MID BLUE	21 DARK BLUE

Supplied in 1-2-4-7 and 14 lb. (Free) Tins.

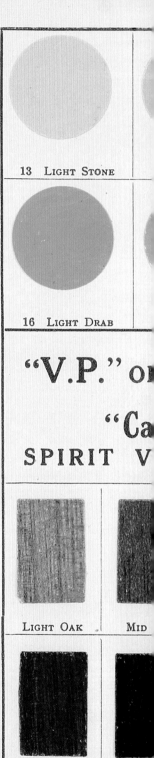

13 LIGHT STONE

16 LIGHT DRAB

"V.P." O

"Ca

SPIRIT V

LIGHT OAK   MID

MAHOGANY   ROSEW

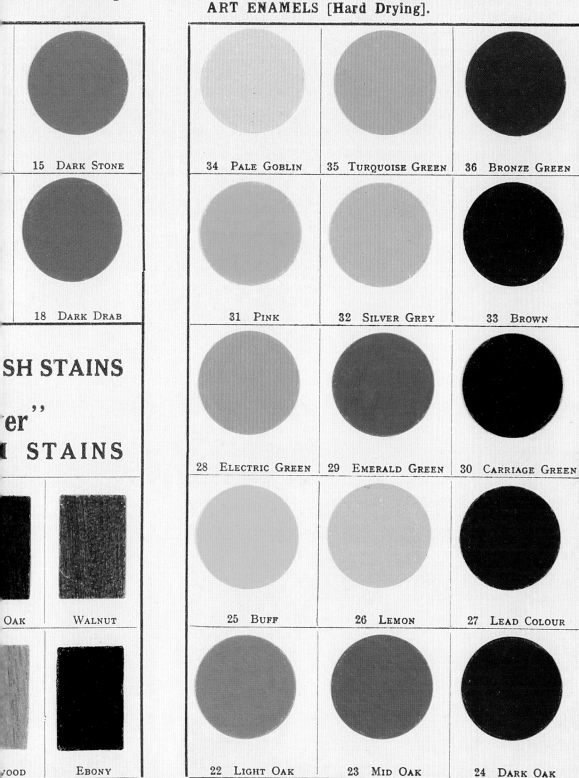

Ready Mixed Paints

ART ENAMELS [Hard Drying].

15 DARK STONE	34 PALE GOBLIN	35 TURQUOISE GREEN	36 BRONZE GREEN
18 DARK DRAB	31 PINK	32 SILVER GREY	33 BROWN

SH STAINS

''er''

STAINS

	28 ELECTRIC GREEN	29 EMERALD GREEN	30 CARRIAGE GREEN
OAK	WALNUT	25 BUFF	26 LEMON	27 LEAD COLOUR
OOD	EBONY	22 LIGHT OAK	23 MID OAK	24 DARK OAK

Also in BLACK, WHITE, CREAM and RED OXIDE.

In 1907 one of the most prolific British authors on painting and decorating, Arthur Seymour Jennings, wrote in *Paint and Colour Mixing*: 'If half-a-dozen practical painters, experienced in colour mixing, were asked separately to mix a given colour, say a sea green, it is almost certain that when the six colours were compared there would not be two alike...' The explanation is that opinions differ as to what is a 'sea green'. In the early twentieth century, the requirement for a system to arrange and standardize colours sparked much interest. This section describes the most influential colour standards and systems published, from *Répertoire de couleurs* (1905) designed originally to more accurately determine the colour of chrysanthemums, to *The Horticultural Colour Chart* (1939–42), which gave equivalent colour references to four other colour systems in use.

[OPPOSITE] Pages from Elizabeth Burris-Meyer's *Historical Color Guide* (1938).

PERSIAN MINIATURE

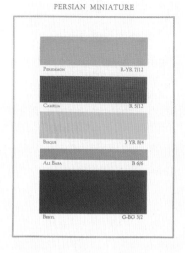

Persimmon	R-YR 7/12
Camelia	R 5/12
Bisque	3 YR 8/4
Ali Baba	B 6/6
Beryl	G-BG 3/2

RUSSIAN

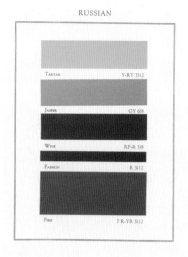

Tartar	Y-RY 7/12
Jasper	GY 6/8
Wine	RP-R 3/8
Passion	R 3/12
Fire	7 R-YR 5/12

SWEDISH

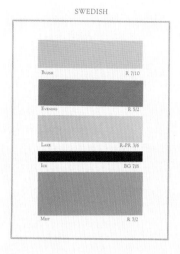

Blush	R 7/10
Evening	R 5/2
Lake	R-PR 3/6
Ice	BG 7/8
Mist	R 7/2

PERUVIAN

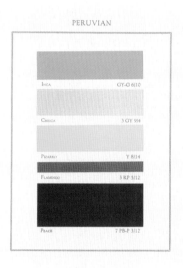

Inca	GY-G 6/10
Chilca	3 GY 9/4
Pizarro	Y 8/14
Flamingo	3 RP 5/12
Peace	7 PB-P 3/12

VAN GOGH

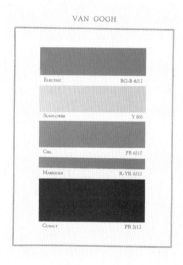

Electric	BG-B 6/12
Sunflower	Y 8/6
Ciel	PB 6/10
Marigold	R-YR 6/10
Cobalt	PB 3/12

GAUGUIN

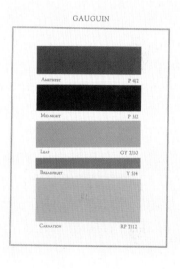

Amethyst	P 4/2
Mid-night	P 3/2
Leaf	GY 7/10
Breadfruit	Y 5/4
Carnation	RP 7/12

MEXICAN

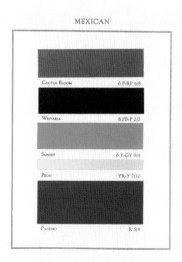

Cactus Bloom	6 P-RP 6/8
Wistaria	8 PB-P 2/2
Sunset	6 Y-GY 9/4
Peon	YR-Y 7/10
Pancho	R 5/4

PERSIAN FRESCO

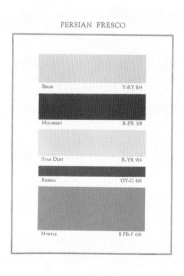

Brier	Y-RY 8/4
Mulberry	R-PR 3/8
Star Dust	R-YR 9/4
Reseda	GY-G 4/6
Myrtle	8 PB-P 6/6

CHINESE, SUNG

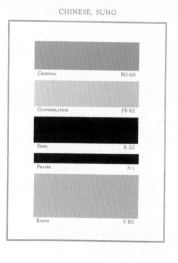

Celestial	BG 6/6
Contemplation	PB 9/2
Sung	R 2/2
Prayer	N 1
Earth	Y 8/2

RÉPERTOIRE DE COULEURS –
SOCIÉTÉ FRANÇAISE DES CHRYSANTHÉMISTES

The chrysanthemum was first brought to Europe in the seventeenth century. Linnaeus named it from the Greek words *chrysous*, meaning 'golden' (the colour of the original flowers), and *anthemon*, meaning 'flower'.

It was not until the beginning of the nineteenth century that the blooms were cultivated in France. In the 1860s, horticulturalists introduced new varieties of the chrysanthemum, namely the pompon variety, which became especially popular in that country. By the turn of the twentieth century, the assortment of chrysanthemum colours had become so extensive that the Société française des chrysanthémistes published *Répertoire de couleurs* (1905), which then came to be used as a colour catalogue in many other fields.

The full title of the work was the *Répertoire de couleurs pour aider à la détermination des couleurs des fleurs, des feuillages et des fruits* (Colour directory to assist in the determination of colours of flowers, foliage and fruit) and it was primarily the work of René Oberthür, with the help of Henri Dauthenay and also Julien Mouillefert, C. Harman Payne, Max Leichtlin

and N. Severi. It was published in two volumes comprising 365 plates and explanatory text. The colours were selected particularly in connection with the colours of fruit, flowers and foliage. The names of each were given in English, German, Spanish and Italian.

Four shades were provided for each colour, together with a brief description of where each one could be seen. For example, under Rose Nilsson it was noted, among other things, that Tones 1 and 4 were the colours of the single petals from the adult flower of the 'Belle Siebrecht' rose rather than the internal reflections seen within the flower itself. Tone 3 resembles the *Pelargonium* 'Constance' and Tone 2 is the colour of the reverse of the petals at the centre of the 'La France' rose. Pourpre de Tyr (see p. 230), known as Tyrian, imperial, or royal purple, is an expensive pigment made from the shells of sea snails *Bolinus brandaris*.

[A] Cover of *Réptertoire de couleurs* (1905). [B] French line infantry drummer by François Hippolyte Lalaisse. The washed-out colour of old infantry trousers was described as Rouge Garance passé.

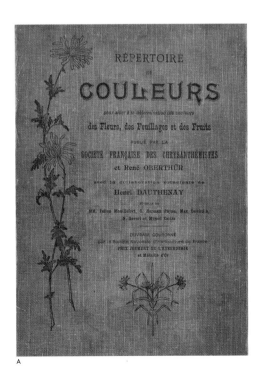

A

B

Rouge Garance passé

Origine : Nuance des pantalons rouges de l'Infanterie de ligne française en cours d'usage.

Synonymes français : néant.

1

2

3

4

Synonymes étrangers :

All. : Trüb Krapprot. Verbleicht Krapplack.
Angl. : Dull Madder red.
Esp. : Rojo Garange pasado.
Ital. : Rosso Robbia appasita.

Remarques :

Tons 1 et 2 : Nuances observées sur fleurs du *Sophronitis grandiflora*.

Tons 1 à 4 : Tonalité générale du Chrysanthème *Gloire Poitevine*, la vue tombant verticalement ou à peu près, sur le capitule entièrement développé.

Rouge Sang-Dragon

Origine : Couleur de la résine provenant d'incisions faites au Dragonnier (*Dracæna Draco*).

Synonymes français : néant.

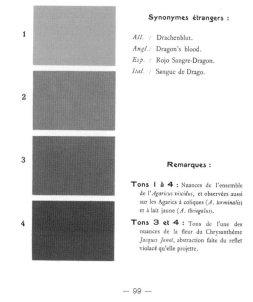

1

2

3

4

Synonymes étrangers :

All. : Drachenblut.
Angl. : Dragon's blood.
Esp. : Rojo Sangre-Dragon.
Ital. : Sangue de Drago.

Remarques :

Tons 1 à 4 : Nuances de l'ensemble de l'*Agaricus viscidus*, et observées aussi sur les Agarics à coliques (*A. torminalis*) et à lait jaune (*A. theiogalus*).

Tons 3 et 4 : Tons de l'une des nuances de la fleur du Chrysanthème *Jacques Janot*, abstraction faite du reflet violacé qu'elle projette.

Rouge Étrusque

Origine : Nuance souvent observée sur les poteries d'origine étrusque.

Synonymes français : Vieux-rouge.

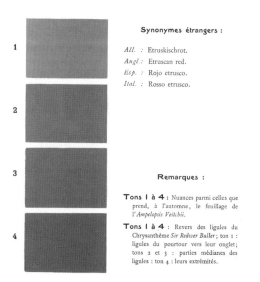

1

2

3

4

Synonymes étrangers :

All. : Etruskischrot.
Angl. : Etruscan red.
Esp. : Rojo etrusco.
Ital. : Rosso etrusco.

Remarques :

Tons 1 à 4 : Nuances parmi celles que prend, à l'automne, le feuillage de l'*Ampelopsis Veitchii*.

Tons 1 à 4 : Revers des ligules du Chrysanthème *Sir Redwer Buller* ; ton 1 : ligules du pourtour vers leur onglet ; tons 2 et 3 : parties médianes des ligules : ton 4 : leurs extrémités.

Carmin de Cochenille

Origine : Le modèle de cette planche a été obtenu par le délayage de la poudre de Carmin de Cochenille. En traitant ce produit par différents procédés, on obtient le Carmin fin, le Carmin extra, la Laque carminée et le Rouge Cardinal. — Il se fabrique aujourd'hui un Carmin d'Alizarine.

Synonymes français : Rouge de Perse (Lor.). Laque rose extra (Bourg.). Carmin fin. — Analogue : Laque carminée rose (Bourg.).

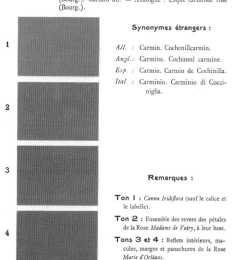

1

2

3

4

Synonymes étrangers :

All. : Carmin. Cochenillcarmin.
Angl. : Carmine. Cochineal carmine.
Esp. : Carmin. Carmin de Cochinilla.
Ital. : Carminio. Carminio di Cocciniglia.

Remarques :

Ton 1 : *Canna Iridiflora* (sauf le calice et le labelle).

Ton 2 : Ensemble des revers des pétales de la Rose *Madame de Vatry*, à leur base.

Tons 3 et 4 : Reflets intérieurs, macules, marges et panachures de la Rose *Marie d'Orléans*.

Blanc Ambré, Ambre

Origine : Couleur de l'Ambre travaillé du commerce.

Synonymes français : Blanc Succin.

Synonymes étrangers :

All. : Ambraweiss. Bernsteinweiss.
Angl. : Amber white. Succinum.
Esp. : Blanco de Ambar, B. de Sucino. B. de Carabe.
Ital. : Bianco di Ambra, B. di Succino.

Remarques :

Tons 1 et 2 : Revers des jeunes ligules (1) et reflets du cœur (2) du Chrysanthème Mlle Lucie Faure.

Tons 3 et 4 : Centre des capitules du Chrysanthème *Comte Tornielli* (sans en considérer la panachure vieux rose, plus ou moins accentuée).

Ton 4 : Quelques ligules centrales dans le Chrysanthème *J. B. Galland*.

— 12 —

Jaune d'Auréoline

Origine : Nom d'une matière colorante obtenue par un mélange d'hypochlorite de soude et de fluorescéine, précipité par un acide ; remplacée aujourd'hui par un Jaune de Cobalt. — Reproduction du *Flavus* du professeur Saccardo.

Synonymes français : Jaune auréolin. Jaune d'Or. Jaune Bouton d'or. Jaune de Cobalt.

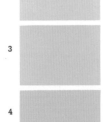

Synonymes étrangers :

All. : Aureolingelb. Butter-blume gelb.
Angl. : Aureoline yellow. Butter-cup yellow.
Esp. : Amarillo de Aureolina. A. de Francesilla.
Ital. : Giallo d'Aureolina. G. Ranuncolo.

Remarques :

Tons 1 à 4 : Couleur d'ensemble du Chrysanthème *Phœbus* ; ton 4 : reflets du cœur.

Ton 3 : Reflets dans le cœur du Chrysanthème *Congrès de Bordeaux* lorsque la fleur n'est ouverte que depuis peu. (Cette variété est jaune de Chrome citron).

— 22 —

Jaune de Chrome citron

Origine : Désignation commerciale de cette couleur (Bourgeois). Correspond au Jaune de Chrome n° 3 de Lorilleux.

Synonymes français : Jaune clair (Le Ripolin). Jaune d'or des horticulteurs (impropre).

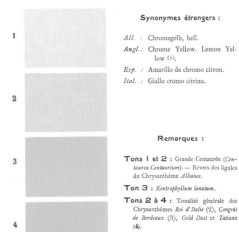

Synonymes étrangers :

All. : Chromegelb, hell.
Angl. : Chrome Yellow. Lemon Yellow [1].
Esp. : Amarillo de chromo citron.
Ital. : Giallo cromo citrino.

Remarques :

Tons 1 et 2 : Grande Centaurée (*Centaurea Centaurium*). — Revers des ligules du Chrysanthème *Alliance*.

Ton 3 : *Kentrophyllum lanatum*.

Tons 2 à 4 : Tonalité générale des Chrysanthèmes *Roi d'Italie* (2), *Congrès de Bordeaux* (3), *Gold Dust* et *Tatiana* (4).

[1] W. B. Warhurst, *A Col. Dict.*

— 20 —

Jaune indien

Origine : Dénomination commerciale de cette couleur. Le Jaune indien vrai vient du Bengale. Il est le produit de la fermentation de l'urine de vache avec des feuilles de Mangoustan (*Garcinia Mangostana*). L'industriel est obtenu par un mélange de dérivés nitrés, ou par une solution d'acide euxanthique, sulfate de magnésie, alun et sel ammoniac.

Synonymes français : Jaune indien vrai : Purrey, Pioury. — Jaune indien industriel : Jaune azo, Azoflavine, Jaune nouveau, Curcumine.

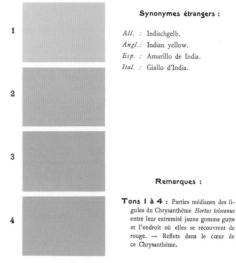

Synonymes étrangers :

All. : Indischgelb.
Angl. : Indian yellow.
Esp. : Amarillo de India.
Ital. : Giallo d'India.

Remarques :

Tons 1 à 4 : Parties médianes des ligules du Chrysanthème *Hortus tolosanus* entre leur extremité jaune gomme gutte et l'endroit où elles se recouvrent de rouge. — Reflets dans le cœur de ce Chrysanthème.

— 27 —

Pierre-de-Fiel

Origine : Dénomination de cette couleur (Bourg.) fabriquée avec les pierres ou calculs qu'on trouve dans les fiels du bœuf.

Synonymes français : Jaune de fiel.

1

2

3

4

Synonymes étrangers :

All. : Gallstein.
Angl. : Gallstone or reddish chrome.
Esp. : Amarillo de fiel.
Ital. : Giallo fiele.

Remarques :

Tons 1 et 2 : Couleur d'ensemble des fleurs, complètement épanouies, de la Giroflée (*Cheirantus Cheiri*) *jaune d'or naine hâtive.*

Tons 1 à 4 : Coloration observée sur les sépales d'un exemplaire du *Lælio-Cattleya Cappei.*

Tons 2 à 4 : Coloration observée sur les sépales d'un hybride *Lælia cinnabarina glauca.*

— 51 —

Jaune du Japon

Origine : Désignation commerciale de cette couleur (Bourgeois).

Synonymes français : Jaune Grenadine.

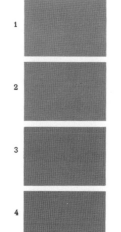

1

2

3

4

Synonymes étrangers :

All. : Japonischgelb.
Angl. : Japanese yellow.
Esp. : Amarillo del Japon.
Ital. : Giallo del Giappone.

Remarques :

Tons 1 à 4 : Tons d'une nuance très fréquente sur les fleurs de plusieurs espèces et variétés d'Œillets d'Inde (*Tagetes patula, T. signata*) et de Rose d'Inde (*Tagetes erecta*).

Tons 3 et 4 : Tige florale, avec ses bractées colorées, du *Calathea crocata.*

Ton 4 : Coloration observée sur les pétales latéraux d'un hybride *Lælia cinnabarina glauca.*

— 52 —

Abricot

Origine : Ensemble des nuances les plus fréquentes de l'épiderme de l'Abricot.

Synonymes français : Jaune de Chrome foncé (tons clairs, Bourg.).

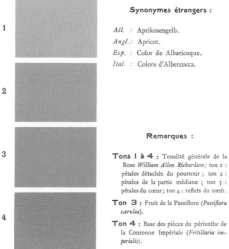

1

2

3

4

Synonymes étrangers :

All. : Aprikosengelb.
Angl. : Apricot.
Esp. : Color de Albaricoque.
Ital. : Colore d'Albercocca.

Remarques :

Tons 1 à 4 : Tonalité générale de la Rose *William Allen Richardson*; ton 1 : pétales détachés du pourtour ; ton 2 : pétales de la partie médiane ; ton 3 : pétales du cœur ; ton 4 : reflets du cœur.

Ton 3 : Fruit de la Passiflore (*Passiflora cærulea*).

Ton 4 : Base des pièces du périanthe de la Couronne Impériale (*Fritillaria imperialis*).

— 53 —

Rouge Carotte

Origine : Nuances de la Carotte adulte et épluchée fraîche.

Synonymes français : Laque Capucine (Bourg.).

1

2

3

4

Synonymes étrangers :

All. : Gelbrübenfarbig.
Angl. : Carrot red. Capucine lake.
Esp. : Rojo de Zanahoria.
Ital. : Rosso di Carota.

Tons 1 à 4 : Les diverses nuances de l'extérieur des fleurs du *Tritoma Uvaria* (*Kniphophia aloides*), après qu'elles viennent de s'ouvrir.

Tons 3 et 4 : La plus vive des diverses nuances observées sur la fleur de la Couronne Impériale (*Fritillaria imperialis*), notamment sur la nervure centrale des pièces du périanthe.

— 55 —

Pourpre de Tyr

Origine : Désignation commerciale de cette couleur, qui rappelle la plus belle nuance des étoffes pourpres sorties des teintureries de Tyr et de Sydon, dans l'antiquité.

Synonymes français : Rouge de Tyr. Rose de Tyr.

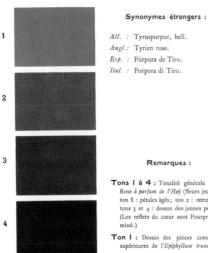

Synonymes étrangers :

All. : Tyruspurpur, hell.
Angl. : Tyrian rose.
Esp. : Púrpura de Tiro.
Ital. : Porpora di Tiro.

Remarques :

Tons 1 à 4 : Tonalité générale de la Rose à parfum de l'Haÿ (fleurs jeunes); ton 1 : pétales âgés; ton 2 : retroussis; tons 3 et 4 : dessus des jeunes pétales. (Les reflets du cœur sont Pourpre carminé.)

Ton 1 : Dessus des pièces corollaires supérieures de l'*Epiphyllum truncatum*.

Pourpre

Origine : Reproduction du *Purpureus* du professeur Saccardo. — Les Anciens tiraient leur Pourpre de plusieurs mollusques (*Murex brandaris, M. trunculus ; Purpura hemostoma, P. Papillus*, etc.) — La teinturerie moderne emploie aujourd'hui un Pourpre tiré des dérivés de la Houille et dit Pourpre de Hesse.

Synonymes français : Laque Amarante (Lorilleux); Laque de Garance pourpre (Bourgeois).

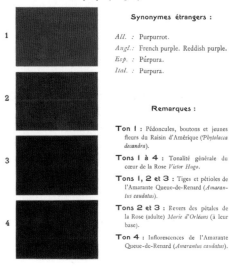

Synonymes étrangers :

All. : Purpurrot.
Angl. : French purple. Reddish purple.
Esp. : Púrpura.
Ital. : Purpura.

Remarques :

Ton 1 : Pédoncules, boutons et jeunes fleurs du Raisin d'Amérique (*Phytolacca decandra*).

Tons 1 à 4 : Tonalité générale du cœur de la Rose *Victor Hugo*.

Tons 1, 2 et 3 : Tiges et pétioles de l'Amarante Queue-de-Renard (*Amarantus caudatus*).

Tons 2 et 3 : Revers des pétales de la Rose (adulte) *Marie d'Orléans* (à leur base).

Ton 4 : Inflorescences de l'Amarante Queue-de-Renard (*Amarantus caudatus*).

Lie-de-Vin

Origine : Couleur la plus ordinaire de la lie du vin. — Reproduction du *Vinosus* du professeur Saccardo.

Synonymes français : néant.

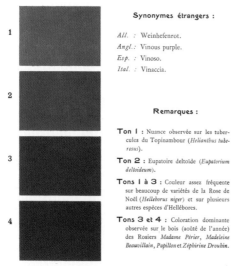

Synonymes étrangers :

All. : Weinhefenrot.
Angl. : Vinous purple.
Esp. : Vinoso.
Ital. : Vinaccia.

Remarques :

Ton 1 : Nuance observée sur les tubercules du Topinambour (*Helianthus tuberosus*).

Ton 2 : Eupatoire deltoïde (*Eupatorium deltoideum*).

Tons 1 à 3 : Couleur assez fréquente sur beaucoup de variétés de la Rose de Noël (*Helleborus niger*) et sur plusieurs autres espèces d'Hellébores.

Tons 3 et 4 : Coloration dominante observée sur le bois (août de l'année) des Rosiers *Madame Périer, Madeleine Beauvillain, Papillon* et *Zéphirine Drouhin*.

Mauve (vrai)

Origine : Couleur des fleurs de la Mauve la plus commune : *Malva rotundifolia* (tons 1 et 2).

Synonymes français : néant.

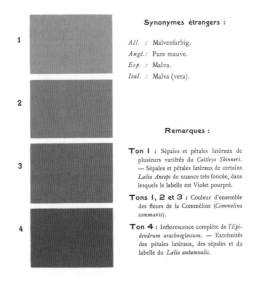

Synonymes étrangers :

All. : Malvenfarbig.
Angl. : Pure mauve.
Esp. : Malva.
Ital. : Malva (vera).

Remarques :

Ton 1 : Sépales et pétales latéraux de plusieurs variétés du *Cattleya Skinneri*. — Sépales et pétales latéraux de certains *Lælia Anceps* de nuance très foncée, dans lesquels le labelle est Violet pourpré.

Tons 1, 2 et 3 : Couleur d'ensemble des fleurs de la Comméline (*Commelina communis*).

Ton 4 : Inflorescence complète de l'*Epidendrum arachnoglossum*. — Extrémités des pétales latéraux, des sépales et du labelle du *Lælia autumnalis*.

Violet Évêque

Origine : Désignation de cette couleur dans le commerce des laines, soieries et étoffes. — Reproduction lithographique du Violet clair extra de Bourgeois. — Allusion à la couleur usitée dans le vêtement des évêques.

Synonymes français : Magenta (n° 2, Friant).

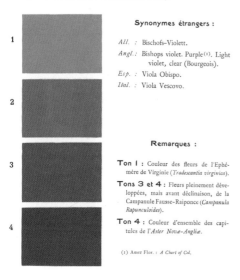

1
2
3
4

Synonymes étrangers :

All. : Bischofs-Violett.

Angl. : Bishops violet. Purple[1]. Light violet, clear (Bourgeois).

Esp. : Viola Obispo.

Ital. : Viola Vescovo.

Remarques :

Ton 1 : Couleur des fleurs de l'Ephémère de Virginie (*Tradescantia virginica*).

Tons 3 et 4 : Fleurs pleinement développées, mais avant déclinaison, de la Campanule Fausse-Raiponce (*Campanula Rapunculoides*).

Ton 4 : Couleur d'ensemble des capitules de l'*Aster Novæ-Angliæ*.

(1) Amer Flor. : *A Chart of Col.*

— 189 —

Violet Pétunia

Origine : Couleur se rencontrant assez souvent sur les fleurs des Pétunias cultivés.

Synonymes français : Violet clair extra (Bourgeois, tons foncés).

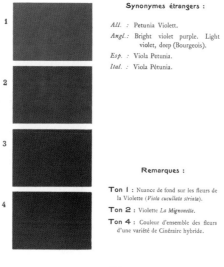

1
2
3
4

Synonymes étrangers :

All. : Petunia Violett.

Angl. : Bright violet purple. Light violet, deep (Bourgeois).

Esp. : Viola Petunia.

Ital. : Viola Pétunia.

Remarques :

Ton 1 : Nuance de fond sur les fleurs de la Violette (*Viola cucullata striata*).

Ton 2 : Violette *La Mignonette*.

Ton 4 : Couleur d'ensemble des fleurs d'une variété de Cinéraire hybride.

— 190 —

Violet Pensée

Origine : Tons se rencontrant fréquemment sur les fleurs de la Pensée (*Viola tricolor hortensis*).

Synonymes français : Violet solide (Nos 52 et 57, Lefranc).

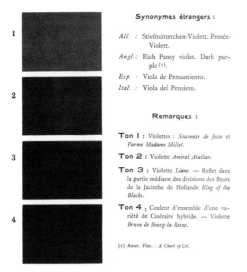

1
2
3
4

Synonymes étrangers :

All. : Stiefmütterchen-Violett. Pensée-Violett.

Angl. : Rich Pansy violet. Dark purple[1].

Esp. : Viola de Pensamiento.

Ital. : Viola del Pensiero.

Remarques :

Ton 1 : Violettes : *Souvenir de Josse* et *Parme Madame Millet*.

Ton 2 : Violette *Amiral Avellan*.

Ton 3 : Violette *Liane*. — Reflet dans la partie médiane des divisions des fleurs de la Jacinthe de Hollande *King of the Blacks*.

Ton 4 : Couleur d'ensemble d'une variété de Cinéraire hybride. — Violette *Brune de Bourg-la-Reine*.

(1) Amer. Flor. : *A Chart of Col.*

— 191 —

Violet de Violette

Origine : Couleur de la Violette odorante (*Viola odorata*) dite " de Paris ".

Synonymes français : néant.

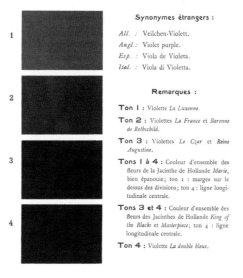

1
2
3
4

Synonymes étrangers :

All. : Veilchen-Violett.

Angl. : Violet purple.

Esp. : Viola de Violeta.

Ital. : Viola di Violetta.

Remarques :

Ton 1 : Violette *La Luxonne*.

Ton 2 : Violettes *La France* et *Baronne de Rothschild*.

Ton 3 : Violettes *Le Czar* et *Reine Augustine*.

Tons 1 à 4 : Couleur d'ensemble des fleurs de la Jacinthe de Hollande *Marie*, bien épanouie ; ton 1 : marges sur le dessus des divisions ; ton 4 : ligne longitudinale centrale.

Tons 3 et 4 : Couleur d'ensemble des fleurs des Jacinthes de Hollande *King of the Blacks* et *Masterpiece* ; ton 4 : ligne longitudinale centrale.

Ton 4 : Violette *La double bleue*.

— 192 —

THE MUNSELL COLOUR SYSTEM

Albert H. Munsell was an artist and professor of art at the Massachusetts Normal Art School, now known as the Massachusetts College of Art and Design. He felt that the use of vague colour names was both 'foolish' and 'misleading' and wanted to create an accurate rational way to describe colour that he could teach to his students. He first started work on his colour system in 1898 and published it in full form as *A Color Notation* in 1905.

Munsell began his book with a lengthy quotation from Robert Louis Stevenson that perfectly summed up the kind of dilemma that anyone working with colour might still encounter. Writing from Samoa on 8 October 1892, to Sidney Colvin in London, Stevenson proposed:

> Perhaps in the same way it might amuse you to send us any pattern of wall paper that might strike you as cheap, pretty and suitable for a room in a hot and extremely bright climate. It should be borne in mind that our climate can be extremely dark, too. Our sitting room is to be varnished in wood. The room I have particularly in mind is a sort of bed and sitting room, pretty large, lit on three sides, and the colour in favour of its proprietor at present is a topazy yellow. But then with what colour to relieve it? For a little work-room of my own at the back, I should rather like to see some patterns of unglossy – well, I'll be hanged if I can describe this red – it's not Turkish and it's not Roman and it's not Indian, but it seems to partake of the two last, and yet it can't be either of them because it ought to be able to go with vermilion. Ah what a tangled web we weave – anyway, with what brains you have left, choose me and send me some – many – patterns of this exact shade.

In normal everyday usage, there still exists the problem of one man's garnet being another man's burgundy, and what exactly is meant by navy blue? However, with the introduction of a widely recognized system of colour notation, it was possible to convey a precise colour description without both parties being able to see the object concerned.

Munsell devised a system that gave each colour three attributes: hue, value and chroma. These three represent the colour family, the lightness or darkness and the colour strength.

HUE

The term 'hue' refers to the attribute that distinguishes one family of colours from another, for example, whether an object is red or green or yellow or blue. Munsell called red, yellow, green, blue and purple the 'principal hues' and placed them at equal intervals around the hue circle. He then inserted five intermediate hues between them: yellow-red, green-yellow, blue-green, purple-blue and red-purple, making ten hues altogether. For simplicity, he used the initials as symbols to designate the ten hue families: R, YR, Y, GY, G, BG, B, PB, P and RP.

Each of these ten hue families was further subdivided into ten more hue families, with the number '5' designating the centre or the most 'true' representation of that hue family and the number '10' designating the hue family that is halfway between two adjacent 'true' hues. This gave one hundred hues in total, although in practice, Munsell colour charts conventionally specified forty hues, in increments of 2.5, progressing as for example 10YR to 2.5GY to 5GY.

VALUE

Value is the quality that distinguishes a light colour from a dark one. Colour values are the same as tints or shades, with tints referring to a light colour. To a painter, a tint is a colour that is mixed with white paint. A shade indicates a dark colour, or any colour that is mixed with black.

The lightness of a colour depends on the amount of light that is reflected from the surface. The lightest colour is white and it reflects most of the light hitting it. The darkest colour is black and no light is reflected. Grey is seen when some of the light is reflected and some absorbed.

A neutral grey scale can be constructed that shows visually equal steps between black and white. These neutral colours, which have no hue, are designated in Munsell notation by an N followed by a whole number and a slash, as in N 2/. Absolute black is written as N 0/ and absolute white as N 10/, although neither of these are technically possible. Colours that have a hue are called 'chromatic colours'.

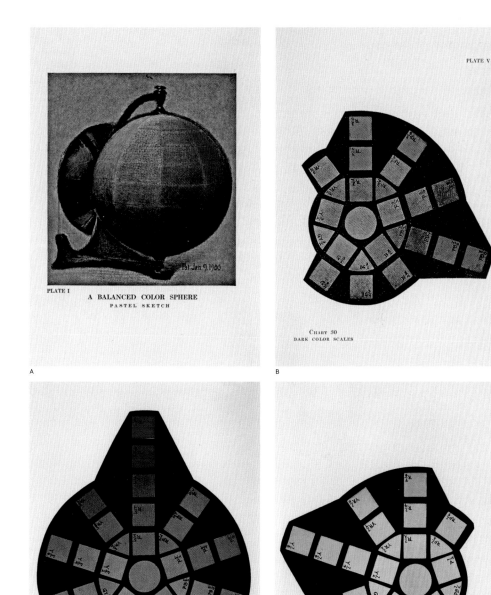

A

B

C

D

Images from *A Color Notation* (1905; this edition, 1911) by Albert H. Munsell,: [A] 'Since the three dimensions of color must be as readily understood as the three dimensions of a box, it is necessary to have in mind some simple, orderly arrangement of all colors, in which HUE, VALUE, and CHROMA are separately identified and yet comprehended together. A sphere serves this purpose.' [B] Chart 30: Dark Color Scales. A horizontal section through the colour solid. All its colours reflect 30 per cent of the incident light. [C] Chart 50: Middle Color Scales. Its colours reflect 50 per cent of the incident light. [D] Light Color Scales, reflecting 70 per cent of the incident light.

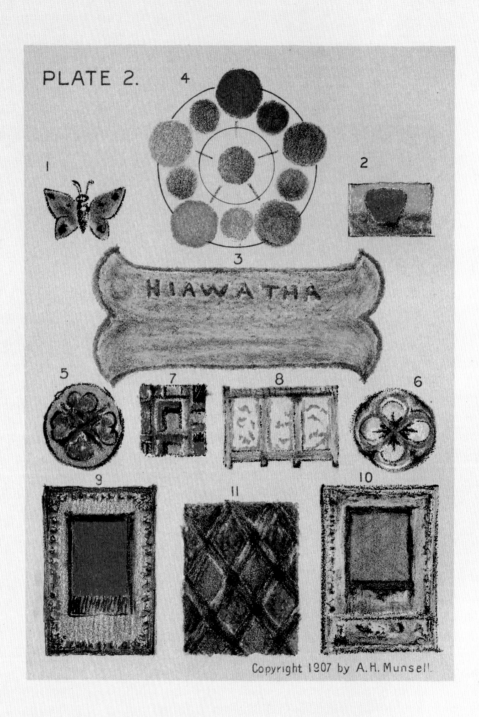

Plates from *A Color Notation* (1905), Albert. H. Munsell. Plate 2: 'Color Studies with TUNED CRAYONS in the Lower Grades. Children have made every example on this plate, with no other material than the five crayons of middle hue, tempered with gray and black. A color sphere is always kept in the room for reference, and five color balls to match the five middle hues are placed in the hands of the youngest pupils. Starting with these middle points in the scales of Value and Chroma, they learn to estimate rightly all lighter and darker values, all weaker and stronger chromas, and gradually build up a disciplined judgment of color.'

Plate 3: 'Color Studies with TUNED WATER COLORS in the Upper Grades. Previous work with measured scales, made by the tuned crayons and tested by reference to the color sphere, have so trained the color judgment that children may now be trusted with more flexible material. They have memorized the equable degrees of color on the equator of the sphere, and found how lighter colors may balance darker colors, how small areas of stronger chroma may be balanced by larger masses of weaker chroma, and in general gained a disciplined color sense. Definite impressions and clear thinking have taken the place of guess-work and blundering.'

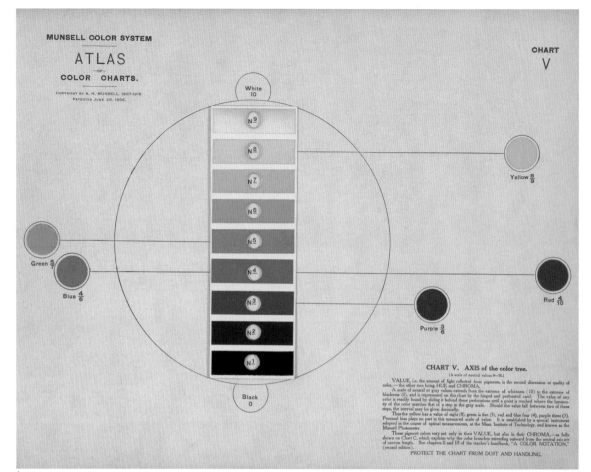

A

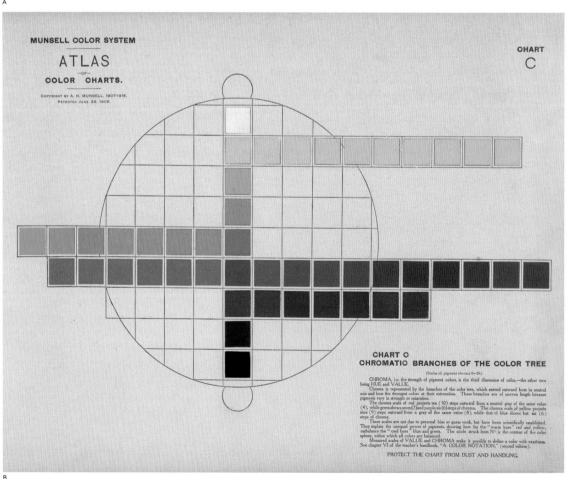

B

CHROMA

The third attribute is chroma. This is the strength of the colour. It is the means by which a strong colour is distinguished from a dull one. Neutralized or greyish colours display a weak (low) chroma, whereas intense colours show a strong (high) chroma. The result of this unevenness is that a three-dimensional solid representation of the Munsell system is highly asymmetrical. It is not a sphere.

While hue and value scales have a definite beginning and end, chroma scales vary. For example, it is possible to create more perceptually equal steps between grey and red, than between grey and blue-green. As new pigments have become available, Munsell colour chips of higher chroma have been made for many hues and values. The chroma scale for normal reflecting materials extends beyond /20 in some cases.

MUNSELL NOTATION

The Munsell notation of a colour is written in the form of the hue number and letter designation followed by the value number placed over the chroma number in the form of a fraction. As an example 5R 5/18 is the 5R red, value 5, chroma 18. This is a 'pure' red, which is medium dark and very strong.

The notation of neutral grey colours is slightly different and the values are designated on the neutral axis by writing them N. Theoretical black is defined as N0, while in actual paint N1 is a more realistic notation for black. Pure white is N10, with N5 denoting a middle grey.

The key advantage with a system of notation like this is that not only are numbers infinitely divisible, making it possible to account for small variations in hue, but also the system is extendable. As new pigments are introduced, the number of colour samples can be increased.

THE COLOUR SOLID

As each colour has three dimensions, an arrangement of all colours takes a three-dimensional form. Initially, Munsell thought that the colour solid would be a perfect sphere, but experiments demonstrated that not all hue families contain the same number of colours. For example, an intense yellow is a light colour with a large number of uniform steps between it and grey, but the purest purple is a dark colour with fewer steps between it and grey.

The Munsell colour solid is therefore an irregular solid. Hue, measured by degrees around horizontal circles; value, measured vertically from 0 (black) at the base to 10 (white) at the top; and chroma, measured radially outward from the neutral (grey) vertical axis. Munsell determined the spacing of colours along each of these dimensions by taking measurements of human visual responses. In each dimension, Munsell colours are as close to being perceptually uniform as he could make them, which makes the resulting solid quite irregular. As Munsell explained:

> Desire to fit a chosen contour, such as the pyramid, cone, cylinder or cube, coupled with a lack of proper tests, has led to many distorted statements of color relations, and it becomes evident, when physical measurement of pigment values and chromas is studied, that no regular contour will serve.

The Munsell colour solid has been described as resembling a deformed grapefruit. Until the appearance of the Ministry of Education's *Building Bulletin No. 9* in 1953, the Munsell colour system was little known in the United Kingdom. However, it was in this publication that the forty-seven colours that came to be known as the Archrome (Munsell) range were seen for the first time (see pp. 296 and 318).

Although little used in the decorative field, the Munsell colour system is employed to measure a wide variety of surfaces and it also features strongly in the sciences, including archaeology, botany, environmental studies, geology and soil science.

[A] Value is shown in Chart V. The scale of neutral values extends from white (10) to black (0). In this chart the value of a colour can be found by sliding it underneath the grey scale and noting which matches its depth. Should the value fall between two steps the interval may be given decimally.
[B] Chroma is the strength of a colour. It extends outwards from the neutral axis and each colour is of uneven length because some are brighter than others – light yellow colours, for example, have more chroma than light purples. This is an early chart and the range has been widened with the introduction of new pigments.

MUNSELL COLOR SYSTEM

ATLAS
—OF—
COLOR CHARTS.

COPYRIGHT BY A. H. MUNSELL. 1907-1915.
PATENTED JUNE 26, 1906.

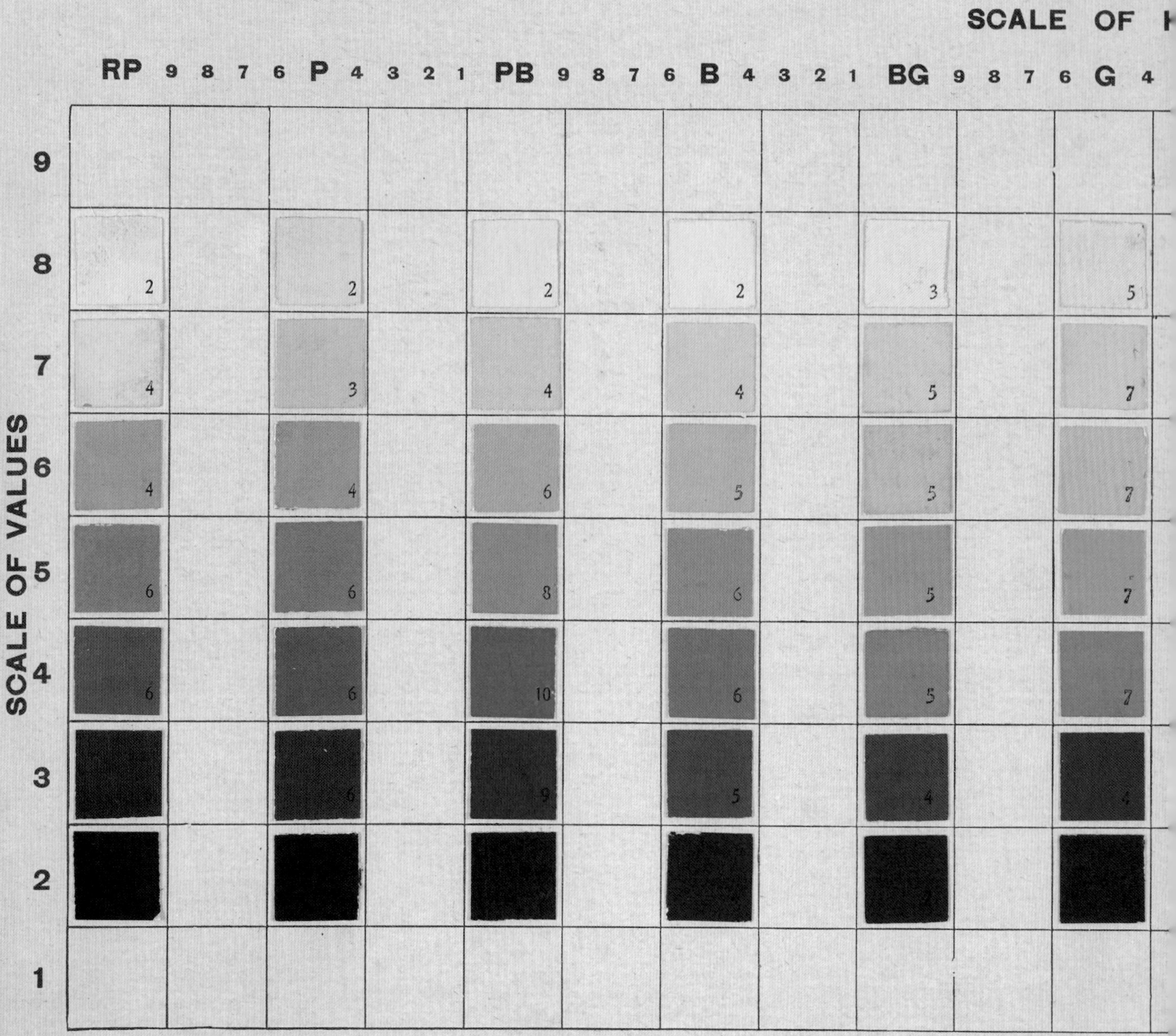
SCALE OF
RP 9 8 7 6 P 4 3 2 1 PB 9 8 7 6 B 4 3 2 1 BG 9 8 7 6 G 4
SCALE OF VALUES
9
8
7
6
5
4
3
2
1
2 2 2 2 3 5
4 3 4 4 5 7
4 4 6 5 5 7
6 6 8 6 5 7
6 6 10 6 5 7
6 9 5 4 4

CHART H.

INDEX FOR COLOR NOTATION.

This chart suggests all color paths and records each step by a simple NOTATION. The ten steps of hue are written RP (red-purple), P (purple), PB (purple-blue), B (blue), BG (blue-green), G (green), GY (green-yellow), Y (yellow), YR (yellow-red or orange), and R (red).

Initials at the top of the chart trace the Sequence of Hues; numerals at the side trace the Sequence of Values and the small numeral printed on each color step is an index of its Chroma i,e. strength or saturation. The color step made of vermilion bears the chroma numeral 10;- it is at the value level 4:- and in the red column R. This step is written $5R\frac{4}{10}$ as explained in a previous introduction and in chapter VI of "A Color Notation."

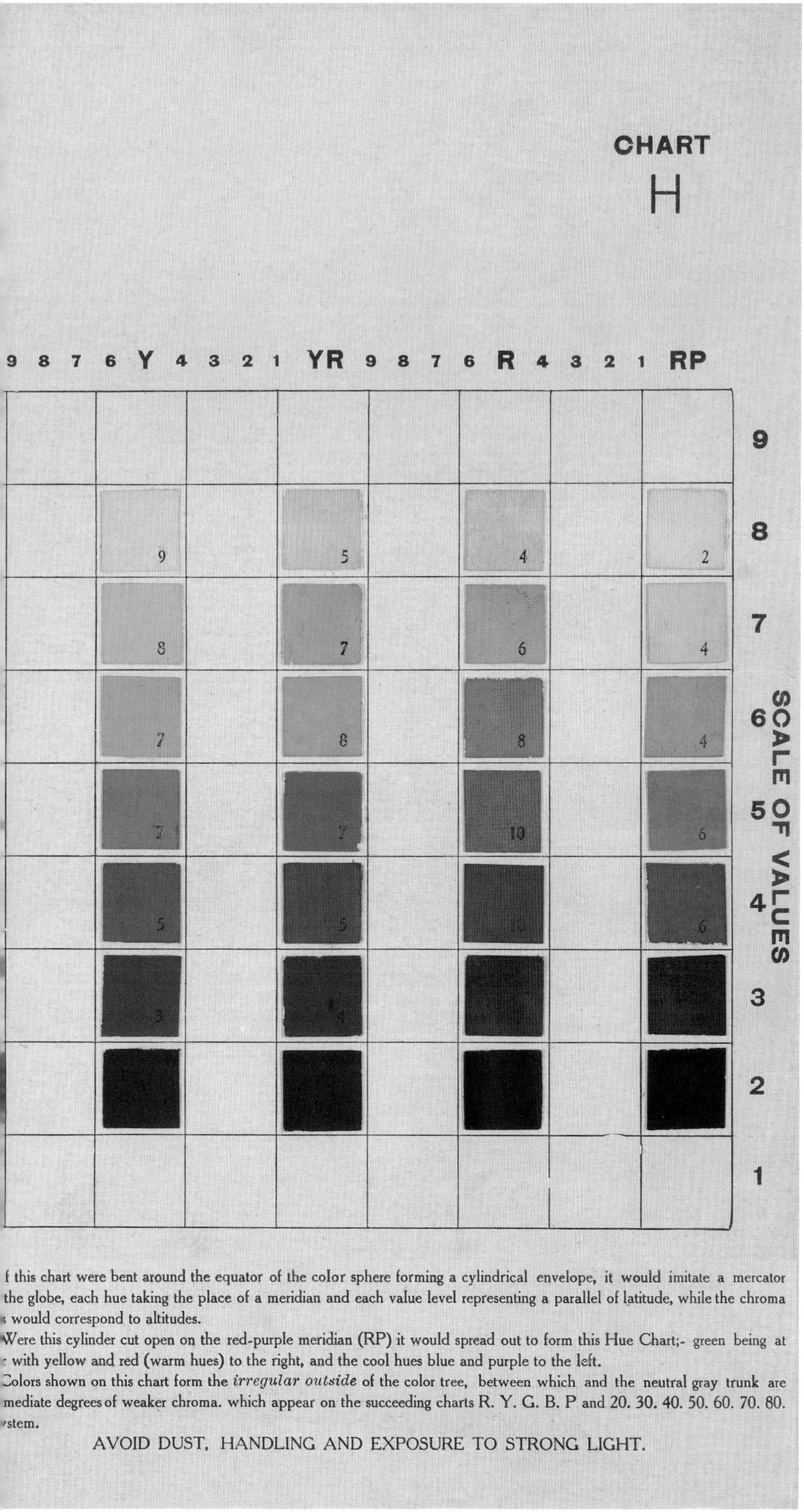

ii. COLOUR SYSTEMS AND STANDARDS, 1900–1945   239

This chart shows the hues horizontally arranged across the page: RP (red-purple), P (purple), PB (purple-blue), B (blue), BG (blue-green), G (green), GY (green-yellow), Y (yellow), YR (yellow-red), R (red) and back to RP (red-purple). The values are seen arranged vertically under each hue and range from the darkest (2) to the lightest (8). The small number printed on each colour is the chroma.

[P. 240] [A] Chart R is the red and blue-green chart. This shows the complementary colours branching out from the neutral axis N. Among other things, this demonstrates how the chroma is stronger for red than blue-green. [B] Chart Y is the yellow and purple-blue chart. Again, this shows the complementary colours branching out from the neutral axis N.

[P. 241] [A] Chart G is the green and red-purple chart. This too shows the complementary colours branching out from the neutral axis N. It also shows that the chroma are more equally balanced, but not as bright as red and yellow. [B] Chart B is the blue and yellow-red chart. Once again this shows the complementary colours branching out from the neutral axis N. Blue can be seen to have a lower chroma than yellow-red.

[P. 242] [A] Chart 30 is a horizontal section through the colour solid where all the colours reflect 30 per cent of the incident light. [B] Chart 40 is a horizontal section through the colour solid where all the colours reflect 40 per cent of the incident light.

[P. 243] [A] Chart 50 is a horizontal section through the colour solid showing all colours of middle value. [B] Chart 60 is a horizontal section through the colour solid where all the colours reflect 60 per cent of the incident light.

9 8 7 6 **Y** 4 3 2 1 **YR** 9 8 7 6 **R** 4 3 2 1 **RP**

SCALE OF VALUES

9

8   9   5   4   2

7   8   7   6   4

6   7   8   8   4

5   7   7   10   6

4   5   5   6

3   3   4

2

1

f this chart were bent around the equator of the color sphere forming a cylindrical envelope, it would imitate a mercator
the globe, each hue taking the place of a meridian and each value level representing a parallel of latitude, while the chroma
s would correspond to altitudes.
Were this cylinder cut open on the red-purple meridian (RP) it would spread out to form this Hue Chart;- green being at
with yellow and red (warm hues) to the right, and the cool hues blue and purple to the left.
Colors shown on this chart form the *irregular outside* of the color tree, between which and the neutral gray trunk are
mediate degrees of weaker chroma. which appear on the succeeding charts R. Y. G. B. P and 20. 30. 40. 50. 60. 70. 80.
stem.

AVOID DUST, HANDLING AND EXPOSURE TO STRONG LIGHT.

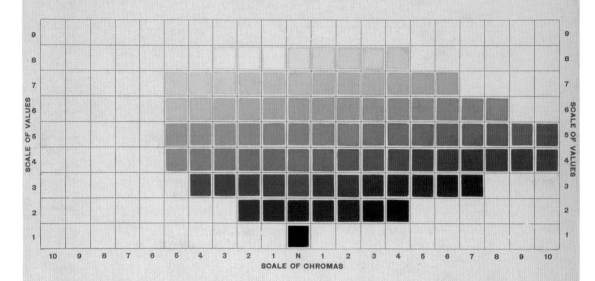

RED AND BLUE-GREEN CHART.

This chart presents a vertical plane passed through the axis of the color solid and bearing the complementary hues, red and blue-green. This pair of opposite hues is shown in regular measured scales from black to white, and from greyness to the strongest color made in stable pigment.

VALUES of red and blue-green range vertically from black (0) to white (10). CHROMAS or strengths of color range horizontally from neutral gray to the maximum (10).

Each step in these color scales bears an appropriate symbol describing its light and its strength. Thus R1/1 is vermilion, the standard red of the system, which exhibits 100% of chromatic strength and reflects 40% of the incident light. Its opposite BG1 reflects the same percentage of light but only 50% of chroma. To balance this pair the areas must be inversely as the chroma, i. e., since

blue-green is but half as strong as vermilion red, twice as much is required for a balance. Attention to these measures leads to pleasing combinations.

Any chosen steps of red and blue-green upon this chart may be balanced by noting their symbols:- thus light blue-green (BG1) balances dark red (R1) when the areas are inversely as the product of the symbols viz:- six parts of light blue-green and twenty-four parts of dark red.

Chapters III and IV of the handbook, "A Color notation," describe these balances and their combinations with other hues. The symbol on each color step is its NAME, a measure of its light and strength by which it is to be memorized, written and reproduced.

AVOID DUST, HANDLING AND EXPOSURE TO STRONG LIGHT.

A

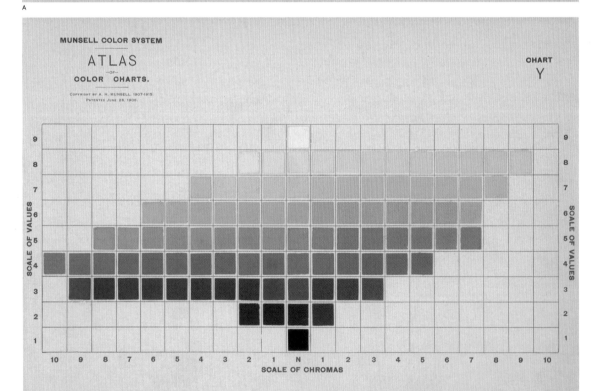

YELLOW AND PURPLE-BLUE CHART.

This chart presents a vertical plane passed through the axis of the color solid and bearing the complementary hues, yellow and purple-blue. This pair of opposite hues is shown in regular measured scales from black to white, and from greyness to the strongest color made in stable pigment.

VALUES of yellow and purple-blue range vertically from black (0) to white (10). CHROMAS or strengths of color range horizontally from neutral gray to the maximum (10).

Each step in these color scales bears an appropriate symbol describing its light and its strength. Thus Y1 is zinc yellow, the strongest permanent yellow, which exhibits 90% of chromatic strength and reflects 80% of the incident light. Its opposite PB1 reflects the same percentage of light but only 20% of chroma. To balance this pair the areas must be inversely as the chroma, i. e., since

purple-blue is but two ninths as strong as zinc yellow, it requires nine parts of purple-blue to balance two parts of the yellow. Attention to these measures leads to pleasing combinations.

Any chosen steps of yellow and purple-blue upon this chart may be balanced by noting their symbols:- thus light yellow (Y1) balances dark purple-blue (PB1), when the areas are inversely as the product of the symbols viz:- twenty-seven parts of light yellow and seventy-two parts of dark purple-blue.

Chapters III and IV of the handbook, "A Color notation," describe these balances and their combinations with other hues. The symbol on each color step is its NAME, a measure of its light and strength by which it is to be memorized, written and reproduced.

AVOID DUST, HANDLING AND EXPOSURE TO STRONG LIGHT.

B

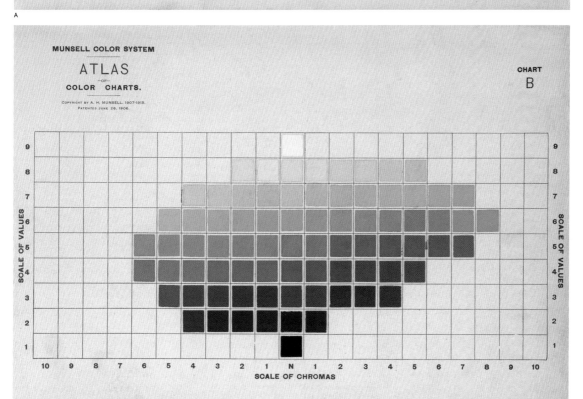

MUNSELL COLOR SYSTEM

ATLAS
—OF—
COLOR CHARTS.

COPYRIGHT BY A. H. MUNSELL. 1907-1915.
PATENTED JUNE 26, 1906.

CHART
G

SCALE OF VALUES

9 8 7 6 5 4 3 2 1

SCALE OF VALUES

10 9 8 7 6 5 4 3 2 1 N 1 2 3 4 5 6 7 8 9 10

SCALE OF CHROMAS

GREEN AND RED-PURPLE CHART.

This chart presents a vertical plane passed through the axis of the color solid and bears the complementary hues, green and red-purple. This pair of opposite hues is shown in regular measured scales from black to white and from greyness to the strongest color made in stable pigment.

VALUES of green and red-purple range vertically from black (0) to white (10). CHROMAS or strengths of color range horizontally from neutral gray to the maximum (10).

Each step in these color scales bears an appropriate symbol describing its light and its strength. Thus G⅟ is emerald green, the strongest permanent green, which exhibits 70% of chromatic strength and reflects 50% of the incident light. Its opposite RP⅟ reflects the same percentage of light but only 60% of chroma. To balance this pair the areas must be inversely as the chroma, i. e., since

red-purple is one seventh less strong than green, seven parts of red-purple will balance six parts of the green. Attention to these measures leads to pleasing combinations.

Any chosen steps of green and red-purple upon this chart may be balanced by noting their symbols; thus light green (G⅟) balances dark red-purple (RP⅟), when the areas are inversely as the product of the symbols viz:- forty parts of dark red-purple and four parts of light green.

Chapters III and IV of the handbook, "A Color notation," describe these balances and their combinations with other hues. The symbol on each color step is its NAME, a measure of its light and strength by which it is to be memorized, written and reproduced.

AVOID DUST, HANDLING AND EXPOSURE TO STRONG LIGHT.

MUNSELL COLOR SYSTEM

ATLAS
—OF—
COLOR CHARTS.

COPYRIGHT BY A. H. MUNSELL. 1907-1915.
PATENTED JUNE 26, 1906.

CHART
B

SCALE OF VALUES

9 8 7 6 5 4 3 2 1

SCALE OF VALUES

10 9 8 7 6 5 4 3 2 1 N 1 2 3 4 5 6 7 8 9 10

SCALE OF CHROMAS

BLUE AND YELLOW-RED CHART.

This chart presents a vertical plane passed through the axis of the color solid and bears the complementary hues, blue and yellow-red. This pair of opposite hues is shown in regular measured scales from black to white, and from greyness to the strongest color made in stable pigment.

VALUES of blue and yellow-red range vertically from black (0) to white (10). CHROMAS or strengths of color range horizontally from neutral gray to the maximum (10).

Each step in these color scales bears an appropriate symbol describing its light and its strength. Thus B⅟ is cobalt, the strongest permanent blue, which exhibits 60% of chromatic strength and reflects 40% of the incident light. Its opposite YR⅟ reflects the same percentage of light but only 50% of chroma. To balance this pair the areas must be inversely as the chroma, i. e., since

the yellow-red exhibits one sixth less strength than the blue, six parts of the yellow-red will balance five parts of blue. Attention to these measures leads to pleasing combinations.

Any chosen steps of blue and yellow-red upon this chart may be balanced by noting their symbols;- thus light yellow-red (YR⅟) balances dark blue (B⅟), when the areas are inversely as the product of the symbols viz:- twenty parts of light yellow-red ("orange") and forty-eight parts of dark blue.

Chapters III and IV of the handbook, "A Color Notation," describe these balances and their combinations with other hues. The symbol on each color step is its NAME, a measure of its light and strength by which it is to be memorized, written and reproduced.

AVOID DUST, HANDLING AND EXPOSURE TO STRONG LIGHT.

A

B

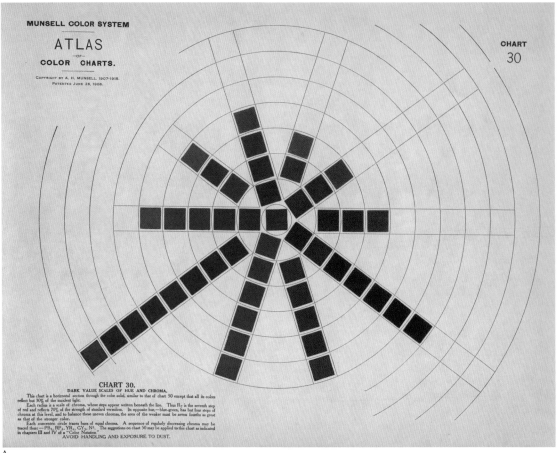

CHART 30.
DARK VALUE SCALES OF HUE AND CHROMA.

A

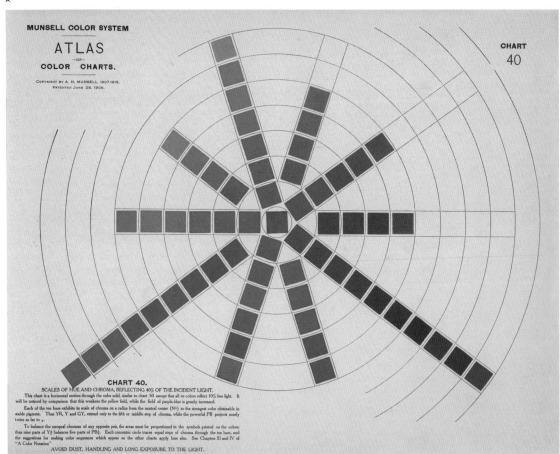

CHART 40.
SCALES OF HUE AND CHROMA, REFLECTING 40% OF THE INCIDENT LIGHT.

B

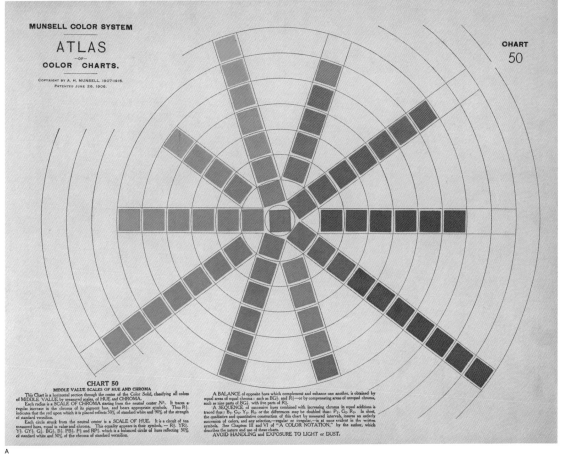

MUNSELL COLOR SYSTEM

ATLAS
—OF—
COLOR CHARTS.

COPYRIGHT BY A. H. MUNSELL, 1907-1915.
PATENTED JUNE 26, 1906.

CHART
50

CHART 50
MIDDLE VALUE SCALES OF HUE AND CHROMA

This Chart is a horizontal section through the center of the Color Solid, classifying all colors of MIDDLE VALUE by measured scales of HUE and CHROMA.

Each radius is a SCALE OF CHROMA starting from the neutral center N^5. It traces a regular increase in the chroma of its pigment hue, and bears appropriate symbols. Thus $R\frac{5}{2}$ indicates that the red upon which it is placed reflects 50% of standard white and 50% of the strength of standard vermilion.

Each circle struck from the neutral center is a SCALE OF HUE. It is a circuit of ten measured hues, equal in value and chroma. This equality appears in their symbols, — $R\frac{5}{2}$, $YR\frac{5}{2}$, $Y\frac{5}{2}$, $GY\frac{5}{2}$, $G\frac{5}{2}$, $BG\frac{5}{2}$, $B\frac{5}{2}$, $PB\frac{5}{2}$, $P\frac{5}{2}$ and $RP\frac{5}{2}$, which is a balanced circle of hues reflecting 50% of standard white and 50% of the chroma of standard vermilion.

A BALANCE of opposite hues which complement and enhance one another, is obtained by equal areas of equal chroma; such as $BG\frac{5}{2}$, and $R\frac{5}{2}$ — or by compensating areas of unequal chroma, such as nine parts of $BG\frac{5}{2}$, with five parts of $R\frac{5}{2}$.

A SEQUENCE of successive hues combined with increasing chroma in equal additions is traced thus: B_3, G_5, Y_7, R_9, or the differences may be doubled thus: P_1, G_5, R_9. In short, the qualitative and quantitative construction of this chart by measured intervals, insures an orderly succession of colors, and any selection, — regular or irregular, — is at once evident in the written symbols. See Chapters III and IV of "A COLOR NOTATION," by the author, which describes the nature and use of these charts.

AVOID HANDLING and EXPOSURE TO LIGHT or DUST.

A

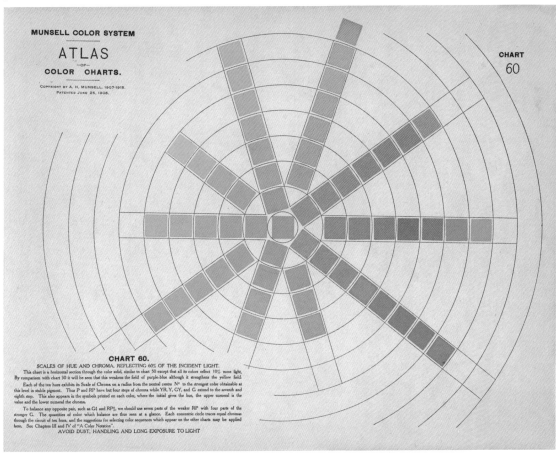

MUNSELL COLOR SYSTEM

ATLAS
—OF—
COLOR CHARTS.

COPYRIGHT BY A. H. MUNSELL, 1907-1915.
PATENTED JUNE 26, 1906.

CHART
60

CHART 60.
SCALES OF HUE AND CHROMA, REFLECTING 60% OF THE INCIDENT LIGHT.

This chart is a horizontal section through the color solid, similar to chart 50 except that all its colors reflect 10% more light. By comparison with chart 30 it will be seen that this weakens the field of purple-blue although it strengthens the yellow field.

Each of the ten hues exhibits its Scale of Chroma on a radius from the neutral centre N^6 to the strongest color obtainable at this level in stable pigment. Thus P and RP have but four steps of chroma while YR, Y, GY, and G extend to the seventh and eighth step. This also appears in the symbols printed on each color, where the initial gives the hue, the upper numeral is the value and the lower numeral the chroma.

To balance any opposite pair, such as $G\frac{6}{5}$ and $RP\frac{6}{4}$, we should use seven parts of the weaker RP with four parts of the stronger G. The quantities of color which balance are thus seen at a glance. Each concentric circle traces equal chromas through the circuit of ten hues, and the suggestions for selecting color sequences which appear on the other charts may be applied here. See Chapters III and IV of "A Color Notation".

AVOID DUST, HANDLING AND LONG EXPOSURE TO LIGHT

B

THE RIDGWAY COLOUR SYSTEM

Robert Ridgway was an American ornithologist, who was the first full-time curator of birds at the United States National Museum. He served there from 1880 until his death in 1929. Ridgway also published one of the first and most important colour systems for bird identification, with his book *A Nomenclature of Colors for Naturalists* (1886). In 1912 he self-published a larger work on colour nomenclature – *Color Standards and Color Nomenclature* – and this is the work that is being considered here. In the preface, Ridgway noted:

> Many works on the subject of colour have been published, but most of them are purely technical, and pertain to the physics of colour, the painter's needs, or to some particular art or industry alone, or in other ways are unsuited for the use of the zoologist, the botanist, the pathologist, or the mineralogist; and the comparatively few works on colour intended specially for naturalists have all failed to meet the requirements, either because of an insufficient number of colour samples, lack of names or other means of easy identification or designation, or faulty selection and classification of the colours chosen for illustration.

The work consists of an introduction, with clear definitions of colour terminology, a breakdown of the components in the hues and tones, and an alphabetical list of the 1,115 colours represented on the fifty-three coloured plates that make up the bulk of the work. The plates show a gradual change of hue.

Ridgway informs his readers that, for pictorial reasons, thirty-six is the practicable number of segments in the ideal chromatic circle. However, these colours are not evenly spaced; furthermore, the number of intermediates required on either side of orange is different: four in the red-orange series and five in the orange-yellow, for example. Six are required for the violet-red series, whereas four will suffice for the blue-violet hues.

At the time of Ridgway writing, one of the best ways of establishing the proportion of one colour to another, and thus allowing for its accurate reproduction, was to use a Maxwell disc, as represented on the cover of *Color Standards and Color Nomenclature* (below). It consists of interlocking cardboard discs of different colours with a scaled graduated circle of one hundred segments around the disc. When rotated, the colours merge and different colours are produced by altering the amount of each one displayed. Once the required colour is revealed, the proportions of each component can be read from the scale. In this example of a Maxwell disc, samples of red, green and violet are adjusted to present, respectively, 32, 42 and 26 per cent of the circumference. Superimposed on these is a single smaller disc of neutral grey, and on this two still smaller discs of black and white, the former occupying 79 per cent and the latter 21 per cent of the area. The result of this combination of colours, when the discs are rotated rapidly, is that the whole surface becomes a uniform grey, like the middle disc.

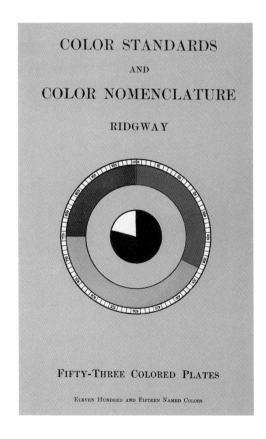

COLOR STANDARDS

AND

COLOR NOMENCLATURE

RIDGWAY

FIFTY-THREE COLORED PLATES

ELEVEN HUNDRED AND FIFTEEN NAMED COLORS

[OPPOSITE] [A] Pure spectrum colours and intermediate hues unmixed with grey (plates I–XII). [PP. 246–248] [B] Spectrum colours and intermediate hues containing 32 per cent neutral grey (plates XIII–XXIV). [C] Spectrum colours and intermediate hues containing 58 per cent neutral grey (plates XXVII–XXXVIII). [D] Spectrum colours and intermediate hues containing 77 per cent neutral grey (plates XXXIX–XLIV). [E] Spectrum colours and intermediate hues containing 90 per cent neutral grey (plates XLV–L).

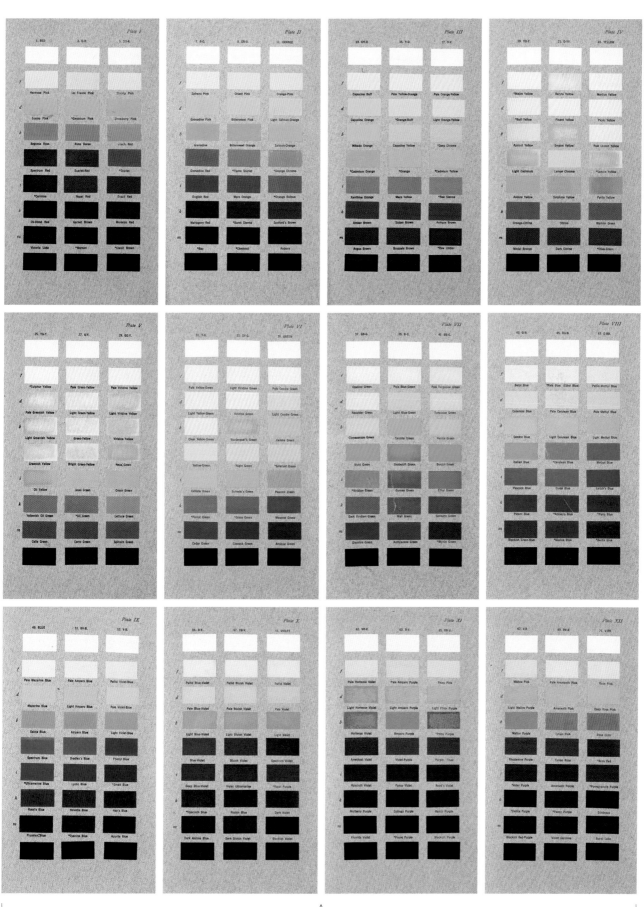

A

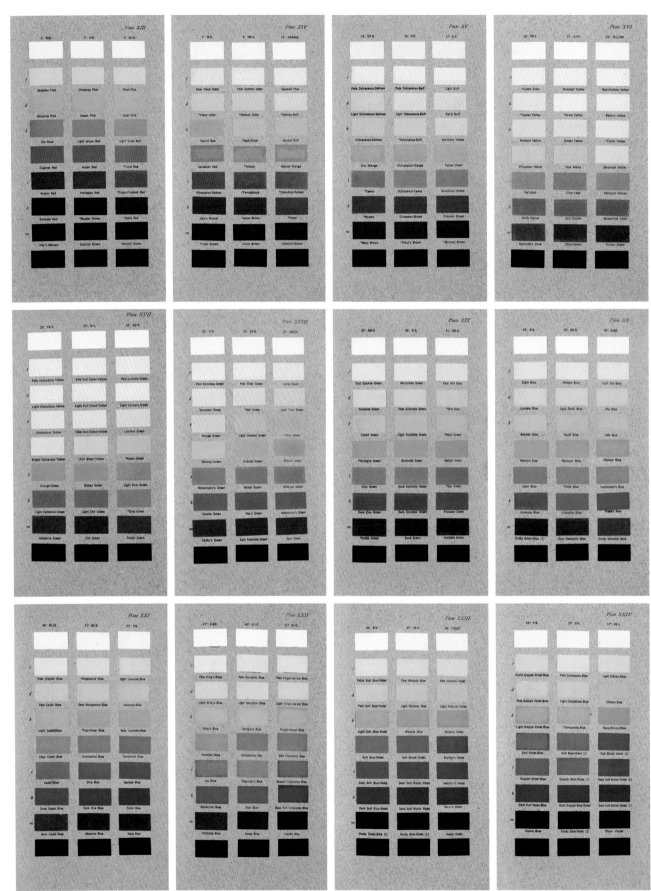

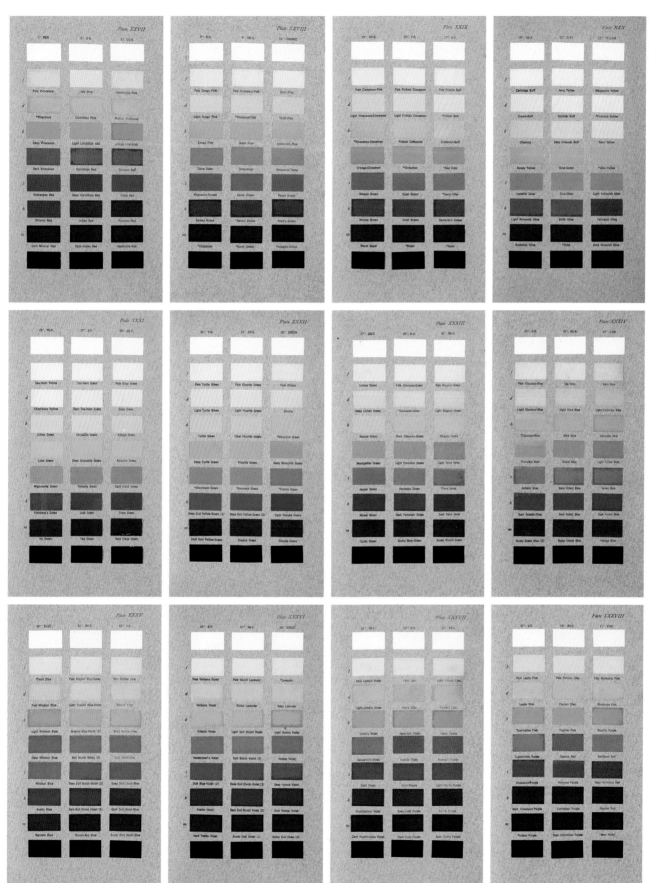

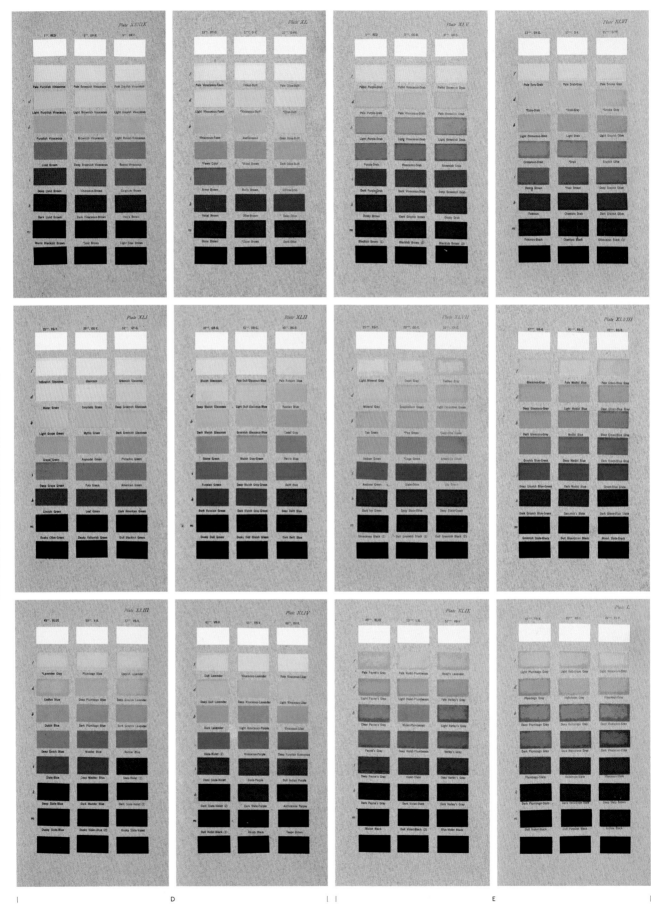

With the spectrum colours as a base, Ridgway mixed a number of fixed colours in definite percentages. In this way, he could produce a series of named colours that could be duplicated at any time. This was important because he had learnt with his earlier work that colours tended to fade.

In the book, the first series of plates (I to XII) show the pure, full spectrum colours and intermediate hues on the middle horizontal line, each with its vertical scale of tints upwards and its shades downwards. The remaining plates show these same thirty-six colours or hues in exactly the same order but dulled by the admixture of neutral grey: the second series (plates XIII to XXVI) contains 32 per cent of neutral grey, the third (plates XXVII to XXXVIII) 58 per cent, the fourth (plates XXXIX to XLIV) 77 per cent, and the fifth (plates XLV to L) 90 per cent. The last three plates (LI to LIII) show the six spectrum colours further dulled by the admixture of 95.5 per cent neutral grey.

Ridgway's *Color Standards and Color Nomenclature* was published in an edition of 5,000 copies by A. Hoen and Co. of Baltimore, Maryland. In order to ensure uniformity, each colour was produced in sufficient quantity for the entire edition. At once, the work came into general use not only among naturalists but also among florists as well as manufacturers of paints, chemicals, wallpapers and a variety of other goods.

Ridgway commented on the constant misuse of terms relating to colour and offered clear definitions for each. In brief these were:

COLOUR | The term that covers the entire range of 'chromatic manifestation' – the spectrum colours – being red, orange, yellow, green, blue and violet (together with those between violet and red, not shown in the spectrum).

HUE | Those lying between any contiguous pair of spectrum colours – for example 'an orange hue of red' or 'a yellow hue of orange'.

TINT | Any colour weakened by the addition of white.

SHADE | Any colour darkened by the addition of black.

TONE | Each step in a colour scale is a tone of that colour. Each of the coloured samples in the vertical scales of the plates in the book represents a separate tone of that colour.

COLOUR SCALE | A linear series of colours showing a gradual transition from one to another or a similar series of tones of one colour. The first is a chromatic scale (or scale of colours and hues) and in the plates in Ridgway's book is represented by each horizontal series. The second is a tone scale, which is shown on each plate running vertically from the centre, to a pale tint at the top and a dark shade at the bottom.

Like many who work with colour in a serious capacity, Ridgway had strong views on the naming of colours:

For obvious reasons it has, of course, been necessary to ignore many trade names, through which the popular nomenclature of colours has become involved in really chaotic confusion rendered more confounded by the continual coinage of new names, many of them synonymous and most of them vague and variable in their application. Most of them are invented, apparently without care or judgement, by the dyer or manufacturer of fabrics, and are as capricious in their meaning as in their origin; for example: Such fanciful names as 'zulu', 'serpent green', 'baby blue', 'new old rose', 'London smoke', etc., and such nonsensical names as 'ashes of roses' and 'elephant's breath'. An inspection of the sample books of manufacturers of fancy goods (such as embroidery silks and crewels, ribbons, velvets, and other dress- and upholstery-goods) is sufficient not only to illustrate the above observations, but to show also the absolute want of system or classification and the general unavailability of these trade names for adoption in a practical colour nomenclature. This is very unfortunate, since many of these trade names have the merit of brevity and euphony and lack only the quality of stability.

Interestingly, many of the old names are being trotted out by modern paint manufacturers.

Among the many works that Ridgway referred to when naming the colours were Werner's *Nomenclature of Colours*; Hay's *Nomenclature of Colours* and *Réptertoire de couleurs* produced by the Société française des chrysanthémistes.

THE OSTWALD COLOUR SYSTEM

Friedrich Wilhelm Ostwald was a Latvian-German chemist who received the Nobel Prize in Chemistry for his work on catalysis. He was also an amateur painter who made his own pigments and was particularly interested in the stability of painting materials. It was soon after producing a handbook titled *Malerbriefe* (Letters to a Painter), in 1904, that he met the American painter Albert H. Munsell. The latter had recently developed a 'colour atlas', and their meeting prompted Ostwald to spend much of the next decade working on colour theory.

Ostwald had seen that some combinations of colour were harmonious, whereas others were decidedly unpleasant. He wondered whether a law could be formulated to ensure harmony, and proceeded on the basis that harmony was created by colour order. The result of this research was the publication of *Die Farbenfibel* (The Colour Primer) in 1916. This was refined by *Die Harmonie der Farben* (The Harmony of Colours), which followed two years later. In his work, the colours were laid out in a regular, evenly spaced fashion, as judged by the eye.

Simply, Ostwald believed that all colours could be divided into three classes. Firstly, the neutral colours: those that have no colour and are composed only of black and white. Secondly, there are the hues or colours in the narrow sense of the word. These hues or 'full colours', when pure, contain no black or white in their make-up. Thirdly, the mixed colours: those that are mixtures of hues with black and white, either singly or in combination in all conceivable proportions. These constitute the majority of the colours that are encountered in everyday life.

Ostwald believed that the painter Leonardo da Vinci and the physiologist Ewald Hering were both correct in asserting that there were four basic hues. He called these yellow, red, blue and sea green. Four further hues were then placed between these: orange between yellow and red; purple between red and blue; turquoise between blue and sea green; and leaf green between sea green and yellow. He then placed two more hues between each of these eight, resulting in a circle of twenty-four evenly spaced hues.

He acknowledged that there was no such thing as 100 per cent black, 100 per cent white or even 100 per cent pure colour. The maximum limits were 96.5 per cent, 89 per cent and 85.5 per cent, respectively. In view of the fact that neither black nor white were 100 per cent pure, a scale of neutrals could not be made by simply mixing equal parts of black and white to arrive at an exact intermediate (50 per cent) grey. Nor could one produce a grey at one quarter of the distance from black that would contain 75 per cent black and 25 per cent white.

Carrying out a number of experiments with a spinning disc with black and white sections, Ostwald discovered that in order to achieve a mid-grey, the proportions were about 17 per cent white to 83 per cent black. Further experiments resulted in a set of fifteen uniform shades. However, when these were applied to the twenty-four hues, the result was 2,535 individual colours, which was not considered commercially practical. For technical purposes, the number of neutrals was trimmed to eight equidistant neutrals, which Ostwald called his 'practical grey scale', thereby giving a system of 680 colours.

When the colours were organized three-dimensionally, the vertical axis of eight neutrals was placed in the centre, resulting in two equilateral monochromatic triangles each with a 'full colour' at its apex. These full colours (labelled 'pa' in the diagrams) were complementary colours – thus blue (14) was directly opposite yellow (2), and red (8) was directly opposite sea green (21), for example. Every triangle was divided by lines drawn parallel to the sides into twenty-eight rhombuses, each of which represented a variation on the full colour with varying amounts of black or white added.

Ostwald's ideas about the standardization of colour spread quickly. *The Colour Primer* was read by members of the Dutch De Stijl movement to whom the geometrical aesthetic appealed, and the first painter who showed an interest in the concept of harmonizing colours by modifying them with black and white was Piet Mondrian. His treatment of colour in the years immediately after the publication had much in common with Ostwald's theories.

The Ostwald system has since been largely superseded by the American Munsell and the Swedish Natural Colour systems. The main reason, apart from the complexity of the notation, is because the original colours chosen by Otswald were laid out in such a way that they could not be modified or extended as brighter pigments and dyes became available.

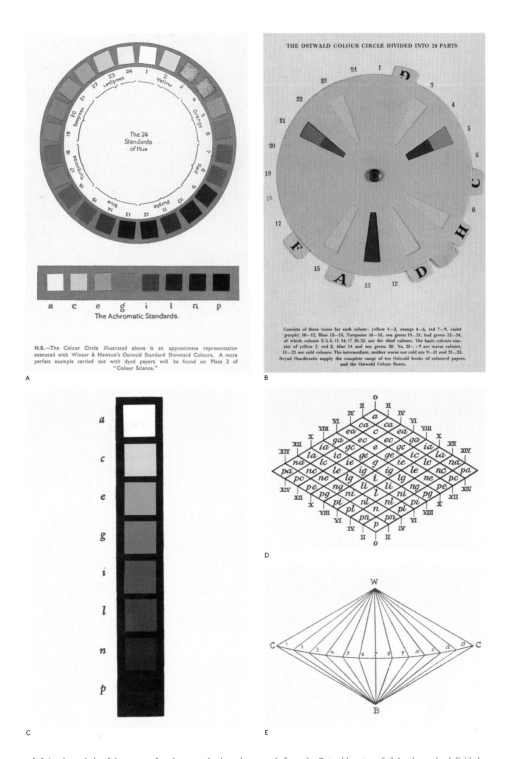

[A] A colour circle of the twenty-four hue standards and grey scale from the Ostwald system. [B] A colour wheel divided into twenty-four parts, each having the same interval of tone between them. By covering tab B a complete triad can be seen, with orange at 5, violet at 12 and sea green at 21. Shaded colours (pure hues mixed with black) are close to the centre.
[C] The grey scale, where 'a' = 89% white and 11% black and 'p' = 3.5% white and 96.5% black. [D] Two monochromatic triangles on a common grey central axis with white 'a' at the top, black 'p' at the base and the purest colour 'pa' at each extreme. [E] The Ostwald colour solid created by splitting the twenty-four hue standards into twelve of the double triangles shown above. The circle of twenty-four purest colours 'pa' is situated on the equator. [OVERLEAF] Ostwald colour standards.

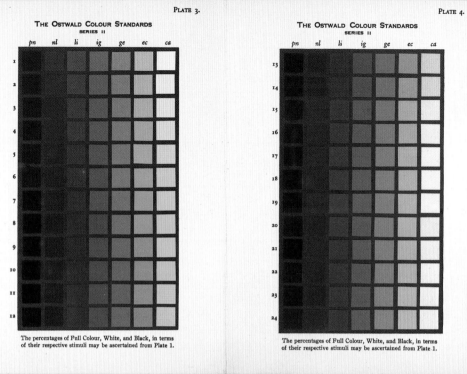

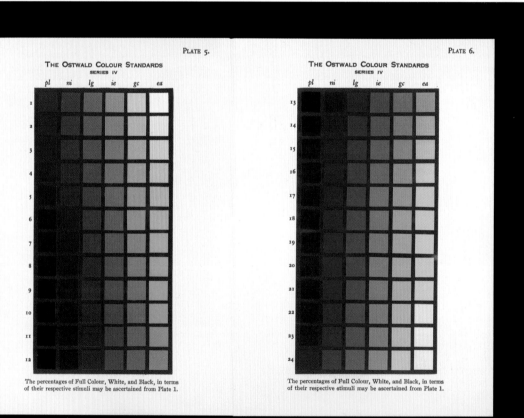

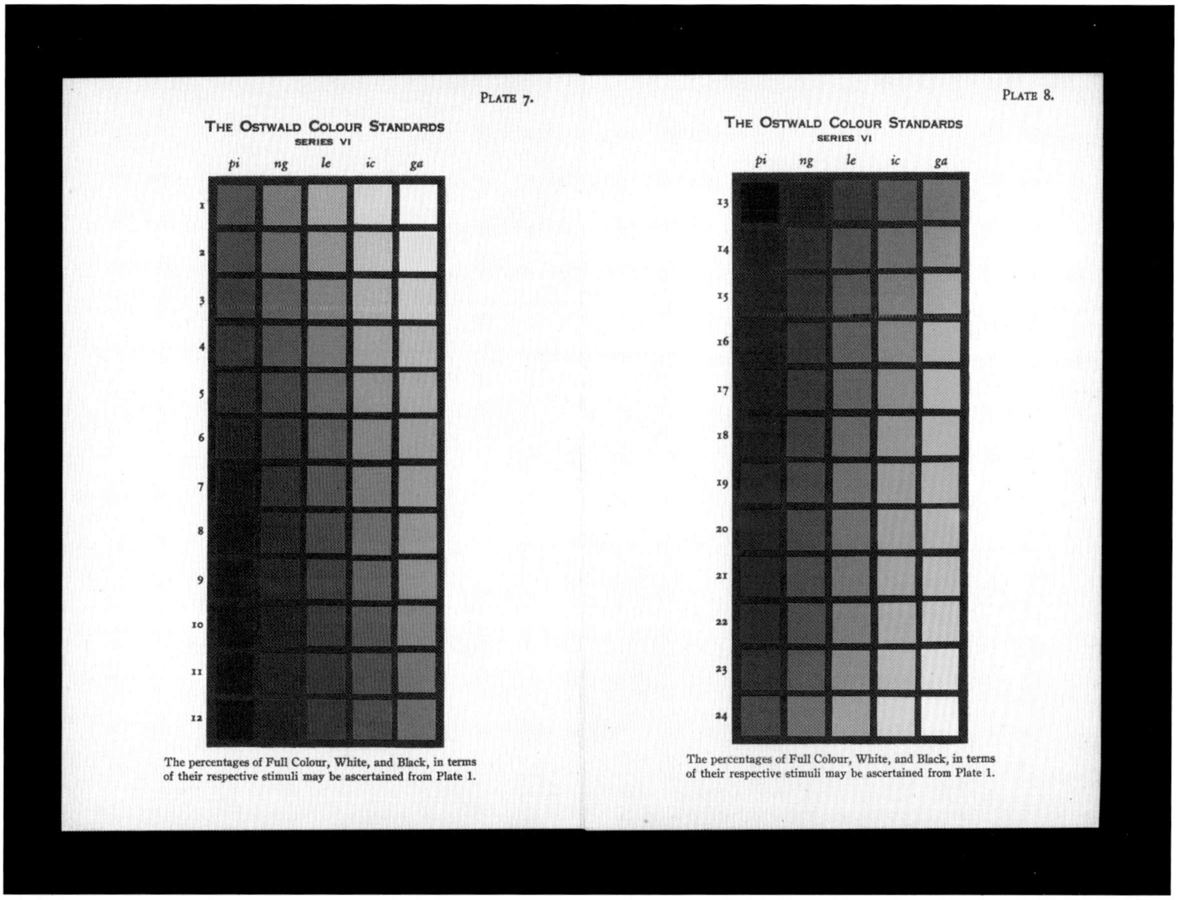

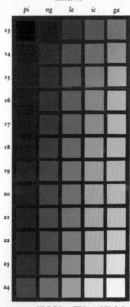

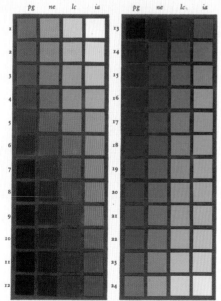

PLATE 7.

THE OSTWALD COLOUR STANDARDS
SERIES VI

The percentages of Full Colour, White, and Black, in terms of their respective stimuli may be ascertained from Plate 1.

PLATE 8.

THE OSTWALD COLOUR STANDARDS
SERIES VI

The percentages of Full Colour, White, and Black, in terms of their respective stimuli may be ascertained from Plate 1.

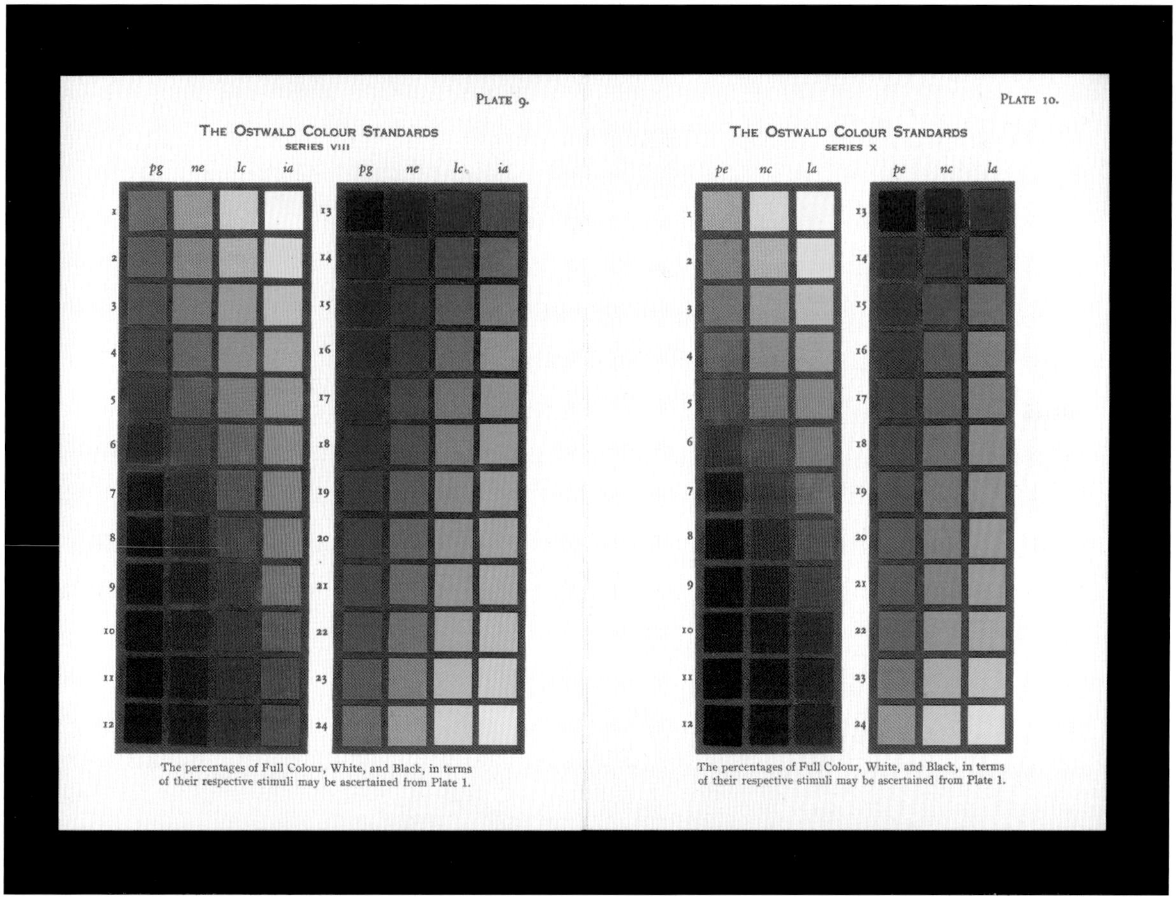

PLATE 9.

THE OSTWALD COLOUR STANDARDS
SERIES VIII

The percentages of Full Colour, White, and Black, in terms of their respective stimuli may be ascertained from Plate 1.

PLATE 10.

THE OSTWALD COLOUR STANDARDS
SERIES X

The percentages of Full Colour, White, and Black, in terms of their respective stimuli may be ascertained from Plate 1.

HISTORICAL COLOURS

Although neither a colour standard nor a colour order system, Thomas Parsons' *A Tint Book of Historical Colours* (often known simply as 'Parsons') was one of the most significant commercial ranges of paint colours produced in the United Kingdom. The range was first published in 1934 and is still available today.

Thomas Parsons & Sons was founded in 1802 in London. The quality of its varnishes and colours was renowned and many a smart carriage, neighbouring theatre and lordly mansion bore witness to the excellence of the firm's products. By 1915 Parsons was offering more than five hundred thousand new colours, achieved with a 'new instrument of science' called the 'Parsons' colourmeter'. The company ceased trading in the 1960s but left behind legacy in the form of *Historical Colours* and other publications.

PARSONS' COLOUR FAMILIES

Historical Colours contained 136 colours that were taken from the decorative and applied arts. The colours were split into 'family' groups according to use or origin. The group of colours from ancient Egypt was sourced from mummy cases, furnishings and wall paintings and it was limited to primaries of mineral origin: red from haematite or yellow ochre, burnt to redness; malachite for green; cobalt and copper for blue; and orpiment for bright yellow.

The pottery and fabrics of China and Persia provided a wealth of wonderful 'oriental' colours, from the delicate blue-green glaze of early Fen Ching porcelain and the celadon glazes to the brilliant turquoises of Chinese and Persian pottery. Reds included rouge de fer, characteristic of exported Chinese porcelain and sang de boeuf of the Qing dynasty.

The Pompeian colours were taken from 'this Brighton of the Romans' (as charmingly described in Parsons'). There, the ash had caused the colours of the walls to remain as fresh as when they were painted. Once again, these were based on indigenous ochres deepened with haematite. Porphyry red was a colour taken from the igneous rock and Etruscan red from Etruscan red-figure pottery of ancient Tuscany.

One of the largest families of coloured artefacts was that concerning tapestry. The dyers of the Verdure, Aubusson, Beauvais and Mortlake tapestries were renowned for their skill in fixing colour. Michel-Eugène Chevreul worked as the director of the dye works at Les Gobelins tapestry works in Paris, where he noticed that the perceived colour of a particular thread was influenced by its surrounding threads, a phenomenon he called simultaneous contrast. His work on colour has had a lasting influence on painting and the decorative arts.

Owen Jones' use of primary colours in his decorative scheme for the interior of the Great Exhibition of 1851 was based on his meticulous study of the Alhambra, the seat of the ancient Moorish kingdom. A selection of these Moorish colours is also shown.

Named after the two great patrons of art, Catherine and Marie de Medici, the Medici colours are useful for emphasizing the features of a structure or as a background for ornaments.

Josiah Wedgwood founded a firm that created not only the famous Wedgwood blue, but also the various Jasper colours. In addition to the Wedgwood range are the colours of the Grès de Flandres (stoneware of Flanders, originally made in Cologne, the Low Countries and the Rhineland), and of the distinctive blue of Royal Worcester. Pages of Delftware colours and those used on the Majolica bas reliefs of Luca della Robbia can also be found in *Historical Colours*.

Historical Colours was extremely influential in the days of limited paint colours and formed the inspiration for a similar book in the United States and a number of later commercial paint ranges. Some four years after the first edition of Parsons' *Historical Colours*, Elizabeth Burris-Meyer, described as the 'Dean of the School for Fashion Careers' in New York, published a work that was clearly based on it: *Historical Color Guide* (1938, see pp. 258–261). Although itself not a scholarly work, Parsons' *Historical Colours* set out to show colours that were actually used on decorative artefacts. However, the colours in the American work were far more abstract and included macaroni (an off-white), designed to convey the eighteenth-century English fop, and cactus bloom (a pink) to suggest a Mexican palette. Samples of metallic colours were also present. Apparently undertaken 'in answer to a demand for workable information on the derivation of schemes for artistic, business and industrial use', the colours were generally far more vibrant and perhaps less useful for interior decoration than those in *Historical Colours*.

COLOURS OF EGYPT

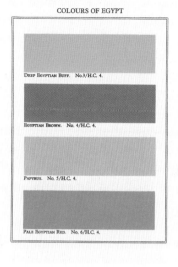

Deep Egyptian Buff. No.3/H.C. 4.

Egyptian Brown. No. 4/H.C. 4.

Papyrus. No. 5/H.C. 4.

Pale Egyptian Red. No. 6/H.C. 4.

COLOURS OF EGYPT

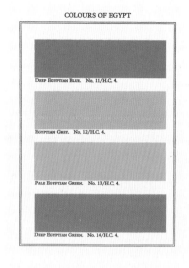

Deep Egyptian Blue. No. 11/H.C. 4.

Egyptian Grey. No. 12/H.C. 4.

Pale Egyptian Green. No. 13/H.C. 4.

Deep Egyptian Green. No. 14/H.C. 4.

COLOURS OF EGYPT

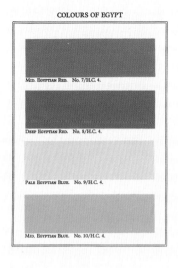

Mid. Egyptian Red. No. 7/H.C. 4.

Deep Egyptian Red. No. 8/H.C. 4.

Pale Egyptian Blue. No. 9/H.C. 4.

Mid. Egyptian Blue. No. 10/H.C. 4.

TYRIAN AND OTHER COLOURS

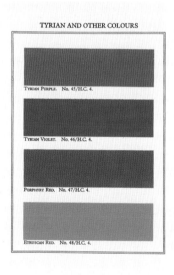

Tyrian Purple. No. 45/H.C. 4.

Tyrian Violet. No. 46/H.C. 4.

Porphyry Red. No. 47/H.C. 4.

Etruscan Red. No. 48/H.C. 4.

POMPEIAN COLOURS

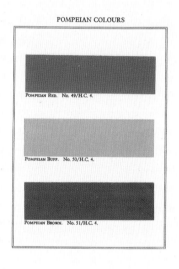

Pompeian Red. No. 49/H.C. 4.

Pompeian Buff. No. 50/H.C. 4.

Pompeian Brown. No. 51/H.C. 4.

MEDICI BLUE

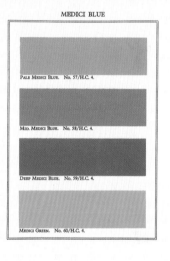

Pale Medici Blue. No. 57/H.C. 4.

Mid. Medici Blue. No. 58/H.C. 4.

Deep Medici Blue. No. 59/H.C. 4.

Medici Green. No. 60/H.C. 4.

ADAM BROTHERS

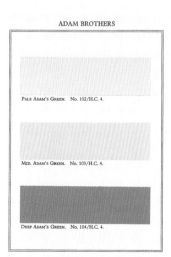

Pale Adam's Green. No. 102/H.C. 4.

Mid. Adam's Green. No. 103/H.C. 4.

Deep Adam's Green. No. 104/H.C. 4.

TREILLAGE GREEN, ISABELLE & LINCOLN GREEN

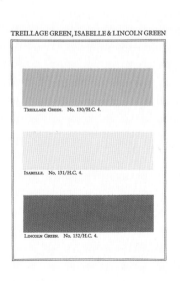

Treillage Green. No. 130/H.C. 4.

Isabelle. No. 131/H.C. 4.

Lincoln Green. No. 132/H.C. 4.

EMPIRE GREEN AND OTHER COLOURS

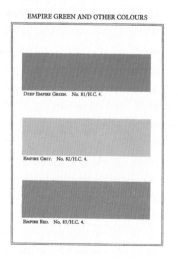

Deep Empire Green. No. 81/H.C. 4.

Empire Grey. No. 82/H.C. 4.

Empire Red. No. 83/H.C. 4.

GRÈS DE FLANDRES COLOURS

PALE GRÈS DE FLANDRES GREY.   No. 65/H.C. 4.

GRÈS DE FLANDRES BLUE GREY.   No. 66/H.C. 4.

PALE GRÈS DE FLANDRES BLUE.   No. 67/H.C. 4.

DEEP GRÈS DE FLANDRES BLUE.   No. 68/H.C. 4.

GRÈS DE FLANDRES COLOURS

GRÈS DE FLANDRES BUFF.   No. 69/H.C. 4.

PALE GRÈS DE FLANDRES BROWN.   No. 70/H.C. 4.

DEEP GRÈS DE FLANDRES BROWN.   No. 71/H.C. 4.

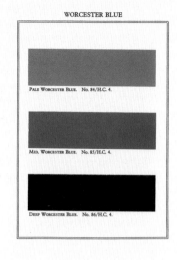

WORCESTER BLUE

PALE WORCESTER BLUE.   No. 84/H.C. 4.

MID. WORCESTER BLUE.   No. 85/H.C. 4.

DEEP WORCESTER BLUE.   No. 86/H.C. 4.

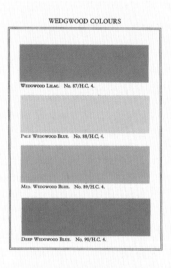

WEDGWOOD COLOURS

WEDGWOOD LILAC.   No. 87/H.C. 4.

PALE WEDGWOOD BLUE.   No. 88/H.C. 4.

MID. WEDGWOOD BLUE.   No. 89/H.C. 4.

DEEP WEDGWOOD BLUE.   No. 90/H.C. 4.

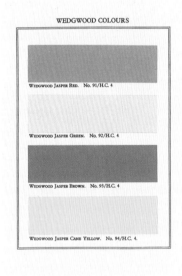

WEDGWOOD COLOURS

WEDGWOOD JASPER RED.   No. 91/H.C. 4

WEDGWOOD JASPER GREEN.   No. 92/H.C. 4

WEDGWOOD JASPER BROWN.   No. 93/H.C. 4

WEDGWOOD JASPER CANE YELLOW.   No. 94/H.C. 4.

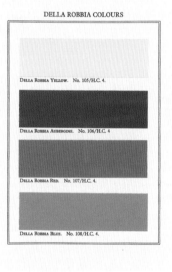

DELLA ROBBIA COLOURS

DELLA ROBBIA YELLOW.   No. 105/H.C. 4.

DELLA ROBBIA AUBERGINE.   No. 106/H.C. 4

DELLA ROBBIA RED.   No. 107/H.C. 4.

DELLA ROBBIA BLUE.   No. 108/H.C. 4.

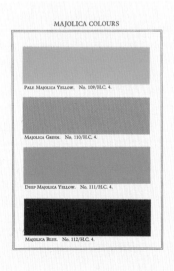

MAJOLICA COLOURS

PALE MAJOLICA YELLOW.   No. 109/H.C. 4.

MAJOLICA GREEN.   No. 110/H.C. 4.

DEEP MAJOLICA YELLOW.   No. 111/H.C. 4.

MAJOLICA BLUE.   No. 112/H.C. 4.

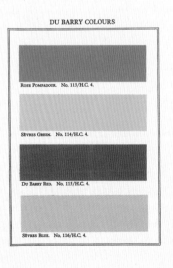

DU BARRY COLOURS

ROSE POMPADOUR.   No. 113/H.C. 4.

SÈVRES GREEN.   No. 114/H.C. 4.

DU BARRY RED.   No. 115/H.C. 4.

SÈVRES BLUE.   No. 116/H.C. 4.

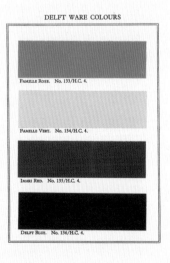

DELFT WARE COLOURS

FAMILLE ROSE.   No. 133/H.C. 4.

FAMILLE VERT.   No. 134/H.C. 4.

IMARI RED.   No. 135/H.C. 4.

DELFT BLUE.   No. 136/H.C. 4.

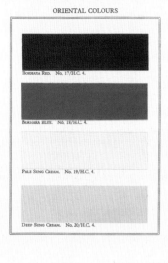

ORIENTAL COLOURS

Bokhara Red.   No. 17/H.C. 4.

Bokhara Blue.   No. 18/H.C. 4.

Pale Sung Cream.   No. 19/H.C. 4.

Deep Sung Cream.   No. 20/H.C. 4.

ORIENTAL COLOURS

Sung Grey Mauve.   No. 25/H.C. 4.

Mazarine Blue.   No. 26/H.C. 4.

Tang Green.   No. 27/H.C. 4.

Tang Yellow.   No. 28/H.C. 4.

ORIENTAL COLOURS

Pale Powder Blue.   No. 33/H.C. 4.

Deep Powder Blue.   No. 34/H.C. 4.

Claire de Lune.   No. 35/H.C. 4.

Pale Apple Green.   No. 36/H.C. 4.

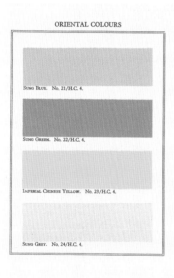

ORIENTAL COLOURS

Sung Blue.   No. 21/H.C. 4.

Sung Green.   No. 22/H.C. 4.

Imperial Chinese Yellow.   No. 23/H.C. 4.

Sung Grey.   No. 24/H.C. 4.

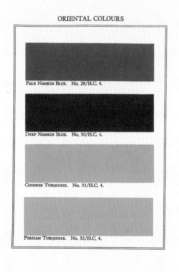

ORIENTAL COLOURS

Pale Nankin Blue.   No. 29/H.C. 4.

Deep Nankin Blue.   No. 30/H.C. 4.

Chinese Turquoise.   No. 31/H.C. 4.

Persian Turquoise.   No. 32/H.C. 4.

ORIENTAL COLOURS

Deep Apple Green.   No. 37/H.C. 4.

Rouge de Fer.   No. 38/H.C. 4.

Pale Celadon Green.   No. 39/H.C. 4.

Mid. Celadon Green.   No. 40/H.C. 4.

GOBELIN TAPESTRY COLOURS

Gobelin Blue.   No. 95/H.C. 4.

Gobelin Yellow.   No. 96/H.C. 4.

Pale Gobelin Brown.   No. 97/H.C. 4.

Deep Gobelin Brown.   No. 98/H.C. 4.

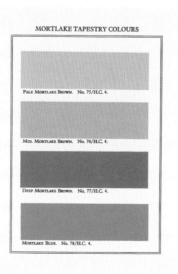

MORTLAKE TAPESTRY COLOURS

Pale Mortlake Brown.   No. 75/H.C. 4.

Mid. Mortlake Brown.   No. 76/H.C. 4.

Deep Mortlake Brown.   No. 77/H.C. 4.

Mortlake Blue.   No. 78/H.C. 4.

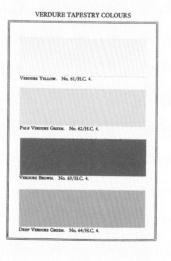

VERDURE TAPESTRY COLOURS

Verdure Yellow.   No. 61/H.C. 4.

Pale Verdure Green.   No. 62/H.C. 4.

Verdure Brown.   No. 63/H.C. 4.

Deep Verdure Green.   No. 64/H.C. 4.

PRIMITIVES

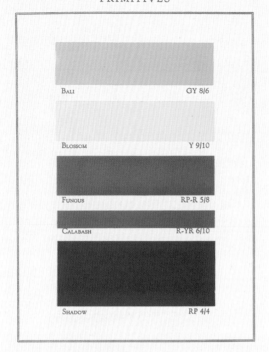

BALI	GY 8/6
BLOSSOM	Y 9/10
FUNGUS	RP-R 5/8
CALABASH	R-YR 6/10
SHADOW	RP 4/4

EGYPTIAN

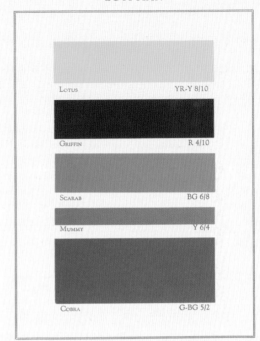

LOTUS	YR-Y 8/10
GRIFFIN	R 4/10
SCARAB	BG 6/8
MUMMY	Y 6/4
COBRA	G-BG 5/2

CRETAN

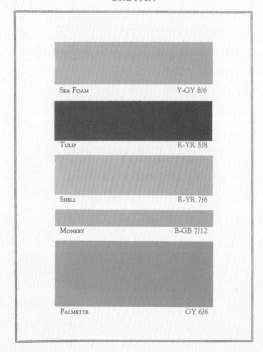

SEA FOAM	Y-GY 8/6
TULIP	R-YR 5/8
SHELL	R-YR 7/6
MONKEY	B-GB 7/12
PALMETTE	GY 6/6

GREEK

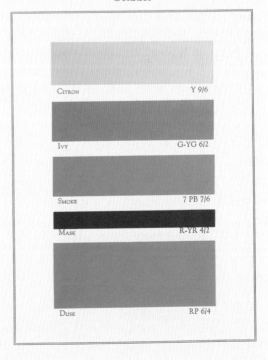

CITRON	Y 9/6
IVY	G-YG 6/2
SMOKE	7 PB 7/6
MASK	R-YR 4/2
DUSK	RP 6/4

GRECO ROMAN
(Pompeians)

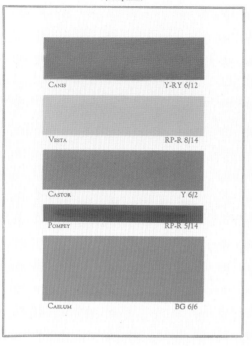

Canis	Y-RY 6/12
Vesta	RP-R 8/14
Castor	Y 6/2
Pompey	RP-R 5/14
Caelum	BG 6/6

ITALIAN PRIMITIVE

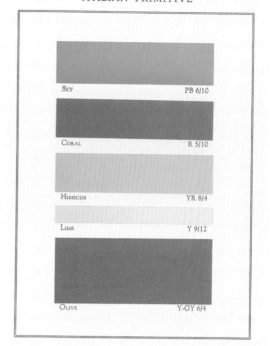

Sky	PB 6/10
Coral	R 5/10
Hibiscus	YR 8/4
Lime	Y 9/12
Olive	Y-GY 6/4

ITALIAN RENAISSANCE

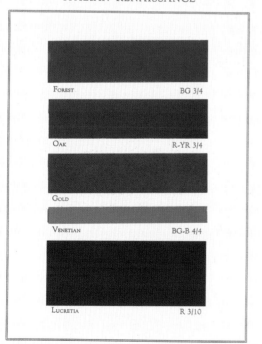

Forest	BG 3/4
Oak	R-YR 3/4
Gold	
Venetian	BG-B 4/4
Lucretia	R 3/10

FLEMISH PRIMITIVE

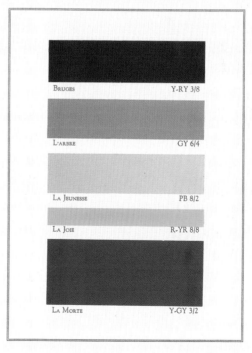

Bruges	Y-RY 3/8
L'arbre	GY 6/4
La Jeunesse	PB 8/2
La Joie	R-YR 8/8
La Morte	Y-GY 3/2

FRENCH, LOUIS XV

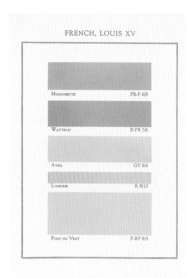

MIGNONETTE	PB-P 6/8
WATTEAU	B-PB 7/6
AVRIL	GY 8/6
L'AMOUR	R 8/10
POUF DU VENT	P-RP 8/4

FRENCH, LOUIS XVI

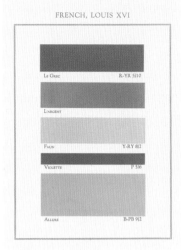

LE GREC	R-YR 5/10
L'ARGENT	
FAUN	Y-RY 8/2
VIOLETTE	P 5/6
ALLURE	B-PB 9/2

FRENCH, EMPIRE

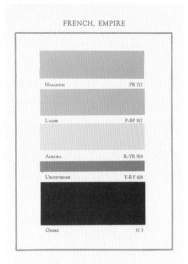

HYACINTH	PB 7/2
L'AUBE	P-BP 9/2
AURORA	R-YR 9/4
L'EGYPTIENNE	Y-RY 6/6
OMBRE	N 3

ENGLISH, 18th CENTURY

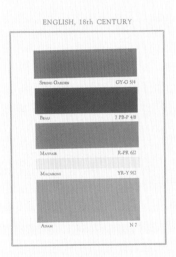

SPRING GARDEN	GY-G 5/4
BEAU	7 PB-P 4/8
MAYFAIR	R-PR 6/2
MACARONI	YR-Y 9/2
ADAM	N 7

ENGLISH, VICTORIAN

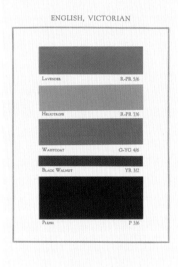

LAVENDER	R-PR 5/6
HELIOTROPE	R-PR 7/6
WAISTCOAT	G-YG 4/6
BLACK WALNUT	YR 3/2
PLUSH	P 3/6

CHINESE, BUDDHIST

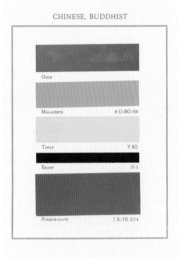

GOLD	
MALACHITE	6 G-BG 6/6
TOPAZ	Y 8/2
EBONY	N 1
POMEGRANATE	7 R-YR 5/14

CHINESE, SUNG

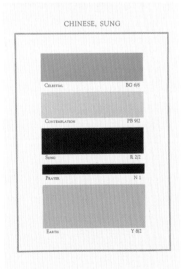

CELESTIAL	BG 6/6
CONTEMPLATION	PB 9/2
SUNG	R 2/2
PRAYER	N 1
EARTH	Y 8/2

INDIAN

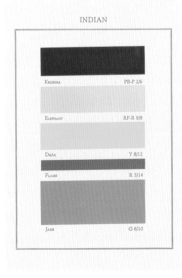

KRISHNA	PB-P 2/6
ELEPHANT	RP-R 8/8
DHÂK	Y 8/12
FLAME	R 5/14
JADE	G 6/10

PERSIAN FRESCO

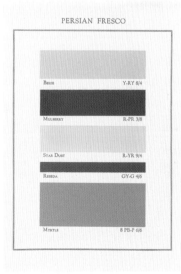

BRIAR	Y-RY 8/4
MULBERRY	R-PR 3/8
STAR DUST	R-YR 9/4
RESEDA	GY-G 4/6
MYRTLE	8 PB-P 6/6

PERSIAN MINIATURE

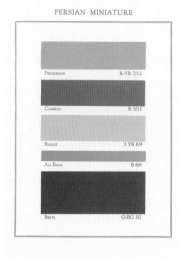

PERSIMMON	R-YR 7/12
CAMELIA	R 5/12
BISQUE	3 YR 8/4
ALI BABA	B 6/6
BERYL	G-BG 3/2

SPANISH, VELASQUEZ

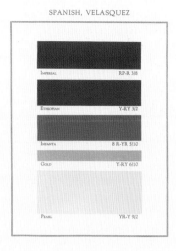

IMPERIAL	RP-R 3/8
ETHIOPIAN	Y-RY 3/2
INFANTA	8 R-YR 5/10
GOLD	Y-RY 6/10
PEARL	YR-Y 9/2

SPANISH, EL GRECO

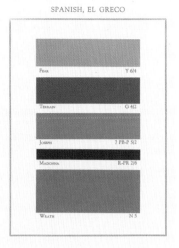

FEAR	Y 6/4
TERRAIN	G 4/2
JOSEPH	7 PB-P 5/2
MADONNA	R-PR 2/6
WRATH	N 5

MEXICAN

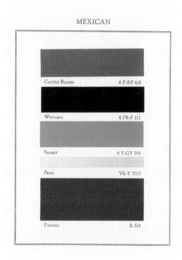

CACTUS BLOOM	6 P-RP 6/8
WISTARIA	8 PB-P 2/2
SUNSET	6 Y-GY 9/4
PEON	YR-Y 7/10
PANCHO	R 5/4

PERUVIAN

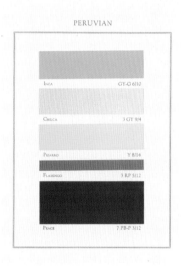

INCA	GY-G 6/10
CHILCA	3 GY 9/4
PIZARRO	Y 8/14
FLAMINGO	3 RP 5/12
PEACE	7 PB-P 3/12

RUSSIAN

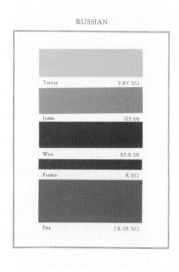

TARTAR	Y-RY 7/12
JASPER	GY 6/8
WINE	RP-R 3/8
PASSION	R 3/12
FIRE	7 R-YR 5/12

SWEDISH

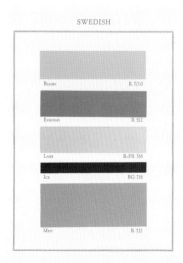

BLUSH	R 7/10
EVENING	R 5/2
LAKE	R-PR 3/6
ICE	BG 7/8
MIST	R 7/2

AMERICAN, SAMPLER

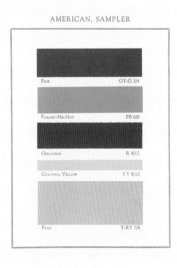

PINE	GY-G 3/4
FORGET-ME-NOT	PB 6/8
GERANIUM	R 4/12
COLONIAL YELLOW	3 Y 8/10
FLAX	Y-RY 7/6

AMERICAN, FRACTUR

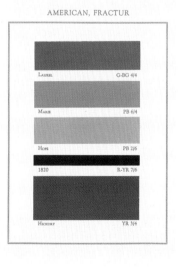

LAUREL	G-BG 4/4
MARIE	PB 6/4
HOPE	PB 2/6
1820	R-YR 7/6
HICKORY	YR 3/4

THE SPREAD OF STANDARDIZATION

During World War I, British Standards were used by the Admiralty, the War Office, the Board of Trade, Lloyd's Register, the Home Office, the Road Board, the London County Council and many of the smaller colonial governments. During the 1920s, standardization spread to Canada, Australia, South Africa and New Zealand. Interest was also developing in the United States and Germany.

It was inevitable that the British Engineering Standards Association (an earlier name of the British Standards Institution) would consider paint colour, and in 1930 *British Standard 381: 1930 Schedule of Colours for Ready Mixed Paints* was published. In order to compare other colours with the standards, a piece of clear celluloid was provided so that it could be placed over them and a fair assessment made.

This range of sixty-four colours was revised in 1931 as *British Standard 381C: 1931 Colours for Ready Mixed Paint,* and it was this version that provided the limited palette of paint colours available from most paint manufacturers throughout the next twenty-five years.

A key event in the introduction of colour standards was the founding of the British Colour Council in 1931. Under its director, the designer Robert Francis Wilson, it was active until the 1960s and produced a number of indexes of named colours for use by government, industry, academia and horticulture. When the British Colour Council came into being, the declared aims and objects included the placing of 'colour determination' for the British Empire in British hands and the provision of standard names for colours for the sake of clarity.

In 1934 the British Colour Council published a *Dictionary of Colour Standards* in two volumes, one showing 220 colours presented on pure silk ribbon – named, numbered and coded – and the other giving the history of each colour, the various names by which each had been known previously and the authority for standardization. Both this and the British Colour Council's subsequent book, *Traditional British Colours* (1937), formed part of later influential standards.

In the same year (1934), the French painter Amédée Ozenfant wrote six articles on colour for the *Architectural Review*. Ozenfant thought colour to be an essential element of architecture, rather than something considered by the architect as his work was being built. He believed that colour always modified the form of the building and should receive careful attention. Ozenfant was in no doubt that a range of paint colours for interior decoration was much needed. He believed strongly that England had a distinct palette, about which he enthused at length:

> There is the strong 'tobacco brown' that one found, with the white and the famous green of fishing boats; there is the authentic old stout-bottle brown; and that of the doors of the aristocratic streets and magnificent squares of the Adam period; the red, blue and green; the dark brown of old timbers; the deep greens beloved of joiners, and of old wagons, and the 'English' vermilion which signifies British, especially on labels of international produce.

Although very keen that a set of standardized colours should be produced, Ozenfant was aware that such a thing would have to be undertaken on a national basis.

THE WILSON COLOUR CHART

The first volume of *The Wilson Colour Chart* appeared in 1938. It showed one hundred colour samples: one per page. It was designed with horticulturalists in mind, but it was recognized that the chart would also 'have a use and value far outside its horticultural scope'.

The aim of producing a collection of colour samples each with a single name that would be recognized by the textile and other colour-referencing industries, as well as by artists' colourmen, was on its way to being met. For at the International Horticultural Conference in Berlin in 1938, *The Wilson Colour Chart* was 'recommended as an international standard'.

[PP. 258-261] Pages from *Historical Color Guide* (1938) by Elizabeth Burris-Meyer. This work contained thirty plates of colours 'from the primitive to the modern', based on Thomas Parsons' *A Tint Book of Historical Colours* (1934), but the colours were more vibrant and perhaps less practical for decorative use. However well meant, such distortions only underlined the need for standard references. [OPPOSITE] Pages from the first range of British Standard colours – BS 381: 1930 *Schedule of Colours for Ready Mixed Paints.* [PP. 264-267] *The Horticultural Colour Chart* (1939-42) was a direct development of *The Wilson Colour Chart*. It provided equivalent colour names from four other systems: British Colour Council, Ridgway, *Répertoire de couleurs* and Ostwald.

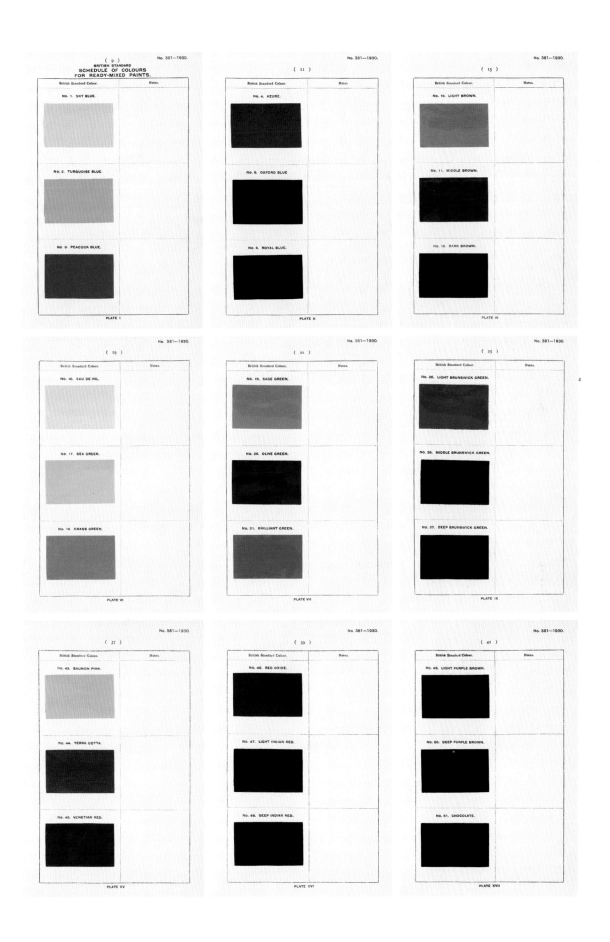

MAJOLICA YELLOW o9

EQUIVALENT TO

BRITISH COLOUR COUNCIL :	Nil
RIDGWAY	Ochraceous Orange 15′
REPERTOIRE	Ocre (Vraie) 313/4
OSTWALD	

History :

The typical yellow colour of the pottery ware which resembles porcelain. The name being derived from the Italian *Maiolica* for Majorca from whence the first specimens came.

o9/₃

Foreign Synonyms :

Dutch :	*Majolica geel*
French :	*Jaune majolique*
German :	*Majolikagelb*
Italian :	*Giallo Maiolica*
Latin :	*Flavus majolicanus*
Spanish :	*Amarillo mayólica*

o9/₂

Horticultural Examples :

o9/₃

o9/₂

o9/₁

o9/₁

o9

o9 *Primula aurantiaca*
Crepis aurea

102

BARIUM YELLOW 503

EQUIVALENT TO

BRITISH COLOUR COUNCIL :	Nil
RIDGWAY	Baryta Yellow 21 f
REPERTOIRE	Jaune Succin 28/2
OSTWALD	

History :

A name which has been in use for over 100 years, especially in the paint trade, Barium being the metallic basis of Oxide of Barium.

503/₃

Foreign Synonyms :

Dutch :	*Barium geel*
French :	*Jaune de baryum*
German :	*Baryumgelb*
Italian :	*Giallo bario*
Latin :	*Luteus baryticus*
Spanish :	*Amarillo de bario*

503/₂

Horticultural Examples :

503/₃

503/₁

503/₂

503/₁

503

503

131

MIMOSA YELLOW 602

EQUIVALENT TO

BRITISH COLOUR COUNCIL :	Nil
RIDGWAY	Nil
REPERTOIRE	Jaune Soufre 18/4
OSTWALD	

History :

A colour name which has been used for many years in the textile trade. The colour here shown is a general representation of the yellow of the flowers of the shrub.

602/₃

Foreign Synonyms :

Dutch :	*Mimosageel*
French :	*Jaune Mimosa*
German :	*Mimosengelb*
Italian :	*Giallo Mimosa*
Latin :	*Mimosinus*
Spanish :	*Amarillo mimosa*

602/₂

Horticultural Examples :

602/₃ *Tulipa primulina*

602/₂ *Pomaderris elliptica*

602/₁ *Corydalis thalictrifolia*

602 *Raffenaldia primuloides*
Linum campanulatum
Sedum acre
Paeonia Potanini trollioides

602/₁

602

143

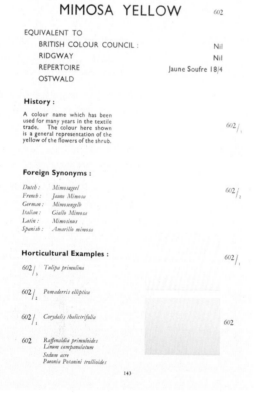

CHROME YELLOW 605
(Light)

EQUIVALENT TO

BRITISH COLOUR COUNCIL :	Nil
RIDGWAY	Nil
REPERTOIRE	Jaune de Chrome moyen 26/1
OSTWALD	

History :

A paint name for this colour which has been in use since the beginning of the 19th Century.

605/₃

Foreign Synonyms :

Dutch :	*Chromiumgeel*
French :	*Jaune de Chrome*
German :	*Chromgelb*
Italian :	*Giallo cromo*
Latin :	*Luteus chromatinus*
Spanish :	*Amarillo cromo*

605/₂

Horticultural Examples :

605/₃

605/₂

605/₁

605 *Rose "Mrs. Wemyss Quin"*
Hypericum Androsaemum

605/₁

605

144

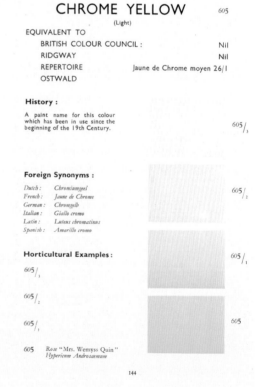

BLUEBIRD BLUE o42

EQUIVALENT TO

BRITISH COLOUR COUNCIL :   Nil
RIDGWAY   Dull Violet-Blue 53*
REPERTOIRE   Nil
OSTWALD   VIII 13 ia

History :

General representation of the plumage of the Bluebird *(Sialia sialis)* found in North America. A more intense blue appears in some individual feathers in the wings and on the body.

o42/₃

Foreign Synonyms :

Dutch :   Sialiablauw
French :   Bleu sialia
German :   Sialiablau
Italian :   Azzurro sialia
Latin :   Caeruleus sialianus
Spanish :   Azul sialia

o42/₂

Horticultural Examples :

o42/₃

o42/₂   *Jasione montana*
    Fuchsia procumbens (stamens)
    Globularia vulgaris

o42/₁

o42/₁

o42

o42

118

SEA BLUE o43

EQUIVALENT TO

BRITISH COLOUR COUNCIL :   Nil
RIDGWAY   Nil
REPERTOIRE   Bleu Marine 211/2
OSTWALD

History :

A descriptive colour name which has long been associated with this colour.

o43/₃

Foreign Synonyms :

Dutch :   Zee blauw
French :   Bleu de mer
German :   Meerblau
Italian :   Azzurro mare
Latin :   Azureus marinus
Spanish :   Azul de mar

o43/₂

Horticultural Examples :

o43/₃

o43/₂

o43/₁   *Allium caeruleum*

o43/₁

o43

o43

119

MOORISH BLUE 739

EQUIVALENT TO

BRITISH COLOUR COUNCIL :   Nil
RIDGWAY   Nil
REPERTOIRE   Nil
OSTWALD

History :

A colour typical of Moorish art especially in tiles and pottery.

739/₃

Foreign Synonyms :

Dutch :   Moorsch blauw
French :   Bleu Moresque
German :   Maurischblau
Italian :   Azzurro Moresco
Latin :   Caeruleus mauricus
Spanish :   Azul Morisco

739/₂

Horticultural Examples :

739/₁

739/₃   *Anemone Hepatica*
    (Hepatica nobilis)

739/₂

739/₁

739

739

163

CORNFLOWER BLUE 742

EQUIVALENT TO

BRITISH COLOUR COUNCIL :   Cornflower B.C.C. 217
RIDGWAY   Nil
REPERTOIRE   Nil
OSTWALD

History :

A colour standardised by the British Colour Council in the Dictionary of Colour Standards and matched to the cultivated Cornflower.

742/₃

Foreign Synonyms :

Dutch :   Korenbloem blauw
French :   Bluet
German :   Kornblumenblau
Italian :   Azzurro di Fiordaliso
Latin :   Cyaninus
Spanish :   Azul Amapola

742/₂

Horticultural Examples :

742/₃   *Lithospermum rosmarinifolium*

742/₂   *Delphinium cinereum*
    Coleus thyrsoideus

742/₁

742/₁

742   *Phacelia campanularia*

742

164

BRICK RED   o16

EQUIVALENT TO

BRITISH COLOUR COUNCIL :	Brick Red BCC 125
RIDGWAY	Nil
REPERTOIRE	Nil
OSTWALD	XII 6 pc

History :

An old colour name dating back to the 17th century. Standard-ised in 1934 in the British Colour Council Dictionary of Colour Standards.

o16/₃

Foreign Synonyms :

Dutch :	Steen rood
French :	Rouge de brique
German :	Zieglrot
Italian :	Rosso di mattone
Latin :	Testaceus
Spanish :	Rojo ladrillo

o16/₂

Horticultural Examples :

o16/₃

o16/₂

o16/₁

o16/₁

o16   Kennedia coccinea (Standard)

o16

106

DUTCH VERMILION   717

EQUIVALENT TO

BRITISH COLOUR COUNCIL :	Nil
RIDGWAY	Nil
REPERTOIRE	Rouge Ponceau 84/3
OSTWALD	

History :

A name given to this particular hue of vermilion due to its fre-quent use by the famous Dutch painters.

717/₃

Foreign Synonyms :

Dutch :	Hollandsch vermiljoen
French :	Vermillon hollandais
German :	Holländischer Zinnober
Italian :	Vermiglio d'Olanda
Latin :	Ruber vermicularis hollandicus
Spanish :	Bermellón holandés

717/₂

Horticultural Examples :

717/₃   Fuchsia parviflora
           Tulipa Veneris

717/₂   Euphorbia fulgens
           Impatiens Holstii

717/₁   Begonia Davisii

717/₁

717   Hippeastrum pratense

717

156

BLOOD RED   820

EQUIVALENT TO

BRITISH COLOUR COUNCIL :	Union Jack Red B.C.C. 210
RIDGWAY	Nil
REPERTOIRE	Rouge Sang 93/3
OSTWALD	

History :

A self explanatory colour name dating back to the 13th century.

820/₃

Foreign Synonyms :

Dutch :	Bloed Rood
French :	Rouge Sang
German :	Blutrot
Italian :	Rosso Sangue
Latin :	Sanguineus
Spanish :	Rojo Sangre

820/₂

Horticultural Examples :

820/₃

820/₂   Cotoneaster × hybrida pendula
           (fruit)

820/₁

820/₁

820

820

166

RHODONITE RED   oo22

EQUIVALENT TO

BRITISH COLOUR COUNCIL :	Nil
RIDGWAY	Eugenia Red I'
REPERTOIRE	Nil
OSTWALD	

History :

Typical colour of Rhodonite—a manganese silicate.

oo22/₃

Foreign Synonyms :

Dutch :	Rhodonietrood
French :	Rouge rhodonite
German :	Rhodonitrot
Italian :	Rosso rodonite
Latin :	Ruber rhodoniticus
Spanish :	Rojo rodonita

oo22/₂

Horticultural Examples :

oo22/₃

oo22/₂

oo22/₁

oo22/₁

oo22

oo22

188

POD GREEN   o61

EQUIVALENT TO

BRITISH COLOUR COUNCIL:	Nil
RIDGWAY	Dull Green Yellow 27'
REPERTOIRE	Vert Cossé 266/4
OSTWALD	XII 24 pe

History:

A colour name which has been in use since the beginning of the 20th century, being a general representation of the pods of fresh peas.

Foreign Synonyms:

Dutch:	*Dop groen*
French:	*Vert Cosse (de pois)*
German:	*Zuckerschotengrün*
Italian:	*Verde buccia di Pisello*
Latin:	*Viridis valvalarum (pisorum)*
Spanish:	*Verde de vaina de Guisante*

Horticultural Examples:

o61/₃

o61/₂

o61/₁

o61

o61/₃
o61/₂
o61/₁
o61

120

SCHEELES GREEN   860

EQUIVALENT TO

BRITISH COLOUR COUNCIL:	Nil
RIDGWAY	Nil
REPERTOIRE	Nil
OSTWALD	X 23 pe

History:

A colour named after the Swedish chemist Karl Wilhelm Scheele who discovered a dye of this colour in 1775 when investigating the reactions of arsenic.

Foreign Synonyms:

Dutch:	*Scheele's groen*
French:	*Vert Scheele*
German:	*Scheele-grün*
Italian:	*Verde Scheele*
Latin:	*Viridis Scheeleanus*
Spanish:	*Verde Scheele*

Horticultural Examples:

860/₃

860/₂

860/₁

860

175

SPINACH GREEN   o960

EQUIVALENT TO

BRITISH COLOUR COUNCIL:	Nil
RIDGWAY	Nil
REPERTOIRE	Vert Epinard 270/4
OSTWALD	

History:

Name introduced about 1896 for the colour of the vegetable Spinach. (Spinacia oleracea).

Foreign Synonyms:

Dutch:	*Spinaziegroen*
French:	*Vert-epinard*
German:	*Spinatgrün*
Italian:	*Verde spinacio*
Latin:	*Viridis spinaciae*
Spanish:	*Verde espinaca*

Horticultural Examples:

o960/₃

o960/₂ *Magnolia grandiflora* (foliage)

o960/₁

o960 *Anigozanthos Manglesii* (foliage)

o960/₃

o960/₂

o960/₁

o960

187

LAVENDER GREEN   ooo761

EQUIVALENT TO

BRITISH COLOUR COUNCIL:	Nil
RIDGWAY	Nil
REPERTOIRE	Vert Pois 277/1
OSTWALD	

History:

Colour of the mature leaf of the Lavender (Lavandula officinalis).

Foreign Synonyms:

Dutch:	*Lavendelgroen*
French:	*Vert-lavande*
German:	*Lavendelgrün*
Italian:	*Verde lavanda*
Latin:	*Viridis lavandulinus*
Spanish:	*Verde espliego*

Horticultural Examples:

ooo761/₃

ooo761/₂ *Leucadendron argenteum* (foliage)

ooo761/₁ *Lavandula officinalis* (foliage)

ooo761 *Pyrus salicifolia* (foliage)

ooo761/₃

ooo761/₂

ooo761/₁

ooo761

196

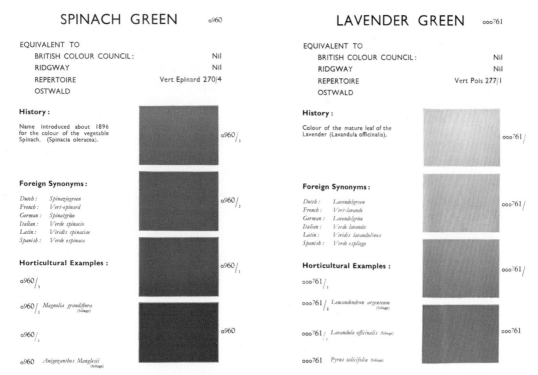

The cool, calming tones and intimate spaces of this bedroom, with a circular sitting area and a sleeping alcove, were designed in *c.* 1930 by the Paris firm Décoration Intérieure Moderne (D.I.M., sometimes known as Joubert et Petit, after its principals).

Émile-Jacques Ruhlmann was one of the foremost furniture and interiors designers of the French
art deco style of the 1920s. This illustration of a bedroom in his Hôtel du Collectionneur demonstrates
his characteristically refined elegance. Its walls were hung with ivory damask, giving an air
of understated luxury that is complemented by pale painted wood- and plasterwork.

Sensory overload caused by clutter and the brightly coloured and strongly patterned wallpapers beloved by the previous generation was sometimes given as the main reason for the preference for straight lines and quiet pale colours in the 1930s. In addition, new building methods allowed for the inclusion of larger windows, and a new-found love of nature required interiors to be decorated in sympathy with the view without.

[OPPOSITE] Images of interiors from *New Rooms for Old* (1935), Pinchin Johnson & Co. [OVERLEAF] [P.272 TOP] The modern part of Eltham palace was built for Stephen and Virginia Courtauld in the early 1930s. The entrance hall was created by the Swedish designer Rolf Engströmer. Its walls are lined with blackbean veneer and decorated with marquetry. The Engströmer furniture and Dorn rug are recreations of the originals. [P.272 BOTTOM] Virginia Courtauld's bedroom was lined with veneer and marquetry details with classical references. The wood in this room and in the entrance hall darkened with time, and slight adjustments had to be made to the colour of the ceilings more recently in order to reduce the contrast. [P.273] The landing and top of the spiral staircase at the modernist country villa The Homewood in Surrey. Designed by architect Patrick Gwynne for his family, it was completed in 1938. The colours are light and the surfaces reflective.

THE NEW CLEAN LINES

During the 1930s new methods of building houses using concrete meant that walls were no longer load-bearing and wider metal-framed and French windows could be fitted. There was also a tendency to build houses as far from the street as possible, and to open rooms onto the garden if circumstances allowed. The recognition of the health-giving properties of sunlight brought about a real 'return to nature', and the 'new architecture' – with its large windows and wide glass doors – once more brought the outside in. More than a hundred years previously, there had been a similar celebration of the new when Humphry Repton contrasted the 'modern living room' with 'the ancient cedar parlour' in his *Fragments on the Theory and Practice of Landscape Gardening* (1816, see p. 91).

One of the consequences of this new approach in architecture was the need for restraint in the choice of colour and ornament in interiors. With more of the outside world now visible, there was a greater tendency for discordant effects – with the indoors competing with the outdoors. This did not necessarily demand white walls and ceilings, with plain-coloured upholstery and neither pictures nor sculptures. It did, however, mean that colours should be pale and soft and that works of art should be subordinate to the room rather than dominate it.

The clean lines created by the new building methods had a noticeable effect on existing houses as many underwent cosmetic refurbishment. New windows were installed; rooms were made to appear taller by the removal of picture rails and chair rails; and clutter was reduced to produce a more streamlined look. Panelled doors and staircase balustrades were smoothed out, by being covered with three-ply board, and modern lighting was introduced.

Paint too played a major part in the modernization of the interior, with durable enamel paints becoming more readily available. Light-reflective finishes in pale tints were introduced and paints with a high degree of gloss were used in a way not seen before.

Generally, it was felt that north rooms needed warm tones – colours containing red, orange or yellow. Rooms with a southern aspect were believed to get the most out of the sunlight outside if they were coloured in light neutral tints such as light grey, cream or ivory. Blue absorbs light, thus making the room seem cold; whereas green in its lighter tones and yellow most of all were thought to stimulate the mind and make the room cheerful. At the same time, it was understood that the warmer colours stood out more, thus making the room appear smaller, whereas walls painted in colder tones had a tendency to recede, which seemed to increase the size of the room.

A good account of this new approach to finish and colour was given in some of the publicity material being produced by several of the paint companies at the time.

NEW ROOMS FOR OLD

The images in this section come largely from a work published in 1935 by Pinchin Johnson & Co. It was titled *New Rooms for Old. Some helpful designs and details for transforming the ordinary interior into the ultra modern.* The title is clear enough, and each room of the house is shown before and after modernization.

The type of paints produced by Pinchin Johnson & Co. were very similar to those manufactured by Thomas Parsons & Sons, some of whose products are featured on these pages. Colours from the latter's extensive catalogue have been selected to indicate the closest match, should readers want to draw inspiration from these images. In most instances, a reasonable likeness can be found, but some colours would need adjustment if a fully accurate copy were to be achieved.

In each case, there is a brief commentary, emphasizing the differences between the old and the new rooms, and offering a few thoughts on the paints. Of particular note throughout these images is the theme of 'streamlining':

(1) the 'heightening' of rooms by the elimination of chair and picture rails;

(2) the smoothing-off of surfaces and the consequent reduction of dust traps;

(3) the replacement of wallpaper with paint;

(4) the increased light produced by changing the windows, improving the artificial lighting and the use of lighter colours in shinier paint; and

(5) the provision of storage spaces to reduce clutter.

PALE ART GREEN PARLYTE

PERMANENT BROWN NO.4 ENAMEL

BROKEN WHITE ENAMEL

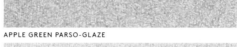

APPLE GREEN PARSO-GLAZE

IVORY PARSO-GLAZE

BROKEN WHITE PARLYTE

THE HALL

The room descriptions in this section are those found in the original book. The caption below the Hall image reads as follows:

> An exceptionally attractive air of spaciousness and charm has been secured in this, otherwise quite ordinary hall by the sample means of covering the doors with three-ply, or composition board, boxing in the old-fashioned balustrade and building out a corner cupboard for the storage of overcoats, umbrellas, etc. A wall lighting fitting of modern and inexpensive design replaces the hanging light and the whole is finished in shades of Deydol Water Paint and Satinette Enamel.

In this case, the walls were painted in an eau-de-Nil shade. Deydol water paint was what is known as an oil-bound distemper, very similar to Thomas Parsons' Parlyte water paint. The satinette enamel was a white gloss enamel, presumably similar to one of the Parsons' gloss enamels.

The colours shown here are approximations to the Hall colours from the Parsons' range.

THE MORNING ROOM

Most houses have a room with a French casement leading to the garden. The conversion of such an interior into a morning, or breakfast-room, is quite a simple matter. The old-fashioned fireplace is removed and replaced by one of modern design, with a lighting unit of character on either side. The recess is filled in with a comfortable settee, and a small writing-table – a handy feature in such a room – is also introduced. The decoration is effected by means of Hygeia Flat Wall Finish and Veritone Scumble varnished with Gripon Supervar.

All mod cons are shown in this image: telephone, electric wall light and electric fire.

The walls and joinery appear to have been given a glazed finish – a ground coat of a flat oil finish (although an eggshell might have been used) with a coat of tinted scumble glaze stippled on top, before being given a coat of varnish (presumably matt or eggshell). The nearest Parsons' green-coloured scumble glaze is far too bright and yellow, but it does show the technique well.

The colours shown here are broad approximations to the Morning Room colours from the Parsons' range.

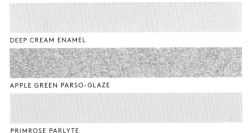

DEEP CREAM ENAMEL

APPLE GREEN PARSO-GLAZE

PRIMROSE PARLYTE

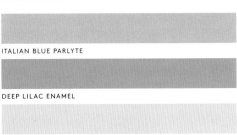

ITALIAN BLUE PARLYTE

DEEP LILAC ENAMEL

PRIMROSE ENAMEL

THE LOUNGE

In this view of the lounge, the two recesses beside the fireplace are filled; on the one side, with a lounge settee of the most comfortable description; and on the other, with a cocktail cabinet. The old fireplace is replaced by a modern panel type electric fire and the lighting is secured by means of tubular lamps placed on either side of the mirror. The window shown is of metal type in wood-surround. The decorating materials employed are Satinette Enamel, Deydol Water Paint, Veritone Scumble and Gripon Supervar.

Once again, all mod cons are featured in this room: wall lighting and a rather useful-looking directional lamp beside the 'lounge settee', an electric fire and a magnificently equipped cocktail cabinet.

From the description, it seems that the walls would have been given a glazed and varnished finish, the ceiling was painted in a water paint and the joinery in a gloss enamel. The Parsons' green stippled finish is obviously too bright and yellow, but again it does show the technique well.

The colours shown here are rough approximations to the Lounge colours from the Parsons' range.

THE LIVING ROOM

The building-out of the fireplace and the construction of one settee beneath the window and another facing it on this side of the fireplace has introduced an air of complete comfort and spaciousness into what was previously an average, plain living or drawing room. It will be observed that provision has been made for a gramophone or wireless cabinet – the cupboards, on either side of the settees, forming handy receptacles for records. The bright effect of the blue upholstery is heightened by the colouring of the walls and woodwork. The materials used are Satinette Enamel, Velveteen Flat Wall Paint and Figaro Hard Enamel Gloss Paint.

The modern lighting would have been enhanced by the satinette enamel on the walls and the very shiny joinery, which was based on 'home entertainment' of a most sophisticated kind. Note also the clock, which has been built into the wall. The use of complementary colours – blue and yellow – would have made the whole effect very crisp.

The colours shown here are good approximations to the Living Room colours from the Parsons' range.

BRILLIANT YELLOW PARLYTE

DARK BATH STONE PARSO-STONE

REGENT GREEN ENAMEL

CAVENDISH GREY PARLYTE

DEEP CREAM ENAMEL

PERMANENT BROWN NO.4 ENAMEL

THE DINING ROOM

The awkward recess occasioned in this room by the bay window is pressed into useful service in our adaptation by being made an auxiliary to the table. This latter is secured to the floor, which enables the top to project far enough to allow comfortable leg space everywhere. The sideboard with its accompanying lounges on either side lends a great deal of character to the room itself. The casement windows have been removed and replaced by those of metal type. Lighting panels are let into the wall. The decoration is provided by means of Deydol Water Paint, Cementilk The Perfect Rough Surface Decorative Material and Satinette Enamel.

This is a very interesting development. The space-saving, albeit rather curious, table would surely have resulted in some guests sitting with their backs to their neighbours. The bronze panther statue on the glass display case is a classic piece of art deco decoration. Of particular interest is the juxtaposition of rough-textured walls with shiny smooth surfaces.
The colours shown here are approximations to the Dining Room colours from the Parsons' range. The stone textured paint is too pale.

THE STUDY

It has been said that books form the finest decorative background that it is possible to have. In most homes the books are housed in a bureau or old type bookcase and so lose half their decorative value. The interior pictured here has been revised to form a lounge-study, or writing room, in which everything is happily placed both for service and for artistic effect. The decoration carried out with Deydol Water Paint and Satinette Enamel is exceptionally restful and pleasing.

In the Study, the joinery appears to have been painted with something like Parsons' deep cream enamel paint and the flat upper surfaces in permanent brown. The high gloss of these surfaces is evident. The walls have a grey water paint, which is similar to the Parsons' Cavendish grey.
The colours shown here are approximations to the Study colours from the Parsons' range.

IVORY PARSO-GLAZE

PERMANENT BROWN NO.6 ENAMEL

NEW STONE ENAMEL

TERRACOTTA WALL FINISH

PERMANENT BROWN NO.6 ENAMEL

IVORY PARSO-GLAZE

THE BEDROOM

The fitment which has been constructed across the whole of one side of this bedroom replaces both dressing table and wardrobe. Centred upon the window, it is finished in two distinct shades of Satinette Enamel in order to break the monotony of line, and is boxed in at the top to provide space for concealed electric lights. The door has been simplified and a full-length mirror takes the place of panelling. The window is of metal, in wood surround. The walls are pleasantly stippled. The materials used are Hygeia Flat Wall Finish with Satinette Enamel.

The dressing table has been painted in a brown-virtually-black gloss enamel, like Parsons' permanent brown no. 6. The other joinery has also been painted in an enamel in a colour slightly darker than new stone, and the walls have been stippled in something like Parsons' Parso-glaze in Ivory.

The colours shown here are approximations to the Bedroom colours from the Parsons' range.

THE BATHROOM

The delightful and cheerful appearance of this bathroom is attained by the building-in of the bath and wash basin, and by the freshness and charm of its decoration. You must sing in such a bathroom as this. The space beside the foot of the bath is utilized for a most useful cupboard and additional cupboard space is provided on either side of the basin. Artificial lighting is provided by panels let in above the bath and beside the basin. The materials used to create the effect shown in our illustration are Satinette the Perfect Enamel, Hygeia Flat Wall Finish and Gripon Supervar.

The washbasin and cupboard at the foot of the bath seem to have been painted in a gloss enamel similar in colour to Parsons' new stone. The walls were probably painted in a flat wall finish, which no doubt was similar to Parsons' colour terracotta. Underneath the washbasin, the bath panel and wedge-shaped element appear to have been given a marbled effect using scumble glaze and then varnished for protection. It is possible that the skirting of this element has been painted in a colour like permanent brown no. 6.

The colours shown here are approximations to the Bathroom colours from the Parsons' range.

BATH STONE ENAMEL

TURQUOISE GLOSS

MID-BLUE GLOSS

IVORY PARSO-GLAZE

SILVER PARSO-GLAZE

PERMANENT BROWN NO. 4 ENAMEL

THE KITCHEN

A spotless and well-ordered kitchen is a delight and, from an hygienic point of view, an absolute necessity in the modern home. Here is a re-modelled kitchen of which any house-wife would be proud. Everything is placed ready for use and where it is most needed. A window of a more modern character has been introduced and two lighting panels are placed, handily, above the sink. The colour scheme selected is cheerful and bright and purposely in light shades, so that dust and dirt may be instantly detected. These beautiful, sanitary and washable surfaces are created by Figaro Hard Enamel Gloss Paint and Satinette Enamel.

As indicated, all the surfaces were very shiny in this 1930s kitchen. The walls, ceiling and door of the room were covered in an enamel paint in a colour similar to Parsons' Bath stone. A harder gloss paint was applied to the work surfaces, upstand and door architrave in a mid blue, and the same sort of finish was employed in a colour similar to Parsons' turquoise on the kitchen units and the cupboards.

The colours shown here are approximations to the Kitchen colours from the Parsons' range.

THE NURSERY

Many houses have a small room which is neglected or used simply as a lumber room. With the advent of the electric fire, these rooms may be put into service for a variety of purposes. Here such an interior had been converted into a nursery, or play room, for the little folk. The built-out fireplace, with its complement of shelves and cupboards, forms a snug fitment and one which encourages tidiness. The miniature desk and seat should prove an incentive to lessons. The scheme of decoration selected is carried out in Velveteen Flat Wall Paint, Deydol Water Paint, Satinette Enamel and Veritone Scumble, varnished with Gripon Supervar.

The walls have been painted with flat wall paint and scumbled with a glaze similar to Parsons' ivory. The ceiling was painted in a water paint in a colour close to Parsons' beige. The desk unit has been stippled and then given a gloss varnish similar to Parsons' silver Parso-glaze. The door has been 'flushed' with a sheet of plywood and painted in an enamel similar to Parsons' permanent brown no. 4.

The colours are rough approximations to the Nursery colours from the Parsons' range.

PRACTICAL GRAINING AND MARBLING (1902)
PAUL N. HASLUCK

A very detailed little work edited by the author of many such useful works. The tools, materials and processes for what Paul N. Hasluck (1854–1931) describes as an 'English art' are itemized. Although successfully practised for more than a hundred years (i.e. from the beginning of the nineteenth century) it did not reach its peak of perfection and popularity until the mid-century. Hasluck acknowledges that some claimed that such techniques were an 'exhibition of artistic ignorance', but felt that such criticisms had largely abated.

Provided that painted imitations are employed where the genuine article could properly be used they were no more objectionable than plaster imitations of carved stonework and picture frames treated to resemble gold.

This work is still of use to the modern practitioner and most of the tools and brushes illustrated are identical to those in use in today.

A FEW SUGGESTIONS FOR ORNAMENTAL DECORATION (1908)
F. SCOTT MITCHELL

This was one of the many highly finished promotional publications produced by the firm of Thomas Parsons & Sons. It shows a compilation of colour schemes for rooms of all types, decorative panels, borders and motifs in period and contemporary styles.

Clearly, the aim was to sell Parsons' products, but the many illustrations and enclosed colour samples reveal a lot about decorative trends at the beginning of the twentieth century. The different approaches to panelling the walls of a room by the use of paint rather than mouldings are illustrated, too. As if this were not sufficient, examples of decorative effects are also provided, including a Moorish niche and vase; Assyrian panels, borders and spandrels, and Byzantine borders and panels.

It is interesting to compare the products and the colours with those that appear in Parsons' extensive catalogue of the 1930s. The historical nature of decoration is evident – even more so in their classic work *A Tint Book of Historical Colours* (1934, see p. 254).

HOUSE PAINTING AND DECORATION (1912)
ARTHUR SEYMOUR JENNINGS

Arthur Seymour Jennings (1860–1928) wrote numerous books on the subject of painting and decorating. This, he tells readers, is an updated one of another that he wrote in 1905 under the nom-de-plume 'Herbert Arnold'. He emphasizes that the present work is aimed at the non-specialist at a price that is affordable. With this book, the reader would know what to use for different painting jobs; for whitewashing; paperhanging and varnishing.

The folly of using cheap brushes and bad tools is explained, as is the method of cleaning and storing good ones. A step-by-step description of how to decorate a room is given, as is the repainting of outside work. Perhaps somewhat ambitiously, Jennings also runs through the process of wood graining so that one might end up with a kitchen that will not show finger marks.

The chapter on colour mixing is especially useful as so many of the recipes are identical to those of a century or more before.

PAINTERS' AND DECORATORS' WORKS (1916)
HENRY GEO. DOWLING

This work by Henry Dowling was aimed at the young painter and decorator and was designed to supplement the information that he picked up during his apprenticeship.

The chapters deal with the purpose of painting; the tools, appliances and materials of the trade; and the various techniques that might be required. The book includes paper-hanging, imitative painting and even sign-writing and gilding. It is laid out like a course book, with questions posed at the end of each chapter to ensure a full understanding of the preceding pages.

The illustrations are particularly charming (see p. 80) and the three coloured plates showing suggested colour schemes are most helpful. It is believed that these were produced by the author.

The questions in the appendices are quite demanding, for example: What would you use to give an acid-resisting coat (colour immaterial) to a wooden vessel which is to contain a 10 per cent solution of sulphuric acid? What description of paint would you use for a stable to be finished in a light tint?

Also included is a section of cornice (see p. 168) asking how two olive greens and a light biscuit colour might be applied for best effect.

*THE HOME PAINTING
MANUAL* (1920)
THE SHERWIN-WILLIAMS CO.

*PAINTING AND DECORATING
WORKING METHODS* (1922)
F. N. VANDERWALKER

*THE DECORATION AND RENOVATION
OF THE HOME* (1924)
ARTHUR SEYMOUR JENNINGS

*OUTLINES OF PAINT
TECHNOLOGY* (1928)
NOEL HEATON

Although produced by a commercial paint company, the information contained in this manual would have been of use to any homeowner of the time.

The instructions for applying varnish, and for rubbing down a gloss varnish with powdered pumice-stone and rubbing oil to give a dull finish, are superb (matt varnishes came later). The treatment of floors and the staining and varnishing of wood are covered in great detail. Glazing and stencilling is dealt with, as is the tricky business of estimating quantities. Much is still relevant today, including such pieces of common sense as:

> To say that straight 'lead and oil' paint today is the best, would be to say that the world has progressed in every other industry but that of paint making.

Basic practical advice on colour is given, and the extensive range of sample specifications is particularly revealing about contemporary fashions. Readers are shown how to deal with, among other things, a 'Colonial Bedroom'; a 'Dining-Room in the Spirit of Old Colony Days'; a 'Homey Living-Room' and a 'Hospitable Hall'. These might have been in a 'Cosy Little Farm Cottage', or a 'Small English Stucco Residence'.

Fred Norman Vanderwalker (1885–1945) wrote a number of books on painting and decorating and colour-mixing from the 1920s to the 1940s. They are all useful.

Very much aware that the apprentice system had broken down in the United States by the end of the nineteenth century, the International Association of Master House Painters and Decorators of the United States and Canada began to seek a better method for training young men in the business of painting and decorating.

The expressed purpose of this book was to help educate boys and young men to be first-class journeymen house-painters. It was acknowledged that the scope was limited, but with the information in the book as a grounding and with practical work with an employer, it was felt that a competent workman would result.

As might be imagined, the contents are comprehensive and clear. The instructions for mixing and applying calcimine (soft distemper) are most useful and more detailed than usually found. It is well illustrated and has twenty examples of colours that can be mixed following the instructions given.

This book was written in response to the many requests for practical advice regarding decorating in the home that the author received in his capacity as editor of *The Decorator* magazine.

The aim of Jennings' book was threefold. The first was to provide examples of the many different colour combinations suitable for the decoration of rooms of all kinds. The second was to give practical information on all aspects of house-painting and decoration, with particular reference to the renovation of old houses to enable the architect, owner or tenant to give exact details of his requirements to his decorator or builder. The third aim was to explain modern methods of decoration with regard to the materials used and the effects that could be obtained, for example, the broken colour effects produced by the use of tinted scumble glazes and panelled work in wallpaper decoration.

Many of the advertisements shown on pages 214–215 can be found in this book.

This book was originally intended to form the seventh edition of an older classic, G. H. Hurst's *Painters' Colours, Oils, and Varnishes* (1892), but as the revision progressed it was realized that it would have to be entirely rewritten. First published in 1928, this work was revised extensively in 1946 and then amended further in 1956.

The format is similar to the older book: it is divided into three parts, and contains very detailed information on pigments, their properties and preparation; oils, solvents and resins; and paints and varnishes. It is one of the few technical works that should form part of the analyst's library.

Noel Heaton's book probably contains far more than is necessary for the general student of paint and colour. The chapters on oil paints and on water paints are very useful, however, and are well worth reading by student and professional alike. The detailed information on the different forms of distemper helps cut through the woolly thinking that often arises when this subject is raised.

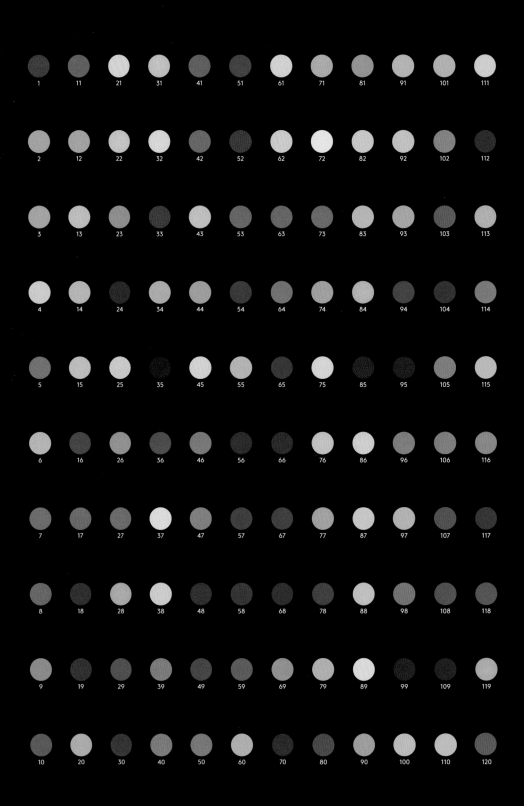

IV.

PAINTS, COLOUR STANDARDS AND INTERIORS

1945 – 1960

120 COLOURS DERIVED FROM

THE DICTIONARY OF COLOURS FOR INTERIOR DECORATION (1949), BRITISH STANDARDS COUNCIL

(SEE PP. 288 – 291)

1. BRONZE	31. SAFFRON YELLOW	61. PORCELAIN GREEN	91. OPALINE GREEN
2. GOLDEN BUFF	32. LOTUS PINK	62. ABSINTHE	92. PINK BEIGE
3. EMPIRE ROSE	33. CHERRY	63. ALMOND GREEN	93. QUARTZ GREEN
4. LEMON YELLOW	34. CAMBRIDGE BLUE	64. BRACKEN BROWN	94. COFFEE BROWN
5. MOSS GREEN	35. ACONITE VIOLET	65. TEAL BLUE	95. SCARLET RED
6. LAVENDER GREY	36. WOODLAND BROWN	66. PEONY RED	96. STEEL GREY
7. GROTTO BLUE	37. REGENCY CREAM	67. WINCHESTER GREEN	97. MISTLETOE
8. DONKEY BROWN	38. TOPAZ	68. DERBY BLUE	98. DELFT ROSE
9. VIOLET SLATE	39. CHINESE ROSE	69. AMARANTH PINK	99. ROYAL PURPLE
10. FLORENTINE BLUE	40. MARIGOLD	70. BEAGLE GREEN	100. SILVER SAGE
11. SMALT	41. BLUE FIG	71. VERBENA MAUVE	101. LEAF BEIGE
12. LETTUCE GREEN	42. MALACHITE GREEN	72. SKY BLUE	102. BRUNSWICK GREEN
13. KASHMIR BEIGE	43. MAZARINE BLUE	73. RUSSET GOLD	103. PERSIAN ROSE
14. MEDICI BLUE	44. ROSE POMPADOUR	74. ROCKINGHAM GREEN	104. YEW GREEN
15. LILAC HAZE	45. CHINESE YELLOW	75. PEACH	105. MADONNA BLUE
16. JUNIPER	46. FRENCH TURQUOISE	76. MAIZE YELLOW	106. LAUREL GREEN
17. POPPY	47. DUESBURY GREEN	77. GRENADINE RED	107. AMETHYST VIOLET
18. CYANINE BLUE	48. BOKHARA GREEN	78. FOREST GREEN	108. COCONUT BROWN
19. CLARET	49. BRONZE GREEN	79. NEPTUNE GREEN	109. DELFT BLUE
20. CYCLAMEN PINK	50. LEEK GREEN	80. ROSE RED	110. MOONSTONE GREY
21. SEACREST GREEN	51. LINCOLN GREEN	81. PHLOX MAUVE	111. GENOESE PINK
22. BUTTERCUP YELLOW	52. PETUNIA PURPLE	82. LEAF GREEN	112. SPECTRUM VIOLET
23. BLUE LAVENDER	53. CAMPANULA MAUVE	83. GREENGAGE	113. SALMON PINK
24. WOOD VIOLET	54. ULTRAMARINE	84. NECTARINE	114. BLUEBIRD
25. ZIRCON BLUE	55. TROPIC TURQUOISE	85. RUBY	115. PEA GREEN
26. OLIVE GREEN	56. ENGLISH GREEN	86. APRICOT	116. FLAME
27. CAMEO VIOLET	57. ROYAL BLUE	87. FJORD BLUE	117. RIVER BLUE
28. MAJOLICA ORANGE	58. PURPLE LILAC	88. CHINESE JADE	118. EMPIRE GREEN
29. BERYL GREEN	59. MORTLAKE BROWN	89. LIME GREEN	119. SPANISH ORANGE
30. VICTORIA VIOLET	60. EGGSHELL GREEN	90. TYROLITE GREEN	120. PIMENTO

'Our interiors of today often depend rather more on colour than on architectural form. This is perhaps not the fault of the architect. He has to build for economy, both in terms of space and money, and he also has to use prefabricated members for his flat, house or bungalow. He therefore resorts to colour to improve or add variety to an interior, and it is remarkable what a difference can be effected wholly by colour.'* This section reviews the development of emulsion paints and the wide variety of colour ranges that emerged after World War II, together with the new popular interest in interior decoration by the homeowner.

*Noel Carrington, *Colour and Pattern in the Home* (1954)

BRITISH STANDARD
COLOURS FOR FLAT FINISHES
FOR WALL DECORATION

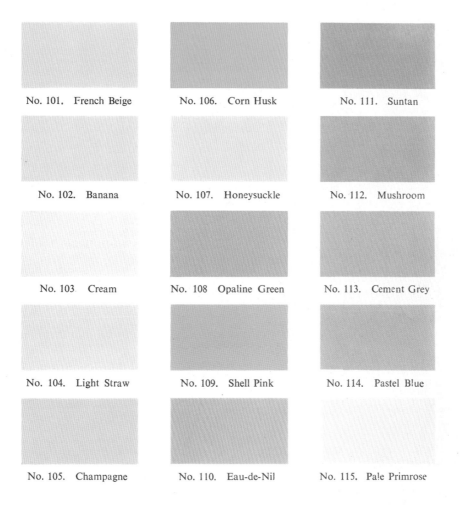

No. 101. French Beige	No. 106. Corn Husk	No. 111. Suntan
No. 102. Banana	No. 107. Honeysuckle	No. 112. Mushroom
No. 103 Cream	No. 108 Opaline Green	No. 113. Cement Grey
No. 104. Light Straw	No. 109. Shell Pink	No. 114. Pastel Blue
No. 105. Champagne	No. 110. Eau-de-Nil	No. 115. Pale Primrose

British Standard 1572: 1949 Colours for Flat Finishes for Wall Decoration was a range of paint colours designed for the Ministry of Works for the purpose of interior decoration. This range of seventeen colours – two were not displayed on the card: white and off-white (ivory) – superseded an earlier *British Standard, BS 381WD: 1945 Flat Colours for Wall Decoration*, which showed only ten colours.

Some of the best sources of information on the paint colours in use in the immediate post-war period were produced by the Ministry of Works in conjunction with the British Standards Institution. The published standards illustrate the limited colours selected for use in government buildings. *British Standard 1572: 1949 Colours for Flat Finishes for Wall Decoration* was a range of seventeen paint colours designed for the Ministry of Works for the purpose of interior decoration. It superseded an earlier standard (1945), which showed only ten colours:

101	French Beige
102	Banana
103	Cream
104	Light Straw
105	Champagne
106	Corn Husk
107	Honeysuckle
108	Opaline Green
109	Shell Pink
110	Eau de Nil

Five new colours were added in 1949 (two were not displayed on the colour card – white and off-white):

111	Suntan
112	Mushroom
113	Cement Grey
114	Pastel Blue
115	Pale Primrose

It is not known which type of 'flat finishes' the title of this small range refers to. It could be flat oil, such as Unicote flat wall finish, or water paint such, as Parsons' Duresco or Walpamur.

COLOUR SCHEMES

In 1952 HMSO published a set of short-term standards in the form of a colour card titled *Ministry of Works Colour Schemes for Interior Decoration of Normal Office Accommodation*. It was designed to show how the colours in *BS 1572: 1949* might be used – on which surfaces and in which types of paint. Within its pages are five sample schemes with colour chips suggesting how to decorate offices on different sides of a building. Scheme one is labelled 'General Scheme' and it was recommended

for the redecoration of single rooms where the existing general scheme was cream and green. The remaining schemes were based on their outlook – the warm schemes were recommended for rooms facing north-west to south-east (cool aspects) or on occasion for rooms facing south-east to north-west if they were over-shadowed and did not receive direct sunlight. The cool scheme was recommended for well-lit rooms that received direct sunlight.

The colours referred to were taken from *BS 1572: 1949*, which relates to colours for flat finishes, and from *BS 381C*, which relates to colours for gloss finishes. The broken white shown was not a British Standard colour, but had been adopted as standard for these schemes.

In the example designed for a well-lit room, it was recommended that the walls, skirtings, door frames and architraves be painted in cement grey (113). Whereas the walls should be painted in a semi-gloss finish, the woodwork should be in a more practical gloss paint. Ceilings and beams should be painted with French beige (101). In this case, the recommended finish was non-washable distemper (either a soft distemper or a product such as Ceilingite). Windows, reveals and window boards should be painted in a broken white gloss paint. On the back of the colour card the following notes were provided:

[A] All wall surfaces should be in semi-gloss finish and ceilings should be in non-washable distemper.

[B] Borrowed lights, cover strips and picture rails should be taken in with the general wall treatment. All other woodwork should be in gloss finish.

[C] Skirtings in schemes 2 to 5 should match the wall colour (but in gloss finish) in rooms of ordinary size and should vary in colour only in large rooms.

[D] Pipes at skirting level and radiators should match the background colour but be in gloss finish. Pipes etc. above skirting level should be taken in with the background.

[OPPOSITE] *Ministry of Works Colour Schemes* (Official Colour Card No. 1 1952) was an aid to the decoration of Ministry of Works offices of the early 1950s.

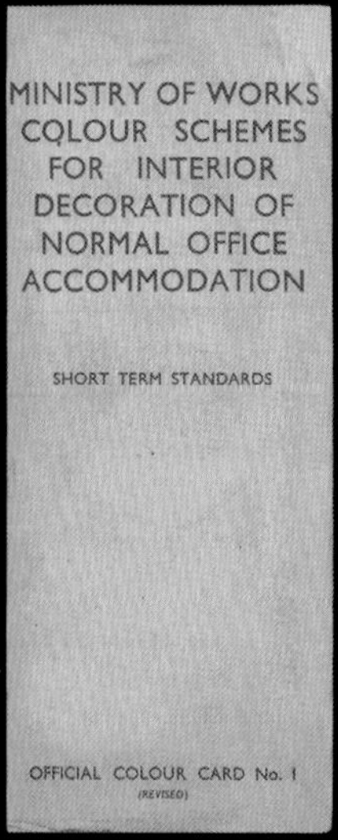

MINISTRY OF WORKS COLOUR SCHEMES FOR INTERIOR DECORATION OF NORMAL OFFICE ACCOMMODATION

SHORT TERM STANDARDS

OFFICIAL COLOUR CARD No. 1
(REVISED)

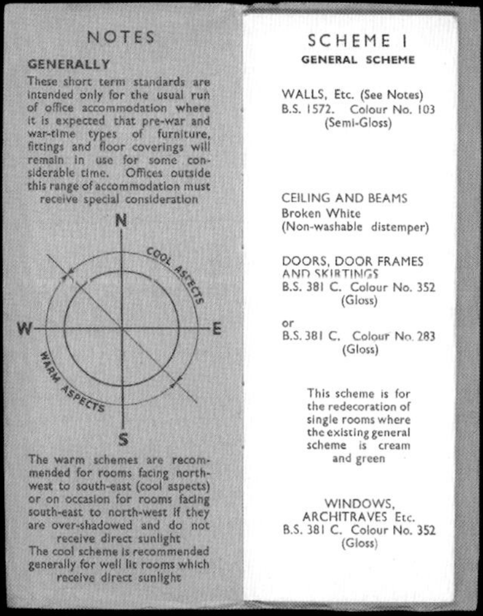

NOTES

GENERALLY

These short term standards are intended only for the usual run of office accommodation where it is expected that pre-war and war-time types of furniture, fittings and floor coverings will remain in use for some considerable time. Offices outside this range of accommodation must receive special consideration

The warm schemes are recommended for rooms facing north-west to south-east (cool aspects) or on occasion for rooms facing south-east to north-west if they are over-shadowed and do not receive direct sunlight
The cool scheme is recommended generally for well lit rooms which receive direct sunlight

---

SCHEME 1
GENERAL SCHEME

WALLS, Etc. (See Notes)
B.S. 1572.   Colour No. 103
(Semi-Gloss)

CEILING AND BEAMS
Broken White
(Non-washable distemper)

DOORS, DOOR FRAMES
AND SKIRTINGS
B.S. 381 C. Colour No. 352
(Gloss)

or

B.S. 381 C.   Colour No. 283
(Gloss)

This scheme is for the redecoration of single rooms where the existing general scheme is cream and green

WINDOWS,
ARCHITRAVES Etc.
B.S. 381 C. Colour No. 352
(Gloss)

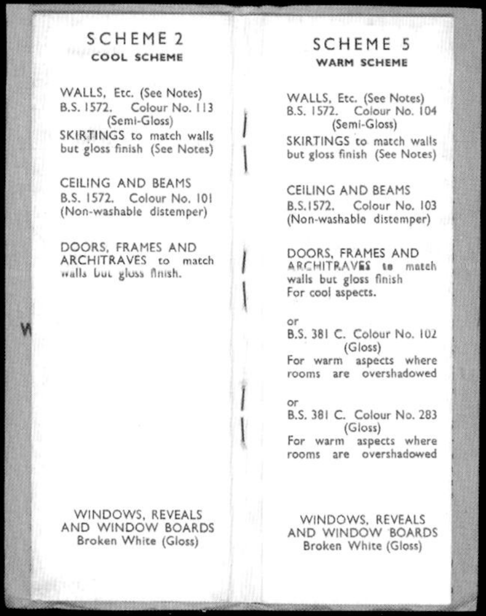

SCHEME 2
COOL SCHEME

WALLS, Etc. (See Notes)
B.S. 1572.   Colour No. 113
(Semi-Gloss)
SKIRTINGS to match walls
but gloss finish (See Notes)

CEILING AND BEAMS
B.S. 1572.   Colour No. 101
(Non-washable distemper)

DOORS, FRAMES AND
ARCHITRAVES to match
walls but gloss finish.

WINDOWS, REVEALS
AND WINDOW BOARDS
Broken White (Gloss)

SCHEME 5
WARM SCHEME

WALLS, Etc. (See Notes)
B.S. 1572.   Colour No. 104
(Semi-Gloss)
SKIRTINGS to match walls
but gloss finish (See Notes)

CEILING AND BEAMS
B.S.1572.   Colour No. 103
(Non-washable distemper)

DOORS, FRAMES AND
ARCHITRAVES to match
walls but gloss finish
For cool aspects

or

B.S. 381 C. Colour No. 102
(Gloss)
For warm aspects where
rooms are overshadowed

or

B.S. 381 C. Colour No. 283
(Gloss)
For warm aspects where
rooms are overshadowed

WINDOWS, REVEALS
AND WINDOW BOARDS
Broken White (Gloss)

SCHEME 4
WARM SCHEME

WALLS, Etc. (See Notes)
B.S. 1572.   Colour No. 101
(Semi-Gloss)
SKIRTINGS to match walls
but gloss finish (See Notes)

CEILING AND BEAMS
Broken White
(Non-washable distemper)

DOORS, FRAMES AND
ARCHITRAVES to match
walls but gloss finish
For cool aspects

or

B.S. 381 C. Colour No. 283
(Gloss)
For warm aspects where
rooms are overshadowed

WINDOWS, REVEALS
AND WINDOW BOARDS
Broken White (Gloss)

NOTES continued

APPLICATION

The following points should be observed

(a) All wall surfaces should be in semi-gloss finish and ceilings should be in non-washable distemper

(b) Borrowed lights, cover strips and picture rails should be taken in with the general wall treatment. All other woodwork should be in gloss finish

(c) Skirtings in schemes 2 to 5 should match the wall colour (but in gloss finish) in rooms of ordinary size and should vary in colour only in large rooms

(d) Pipes at skirting level and radiators should match the background colour but be in gloss finish. Pipes etc. above skirting level should be taken in with the background

BRITISH STANDARD NUMBERS

B.S. 1572 relates to colours for flat finishes and B.S. 381C to colours for gloss finishes. The Broken White shown has been adopted as standard for these schemes

British Standard Colours are reproduced by permission of the
BRITISH STANDARDS INSTITUTION
24/28, Victoria Street, London, S.W.1

Wt 3829 K 143   31-108

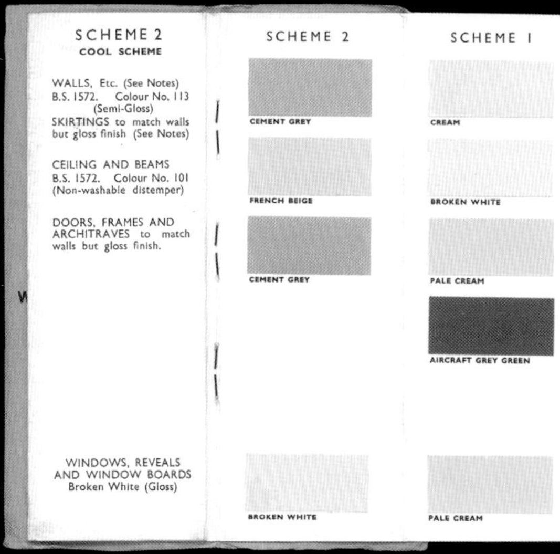

SCHEME 2
COOL SCHEME

WALLS, Etc. (See Notes)
B.S. 1572.   Colour No. 113
(Semi-Gloss)
SKIRTINGS to match walls
but gloss finish (See Notes)

CEILING AND BEAMS
B.S. 1572.   Colour No. 101
(Non-washable distemper)

DOORS, FRAMES AND
ARCHITRAVES to match
walls but gloss finish.

WINDOWS, REVEALS
AND WINDOW BOARDS
Broken White (Gloss)

SCHEME 2

CEMENT GREY

FRENCH BEIGE

CEMENT GREY

BROKEN WHITE

SCHEME 1

CREAM

BROKEN WHITE

PALE CREAM

AIRCRAFT GREY GREEN

PALE CREAM

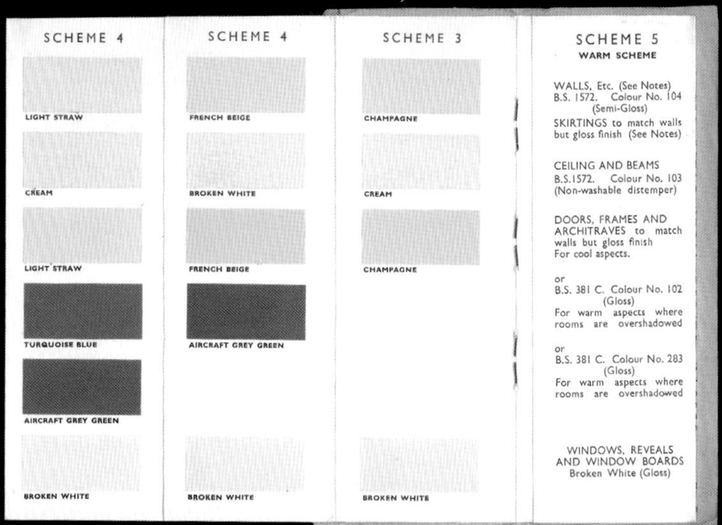

SCHEME 4

LIGHT STRAW

CREAM

LIGHT STRAW

TURQUOISE BLUE

AIRCRAFT GREY GREEN

BROKEN WHITE

SCHEME 4

FRENCH BEIGE

BROKEN WHITE

FRENCH BEIGE

AIRCRAFT GREY GREEN

BROKEN WHITE

SCHEME 3

CHAMPAGNE

CREAM

CHAMPAGNE

BROKEN WHITE

SCHEME 5
WARM SCHEME

WALLS, Etc. (See Notes)
B.S. 1572.   Colour No. 104
(Semi-Gloss)
SKIRTINGS to match walls
but gloss finish (See Notes)

CEILING AND BEAMS
B.S.1572.   Colour No. 103
(Non-washable distemper)

DOORS, FRAMES AND
ARCHITRAVES to match
walls but gloss finish
For cool aspects.

or

B.S. 381 C. Colour No. 102
(Gloss)
For warm aspects where
rooms are overshadowed

or

B.S. 381 C. Colour No. 283
(Gloss)
For warm aspects where
rooms are overshadowed

WINDOWS, REVEALS
AND WINDOW BOARDS
Broken White (Gloss)

DICTIONARY OF COLOURS FOR INTERIOR DECORATION

In 1949 the British Colour Council published the *Dictionary of Colours for Interior Decoration*. It consisted of three volumes, two of colour samples and the other a slim list of names and a history of the colours.

The 378 colours illustrated were shown on three surfaces: matt, gloss and a pile fabric (like carpet). One reference name and number was given for each colour depicted, and it was stressed that the surface required should be made clear to the contractor when the *Dictionary* was used to specify a colour match. For some colours, only paint examples were shown because it was not considered advisable to dye that particular colour on pile fabric due to the possibility of fading or discoloration.

Where colours were repeated from the earlier *Dictionary of Colour Standards* (1934), the same standard name was given (this applied to 131 of the 378 colours). Colours were cross-referenced with many of the leading international standards, such as:

[1]   British Standards Institution. *BS 381C: 1948 Colours for Ready Mixed Paints.*
[2]   British Colour Council. *Machinery Colours, Safety Colour Code, Pipe Identification Colours,* 1949.
[3]   College of Arms. *Heraldic Colours.*
[4]   A. Maerz and M. Rea Paul. *A Dictionary of Color,* 1930.
[5]   *Répertoire de couleurs,* published by the Société française des chrysanthémistes, in 1905.
[6]   British Colour Council. *Colours for Vitreous Enamels,* 1945.
[7]   Robert F. Wilson for the Royal Horticultural Society. *The Wilson Colour Chart,* 1938.

COLOUR NAMES

The colour names given by the British Colour Council were particularly descriptive and often referred to flora or fauna, with titles such as blue anemone (CC 153), flamingo (CC 26), kermes and squirrel brown.

The names and references became standards for identifying colours used in a wide range of applications, from the Royal Horticultural Society leek green (CC 335) and phlox mauve (CC 164), to the armed services battleship grey, (CC 322), rifle green (CC 264) and scarlet red

(CC 22), and the Royal Mail oriental red (also known as Post Office red, CC 29). Whereas a number of references were given for the colours used in flags, for example scarlet red also known as Union Jack red (CC 22), others were used as a reference for seasonal textile ranges, such as blue conifer (CC 342) and petrol blue (CC 269).

Although by their nature not given to exact specification, most of the colours used in heraldry were also illustrated. A more complete representation was given in the earlier *Dictionary of Colour Standards* (1934), and these are cross-referenced in volume three of the later work.

Due to their subtlety of hue in comparison with previous standards, the colours were useful for the fairly precise colour referencing in fields as diverse as tapestry (Mortlake rose, CC 10) and the classification of Chinese porcelain (Ming blue, CC 287).

In addition, the two editions of the *Dictionary of Colour Standards* have been used by many universities to designate the shades prescribed for the facings and linings of their academic robes and hoods. In more recent years, the green background of the flag of the South African National Defence Force (1994–2003) was specified as green beetle (CC 100).

WIDESPREAD USE

The British Colour Council was very active in the years immediately after World War II, and the *Dictionary of Colour Standards* was employed by a number of interior decorators as it was designed to be used:

So many shades are now available that you must be very exacting not to find what you want with one firm or another. Alternatively you can consult the British Colour Council Dictionary and specify the colour which you want to have matched...

It was superseded by the introduction of the Archrome (Munsell) colour range in 1953 and the BS 2660: 1955 *Colours for Building and Decorative Paints* two years after that (see p. 296).

[OPPOSITE AND OVERLEAF] Pages from the *British Colour Council Dictionary of Colours for Interior Decoration* (1949). Each colour is shown in three finishes: matt, gloss and a pile fabric.

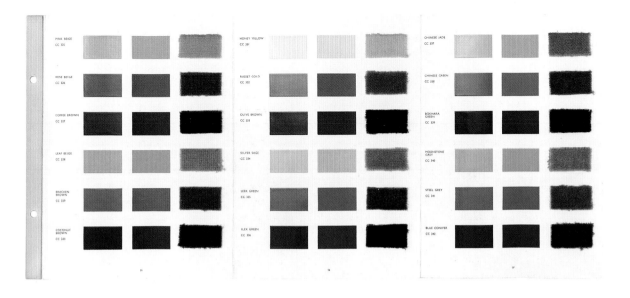

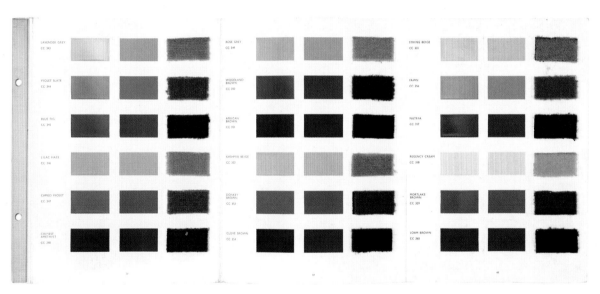

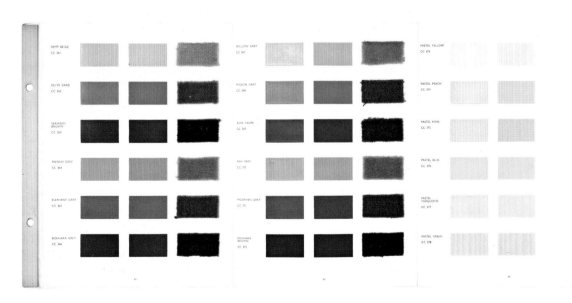

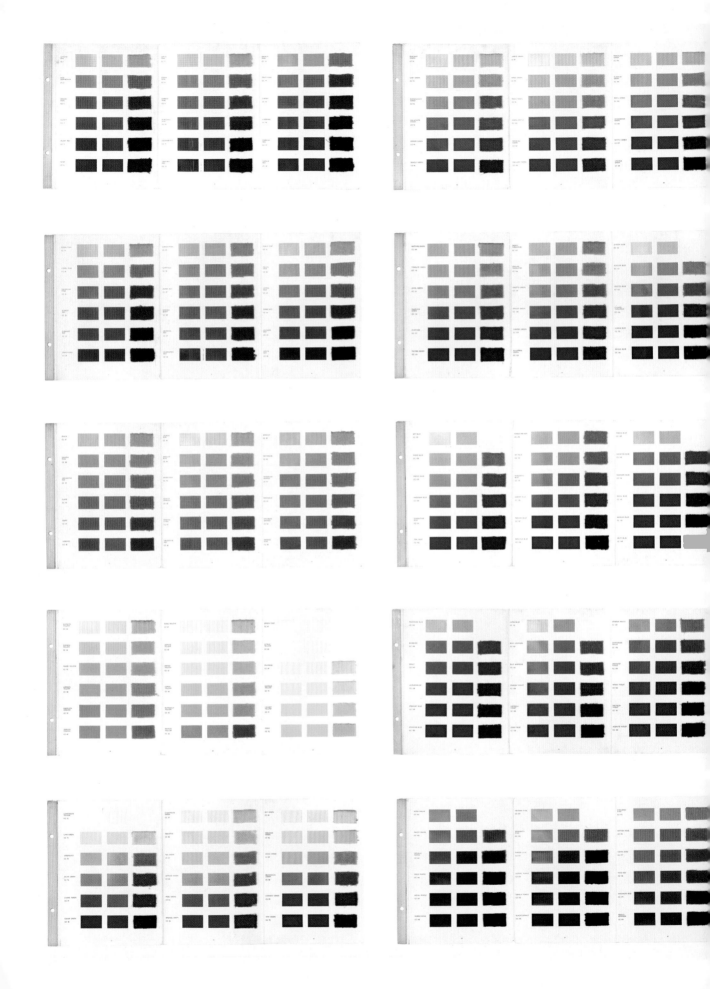

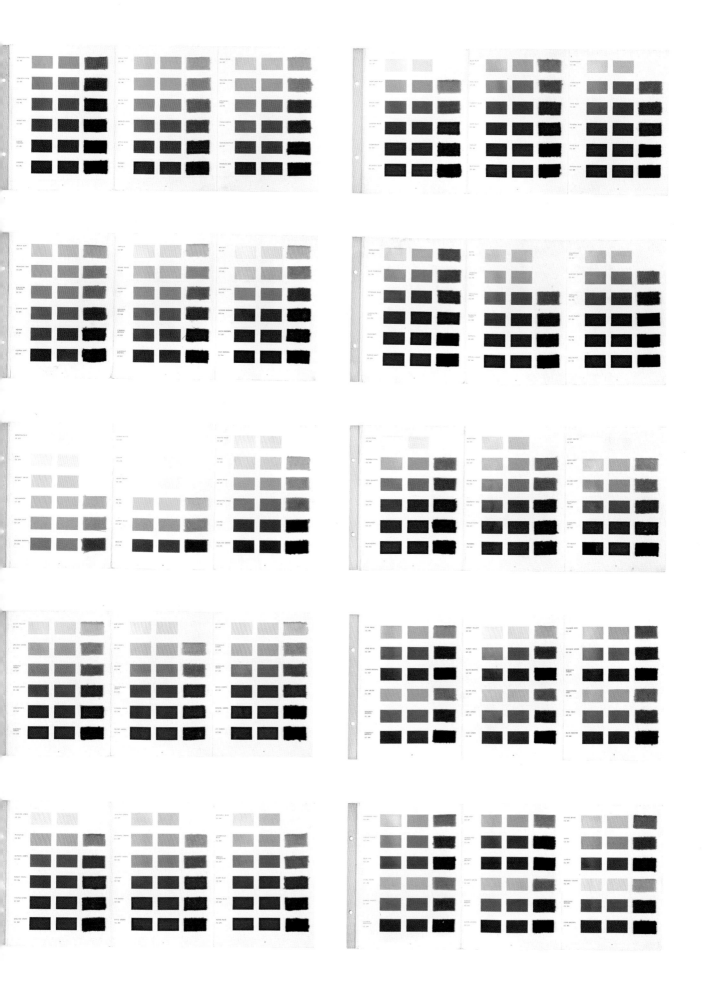

Peder Hald's *Maleeriets Teknik*,
or *Techniques of Painting* (1950).
Described by a Danish artist as the
'bible', the book contains a number
of colour samples. The colours were
designed for artists working in oil.

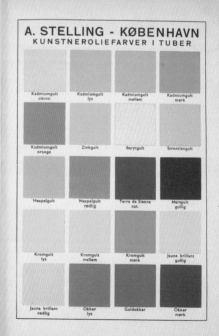

Cinnoberen kendeligt, idet Stoffet gaar over i den sorte Modifikation. Det er derfor med tvivlsom Ret, det har faaet Plads i Normalfarverækken. Af Bindemidler paavirkes Cinnober ikke. Paa Grund af de ovennævnte Egenskaber vil man dog næppe bruge det i Fresko, og ogsaa i de andre Teknikker fortrænges det efterhaanden af Kadmiumrødt. Billige Surrogater bestaar oftest af Mønnie med eller uden Tilsætning af Tjærefarver (f. Eks. Eosin, der hurtigt bleges, eller Helioægterødt, som er meget bestandigt). Ægte Cinnober er ikke giftigt. Stoffet har været kendt af Assyrere og Ægyptere flere Tusind Aar f. Kr.

Kadmiumrødt.

Kadmiumselenid + Kadmiumsulfid. CdSe + CdS.

Fremstilling: Glødning ved 600° af Kadmiumsulfid med 10 % Svovl og 6 % Selen. Tungspat er nødvendigt Substrat.

Egenskaber og Brug. Kadmiumrødt har god Dækkeevne. Olieforbruget er 16—20 %. Det er overordentlig lysægte og er egnet til at afløse Cinnober paa Kunstnerpaletten. Det blev indført i Maleriet ved sidste Aarhundredskifte, men er siden baade fremstillet i flere og smukkere Nuancer og faldet i Pris. Det kan faas i alle Toner fra Orangerødt til dybt Karminrødt, og, tager vi de gule Kadmiumfarver med, spænder denne Gruppe nu over næsten ⅓ af hele Farvekredsen. Kadmiumrødt er kalkægte og har vist god Holdbarhed i Fresko, selv i fri Luft. Det er ikke giftigt.

Mønnie.

Blymellemilte. Pb₃O₄.

Fremstilling: Glødende Bly iltes let til det gule Blyilte (PbO, Sølverglød). Dette Stof ophedes i varm Luftstrøm til ca. 460° og omdannes derved efterhaanden til Mønnie. Med Blyhvidt som Udgangspunkt faas den saakaldte Orangemønnie.

Egenskaber og Brug. Vægtfylde ca. 9. Olieforbrug ca. 7 %. Dækkraften er fremragende. Lysægtheden er ikke stor. Det har derfor ringe Anvendelse i Kunstmaleriet, men bruges i Haandværket som rustbeskyttende Oliefarve. Malingen er tilbøjelig til at stivne ved Lagring. Mønnie har Anvendelse som Substrat for Cinnoberimitationer og bruges endvidere til Mønniekit og keramiske Glasurer. Stoffet er giftigt. Det har været kendt fra Oldtiden.

64

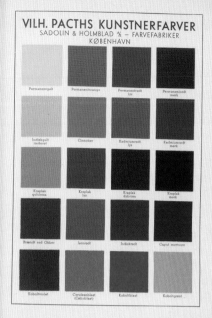

VILH. PACTHS KUNSTNERFARVER
SADOLIN & HOLMBLAD ⅍ – FARVEFABRIKER
KØBENHAVN

Navn	Anvendelig som			Anmærkninger
	Oliefarve	Lime- og Akvarelfarve	Kalkfarve	
Elfenbenssort	+	+	+	
Grønjord	+	+	+	
Jernrødt (og Cap. mort.)	+	+	+	I Akvarel er Aureolin og Hansagult at foretrække for de lyseste Nuancer.
Kadmiumgult	+	+	+	
Kadmiumrødt	+	+	+	
Koboltblaat	+	+	+	
Koboltgrønt	+	+	+	
Koboltviolet (mørk)	+	+	+	
Kridt	÷	+	+	
Kraplak	+	+	÷	De lyse Sorter ikke lysægte. Kun orange Kr. er nogenlunde holdbart i Kalk.
Kromgult	+	+	÷	Ikke lysægte.
Kromgrønt	+	+	÷	
Kromoxyd (dækkende og laserende)	+	+	+	
Lithopone	+	+		Bruges ikke i Kunstmaleri.
Mangansort			+	Bruges kun til Kalk og Cement.
Neapelgult	+			Faren for Sværtning med Svovlbrinte er ringe.
Okker (raa, brændt og Marsgult)	+	+	+	
Pariserblaat	+	+	÷	
Sodsort	+	+	÷	
Terra di Siena (raa og brændt)	+	+	+	Overgaar i flere Henseender Zink- og Blyhvidt.
Titanhvidt				
Tjærefarver	Anvendelige i Udvalg			Flere Røde er bedre end Kraplak.
Ultramarin	+	+	+	Faren for Svovlsyrlingbleguing i Kalk er ringe.
Umbra (raa og brændt)	+	+	+	
Zinkgult	+	+		Svagt vandopløseligt.
Zinkgrønt		+		
Zinkhvidt	+	+	÷	

80

SADOLINS KUNSTNERFARVER
SADOLIN & HOLMBLAD ⅍ – FARVEFABRIKER
KØBENHAVN

S200 MERLON BLUE   S211 VICTORIA GREY

S201 SWANLEY BLUE   S210 CEDAR BANK OFF WHITE

S202 OFFING BLUE   S209 PALE COBWEB

S203 CRAYFORD BLUE   S208 HAVEN GREY

S204 SWALE BLUE   S207 ORCHID GREY

S205 CLIPPER BLUE   S206 SPURN BLUE

S236 CLEAR YELLOW   S247 NATIVE GREEN

S237 HAMLET YELLOW   S246 WINESTEAD GREEN

S238 ELEGANT YELLOW   S245 SARUM GREEN

S239 RADIANT YELLOW   S244 GLADE GREEN

S240 ORPINGTON GREY   S243 MARISH GREEN

S241 BEXLEY GREY   S242 GREYING GREEN

S251 CEDAR BANK OFF WHITE   S256 RUMFORD WHITE   S261 CUTSTONE WHITE

S252 VICTORIA GREY   S257 VIBURNUM WHITE   S262 FRESHSTONE

S253 MOCHRAS GREY   S258 PASTEL PINK   S263 APRICOT

S254 TRANQUIL GREY   S259 PEACH   S264 CORALLITE

S255 SPURN BLUE   S260 RUTLAND GREY   S265 KILN RED

S281 BARTON WHITE   S290 DENGE BLUE   S291 EASTFLEET BLUE

S282 NATIVE GREEN   S288 CRAYFORD BLUE   S292 KILNSEA BLUE

S283 WINESTEAD GREEN   S289 MARSH BLUE   S293 HAWKE BLUE

S284 SARUM GREEN   S286 THORPE GREEN   S294 PORTAL BLUE

S285 GREYING GREEN   S287 GREEN BLACK   S295 BLUE BLACK

* delete for exterior use   * delete for exterior use

A range of paint colours produced by W. H. Screeton in *c.* 1953. A Kent-based firm established in the 1890s, it claims that it was the first to introduce titanium dioxide as a white pigment for paint to replace white lead.

1950S PAINT TYPES AND COLOURWAYS

In the early 1950s, 'washable' or bound distempers were the principal paints for walls, while soft distemper was used on ceilings and oil paints on joinery. Author and designer Noel Carrington pointed out that although washable, these bound distempers could not be scrubbed and they tended to absorb dirt within two or three years. He recommended applying a coat of varnish, but acknowledged that this would alter the colour and was an extra process. However, hope was on the horizon in the form of the new emulsion paints, which some decorators believed would lead to the phasing out of distemper, such was their ease of application and durability.

THE INTRODUCTION OF EMULSION PAINTS

Emulsion paints were still very new when W. P. Matthew published *Modern Home Painting and Decorating* in the early 1950s. He described their superior properties as well as their peculiar and distinctive smell when first applied. He also indicated that flat wall paints (oil-based) provided a 'richer' appearance but were equally durable and washable. It was certainly more economical to use oil paints rather than distemper because they would last for perhaps ten years, even in a dirty city like London, against two or three years for a distemper.

Matthew went on to describe the two principal finishes for interior doors, window frames, skirting boards and other woodwork as gloss paint and varnished graining. He described a plain gloss paint as very pleasing, especially in a room with modern furnishings, but that a nicely grained panelled door was 'substantial looking'. He felt that matt (oil) paints were not usually durable for interior woodwork, but that they played down window pelmets and picture rails that would otherwise appear too prominent.

INCREASING COLOUR RANGES

It took a few years for paint companies to respond to the post-war interest in paint colour. Architect David Medd described how the representative of the first paint company he approached:

> appeared in a three-piece suit from whose waistcoat pocket he withdrew a complete

shade card offering little more than camouflage colours and the likes of primrose and eau de Nil.

Recovery was generally slow in the early 1950s and most paint colour cards looked very similar to the more limited ones of the pre-war era, with creams, browns and greens predominating. In 1951, at the same time as Medd and fellow architect Oliver Cox brought out their colour range (see p. 318), *House & Garden* magazine identified a selection of twenty-four colours that it felt would be useful in decoration. Throughout the 1950s, the colours were updated annually and marketed through a number of stockists. Initially available only in paint, by March 1953 the magazine reported:

> You can now buy almost anything you desire in a *House & Garden* colour – not only paints, distempers, wallpapers and carpets, but kitchen scales, table mats, lamps and tableware.

The *House & Garden* colour range was a dynamic one, subject to frequent changes to accommodate the taste of the moment and to reflect the main developments in interior design. Only three of the original colours – gunmetal, mustard and sandalwood – were on offer six years after the launch. At that stage, the range had been adopted by some 140 manufacturers, and more than ninety leading retail stores in London and the provinces cooperated in the scheme, keeping stocks or samples of the main *House & Garden* colour merchandise.

The magazine felt that it was responsible for the first major attempt to persuade the British people that colour in the home 'not only delights the eye, but raises the spirit and challenges the imagination'. This is, no doubt, true – *House & Garden*'s pages show many exciting, if somewhat vibrant, interiors.

CONTROLLING COLOUR CHOICES

By 1954 the range of colours had become so extensive that Carrington suggested that so many shades were now available that 'you must be very exacting not to find what you want with one firm or another'. Alternatively, homeowners could 'consult the British Colour Council *Dictionary* and specify the colour which [they] want to have matched'.

The Paint Industry Colour Ranges Committee – approached the Royal Institute of British Architects to discuss the problems that were being created by the increasing tendency of users to order special colours or to specify from the ever-increasing number of available colour ranges. With advice from the British Colour Council, a set of approximately one hundred colours was proposed, from which a range of fifty to sixty colours would be selected.

Studies at the government's Building Research Station at Garston had suggested that if colours were laid out in a logical order it would be possible to reduce the number of alternatives, without leaving too many gaps. Existing ranges had not been designed for a particular use and often presented an arbitrary collection of colours that had been extended for various reasons.

At this time, it was unusual to find the colours on existing shade cards arranged in a systematic order, except perhaps for a general grouping in terms of hue. In order to describe the colours accurately, however, further information was required.

THE 1955 BRITISH STANDARD RANGE

In March 1955, an interim range, based heavily on the Archrome colours (see p. 318), was released for use by all government departments. This *Colour Range of Building Paints for Government Departments* was produced in booklet form on the basis that it would be superseded by a new British Standard colour chart. Later in the same year, the Paint Industry Colour Ranges Committee, in conjunction with the Royal Institute of British Architects and a number of government departments, finally agreed on a standard range of 101 colours, which incorporated the majority of the Archrome range. This was adopted by the British Standards Institute as BS 2660: 1955 *Colours for Building and Decorative Paints*. The new standard was, as described by one of those who worked on it, 'an architect-designed range'. It found immediate favour with a great many architects and designers, and gradually became popular as a colour coordinator of manufactured goods.

That there were thousands of lively minded Britons, avid for colour in their homes, was shown by the enthusiasm with which *House & Garden* colours were taken up, first by a group of enterprising manufacturers, and then by the wider (and still increasing) public that insisted on these colours. In addition to the growing number of commercial paint ranges,

the number of colours available increased with the introduction of the 1955 British Standard range, which proved very popular.

A PLETHORA OF COLOURS

Within a short time, this range of 101 colours was available from most paint manufacturers across the United Kingdom. Colour could be specified with confidence. For the more faint-hearted, *House & Garden* pointed out that 'nature also thought up the poppy, the cornflower, and the laburnum.'

However, all these different colours posed a significant problem for the paint shops. In order to stock the full colour range in all sizes and in all finishes, large storage areas and a considerable financial outlay were required. Furthermore, there was the problem of the slow colours, those that proved less popular. All this began to change with the introduction of innovations such as the Robbialac Colorizer system, which offered the customer more than a thousand extra colours and meant that the retailer need only carry a full complement of different base paints and a selection of colourants in sachets. Colours were achieved by squeezing the contents of the relevant sachets into the base paint.

One of the first retailers to adopt this system in the United Kingdom was the newly established Papers and Paints in Chelsea, London. It proved sufficient for a while, but variations were soon required and it was not long before a full colour-matching service was offered. This was not unique, but such work was very skilled and labour-intensive.

The late 1950s also saw the introduction of the revolutionary 'plastic emulsion paints', which were altogether more user-friendly. They were adopted quickly and gradually replaced by the long-established water paints, such as Duresco and Walpamur, and the mixing up of soft distemper for the decoration of ceilings.

By the end of the 1950s, the colourman had become the paint shop, where customers could generally obtain advice and find the colour that they required.

[OPPOSITE] The range of colours from BS 2660: 1955 *Colours for Building and Decorative Paints*. One hundred of the 101 colours are shown here: cyclamen 8-091 has been omitted.

CANARY YELLOW 0-001

ORCHIS 1-021

MAPLE 0-041

PINE GREEN 5-061

NARVIK BLUE 7-081

OXLIP 0-002

REEF RED 1-022

RICH CREAM 3-042

YAFFLE GREEN 5-062

PORCELAIN BLUE 7-082

GOLDEN YELLOW 0-003

TAWNY RED 1-023

LIGHT STONE 3-043

MOSS GREEN 5-063

RIBBON BLUE 7-083

MARIGOLD 0-004

CHESTNUT 1-024

GOLDEN BROWN 3-044

BREDON GREEN 5-064

FIESTA BLUE 7-084

POPPY 0-005

CHERRY 1-025

MIDDLE BROWN 3-045

CROFT GREEN 5-065

MARINE BLUE 7-085

POST OFFICE RED 0-006

MELLOW BUFF 2-026

OFF WHITE 4-046

GROTTO 6-066

MIDNIGHT BLUE 7-086

AFGHAN RED 0-007

CYGNET 2-027

SILVER GLEAM 4-047

ATLANTIC GREEN 6-067

STEEL BLUE 8-087

LIME 0-008

FALLOW 2-028

STONE GREY 4-048

MARBLE GREEN 6-068

WEDGWOOD BLUE 8-088

PARAKEET 0-009

COPRA 2-029

EDDYSTONE 4-049

GLACIER 6-069

CASTLE GREY 8-089

VIRIDIAN 0-010

PINK BEIGE 2-030

OLIVE 4-050

PASTEL GREEN 6-070

COLUMBINE 8-090

BALTIC BLUE 0-011

AURORA 2-031

MONTELLA 4-051

EAU-DE-NIL 6-071

REGAL RED 8-092

PACIFIC BLUE 0-012

COCOA 2-032

BUTTERMILK 4-052

APPLE GREEN 6-072

SILVER 9-093

ANCHUSA 0-013

MAGNOLIA 3-033

JONQUIL 4-053

BOTTLE GREEN 6-073

FLAKE GREY 9-094

NIGHTSHADE 0-014

VANILLA 3-034

MIMOSA YELLOW 4-054

MIDDLE GREEN 6-074

MINERVA GREY 9-095

ZEPHYR 10-015

ALABASTER 3-035

JASMINE YELLOW 4-055

HORIZON BLUE 7-075

SARUM GREY 9-096

PINK HAZE 1-016

COBWEB 3-036

MUSTARD 4-056

COURT GREY 7-076

DARK GREY 9-097

ROSE GREY 1-017

BUFFALO 3-037

BRASS 4-057

SHADOW BLUE 7-077

BLUE GREY 9-098

MECCA RED 1-018

CONGO BROWN 3-038

GOSSAMER 5-058

LIGHT GREY 7-078

ASH GREY 9-099

ROYAL MAROON 1-019

CHOCOLATE 3-039

GREENSTONE 5-059

SKY BLUE 7-079

GRAPHITE 9-100

DAYBREAK 1-020

PALE IVORY 3-040

QUARRY GREY 5-060

MANTLE BLUE 7-080

CHARCOAL 9-101

Paints stocked by Cotterell
Brothers Ltd, Bristol, in 1950.

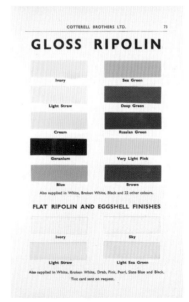

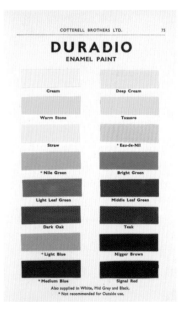

BLUNDELL'S
PAMMEL

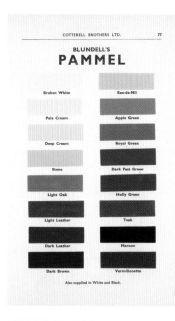

Broken White	Eau-de-Nil
Pale Cream	Apple Green
Deep Cream	Royal Green
Stone	Dark Fast Green
Light Oak	Holly Green
Light Leather	Teak
Dark Leather	Maroon
Dark Brown	Vermillionette

Also supplied in White and Black.

MANDER'S
DURABLE GLOSS PAINT

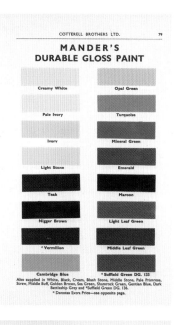

Creamy White	Opal Green
Pale Ivory	Turquoise
Ivory	Mineral Green
Light Stone	Emerald
Teak	Maroon
Nigger Brown	Light Leaf Green
* Vermilion	Middle Leaf Green
Cambridge Blue	* Suffield Green DG. 133

Also supplied in White, Black, Cream, Blush Stone, Middle Stone, Pale Primrose, Straw, Middle Buff, Golden Brown, Sea Green, Shamrock Green, Gentian Blue, Dark Battleship Grey and *Suffield Green DG. 136.
* Denotes Extra Price—see opposite page.

DIXON'S
ENAMEL PAINT AND METSEALA

Ivory	Middle Brunswick Green
Cream	Nut Brown
Light Stone	Windsor Brown
Eau-de-Nil	Purple Brown
Permanent Green	Light Battleship Grey
Beige	Orange
Middle Oak	* Royal Blue
Extra Light Brunswick Green	Light Brunswick Green

Also supplied in White, Black, Middle Stone, Jacobean Oak, Red Oxide, *Lemon Chrome, *Signal Red, Spring Green, Light Oak and Dark Brunswick Green.
*Denotes Extra Price—see opposite page.

COTTERELLS'
READY MIXED PAINT

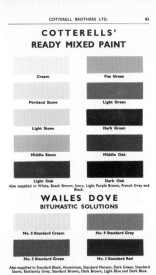

Cream	Pea Green
Portland Stone	Light Green
Light Stone	Dark Green
Middle Stone	Middle Oak
Light Oak	Dark Oak

Also supplied in White, Beech Brown, Ivory, Light Purple Brown, French Grey and Black.

WAILES DOVE
BITUMASTIC SOLUTIONS

No. 8 Standard Cream	No. 9 Standard Grey
No. 5 Standard Green	No. 3 Standard Red

Also supplied in Standard Black, Aluminium, Standard Maroon, Dark Green, Standard Stone, Battleship Grey, Standard Brown, Dark Brown, Light Blue and Dark Blue.

KEYSTONA
FLAT OIL PAINT

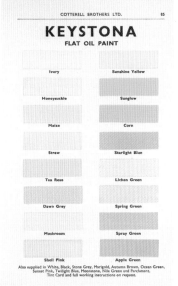

Ivory	Sunshine Yellow
Honeysuckle	Sunglow
Maize	Corn
Straw	Starlight Blue
Tea Rose	Lichen Green
Dawn Grey	Spring Green
Mushroom	Spray Green
Shell Pink	Apple Green

Also supplied in White, Black, Stone Grey, Marigold, Autumn Brown, Ocean Green, Sunset Pink, Twilight Blue, Moonstone, Nile Green and Parchment.
Tint Card and full working instructions on request.

CHROMALO
WATER PAINT

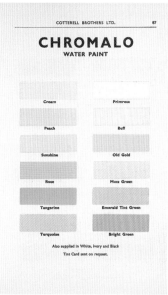

Cream	Primrose
Peach	Buff
Sunshine	Old Gold
Rose	Moss Green
Tangerine	Emerald Tint Green
Turquoise	Bright Green

Also supplied in White, Ivory and Black.
Tint Card sent on request.

KAVECO
WATER PAINT

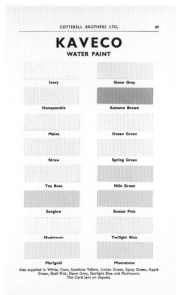

Ivory	Stone Grey
Honeysuckle	Autumn Brown
Maize	Ocean Green
Straw	Spring Green
Tea Rose	Nile Green
Sunglow	Sunset Pink
Mushroom	Twilight Blue
Marigold	Moonstone

Also supplied in White, Corn, Sunshine Yellow, Lichen Green, Spray Green, Apple Green, Shell Pink, Dawn Grey, Starlight Blue and Parchment.
Tint Card sent on request.

WALPAMUR
WATER PAINT

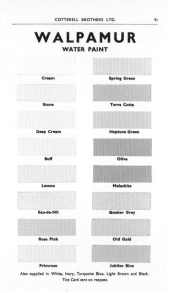

Cream	Spring Green
Stone	Terra Cotta
Deep Cream	Neptune Green
Buff	Olive
Lemon	Malachite
Eau-de-Nil	Quaker Grey
Rose Pink	Old Gold
Primrose	Jubilee Blue

Also supplied in White, Ivory, Turquoise Blue, Light Brown and Black.
Tint Card sent on request.

BELDEC
WATER PAINT

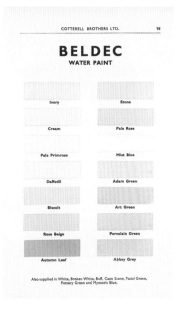

Ivory	Stone
Cream	Pale Rose
Pale Primrose	Mist Blue
Daffodil	Adam Green
Biscuit	Art Green
Rose Beige	Porcelain Green
Autumn Leaf	Abbey Grey

Also supplied in White, Broken White, Buff, Caen Stone, Pastel Green, Pottery Green and Myosotis Blue.

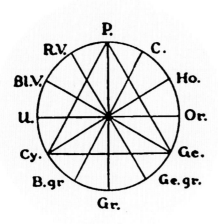

HÖLZEL (1919)

ITTEN (1921)

Adolf Hölzel (1853–1934) studied painting at the Vienna Academy. A founder of the Munich Secession and an early member of the Vienna Secession, he was one of many artists at the time keen to explore the possibilities of art outside the confines of academic tradition.

He made a close study of colour theory – in particular the work of Johann Goethe and Wilhelm von Bezold – and developed his own ideas about colour harmonies. From 1888 to 1905 Hölzel worked in Dachau, Bavaria, where it was said that every tenth person was an artist. It was there that his work moved closer to abstraction, resulting in his *Composition in Red* in 1905, which prefigured Wassily Kandinsky's *Blue Mountain* by a few years. It was also there that he taught the future German expressionist Emil Nolde for a short period.

In 1906 he moved to Stuttgart, where he taught at the Academy of Art and it was there that he further developed his theories on colour and attracted a circle of artists who would later become influential. One of these was Johannes Ittens, who worked as his assistant and who was later to develop his own theories, which were largely based on those of his teacher. In 1909 Hölzel published his twelve-piece chromatic colour circle (above).

Johannes Itten (1888–1967) was a Swiss expressionist painter, designer, teacher, writer and theorist. From 1919 to 1922 he taught at the Bauhaus, where he developed the innovative 'preliminary course' that was to teach students the basics of material characteristics, composition and colour.

Itten's colour star (colour sphere in seven light values and twelve tones) is a sphere that has been opened flat. Each of twelve hues is shown with two steps towards white (in the centre) and two steps towards black (at the points). The star is arranged so that the six complementary colours face each other, for example, red-green and blue-orange. The twelve hues are:

Purpurviolett (violet-purple); Purpur (purple); Karmin (carmine); Zinnober (cinnabar); Orange (orange); Gelb (yellow); Gelbgrün (yellow-green); Grün (green); Blaugrün (blue-green); Cyanblau (cyan blue); Ultramarin (ultramarine); Blauviolett (blue-violet)

It was here that Itten developed his theory of the seven types of colour contrast and devised exercises to teach them. The contrasts were: light and dark; extension; saturation; complements; simultaneous contrast; hue; and warm and cool.

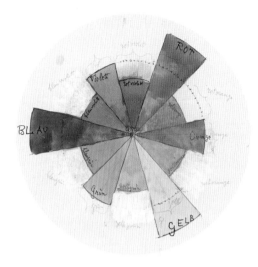

KLEE (1931)

ALBERS (1963)

The Swiss-German artist Paul Klee (1879–1940) studied at the Academy of Fine Arts in Munich. After a slow start he met the Expressionists August Macke and Wassily Kandinsky, and in 1911 joined the group known as *Der Blaue Reiter* (The Blue Rider). These artists shared an interest in the spiritual and symbolic associations of colour and the connection between visual art and music. Klee's artistic breakthrough came in 1914 when he visited Tunisia with Macke and was impressed by the quality of the light there. He wrote, 'Colour has taken possession of me; no longer do I have to chase after it, I know that it has hold of me forever.'

In 1920 Klee was invited by Johannes Itten to teach at the Bauhaus. The two were to influence one another and both artists drew on the same sources, going on to inspire a generation of students. In his colour teaching notes, Klee showed interest in Goethe's 'Theory of Colours', particularly in his colour circle, with red opposite green, orange-red opposite blue, and yellow opposite violet. He then followed Goethe by carrying out experiments with coloured after-images, and by applying complementary colours, in transparent watercolours, over each other. Needless to say, they produced grey.

Josef Albers (1888–1976) was a German-born American artist and teacher whose work formed the basis of some of the most influential and far-reaching art education programmes of the twentieth century.

As a maker of stained glass, he joined the Bauhaus in 1922 and in the following year was teaching handicrafts. Among his students there were Paul Klee and Wassily Kandinsky. After the closure of the Bauhaus in 1933, Albers emigrated to the United States and began teaching in North Carolina. Two notable students at that time were Cy Twombly and Robert Rauschenberg.

In 1950 he moved to Yale, where he spent most of that decade. In 1963 he published his theory of colour in *Interaction of Color*. This contained a series of colour exercises; his introduction to the exercises; a portfolio of 150 silk screen plates, mainly created by his students; and an additional section of Albers' commentaries on the plates.

The colour triangle above shows the three primary colours; the secondaries; the tertiaries and their complements.

Post-war houses were designed to be compact, straightforward and generally in the Modern Style. There was a need for economy and the new buildings were smaller than their predecessors, containing fewer rooms. Houses had, traditionally, been built with many rooms, each with a specific function, but now with less space several became dual-purpose. This gave rise to selective colour use and a more fluid decoration technique. In schools and workplaces, colour was used to brighten the atmosphere and to reduce the incidence of clutter and gloomy corridors.

[OPPOSITE] Lithographs by Ronald Collins from Noel Carrington's *Colour and Pattern in the Home* (1954).

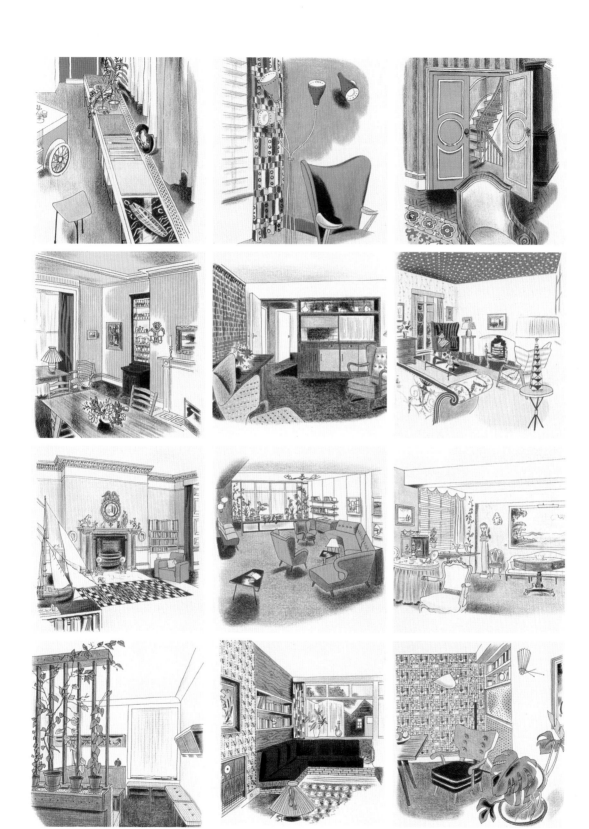

A variety of decor alternatives, *c.* 1957. [OVERLEAF] [P. 306] 'Rooms in the sun: cool white tile sunroom
with comfortable Far Horizon furniture, both by designer John B. Wisner, give an illusion of sun, sand
and surf.' [P. 307] 'Color in Your Home: patio-style room with sky blue walls, maple coffee table, folding
safari chairs, white linen couch, all by Milo Baughman, and Milton Avery painting of waves.'

RESPONDING TO MODERNIST ARCHITECTURE

The 1950s saw a rise in the popularity of modernist architecture characterized by minimal ornamentation, larger windows and open-plan layouts. The increased availability of new materials – plastics, PVC, linoleum and laminates – in a wide range of colours was another major factor behind the radical shift in interior design. Developments in labour-saving technology and the social change created by the upheaval of the two World Wars also led to a different way of living. The greatest change was seen in the kitchen.

After World War II, two innovative exhibitions brought design ideas to the public. The first was 'Britain Can Make It', held in 1946 at the Victoria and Albert Museum. The second was the Festival of Britain, which ran throughout the summer of 1951.

THE RISE OF DIY

Of the houses that had survived the war unscathed, nearly half were at least sixty-five years old and in need of renovation. With so much reconstruction work taking place, labour became more expensive and builders scarce. Consequently, more homeowners took on simple tasks themselves. DIY seemed to consume the nation in the 1950s. Building materials became more readily available after Building Controls were lifted in October 1954, and there were many sources of design ideas.

Television was still new, but it was becoming increasingly popular. In the early 1950s, only 3 per cent of households owned a set, but by 1958 television had overtaken radio as the principal form of home entertainment. An unlikely early 'star' was the handyman W. P. Matthew. He began his media career on radio in the 1930s and would have had his first show on television on 3 September 1939 had Hitler not invaded Poland. He eventually had his own DIY programme from 1947. By the time he died in 1956, he had a loyal following and had published the very popular *Modern Home Painting and Decorating*.

Spurred on by new magazines such as *Practical Householder*, first published in 1955, and the more upmarket *House & Garden*, the whole nation was encouraged to play a part in home improvement and design. By 1957 the annual DIY exhibition at Olympia had grown four times as large as any of its predecessors, and in 1963 *Do It Yourself* magazine called the exhibition 'the Mecca of DIY'.

PAINTING EXTERIORS

For practical advice, Matthew was the man to turn to. He advised that the most important thing to remember when undertaking outside painting was that the paint must be of outside quality. He also pointed out that a certain amount of fading was inevitable except with cream, which usually went rather deeper in shade after exposure to sunlight.

The traditional treatment of browns and greens, with black for the gutters and downpipes, was slowly being replaced by brighter colours, such as reds and blues. It was thought that ordinary-looking houses could be given 'character' by avoiding the conventional approach. Noel Carrington adopted a more artistic strategy when offering advice. For doors, he described yellow as striking, although not for ironwork or windows. A red front door was considered bold, but the red should be Venetian rather than crimson and red for shutters and windows was too like the surrounding brickwork to be acceptable. Blue was becoming popular as an outside colour for doors and shutters but Carrington recommended a blue green rather than a straight blue as it would fade to rather a subtle shade. A pure green was thought to be more successful in town than in the country where it was likely to clash with the vegetation. Black was regarded as 'too funereal to be encouraged' and white was best employed around windows where it reflected light.

In the country, untreated brick or stone was the general convention. The tradition of applying whitewash or colour wash was found only in certain areas. Where mellow brick or stone were in good condition, it made no sense to apply colour, but where these materials had to be patched with cement, a colour wash was described as a great improvement. Pale yellow, cream and pale orange were all favourites for colour-washed cottages.

In many European countries where brickwork was popular, such as the Netherlands, northern France and Denmark, a colour wash was often employed on exposed brickwork to produce a unified effect. Colour might also be introduced in town where a verandah or house wall was, in effect, part of a garden room. Ochre, pale green and pink were recommended as dead white walls would reflect too much glare in summer.

JASMINE

HORIZON BLUE

CYCLAMEN

RIBBON BLUE

REEF RED

FLAKE GREY

THE HALL

It was generally agreed that the entrance hall should have a warm friendly atmosphere, regardless of aspect. The first impression of a home is gained on entering the hall, and a cool scheme tends to give a rather chilly reception. As this area is seen by many people, it warrants an extra degree of smartness and finish.

Colours could be fairly strong and the scheme bold as only a short time was spent in the hall. For example, the ceiling could be in a sunlight yellow, or even in geranium if the height was sufficient to carry so dominant a colour. Walls would be white or a light neutral grey. If desired, the carpet could reflect the ceiling colour.

Given the awkward shape and size of the hall and staircase, redecoration was infrequent. Painted walls and ceilings were suitable because they could be washed down easily. If wallpaper was selected, it was a good idea to hang it above a dado of varnished paper or other hard-wearing material, such as leatherette. If not already hidden, the stair balusters could be covered with hardboard 'which will hide a lot of the ornament and get rid of the monotonous perpendicularity'. The colour of passage walls and bedroom walls should be kept in harmony, as they might be seen together through an open door.

THE BATHROOM

The bathroom was the second room in the house that saw the most change in the 1950s. Early fittings were chunky and square-cut and most washbasins were free-standing. As the decade progressed, flowing lines took over and basins could be set into a counter-top. Baths tended to be fitted against the wall with a panelled side.

Noel Carrington explained that the bathroom was usually left by the builders 'in hygienic purity' – with white bath, white tiles and white paint, although more expensive houses often had a pale green washbasin and bath in 'the very nasty shades that only seem fully realized in porcelain or plastic compounds'. DIY expert W. P. Matthew felt that it was good to have the imagination stirred by bright colours and fanciful effects at the beginning of the day.

Some homeowners took their lead from the brightly coloured bathrooms shown in *House & Garden*. Others adopted a gentler route with pink walls, white woodwork and perhaps a blue ceiling and door. An even quieter approach was to paint most of the walls white, with the wall behind the bath in pink. Tiles made of linoleum, rubber or plastic in biscuit shades and greys were also considered, as well as those arranged in a black and white chequer design.

JASMINE

APPLE GREEN

MARIGOLD

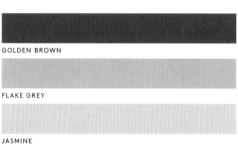

GOLDEN BROWN

FLAKE GREY

JASMINE

THE LIVING ROOM

Several writers pointed out that the living room was intended for rest and relaxation and that the colour scheme, therefore, ought to be 'quiet' – but not dull. A well-planned scheme was more likely to provide a satisfying background for living than a daring scheme that would so quickly pall when the novelty wore off. If selective colouring were to be employed, it should be in a subdued key. Generally, the most suitable areas for selective treatment were the recesses on either side of the chimney breast; however, the wall opposite the fireplace could also be given this treatment, leaving the remaining walls and chimney breast in white or a light neutral tint.

If wallpaper were to be hung in the living room, it was important to be sure that the colour and design would not become distracting after a time. It was advisable to try a different colour or pattern for one wall or one dominant feature only, such as the chimney breast. Alternatively, a textured finish could be employed. As long as the relief was not too pronounced, it was considered restful in shades such as pale grey green or warm grey.

The choice of colour for selected areas would have been governed by the room's furnishings, with colours being either in harmony for a quiet

scheme or in contrast where a livelier effect was desired. If the carpet was of a positive colour, it was considered effective to repeat this colour on the ceiling or to echo it in a paler tint. If the walls were painted in white, an effect of breadth and spaciousness could be achieved.

The tradition of the parlour continued in many houses or, at least, in those that were big enough to have one. Whether it was called the parlour, drawing room, sitting room, living room or even lounge, it was still a 'special' room. It was here that the house-proud would set out to impress visitors or neighbours. Good taste was important.

In spite of the suggestions for a quiet scheme, several of the magazines show that brightly coloured upholstery fabrics tended to be popular in the 1950s. Walls were being painted in bold colours, and patterned wallpaper that featured abstract or geometric designs was being hung in many living rooms. A dark wall was shown to be a most attractive background for pictures, especially if the frames were in light natural wood or painted white. Books also always added to the decorative scheme in a living room.

Advances in heating technology meant that the traditional layout of the living room

TAWNY RED

JASMINE

STEEL BLUE

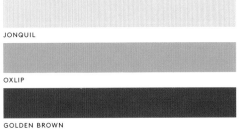

JONQUIL

OXLIP

GOLDEN BROWN

altered. Before World War II, chairs and sofas tended to be grouped around the fire, which was the primary focus of the room. With the introduction of central heating, the fireplace became less of a focal point and its place was taken over by the television set. As an anonymous architect in *The Builder* (2 May 1952) asked of this newcomer:

> Meantime, who televiews - and how much, and when?. Is this the new, vicarious 'life' in the living-room? Is one to 'view' as well as sit in the sitting-room?

Perhaps it was time to consider the television when planning, equipping and furnishing the house. In June 1948 there were 50,000 licence fee-payers; by the coronation of 1953 there were approximately 2 million sets and by 1955 that figure had doubled. Television was becoming a key element in the house, around which the living room took shape.

THE DINING ROOM

Traditionally a room for impressing guests, the dining room was one of the casualties of the post-war period's shortage of space. Very few plans in the architectural journals of the 1950s included a dining room. From then on, it was found combined with the living room or kitchen.

The same period also saw the gradual introduction of labour-saving devices in the form of clean and efficient ovens, refrigerators, washing machines, dryers and even dishwashers. This was fortunate, as the numbers in domestic service had been declining steadily since the end of World War I. With the huge number of council houses built, the maid had been able to move out of the attic and now there was no one to carry dishes from one room to another.

In many households the dining room, where it existed, often retained a more traditional feel than the rest of the interior and may have been decorated in a Regency revival style. DIY expert W. P. Matthew warned against giving it a heavy Victorian effect and suggested that as 'cheerful colours aid digestion and enhance one's enjoyment of food' the colours could be rather on the bright side. Indeed, he went as far as to say that strong, contrasting colours could safely be used in a dining room.

JASMINE

RIBBON BLUE

MARIGOLD

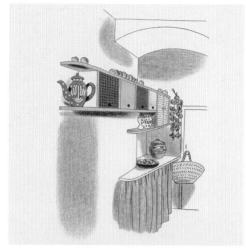

TAWNY RED

JASMINE

STEEL BLUE

THE KITCHEN

As servants and domestic help became a thing of the past, the housewife found herself spending a lot more time in the kitchen than she had done previously. Labour-saving devices such as washing machines, refrigerators and electric kettles began to appear, and a more efficient layout was introduced. In a well-designed kitchen the sink, cooker and refrigerator were positioned so that the 'work flow' formed a triangle between these points.

Kitchens became less utilitarian and altogether more attractive. Formica, a plastic laminate that provided an easy-clean surface, brought colour and pattern onto tables, worktops and unit doors, which had previously been plain wood. This spread to other articles such as storage jars, saucepans, dustpans and buckets, which were available in bright colours, often from the latest *House & Garden* range.

Primary colours were popular and the kitchen was one of the rooms where homeowners could really 'go to town' with colour, although there was a danger of overdoing things. It was important to resist the temptation to 'pick out' the handles, mouldings and shelf edges with red or other bright colours, since this only produced a 'fussy and rather niggling effect'.

In fact, the treatment could be fairly simple, with the ceiling painted in the same colour as the built-in cupboards, for example. Alternatively, broad well-placed areas of colour could be enhanced by larger areas of white or other neutral tints. The ceiling, for example, might be:

blue or eau de Nil, with walls in pale primrose or white and woodwork in pale grey, with the main doors perhaps in a deeper shade of the ceiling colour. The ceiling colour can also be repeated inside cupboards and recesses, with shelves painted white so giving the housewife a prospect of pleasant colour whenever she opens the cupboard door!

The walls of the kitchen were best painted to resist steam and occasional smoke. Bound distemper was one option, but regular renewal was inevitable. W. P. Matthew recommended the best quality hard gloss paint or enamel, not only for the woodwork but also for the walls and ceiling. Wallpapers were designed especially for kitchens, with a protective coating that was impervious to moisture and easily washed. Designs often featured slices of fruit, vegetables and fish, or perhaps images of chianti in raffia flasks.

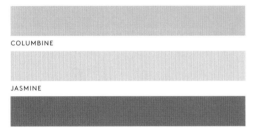

COLUMBINE

FLAKE GREY

JASMINE

BRASS

TAWNY RED

TAWNY RED

THE KITCHEN-DINER

By the beginning of the 1950s, the era of the lavish formal dinner party was coming to an end and a trend for more relaxed entertaining was becoming the norm. Rather than a separate room for eating in, the new smaller flats and houses tended to have a combined kitchen-dining room. The different areas might be demarcated by a room divider, perhaps in the form of a sideboard, or by painting the walls a contrasting colour. Different flooring might also be used.

In a dual-purpose room such as this, it was important to reduce the emphasis on the functional aspects and 'make the room better suited for a meal over which it is pleasant to linger'. The manufacturers helped with this in the design of their refrigerators and cookers. The latter could be set in a wide tiled chimney-piece where 'it is better looking than the old fashioned cast-iron Kitchener'. The same may be said for the stainless steel sink, which replaced the old-fashioned ceramic Belfast sink.

However, with space at a premium, homeowners could opt for the compact, if purely functional, Five-Foot Electric Kitchen that Hotpoint was advertising in 1950. The basic model had an oven with a four-point hob, a cabinet sink (with an optional Disposall® waste

unit) and an under-counter refrigerator covered by a 'beautiful Textolite counter-top to provide an astonishing amount of work surface'. The wall cabinets could accommodate plenty of dishes, all out of sight. If space permitted, a Hotpoint electric dishwasher could be added. The entire workspace was very neat and unobtrusive, without the sprawl of a traditional kitchen.

There was no longer a need to banish the washing-up to the scullery. Conversation could continue as the cook prepared the meal for the guests or family, encouraging collaboration. The ceramic tiles around the stove would most likely have been black, whereas the sink would have been surrounded by tiles of a biscuit colour or another colour to match the tone of the walls.

The table in the kitchen-diner might be covered with patterned linen or a colourful oil-cloth. It might even be covered with a wood grain design Formica, whose finish would supposedly outlive the table.

Colourful china and glass would also help to brighten things up. Bottles were another option as they came in many different shapes and tended to have colourful or appealing labels. Further interest might be given by hanging a few paintings, prints or maps on the walls.

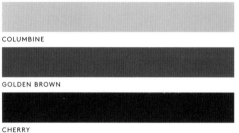

COLUMBINE

GOLDEN BROWN

CHERRY

CHERRY

COPRA

FLAKE GREY

THE BEDROOM

As bedrooms were seldom seen by visitors, they were often the room in which short cuts were made when money was running out. In the 1950s, bedrooms were characterized by their matching furniture. The bed and bedside table were usually of a set, as were the dressing table and wardrobe. Wherever space was sufficient, it was common to find an easy chair or small sofa. In older houses with larger rooms, there might also be a small writing desk and bookcase. The idea was to 'suggest a habit of living as well as sleeping'.

Central heating was rarely installed in bedrooms, so warmth was provided by fabrics in the form of bedspreads and curtains. Chintzes were less fashionable at this time, but where a pale colour or near white was applied to the walls, a strongly patterned bedspread or yak rug was considered a good foil. Fitted carpets were also popular and provided warmth underfoot.

It was generally agreed that the bedroom scheme should be restful. Colours such as primrose, pink or eau de Nil were suggested as being more stimulating than the orthodox white or cream. W. P. Matthew was a bit bolder and considered it better to wake up in a room that had a dash of colour to 're-stimulate mental activity'. He felt that the desired effect could be

obtained by using restful tones for the large wall and ceiling areas, and by using a stronger colour on the wall immediately behind the bed to give a sense of cosiness and security.

The bedroom was considered to be an appropriate place for a tinted ceiling for 'it must be remembered that this is a room to wake up in as well as to sleep in'. It was accepted that most people were rather timid about a coloured ceiling, fearing that it might make the room appear more confined. This was certainly true if the colour was too strong for the height of the room. However, a tinted ceiling could look especially effective when the walls below it, and certainly the cornice, were in white or off-white. This was felt to frame the colour.

For a reasoned approach, the colouring of a bedroom would depend to a certain extent on the aspect. Cool rooms facing north-west to south-east would require light and cheerful shades. Honeysuckle or cream might be applied to the walls, with honeysuckle or rose pink for the ceiling and pale ivory or rose pink for the woodwork. In a well-lit room that received direct sunlight, darker and richer colours could be used. Grey walls or carpet might be offset by crimson hangings or chair covers, or indeed with

MINERVA

OXLIP

SKY BLUE

RIBBON BLUE

REEF RED

STEEL BLUE

several other quite strong colours, because greys will combine with most colours. If a gentler effect were desired, an oyster grey or Delft blue could be employed on the walls, with flesh pink or cream on the ceiling and pale oyster grey or cream on the woodwork.

Wallpapers were popular in bedrooms, too, but caution was necessary with regard to bold patterns, even where the areas of wall were large. If such a design were desired, it might be applied to one wall only as a feature. Simplicity was an advantage in any room of irregular shape where bold patterns, and especially stripes, would have a tendency to emphasize the irregularities and cause distraction. It was suggested that the repeating diagonal pattern of some wallpapers could almost induce delirium in an invalid.

Spare bedrooms were often quite small with little room for much more than a bed and a chair. Care was needed here to achieve a satisfactory balance of colour, because every detail would be scrutinized by a guest.

It was essential for children's bedrooms to have good lighting, warmth and ventilation, as well as hard-wearing furniture. The choice of colour for walls and doors should be of the kind that shows the least signs of hard wear.

THE STUDIO APARTMENT

The studio apartment, or bedsit, was generally occupied by the young setting up home for the first time, the bachelor/spinster or the elderly. In each case, the chief criteria were economy, comfort and simplicity.

With space at a premium, everything had to be thought through. The design had to be functional and compact and the layout planned. Items of furniture would often have to double up, and so the bed might be turned into a sofa if it could not be folded away. Equally, it could be hidden by a screen. Storage tended to be built in rather than free-standing. Cooking and food preparation areas could also be screened or contained within a neat fitted unit. The Hotpoint Five-Foot Electric Kitchen was the ideal response, if it could be afforded.

For the young, in particular, the bedsit was an exercise in setting up home on a small scale and with a limited budget. It offered them the opportunity to experiment and to develop their own taste. Contemporary patterns were popular as were bright paint colours, although white or a 'fresh light' colour was found to help give the appearance of space. 'A bright sunny yellow', particularly BS 0-001 canary, was a very popular choice of colour.

These two illustrations were featured in *Modern Home Painting and Decorating* (undated, early 1950s), edited by DIY expert
W. P. Matthew. 'Despite the small size of this bedroom or bedsitting room, the decoration – in restrained contemporary style –
provides plenty of interest, and encourages a feeling of cosy comfort. A neat wallpaper of modern design is combined
with light grey wall paint, and the small pictures are well placed to add to the interest of the scheme. Well-bound
books in a modern bookcase complete the picture. The ceiling could be in ivory distemper.'

W. P. Matthew commented: 'In an overcrowded room such as this it is best to avoid all "fussiness" in the decorative scheme. A pale blue paper with light dot pattern is used on the walls.'

Two young architects, David Medd and Oliver Cox, were the driving force behind the major development in post-war architectural colour. They had been greatly inspired by Amédée Ozenfant's pre-war articles in the *Architectural Review*. In an address on the application of colour in buildings, with special reference to primary schools, Medd raised several points that had been covered by Ozenfant a decade earlier. Firstly, the need to establish national colour standards. Secondly, that colour and form were literally inseparable. 'All surfaces to be painted are subject to certain natural and functional conditions, such as the degree of daylight falling upon these surfaces, their orientation, and most important, the functions for which these surfaces are forming a background.' Thirdly, colour schemes should stand up to rational analysis.

Medd and Cox developed the Archrome range, initially for their own employers. At first they mixed the colours by eye, then assigned references according to the Ostwald system, then the Munsell. Consisting of forty-seven colours plus black and white, the Archrome (Munsell) range became commercially available almost immediately, with any manufacturer being allowed to produce the colours. The range was brought to a wider audience when published by the Ministry of Education in *Building Bulletin No. 9* in 1953, along with the rationale it employed. This described how workplaces needed to be light, clean and cheerful without being unduly vivid, much of which could be achieved with paint and colour.

In schools, the colours were applied in large plain areas on panels between steel uprights, according to consistent principles. Structural members were generally painted pale grey; classrooms in light, undistracting colours; halls were bright but dignified; and the strongest colours – rich reds, yellows and blues – were reserved for circulation spaces, entrance halls and occasional exterior panels. The principles were codified by Cox, who remembered their effect in the early schools:

> The impact of these schemes on the teachers was tremendous; few had ever seen such bold and striking use of colour in buildings before. Many dressed to match! The children took it completely for granted and carried on painting with a similar palette.

In 1946 the British Colour Council published *Colour and Lighting in Factories and Offices*. The preface by A.W. Garrett, HM Chief Inspector of Factories in 1945, explained the need for such a document:

> Factories were built first to house machines. The conception that they must be places of human habitation for the workers who were to operate the machines came much later. Only today after more than 100 years of steady progress, after the expenditure of an immense amount of constructive effort and applied research and with the added impetus of two great wars fought to a large extent on the 'factory front' have we come to fully realise the implications of that essentially simple requirement that factories should be places fit for people to live in.

It was understood that colour and lighting produce physical and psychological reactions and that their correct use has a direct effect on the health, safety and well-being of personnel, as well as on the working atmosphere as a whole. In a pleasant harmonious environment, absenteeism can be reduced and an increased rate and reliability of output can be ensured. Even the colours of the machinery came under scrutiny:

> Office equipment is available in a limited range of colours only, but most manufacturers supply a light grey finish which is sufficiently neutral to fit most schemes. Old steel furniture in dark green can be repainted to harmonise.

Colour and Lighting in Factories and Offices was reprinted in seven successive years and was revised in 1956 and 1964. The last edition reflected the advances that had been made in industrial lighting and employed paint colours from the British Standard colour range BS 2660: 1955. It consisted of two parts: a forty-four-page booklet with particular colours recommended for different working environments, and a separate colour card showing thirty-seven paint colours. Three sample colour schemes, for varied aspects and lighting, were provided for each of six areas: factories; offices and showrooms; entrance halls, waiting rooms and corridors; cloakrooms and lavatories; rest rooms and welfare clinics; and canteens (see pp. 326–327).

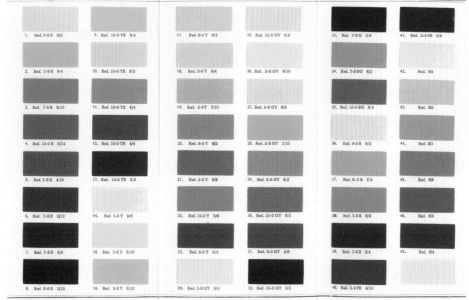

A

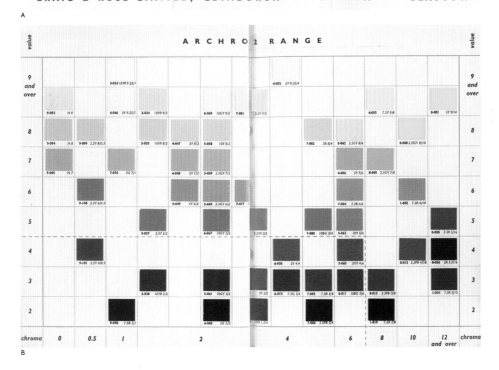

B

[A] This card was produced by the long-established Scottish paint manufacturers Craig & Rose to show that the Archrome colours were available in a wide variety of finishes: gloss enamels and gloss paints for interior and exterior use; semi-gloss, eggshell and flat paint for interior use; flat, eggshell and semi-gloss emulsion paints and oil-bound water paints for interior and exterior use. [B] The second edition of the Ministry of Education's *Colour in School Buildings – Building Bulletin No. 9* – was printed in June 1956. The 1955 British Standard range – *BS 2660: 1955 Colours for Building and Decorative Paints* – had already been released and some of the colours altered to fit in with the new standard.

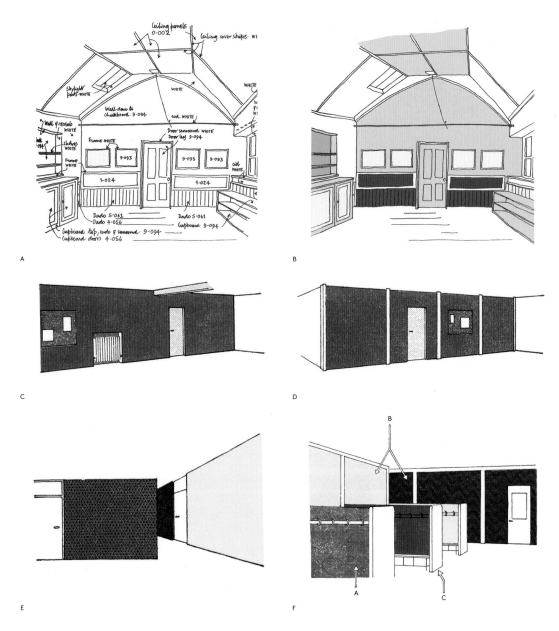

Some useful tips from the Ministry of Education's *Building Bulletin No. 9* (1953). [A, B] Suggestions for the redecoration of an infants' classroom. [C] 'Untidy arrangements of features such as beams, notice boards, radiators and doors are aggravated by strong colour, whose use may consequently be inhibited.' [D] 'Forms of construction in which the stanchions "read" as pilasters make tidy arrangements of doors, and thus strong colours are easier to use.' [E] 'Where there is no regular articulation by stanchions or pilasters, door frames carried to the ceiling simplify wall shapes and may allow the colour to be changed more easily.' [F] 'Bright colours to contrast with full height walls forming background to fittings. Added interest by use of different hues but similar chroma. ... White ends to get full advantage of light source and to bring out full strength of bright colours at right angles.' [G] 'RECEDING COLOUR The dark blue in shadow tends to suggest a void or shadow and thus increases the length of the corridor.' [H] 'ADVANCING COLOUR The bright yellow in good light appears to advance and so shortens the apparent length of the corridor.' [I, J, K, L] 'TUNNEL EFFECTS IN CORRIDORS Dark toned colours in corridors tend to emphasize "tunnel" effects, but by painting one wall in a pale receding tint an effect of greater width is achieved. The receding blue tint on the end wall and the "pinch" effect of strong colour on the side walls tends to increase the length of corridor, but by reversing the colours the length appears to be reduced.' [M, N] 'COLOUR ON AWKWARD SHAPES Strong colour emphasizes unduly the linear arm of the inverted L-shape. It looks more stable and satisfactory in the regular shape of the recess.' [O, P] 'UNINTENDED DISCORD The blue on the ceiling appears darker than the pale yellow walls and is thus in correct tone order, whereas [when] the yellow is now darker than the blue [it] becomes discordant.' [Q] 'Folding models used to illustrate tonal changes when colour is placed *in situ*.'

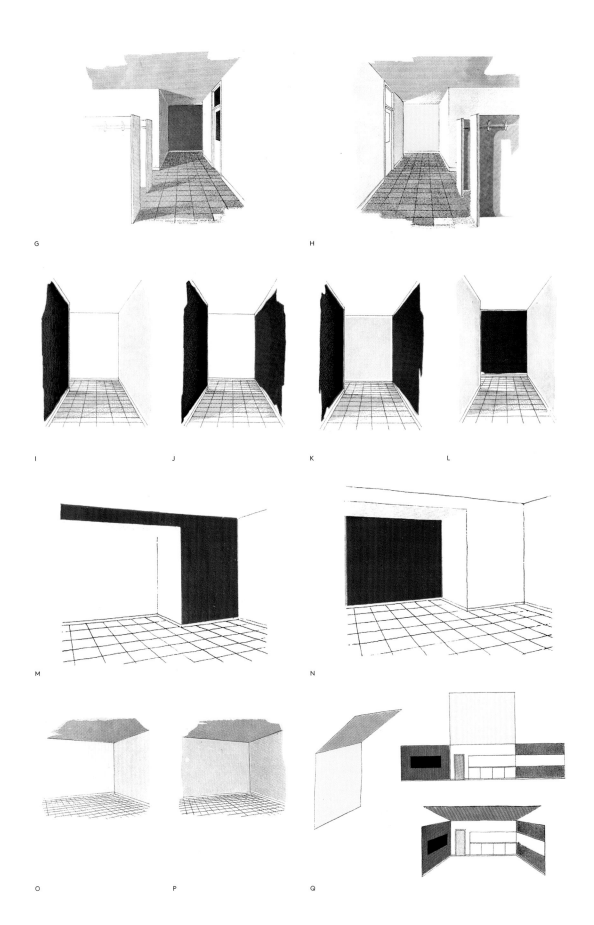

G

H

I

J

K

L

M

N

O

P

Q

A

B

C

D

A

B

C

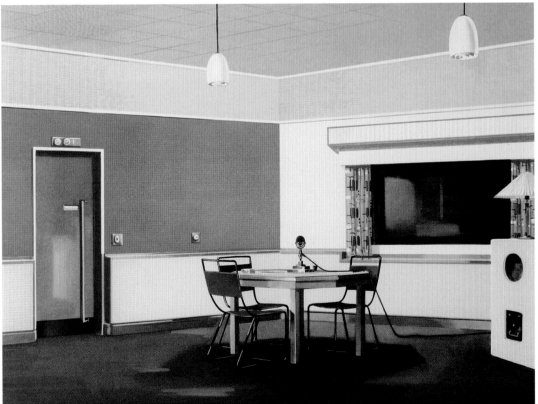

D

[PREVIOUS] [P. 322] Use of colour from a 1955 Walpamur Colour Guide. [A] The Rushton & Carter Home, Lingfield Epileptic Colony, Surrey, staff common rooms. Ceiling in Walpamur water paint intermixing of apricot/white and beams in white. Walls in Peveril emulsion paint ivory and Arctic blue. Doors, skirting and window frames in Duradio enamel paint Paris grey and white. [B] Taunton and Somerset Hospital, Blake Ward. Ceiling in Walpamur water paint shell pink. Doors and architraves French polished medium oak colour. All other surfaces in Duradio enamel paint eau de Nil and cream.

[P. 323] [C] St Catherine's Hospital, Birkenhead, Wirral, H.5 Ward, babies' ward. All surfaces in Duradio enamel paint broken white, Arctic blue, sunlight yellow, shell pink; woodwork intermixing 50/50 shell pink/Arctic blue. [D] Lurgan and Portadown Hospital, Northern Ireland, entrance hall and corridor ward. Ceiling panels and walls in Muromatte flat oil paint, honeydew and cream. Woodwork Paris grey and doors warm stone in Duradio enamel paint.

[P. 324] Use of colour from a 1955 Walpamur Colour Guide. [A] Huwood Mining Machinery Ltd, Gateshead, Tyne and Wear. Ceiling in Darwen satin finish geranium. Walls in Walpamur glossy finish ivory. All other surfaces in Duradio enamel paint Paris grey, peacock blue and broken white. [B] The South Staffordshire Wagon Company Ltd, Dudley, West Midlands New Office Block, Blowers Green and South Corridor. Ceiling and walls in Walpamur water paint French beige, broken white and midnight blue. All other surfaces in Duradio enamel paint broken white, sunlight yellow, Paris grey and golden brown.

[P. 325] [C] Y.M.C.A. Manchester Gymnasium. Upper ceiling panels, lower ceiling flats, upper walls and balcony fronts in Muromatte flat oil paint geranium, broken white and an intermixing of midnight blue/vanilla; and Paris grey/broken white. All other surfaces in Duradio enamel paint, sunlight yellow, broken white, cloud grey and black. [D] The British Broadcasting Corporation, Newcastle-upon-Tyne. Acoustic ceiling tiles as supplied, mouldings in Peveril emulsion paint, light admiralty grey and broken white. Walls in Peveril emulsion paint 50/50 intermixing sunlight yellow and geranium, and broken white. Frieze and dado acoustic units in Darwen satin finish seagull and jasmine.

Charts showing suggested combinations of colours for different areas. The colours shown are taken from BS 2660: 1955 *Colours for Building and Decorative Paints.*

IV. PAINTS, COLOUR STANDARDS AND INTERIORS, 1945–1960 326

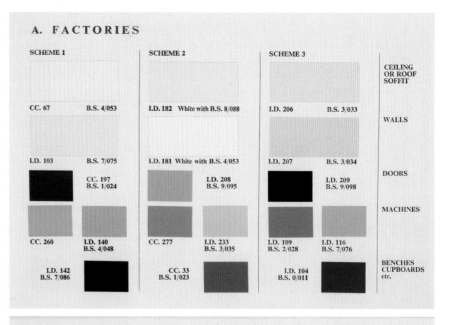

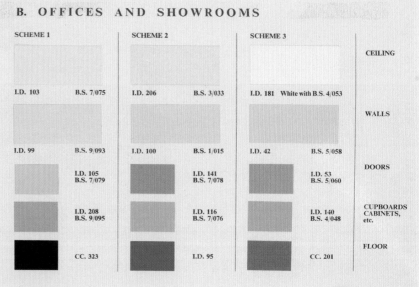

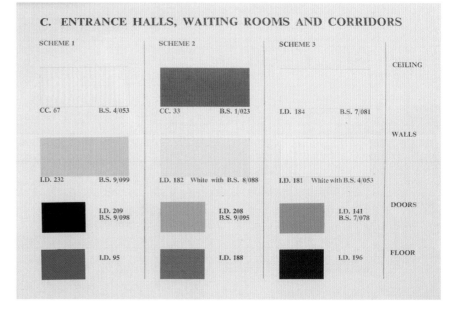

D. CLOAKROOMS AND LAVATORIES

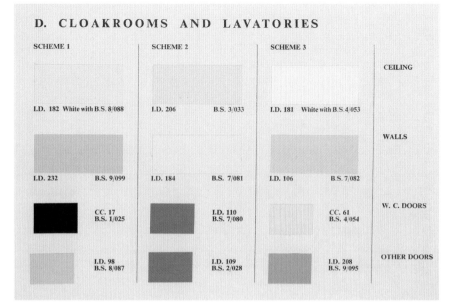

	SCHEME 1	SCHEME 2	SCHEME 3	
CEILING	I.D. 182 White with B.S. 8/088	I.D. 206 B.S. 3/033	I.D. 181 White with B.S. 4/053	
WALLS	I.D. 232 B.S. 9/099	I.D. 184 B.S. 7/081	I.D. 106 B.S. 7/082	
W. C. DOORS	CC. 17 B.S. 1/025	I.D. 110 B.S. 7/080	CC. 61 B.S. 4/054	
OTHER DOORS	I.D. 98 B.S. 8/087	I.D. 109 B.S. 2/028	I.D. 208 B.S. 9/095	

E. REST ROOMS AND WELFARE CLINICS

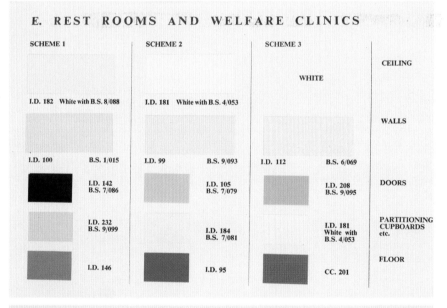

	SCHEME 1	SCHEME 2	SCHEME 3	
CEILING	I.D. 182 White with B.S. 8/088	I.D. 181 White with B.S. 4/053	WHITE	
WALLS	I.D. 100 B.S. 1/015	I.D. 99 B.S. 9/093	I.D. 112 B.S. 6/069	
DOORS	I.D. 142 B.S. 7/086	I.D. 105 B.S. 7/079	I.D. 208 B.S. 9/095	
PARTITIONING CUPBOARDS etc.	I.D. 232 B.S. 9/099	I.D. 184 B.S. 7/081	I.D. 181 White with B.S. 4/053	
FLOOR	I.D. 146	I.D. 95	CC. 201	

F. CANTEENS

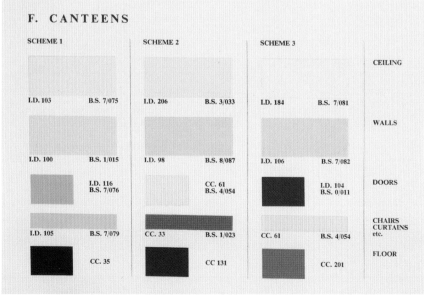

	SCHEME 1	SCHEME 2	SCHEME 3	
CEILING	I.D. 103 B.S. 7/075	I.D. 206 B.S. 3/033	I.D. 184 B.S. 7/081	
WALLS	I.D. 100 B.S. 1/015	I.D. 98 B.S. 8/087	I.D. 106 B.S. 7/082	
DOORS	I.D. 116 B.S. 7/076	CC. 61 B.S. 4/054	I.D. 104 B.S. 0/011	
CHAIRS CURTAINS etc.	I.D. 105 B.S. 7/079	CC. 33 B.S. 1/023	CC. 61 B.S. 4/054	
FLOOR	CC. 35	CC 131	CC. 201	

[OVERLEAF] [P. 328] Use of colour from a 1955 Walpamur Colour Guide. [A] Adams Bros & Shardlow Ltd, Leicester. Roof panels sunlight yellow; purlins, beams, roof lights and side walls in Darwen satin finish pale ivory. End walls, windows, stanchions supporting beam in pompadour Duradio enamel paint. Door, door casing, glazed screen and woodwork in Duradio enamel paint maroon and Paris grey. Machinery in Ferox machinery paint Paris grey. [B] The Wall Paper Manufacturers Limited, Hollins Paper Mills, Darwen, Lancashire. Ceiling in Darwen satin finish sunlight yellow. Beams in Ferox factory paint white. Side walls in Walpamur glossy finish white. End walls in Darwen satin finish 50/50 geranium/ spring green. Girders and stanchions in pompadour, machinery in medium blue and pompadour, fire door in signal red Duradio enamel paint.

[P. 329] [C] McCorquodale & Co Ltd, Newton-le-Willows, Lancashire. Ceiling in Darwen satin finish sunlight yellow. Roof supports and roof light returns in Ferox factory paint white. Walls in Walpamur glossy finish broken white and light blue. Benches in Ferox elastic gloss enamel light grey. All other surfaces in Duradio enamel paint: stanchions pale primrose, door copper glow, door architraves Paris grey. [D] East Lancashire Paper Mill Co. Ltd, Ratcliffe, Greater Manchester. Ceiling in Darwen satin finish sunlight yellow and geranium. Walls and beams in Walpamur glossy finish broken white. Door, lifting girders and stanchions in Duradio enamel paint copper glow and Paris grey. Machinery in Ferox elastic gloss enamel grey green.

[P. 330] Use of colour from a 1955 Walpamur Colour Guide. [A] Smith and Nephew Textiles Limited Weaving Shed, Brierfield, Nelson. Ceiling in Ferox factory paint tinted to match Walpamur water paint Arctic blue and pale primrose. Walls, wooden beams and columns in Duradio enamel paint broken white, pompadour, white and Paris grey. [B] British Bata Shoe Company, Maryport Factory, Cumbria. Ceiling in Ferox paint for factories white and vanilla. Walls in Walpamur glossy finish ivory and light blue. Stanchions and windows in Duradio enamel paint. Machinery in Ferox machinery paint broken white. Machinery in Paris grey and light blue.

[P. 331] [C] Caperns Limited, Yatton, Bristol. Ceiling Walpamur water paint shell pink and Arctic blue. Roof light framework and window frames in Duradio enamel paint ivory. Structural steelwork in Duradio enamel paint white. Walls in Walpamur water paint ivory. Machinery in Duradio enamel paint straw. [D] A.P.V. Co. Ltd, Crawley, West Sussex. All surfaces in Muromatte flat oil paint. Ceiling in broken white, pale primrose and gull grey. End walls in gull grey. Side walls, stage walls and stage ceiling in broken white.

A

B

C

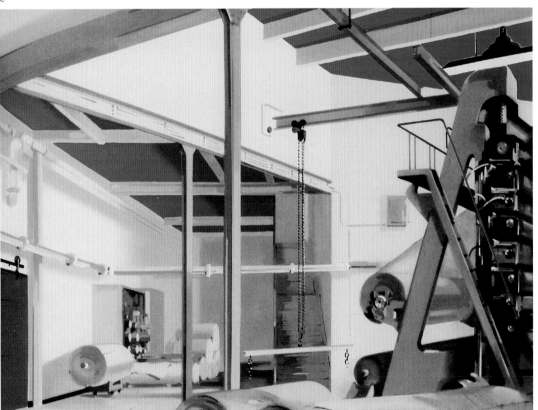

D

A

B

C

D

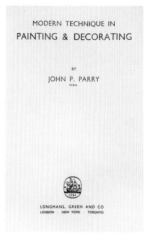

PAINTING AND DECORATING CRAFT PRACTICE (1948)
JAMES LAWRANCE

This small work is a useful introduction to the subject of painting and decorating and it is geared towards the student. James Lawrance wrote a number of weightier books in the first half of the twentieth century that are equally worthwhile.

He devotes many pages to the treatment of different surfaces and is particularly good on how to tackle the various plasters and renders that the decorator might encounter. Failure to employ the correct approach could result in 'sweat out'. The short chapter on gilding is very informative and useful for its explanation of the different types of metal leaf and their dimensions. Details such as this are not found elsewhere. The chapter on special processes is interesting and contains the only reference to the hot-spray process – where dry powdered shellac is blown through a flame direct onto the work – in any of the works examined in this book.

PAINTING AND DECORATING (1949)
A. E. HURST

This, and all the other editions of Hurst's book, are among the more useful of all the manuals published in the twentieth century. The detail is impressive yet the book is accessible to student and professional alike.

Although it has been brought up to date, because of its nineteenth-century origins, it still gives a good idea of some of the more archaic practices of the trade. It seems remarkable to see detailed instructions on the bridling of a brush – something that would have been unchanged from the eighteenth century. Indeed, the instructions for hand-mixing paint provide the sort of information that is taken for granted in the works by John Smith and others, but very useful for understanding the earlier methods.

The chapter on priming new surfaces is one of the most comprehensive of its kind. When readers learn that the amount of water contained in the new brickwork and plaster rendering of an average size room is about one ton, the need to allow the surfaces to dry before applying paint becomes crystal clear.

MODERN TECHNIQUE IN PAINTING AND DECORATING (1950)
JOHN P. PARRY

A useful work from the author of the classic *Parry's Graining and Marbling* (1949). It is sufficiently technical for the specialist, without swamping the homeowner with superfluous detail. All the essential information about decorating is here, yet so much of it relates to materials and processes employed fifty years earlier.

Parry asserts that the craftsman should be capable of advising clients on the use of colour and wallpapers and that it is not enough merely to have an eye for colour — as clients may also claim this distinction. The craftsman needs to possess an understanding of colour nomenclature otherwise his prestige is likely to suffer.

The detailed information on sign writing and heraldry is probably more than might be needed by the homeowner, and is uncommon in such handbooks.

HOME DECORATING (1951)
FREDERICK J. CHRISTOPHER

'The most essential factor to success in home decorating is the unrestricted use of common sense.' So began Frederick Christopher in this little book of top tips. He was an author, journalist, magazine editor and broadcaster who specialized in DIY, and this is one of many such works that appeared at this time.

The basic techniques of decoration are described together with more esoteric hints, such as the stippling of distemper to avoid brush marks and the process of re-enamelling a bath or painting a greenhouse. Brush graining is seldom dealt with in such works, but three pages are devoted to it here.

The book was published just as emulsion paints were making a slow appearance on the market, although there is no mention of them here. However, for a book that could be slipped into the pocket, it is stuffed full of useful detail.

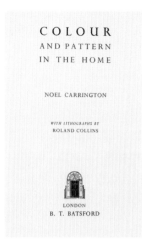

*COLOUR AND PATTERN
IN THE HOME* (1954)
NOEL CARRINGTON

*MODERN HOME PAINTING
AND DECORATING* (c. 1955)
W. P. MATTHEW

COLOUR IN BUILDINGS (1955)
THE WALPAMUR COMPANY LTD

*PRACTICAL HOME DECORATING
AND REPAIRS* (1958)
VARIOUS

Noel Carrington (1895–1989) was a book designer, editor, publisher and the originator of Puffin Books. He was also the brother of the Bloomsbury Group artist Dora Carrington.

This work is a very useful one in many ways. The illustrations – both colourful lithographs and black and white photographs – are real period pieces and show up-to-date decorating ideas on a domestic scale. Carrington offers very practical suggestions for planning a job and explains basic colour harmony in a clear and straightforward fashion. He describes the changes that had taken place in houses after the war and the consequent rationalization of space, such as combined kitchen-dining rooms and dining-living rooms. He also runs through the main colour groups making suggestions for their use. He mentions the work of the British Colour Council and suggests using its dictionary to specify the colour required. Its samples in gloss, matt and fabric show how the same colour can look quite different in different finishes and materials.

Of the 'new emulsion paints', Carrington says that 'Some decorators with whom I have discussed these new paints are so enthusiastic that they foretell the disappearance of distempers.' He also, wisely, points out that 'Some of the fashionable interiors of today will certainly seem equally laughable around the year 2000 and probably long before that', and readers should bear this in mind when considering some of his illustrations.

A very useful book that gives an idea of how houses were decorated in the 1950s and early 1960s. The illustrations are particularly informative, as are the suggested colour combinations for the different rooms. Variations are offered depending on the outlook of the room.

The process of painting is given, with photographs provided of each step. This is another late work with clear instructions on making and applying distemper. The detail is such that anyone could, with no prior knowledge, decorate a bedroom, possibly even employing mottled and clouded effects.

Detailed instructions are provided on wallpapering – as relevant now as they were fifty years ago. This work is very similar to *Practical Home Decorating and Repairs* (1958), and both books contain information that is hard to come by nowadays.

The Walpamur Company produced a number of excellent books at this time. This small book sets out to explain some of the problems of using colour in buildings.

The Munsell colour system is explained, and examples are given of discordant colours and the optical effects that take place when some colours are placed next to others. The different attributes of colours are described, and illustrations are provided that show how rooms can be made to appear bigger or smaller. Selective colouring – the use of strong colours on individual walls – is also explored. This is one of the only contemporary works that mentions this trend and shows how a carefully considered approach can be very effective.

The use of colour in the home and workplace is outlined and the influence of several of the British Colour Council publications is evident here.

A comprehensive account of decoration that might almost have been written fifty years earlier, as many of the materials and tools are unchanged.

The method of painting joinery is explained in great detail, with eighteen separate steps required to deal with an elaborate front door. In the same vein, the long-forgotten fashion for parti-colouring exteriors is demonstrated with a bay window in cream and dark green. The chapter on distempering is probably the clearest and most detailed in all the works examined. This sort of information is so hard to come by now that such materials are obsolete. No detail is too small and there are even clear instructions on how to clean a brush and care for tools. The new technique of 'plastic' (textured) painting is described as well as various paint effects using translucent glazes. The chapter on paint defects is excellent, and still relevant, as is the one that runs through the problems that might be encountered while maintaining a house. General repairs, paperhanging, stencilling and tiling are described, as well as simple electrical work.

This is an excellent book and it is likely that many modern painters, decorators and even homeowners, would benefit from reading it.

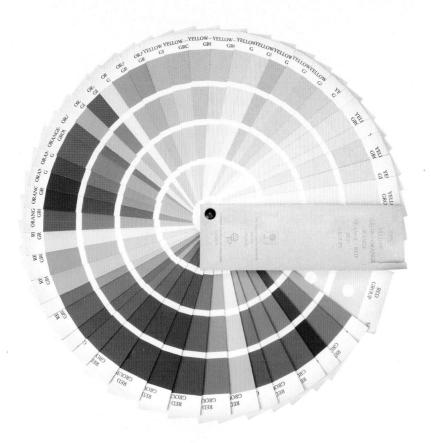

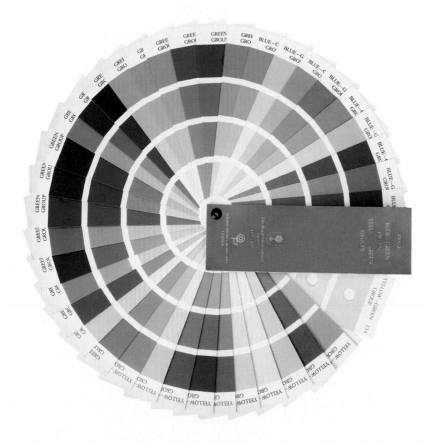

The Royal Horticultural Society Colour Chart is the standard reference for recording plant colours, used by horticulturists worldwide. It resembles a paint chart and has 808 colours that can be matched precisely to flowers, fruits and other plants, in order to record and communicate colours accurately across the world. Each colour has a unique number and letter code as well as a name. For example, among the lavenders, *Lavandula angustifolia* 'Elizabeth' is 88A, while *Lavandula angustfolia* 'Joan Head' is 83A. This colour chart is also used in other industries such as food, cosmetics, pharmaceuticals and fashion. The edition shown here was produced in 1986 in collaboration with the Flower Council of Holland. Note the viewing holes, which made for more accurate matches.

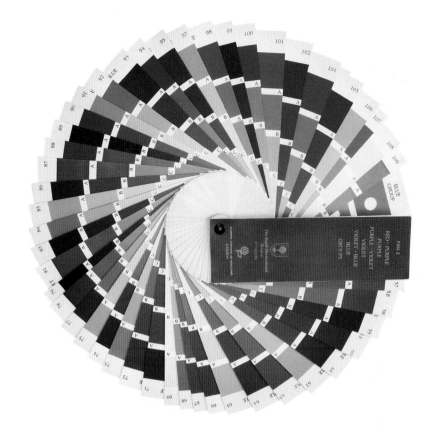

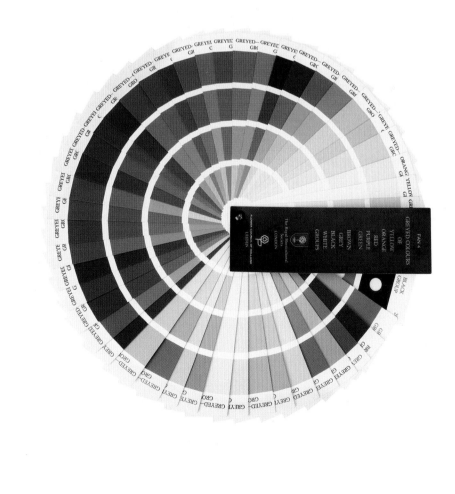

GLOSSARY

ALKYD RESIN | The largest group of resins in use by the modern paint industry. Employed for their durability, weather resistance, paleness of colour and flexibility. Generally found in oil-based paints but they are beginning to appear in some water-based formulations.

APPRENTICE | A young person bound to an employer who undertook to train him/her in every aspect of the craft. The system originated in the 13th century and still exists but in a much altered and reduced form.

ARCHROME RANGE | A range of paint colours introduced in the early 1950s for use in primary schools. It went on to form the basis of the 1955 British Standard paint range.

ASHLAR EFFECT | The imitation of blocks of stone using paint, often textured. The joints are simulated by scoring lines while the paint is still wet.

BINDER | The medium, or adhesive material, used to bind pigment particles together in a paint. In an oil paint it was generally linseed oil and in distemper it was glue size.

BODY | The 'build' or thickness of a coat of paint. This is often related to its coverage and 'hiding power'.

BOILED LINSEED OIL | Linseed oil that has been heated in order to speed up the drying process. Tends to be darker than the raw oil.

BRITISH STANDARD RANGE | Ranges of paint colours published by the British Standards Institution. The first was produced in 1930 and the most recent was revised in 2011.

BROKEN WHITE | White paint that has had the colour softened by the addition of small amounts of pigment.

BRONZING | The application of bronze powder to the highlights in order to simulate that metal.

CALCINED | Roasted in order to produce a chemical change.

CALCIUM CARBONATE | Chalk. Often known as whiting. The main component of soft distemper.

CASEIN-BOUND DISTEMPER (see Water Paint) | An early form of emulsion paint that relied on a milk protein as a binder.

CHALKING | The loose, powdery surface of either an under-bound paint or one that is ageing or weathering.

CHAMBER PROCESS | A form of lead carbonate (white lead) produced by introducing heat and moisture, as steam, together with acetic acid and carbon dioxide into a building containing strips of metallic lead.

CLEARCOLE | White lead ground in water and mixed with glue size. Sometimes used as inexpensive paint or primer.

COLOURANT | Tinting matter that has been dispersed in a medium to colour paint. Designed to ensure complete dispersion and consistent colour.

COMMON COLOURS | Historically the cheapest colours, those that saw everyday use. They included cream colour, lead colour, pearl colour, stone colour, wainscot (or oak) colour and white.

COMPLEMENTARY COLOURS | A pair of colours that when combined cancel each other out. Each reflects those components of white light that the other absorbs.

COPAL | A resin from the copal tree. It was widely used in the nineteenth century in the production of varnishes.

DEAD (as in dead white) | Matt or flatted finish.

DILUENT | Something used to dilute a substance. Generally meaning turpentine or white spirit in an oil paint and water in a distemper.

DISTEMPER (see Soft Distemper and Water Paint) | A water-based coating based on whiting (chalk) and glue size. When dry it produced a matt finish that could be removed by washing (hence 'soft'). Stronger binders, such as oil or casein, were introduced later to produce a more durable finish known as 'water paint'. Both types were replaced by emulsion paint.

DRIERS | Materials added to speed up the drying of oil paint. Usually based on certain metals, such as lead, cobalt and manganese. Terebine drier is a well-known type that is still produced. To be used sparingly and with care.

DRYING OILS | Oils that have the property of changing from a liquid to a solid state when spread out in a thin film and exposed to the air.

DUTCH STACK | The traditional method of manufacturing lead carbonate (lead white). Coils of metallic lead were suspended in a pot above vinegar and subjected to a uniform heat provided by manure or spent tan-bark.

EARTH PIGMENTS | Pigments dug out of the earth rather than manufactured by artificial chemical processes. They include the ochres, siennas and umbers, and the range of colours can be increased by calcination to achieve deeper and warmer hues.

EGGSHELL | A finish that is neither matt nor glossy. A vague term indicating a mid-sheen. Originally meant to indicate the low-sheen seen on the shell of an egg.

EMULSION | A water-based paint that has now replaced the distempers. In its simplest form, the medium was produced by combining oil and water (see Water Paint). When applied to a surface the water evaporates and the dispersed particles flow together and produce a film or coating.

ENAMEL | The term originally indicated a paint made from a small amount of finely ground pigment in a medium of linseed stand oil with or without the addition of resins. The definition has broadened and the term is now usually applied to a good quality high-gloss paint.

EXTENDER | A material that is added to paint for a number of reasons. These might range from cheapening the paint, to providing more bulk (as in an undercoat), to controlling consistency or to prevent settling.

FINISH | This has two meanings: a) a term used to describe the overall appearance of a finished work, for example 'matt', 'gloss' or 'sanded'; b) the final coat in a paint system.

FLAT OIL | An interior-grade oil-based paint designed to present little or no sheen. Now practically obsolete.

FLATTING | A technique for achieving a flat finish with an oil paint. Pigments were ground in turpentine and applied on a still tacky ground coat. This was an expensive process that resulted in a fragile finish.

FLATTING DOWN | The rubbing down of a painted or varnished surface with a fine abrasive in order to produce a matt or eggshell finish.

GLAZE | A clear or semi-transparent coating to which colour can be added to modify the previous coat. This can be used in the imitation of wood or marble or, with more body, for retaining the impression of a brush or tool to produce a paint effect. Sometimes known as scumble glaze.

GLUE SIZE | A weak adhesive made from animal bones, horns or skin. Used for several purposes in decorating, principally as a binder with chalk in soft distemper. Also employed in the making of 'clearcole' and as a cheap primer for plaster.

GOLD SIZE | A slow-drying material prepared from linseed stand oil and yellow ochre and designed to adhere gold leaf to a surface. It is produced with different drying times – typically 12 hours, 3 hours and 1 to 2 hours, but other speeds exist, too.

GRAINING | The imitation of natural wood using paints and glazes. The grain is imparted by special brushes or tools.

(GREEN) COPPERAS | Iron or ferrous sulphate. Sometimes mixed with limewater and applied as a wash to stone or render to give a gingery stone colour.

GROUND | Can have several meanings. a) The past tense of 'grind' – to reduce pigment particles to a state of uniform fineness; b) an opaque coat of paint below a glazed one; and c) an undercoat.

HIDING POWER | The opacity, or ability of a paint to cover the previous coat.

HORSE-MILL | The introduction of horse-mills in the early eighteenth century transformed the market, and the colourman was able to sell pigment ground in oil as a paste for less than he could when ground by hand.

JAPAN | A black enamel with a high sheen. Traditionally made with a bituminous black and varnish.

KNOTS | These are a common defect in timber. Knots occur where a branch has grown out of the trunk. A lot of knots means the timber is difficult to work and is weakened. Unless the surface is sealed, the resin that it contains can bleed and disrupt later coatings.

KNOTTING | A solution, usually based on shellac, designed to be applied to knots in timber in order to prevent resin from exuding and affecting the overlying paint film.

LACQUER | Originally referred to the sap of a tree native to China and employed to produce a varnish used on lacquer work. Many thin coats were applied to result in a durable film that took a fine polish. The term was later used to describe a glossy varnish.

LAKE COLOURS | Pigments made by precipitating soluble dyes onto a mineral base such as chalk and chemically bound to form an insoluble material. They tended to fade when exposed to sunlight.

LEAD CARBONATE | White lead or lead white. The main constituent of traditional oil paints.

LEAD PAINT | A paint made by grinding lead carbonate with linseed oil (usually). Employed in the decoration of houses from *c.* 1600 to *c.* 1960.

LEAD POISONING | Lead carbonate is toxic and poisoning can occur when it builds up in the body, often over a period of months or years. It was once a serious occupational hazard for those employed in the manufacture of lead or the application of paint.

LEVIGATION | The process of washing certain pigments in a series of tanks, each connected to the next and at a lower elevation than the previous one. The finer particles are carried down to the bottom tank with intermediate-sized ones being deposited at different stages on their way down.

LIME | Calcium oxide. Produced from naturally occurring calcium carbonate such as in chalk, limestone or seashells. When these are heated to a high temperature, the carbon dioxide is driven off and quicklime or calcium oxide is formed. This material is not stable and, when cooled, it will spontaneously react with carbon dioxide from the air until, after enough time, it will be completely converted back to calcium carbonate unless slaked with water to produce lime putty.

LIME PUTTY | The clay-like material formed when quicklime is slaked by the addition of water.

LIMEWASH | A cheap and simple form of coating for bricks, plaster or stonework. It has been used for thousands of years and is easily made. A basic limewash is made by slaking lime and adding enough water to give it the consistency of milk.

LINSEED OIL | A drying oil obtained by crushing the seeds of the flax plant. It was the principal oil used in the production of oil-based paints until recently. The 'raw' variety is the basic form and when heated with the addition of driers it becomes darker and is labelled 'boiled' linseed oil. The latter tended to be used in exterior paints, where speedier drying was desirable.

LINSEED STAND OIL | Stand oil is a thickened oil that is produced by heating a pale linseed oil without adding driers. It is very weather resistant and dries to a glossy film.

LITHARGE | A form of lead oxide used as a drier in oil paint.

MILK PAINT | A form of casein-bound water paint, where the milk and lime interact to produce a form of binder. There is no evidence that it saw much use in the United Kingdom.

MULLER AND SLAB | Traditionally made of marble or granite, but also found in glass. A cone-shaped implement (the muller) is used to grind pigment into oil on a flat slab. The purpose is to break down the pigment and to ensure that each particle is surrounded by oil.

MUNSELL COLOUR SYSTEM | A system of colour notation based on hue, value and chroma. Created by the American artist Albert H. Munsell in the early twentieth century.

NUT OIL | An oil obtained largely from the kernels of walnuts and hazelnuts and occasionally used where a very pale oil was required.

OCHRE | A range of earth pigments found all over the world consisting of a mix of silica, alumina and iron oxide. Colours range from lemon yellow through red to dark brown. It is prepared by grinding and levigation. Often the naturally occurring materials are referred to as 'ochres' and the synthesized forms as 'oxides'.

OFF-WHITE | A paint consisting of a white pigment such as chalk, or lead white, with small amounts of visible colouring matter (pigment) added. Sometimes, however, a very small quantity of blue or black was added to a white paint to make it appear 'whiter' (i.e. to appear white). It is often difficult to judge when pigment was added to correct the inherent yellowness of some paints or to impart a slight tint. At the other end of the scale, the difference between an off-white and a pale stone colour is minimal and, as a result, inconsistencies in description are likely to occur.

OIL-BOUND DISTEMPER (see Water Paint) | A water-based coating that has as its binder an emulsion of oil in water. It was supplied in paste form that had to be thinned and stirred before use. It provided a matt finish that was moderately permeable to moisture vapour but had the drawback of flaking when subjected to humidity and peeling when further coats were applied.

OXIDES | Synthesized ochres have been produced for hundreds of years, often as a by-product of other processes. Their chief advantages were more consistent colours, fewer impurities, cost and ease of manufacture.

PAINT | A liquid that is applied to a surface and is then converted to a solid film. Most commonly used to protect or to decorate an object and is composed of the colouring matter known as pigment, a vehicle to carry it, known as the medium or binder, and the diluent or solvent added to make it flow.

PAINT ANALYSIS | The examination of the paint layers applied to a series of representative elements within a room in order to establish how they looked in the past. Comparison of the samples also reveals physical changes that have taken place within the room.

PAINT RESEARCH | A combination of physical and documentary analysis in order to learn something about a building or structure.

PAINT SCRAPE | Also known as a 'scrape'. The process of scratching a painted surface with a sharp implement in order to learn something of previous colours. This is very imprecise and more often likely to confuse than to provide useful information.

PALETTE KNIFE | A knife with a flexible blade used for mixing small amounts of oil and pigment on a slab. Also used to scrape off the resultant paste.

PERMEABLE | A coating that allows a certain passage of moisture vapour. Useful on a plaster surface that is not entirely dry.

PICKING IN | The process of painting a particular area in a different colour than the background. This involves painting the area concerned first and then picking in around it with the background colour. The effect is subtly different to picking out.

PICKING OUT | This is the reverse of picking in. The background is painted first and then particular area is picked out in a different colour. The effect is subtly different to picking in.

PIGMENT | An insoluble substance that imparts colour to a paint. It may be naturally occurring or manufactured and have other characteristics, such as being fast or slow drying, or rust-inhibiting.

POPPY OIL | A very pale oil derived from the seeds of the white poppy, *Papaver somniferum* (opium poppy) and occasionally used where a pale oil was required. Very slow drying.

PRIMER | The initial coat of paint applied to a substrate. It should serve a number of functions: a) to seal the surface and prevent further absorption; b) to provide a surface that subsequent coats can adhere to; c) to form a barrier over chemically active surfaces; and d) to inhibit the rusting of ferrous metal surfaces.

PUMICE | A very light volcanic rock filled with tiny bubbles of gas to produce a material like honeycomb. It can be used as an abrasive, either as small lumps of smooth stone or as a powder.

QUICKLIME | Calcium oxide. Produced from naturally occurring calcium carbonate such as in chalk, limestone or seashells. When these are heated to a high temperature, the carbon dioxide is driven off and quicklime or calcium oxide is formed.

RAL RANGE | In 1927 the German *Reichs-Ausschuß für Lieferbedingungen und Gütesicherung* (Imperial Commission for Delivery Terms and Quality Assurance) created a collection of forty colours under the name of 'RAL 840'. This enabled certain colours to be specified by number. The first British Standard colour range was produced a few years later and both ranges have been developed ever since.

RESTORATION | Returning a place to a known earlier state by removing accretions or by reassembling existing elements without the introduction of new material.

REFURBISHMENT | The repair and redecoration of a building in order to improve its appearance.

ROSIN | A solid form of resin obtained from the pine tree and that could be dissolved into oil by a gentle heat. It was sometimes used to produce a shinier finish in the seventeenth and early eighteenth centuries.

ROTTENSTONE | A fine powdered porous rock used for polishing. It is usually weathered limestone mixed with diatomaceous, amorphous or crystalline silica and has rounded rather than sharp particles. It is used to achieve a more glossy polish after an initial treatment with coarser pumice powder.

SANDING | This has two meanings: a) the rubbing down of a surface with an abrasive before the application of a paint; and b) the strewing of washed fine sand onto a tacky paint in order to suggest the appearance and texture of stone.

SANDPAPER (glasspaper) | An early form of abrasive paper was available in the seventeenth century, but it was not until the 1830s that it was mass-produced.

SATIN | One of a number of terms used to describe a mid-sheen finish.

SCHEME | A series of coats of paints usually applied within days of each other when (re)decoration is carried out. A scheme in oil paint may consist of a primer (initially), one or two undercoats and a top/finish coat.

SCRAPE | See Paint Scrape.

SCUMBLE GLAZE | See Glaze.

SHELLAC | A resin secreted by an insect on trees in the forests of India and Thailand. It is processed and sold as dry flakes and dissolved in methylated spirit to make liquid shellac, which is used as 'knotting', as a spirit varnish and in French polishing.

SLAKING | The process of turning quicklime into lime putty by adding water.

SOFT DISTEMPER | A water-based coating based on whiting (chalk) and glue size. When dry it produced a matt finish that could be removed by washing (hence 'soft').

SOLVENT | A liquid added to paint in order to dissolve or disperse the film-forming constituents. The aim is to create a product that is easier to apply and that presents a smooth finish. The solvent evaporates after application.

STAND OIL | See Linseed Stand Oil.

STIPPLING | The striking of a surface that has just been painted or glazed with a special flat (stippling) brush in order to produce either a smooth effect (in paint) or a shaded effect (in glaze).

STONE COLOUR | A variety of colours ranging from off-whites to quite dark shades. Designed (broadly) to resemble the colour of stone in its many forms (e.g. Bath stone or Portland stone). The difference between a pale stone colour and an off-white is minimal and, as a result, inconsistencies in description are likely to occur.

TEREBINE | A type of metallic drier for oil paint.

THINNERS | See Solvent.

TRIPOLI | See Rottenstone.

TUNG OIL | Also known as China wood oil and is pale amber in colour. When heated it is very water and alkali resistant. Used in flat oil paints in the 1930s and later.

TURPENTINE (turps, white spirit) | A volatile fluid that dries by evaporation, leaving behind little or no resin, depending on its purity. It was added to oil paint in order to help make it flow. It was also employed in the process called 'flatting'.

UNDERCOAT | The coat of paint applied after the primer and before the top coat, or when repainting the first coat. Undercoats have 'body' and are applied to smooth out surfaces, to provide a sound base for the finish coat and often to help with the transition of colour.

VARNISH | A clear coating based on drying oils and natural resin. It was designed to protect a surface and generally had a high-gloss finish. The could be flatted down with fine abrasive in order to produce a matt finish.

VINEGAR | Acetic acid produced from either wine or cider and used in the production of lead carbonate.

WATER PAINT | The correct term for an oil-bound or casein-bound 'distemper'. A primitive emulsion paint that was superseded by emulsion.

WHITE | A paint made up of a white pigment such as chalk, or lead white, with no visible colouring matter (pigment) added. The overall effect would often have been off-white due to the inherent yellowness of the pigment and/or the medium.

WHITE COPPERAS | Zinc sulphate. Sometimes added to paint as a drier.

WHITE LEAD | See Lead Carbonate.

WHITEWASH | A water-based distemper consisting of whiting and bound with glue or casein.

WHITING | Crushed and washed chalk. The main constituent of 'soft distemper' and often added to oil paints as an extender.

BIBLIOGRAPHY

All works that were published appeared first in London, unless otherwise indicated.

Alletz, P. A. *L'Albert moderne: ou Nouveaux secrets éprouvés et licites, recueillis d'après les découvertes les plus récentes*. Paris. 1768.

Anon. *The Painter's and Varnisher's Pocket Manual*. 1825.

Anon. *The Plumber, Painter, and Glazier*. 1865.

Anon. *Valuable Secrets Concerning Arts and Trades*. 1775.

Arrowsmith, H.W. & A. *The House Decorator & Painter's Guide*. 1840

Barber, E. *Painter's, Grainer's, and Writer's Assistant; containing the colors and the quantity to be used in the imitation of fancy woods, marbles, granite, &c. connected with the patent granite and graining machine. etc*. 1852.

Bartholomew, A. *Specifications for Practical Architecture*. 1st edn. 1841. 2nd edn. 1846.

Baty, P. 'Palette of the Past'. *Country Life*, 3 September 1992. 44–47.

Baty, P. 'The Role of Paint Analysis in the Historic Interior.' *The Journal of Architectural Conservation*. March 1995.

Baty, P. 'To Scrape or Not to Scrape?' *Traditional Paint News*, Vol 1, No 2. October 1996. 9–15.

Baty, P. 'Some Tips on Commissioning Paint Analysis,' in *Layers of Understanding: Setting Standards for Architectural Paint Research*. Proceedings of a seminar held on 28 April 2000. Donhead Publishing, Dorset. 2002.

Baty, P. 'The Colour of Chelsea.' The Chelsea Society Report. The Chelsea Society. 2003. 61–67.

Baty, P. 'Inspired by the Past?' in *John Fowler. The Invention of the Country-House Style*, ed. Helen Hughes. Donhead, 2005. 31–40

Baty, P. 'Exterior Colour on the Smaller Town House" in *Materials & Skills for Historic Building Conservation*. Blackwell Publishing, Oxford. 2008. 200–211.

Beard, G. *Craftsmen & Interior Decoration in England, 1660–1820*. John Bartholomew. 1981.

Bersch, J. *The Manufacture of Earth Colours*. 1st German edn. 1918. Scott, Greenwood & Son. 1923.

Braham, W. W. *Modern Color / Modern Architecture*. Aldershot, Ashgate. 2002.

Bristow, I. C. 'The Balcony Room at Dyrham" in *National Trust Studies*. 1980.

Bristow, I. C., 'House Painting in Britain: Sources for American Paints, 1615 to 1830.' *Paint in America – The Colors of Historic Buildings*, ed. Moss, R. W. The National Trust for Historic Preservation, Washington, D.C. 1994. 42–53.

Bristow, I. C. *Architectural Colour in British Interiors 1615–1840*. Yale University Press. 1996.

Bristow, I. C. *Interior House-Painting Colours and Technology 1615–1840*. Yale University Press. 1996.

British Colour Council. *Dictionary of Colours for Interior Decoration*. 1949.

British Standards published by the British Standards Institution:

BS 381: 1930 Schedule of Colours for Ready Mixed Paints.

BS 2660: 1955 Colours for Building and Decorative Paints.

BS 4800: 1981 Paint Colours for Building Purposes.

BS 5252: 1976 Framework for Colour Co-ordination for Building Purposes.

BS 987C: 1942 Camouflage Colours.

'Colour in Buildings: A Scale for Use in Schools.' *The Builder*. 25 February 1949. 251–252.

'Colour in Schools: Factors which heighten the Effects of Visual Interest.' *The Builder*. 27 February 1953. 349–350.

Building Research Station. 'Distempers on Walls and Ceilings'. *Building Research Station Digest*. Garston, Watford, Herts. No 22. September, 1950.

Buck, S. L. 'Bedsteads Should Be Painted Green.' *Old-Time New England*. Vol 73, No 260. Fall 1995. 17–35.

Buck, S. L. 'Interpreting Paint Evidence on the Mount Lebanon Shaker Collection', *Shaker Furniture: The Art of Craftsmanship*. Art Services International: Alexandria, VA. 1995.

Buck, S. L. and Graham, W. 'Paints.' *The Cesapeake House: Architectural Investigation by Colonial Williamsburg*. ed. Carson and Lounsbury, University of NC Press. 2012.

Buck, S. L. 'Teaching Analysis of Architectural Paint Finishes Using Cross-section Microscopy Analysis Techniques'. *Proceedings from Architectural Paint Research: Sharing Information, Sharing Decisions Conference in Lincoln, UK*. London: Archetype. 2014.

Butcher, W. *Smith's Art of House-Painting*. 1821.

Campbell, R. *The London Tradesman*. 1747. Rpt. David & Charles. 1969.

Carrington, Noel. *Colour and Pattern in the Home*. Batsford. 1954.

Castel, L. B. *L'optique des couleurs : fondée sur les simples observations & tournée sur-tout à la pratique de la peinture, de la teinture & des autres arts coloristes*. Paris. 1740.

Chatfield, H. W.(ed.). *Paint and Varnish Manufacture*. George Newnes. 1955.

Chevreul, M. E. *The Laws of Contrast of Colour; and their Application to the Arts*. Translated from the French by John Spanton. 1857.

Clausen, H. 'Zinc-Based Pigments' in *Pigment Handbook*, Vol 1. New York. John Wiley & Sons. 1988.

Cotterell Brothers Ltd. *Catalogue No. 60*. Bristol. 1950.

Crease, J. *Hints for the Preservation of Wood Work Exposed to the Weather*. 1808.

Cruickshank Smith, J. *Oxide of Zinc, Its Nature, Properties and Uses*. The Trade Papers Publishing Co. Ltd. 1909.

Savory, C. 'A Decorator.' *The Paper Hanger, Painter, Grainer and Decorator's Assistant*. Kent & Co. 1879.

Donaldson, T. L. *Handbook of Specifications*. 1859.

Doonan, N. L. 'Historic Exterior Paints.' *Bulletin of the Association for Preservation Technology* (US). Vol xiv, No 4. 1982. 27–29.

Dossie, R. *The Handmaid to the Arts*. 2 vols. 1758. Rev. edn. 1796.

Elliot, J. *Practical House Painting*. The Incorporated Institute of British Decorators, Scottish Branch. 1910.

Elliott, T. *The Modern Painter: A Treatise on Painting, Gilding, Bronzing, Staining, Japanning, Varnishing, Polishing, Etc*. 1842.

Entwisle, E. A. *The Book of Wallpaper*. 1954.

Feller, R. L. 'Barium Sulfate – Natural and Synthetic.' *Artists' Pigments. A Handbook of Their History and Characteristics*. Vol 1. (ed.) Feller R. L. New York, Cambridge University Press. 1986. 47–64.

Fiedler, I. and Bayard, M. A. 'Emerald Green and Scheele's Green' in *Artist's Pigments*. Vol 3. ed. Elisabeth West FitzHugh. National Gallery of Art, Washington. 1997.

Field, G. *Rudiments of the Painters' Art, or a Grammar of Colouring*. 1850.

Fleury, P. *Nouvelles études de faux bois et marbres*. Paris. *c*. 1900.

Fleury, P. *Preparation and Uses of White Zinc Paints*. 1912

Fowler, J. and Cornforth, J. *English Decoration in the 18th Century*. Barrie & Jenkins. 1986. Rpt. of 1st edn. 1974.

Gage, J. *Colour and Culture: Practice and meaning from antiquity to abstraction*. Thames & Hudson. 1993.

Geeson, A. G. (ed.). *The Practical Painter & Decorator*. Virtue and Company Ltd. 1936.

Gerbier, B. *Counsel and Advise to all Builder*. 1663.

Gettens, R. J. and Stout. G. L. *Painting Materials, a Short Encyclopaedia*. New York: Dover Publications Inc. 1966.

Gettens, R. J., Feller, R. L. and Chase, W. T. 'Vermilion and Cinnabar' in *Artists' Pigments: A Handbook of Their History and Characteristics*. Vol 2. (ed. Roy, A.). Oxford, OUP. 1993.

Gloag, H. L. and Medd, D. L. 'Colour in Buildings.' *RIBA Journal*. June, 1956. 334–335.

Gloag, H. L. and Keyte, M. 'Rational Aspects of Colouring in Building Interiors.' *The Architects' Journal*. (1) 14 March 1957. 399–402 and (2) 21 March 1957. 443–448.

Gloag, H. L. and Keyte, M. 'Colour Coordination for the Manufacturer and User.' *Design*. No. 123. March 1959. 34–40.

Goethe, J. W. *Goethe's Theory of Colours*. (Facsimile edition of 1840 John Murray translation of 1810 work). Frank Cass and Company Ltd. 1967.

Goodier, J. H. *Dictionary of Painting and Decorating*. 3rd edn. Charles Griffin & Company Ltd. 1987.

Gunther, R. T. *The Architecture of Sir Roger Pratt*. Oxford, Clarendon Press. 1928.

Harley, R. *Artists' Pigments c. 1600–1835*. 2nd edn. Butterworths. 1982.

Harris, E. *British Architectural Books and Writers 1556–1785*. Cambridge, Cambridge University Press. 1990.

Hasluck, P. N. *Cassell's House Decoration. A Practical guide to Painters' and Decorators' Work*. 1913.

Hasluck, P. N. *House Decoration: Comprising Whitewashing, Paperhanging, Painting, etc*. 1897.

Hay, D. R. *A Nomenclature of Colours, Hues, Tints, and Shades, Applicable to the Arts and Natural Sciences; to Manufactures, and other Purposes of General Utility*. Edinburgh. 1845.

Hay, D. R. *The Laws of Harmonious Colouring adapted to Interior Decorations, with Observations on the Practice of House Painting*. 6th edn. William Blackwood and Sons. Edinburgh and London. 1847.

Hess, M. *Paint Film Defects, Their Causes and Cure*. Chapman & Hall Ltd. 1951.

Colvin, H. M. (ed. 1963–82). *History of the King's Works*. Vol V 1660–1782. HMSO. 1976.

Colvin, H. M. (ed. Crook, J. M and Port, M. H.). Vol VI 1782–1851. HMSO. 1973.

Hobhouse, H. *Thomas Cubitt; Master Builder*. Macmillan. 1971.

Holloway, J. G. E. *The Modern Painter and Decorator*. 3 Vols. Caxton Publishing Company Ltd. 1961.

Holley, C. D. *The Lead and Zinc Pigments*. Chapman & Hall Ltd. 1909.

Hurst, A. E. *Painting and Decorating*. Charles Griffin & Company Ltd. 1949.

Hurst, J. T. *Hurst's Architectural Surveyors' Hand Book*. 1886.

Ionides, B. *Colour and Interior Decoration*. Country Life. 1926.

Itten, J. *The Elements of Color*. Chapman & Hall. 1970.

Jennings, A. S. *House Painting*. Thomas Tofts. 1912.

Jennings, A. S. *Paint and Colour Mixing*. 3rd edn. 1907.

Jennings, A. S. *The Decoration and Renovation of the Home*. 1924.

Jennings, A. S. and Rothery, G. C. *The Modern Painter and Decorator*. Caxton Publishing Company. 1921.

Jenson & Nicholson (pub.). *Paint and its Part in Architecture*. 1930.

Jones, Bernard E. (edl) *House Painting and Decorating*. Cassell and Company. 1924 edn.

Keyte, M. 'The new British Standard colour range of building and decorative paints.' *The Architects' Journal*. 16 February 1956. 212–17.

Klein, A.B. *Colour-Music, the Art of Light*. Crosby Lockwood and Son. 2nd edn. 1930.

Koenig, J. C. *Droguerie, Speerei und Farbwaaren Lexicon*. Munich. 1851.

Koizumi, G. Lacquer Work. *A Practical Exposition of the Art of Lacquering with Valuable Notes for the Collector*. Sir Isaac Pitman & Sons Ltd. 1923.

Lancaster, Michael. *Britain in View. Colour and the Landscape*. Quiller Press. 1984.

Lancaster, Michael. *Colourscape*. Academy Editions. 1996.

Lange, Bente. *The Colours of Copenhagen*. The Royal Danish Academy of Fine Arts School of Architecture Publishers. 1997.

Lange, Bente. *The Colours of Rome*. The Danish Architectural Press and The Royal Danish Academy of Fine Arts School of Architecture Publishers. 1995.

Lawrance, James. *Painting from A to Z*. 1938 edn.

Laxton, W. R. *The Improved Builder's Price Book*. 2nd edn. 1818. 1869.

Leuchs, J. C. *Anleitung zur Bereitung aller Farben und Flüssigkeiten*. Nuremberg. 1825.

Lewis, P. A. *Pigment Handbook*. Vol 1. New York. John Wiley & Sons. 1988.

Libby, W. C. *Color and the Structural Sense*. New Jersey, Prentice-Hall Inc. 1974.

Linton, Harold. *Color Consulting*. New York, Van Nostrand Rheinhold. 1991.

Louw, Hentie. 'Colour Combinations.' *Architects' Journal*. July 1990. pp.44–53.

Lowe, Houston. *Paints for Steel Structures*. Chapman & Hall Ltd. 1910.

McTaggart, P. & A. *A Pigment Microscopist's Notebook*. 1985. 5th edn. 1990.

Mattiello, J. J. (ed.). *Protective & Decorative Coatings: Paints, Varnishes, Lacquers & Inks*. Vol 2. New York. John Wiley. 1942.

Medd, D. 'Colour in Buildings: A Scale for Use in Schools.' *The Builder*, 25 February 1949. 251–252.

Merret, C. *The Art of Glass*. 1662.

Ministry of Education (pub.). *Building Bulletin No 9*. 1953.

Mosca, M. J. 'Historic Paint Research: Determining the Original Colors.' *Old House Journal 9, No. 4*. 1981. 81–83.

Mosca, M. J. 'Pain Decoration at Mount Vernon.' in Moss, R. W. (ed.) *Paint in America: The Colors of Historic Buildings*. The National Trust for Historic Preservation. Washington, D.C. 1994. 105–127.

Morisot, M. R. J. *Tableaux détaillés des prix de tous les ouvrages du bâtiment*. Paris. 1804–1806.

Munsell, A. H. *A Color Notation*. 1905. 3rd edn Geo. H. Ellis Co. Boston, USA. 1913.

Murphy, S. F. (ed.). *Our Homes and How to Make them Healthy*. Cassell & Co. 1883.

Leybourn, W. *The Mirror of Architecture*. 4th edn. 1700.

Lowe, R. *Paints for Steel Structures*. 5th edn. New York: John Wiley & Sons. 1910.

Neve, R. (pseud. Philomath, T. N.). *The City and Countrey Purchaser, and Builder's Dictionary*. 1st edn. 1703. 2nd edn. 1726. 3rd edn. 1736.

Nicholson, P. *An Architectural Dictionary*. Vol II. 1819.

Nicholson, P. *The New Practical Builder*. 1823.

Ozenfant, A. 'Colour: The English Tradition.' *Architectural Review*, 81. January 1937. 41–44.

Ozenfant, A. 'Colour and Method.' *Architectural Review*, 81. February 1937. 89–92.

Ozenfant, A. 'Colour: Experiments, Rules, Facts.' *Architectural Review*, 81. April 1937. 195–198.

Ozenfant, A. 'Colour Solidity.' *Architectural Review*, 81. May 1937. 243–246.

Ozenfant, A. 'Colour in the Town.' *Architectural Review*, 81. July 1937. 41–44.

Ozenfant, A. 'Colour Pro Domo.' *Architectural Review*, 81. August 1937. 77–80.

Patmore, D. *Colour Schemes and Modern Furnishing*. The Studio. 1945.

Pain, W. and Pain, J. *British Palladio*. 1786.

Papworth, W. 'An Attempt to Determine the Periods in England, when Fir, Deal & House Painting were First Introduced.' *Transactions of the RIBA*. 1st series. Vol viii. 1–13. 1857–1858.

Pearce, Walter J. *Painting and Decorating*. Charles Griffin and Co. 1898.

Penn, T. Z. 'Decorative and Protective Finishes, 1750–1850: Materials, Process, and Craft.' M.A. diss., University of Delaware. 1966.

Pincot, J. *Pincot's Treatise on the Practical Part of Coach and House Painting*. c. 1811.

Philips, M. W. 'Discoloration of Old House Paints: Restoration of Paint Colors at the Harrison Gray Otis House, Boston.' APT Bulletin. Vol iii, No 4. 1971. 40–47.

Philips, M. W. 'Acrylic Paints for Restoration.' APT Bulletin. Vol xv, No 1. 1938. 3–11

Philips, M. W. 'The Repainting: Materials and Colors.' Philadelphia Museum of Art Bulletin. Vol 82, Nos 351–352. Summer 1986. 47–51.

Plot, R. *Natural History of Oxfordshire*. Oxford and London. 1677.

Porter, T. *Colour Outside*. The Architectural Press. 1982.

Primatt, S. *The City & Country Purchaser & Builder*. 1667.

Rea, J. T. *How to Estimate: being the Analysis of Builders' Prices giving full details of estimating for builders, and containing thousands of prices, and much useful memoranda*. 2nd edn. B. T. Batsford. 1904.

Riffault, Vergnaud and Toussaint. *Nouveau Manuel Complet du Peintre en batiments*. Paris. 1843.

Rivingtons (pub.). *Notes on Building Construction arranged to meet the requirements of the syllabus of the Science & Art Department of the Committee of Council on Education, South Kensington*. Part I and II.

Rűegg, A. (ed) *Polychromie architecturale: Le Corbusiers Farbenklaviaturen von 1931 und 1959*. Basel, Birkhäuser. 1997.

Sabin, A. H. *Red-Lead and How to Use it in Paint*. John Wiley. New York, USA. 3rd edn. 1920.

Salmon, W. *Palladio Londinensis*. 1734.

Savage, W. L. *Painting Ironwork Steel & Metal*. Austin Rogers & Co. c. 1930.

Smeaton, G. A. *The Painter's, Gilder's, and Varnisher's Manual*. c. 1827.

Smith, J. *The Art of Painting*. (*The Art of Painting in Oyl*.) 1676. 2nd edn. 1687. 5th edn. 1723; 9th edn. 1788.

Snelling, J. *Painting and Decorating Defects, Cause and Cure*. E. & F. N. Spon. 1966.

Société française des chrysanthémistes (pub.). *Répertoire de couleurs*. 1905.

The Shorter Oxford English Dictionary. 3rd edn., rev. Oxford. Clarendon Press. 1986.

Stalker, J. and Parker, G. *A Treatise of Japanning and Varnishing*. 1688.

Taylor, I. *Builder's Price Book*. 1813.

Taylor, J. S. *The Ostwald Colour Album*. Windsor & Newton. 1935.

Thornton, P. *Authentic Décor. The Domestic Interior 1620–1920*. Weidenfeld and Nicholson. 1984.

Tingry, P. F. *The Painter's and Varnisher's Guide*. 1804.

Tingry, P. F. *Painter's and Colourman's Complete Guide*. 1830.

Tressell, R. *The Ragged-Trousered Philanthropist*. 1914.

Tripard, V. *Ocres et peintures décoratives de Provence*. Aix-en-Provence, France. Edisud. 2001.

Trollope, A. *Barchester Towers*. 1857

van Alphen, M. *Paint Film Components*. National Environmental Health Forum Monographs, General Series No 2. Australia. 1998.

Vanherman, T. H. *Every Man his own House-Painter and Colourman*. 1829. (Originally published as: *The Painter's Cabinet, and Colourman's Repository*. 1828.)

Vanderwalker, F. N. *Painting and Decorating Working Methods*. 1922.

Wall, W. E. *Graining, Ancient and Modern*. Charles Griffin and Company Ltd. 1905.

Watin, J. F., *L'art du peintre, doreur, vernisseur*. Paris. 1753. Liege. nouvelle edn. 1778.

Welsh, F. S. 'Who is an Historic Paint Analyst? A Call for Standards'. *Bulletin of the Association for Preservation Technology*. Vol xviii, No 4. 1986. 4–5.

Welsh, F. S. 'The Early American Palette: Colonial Paint Colors Revealed' in, Moss, R. (ed.). *Paint in America: The Colors of Historic Buildings*. 1994.

Welsh, F. S. *Guidelines For Planning Architectural Finishes Investigations*. (They were issued as a special publication with Finish Notes ©, a biannual newsletter produced by the Frank S. Welsh company of Bryn Mawr, Philadelphia, USA, and appeared with the spring 1994 issue.) Philadelphia, USA. 1994.

Whittock, N. *The Decorative Painters', and Glaziers' Guide*. 1827.

Wilson, R. and Mackley, A. *Creating Paradise*. Hambledon. 2000.

Young, F. *Every Man his Own Mechanic*. c. 1890.

Zerr, G. and Rübencamp, R. *A. Treatise on Colour Manufacture*. Charles Griffin and Company. 1908.

SOURCES OF ILLUSTRATIONS

INDEX

ACKNOWLEDGMENTS

I would not be sitting here making a list of all those who have helped me with the book and my studies over the years without the inspiration of three individuals. First, my father Robert Baty, who passed on all that he had learnt during his many years running Papers and Paints and who guided me during my first decade in the business. Second, Dr Ian Bristow, the authority in the field of architectural color, who provided me with my Damascene moment at one of his early lectures and whose published works are unsurpassed and hugely valuable. And last, but by no means least, my wife, Alex, who has been a rock throughout and whose up-to-date knowledge of the subject is seldom recognized. So often do I turn to her for wise words.

The following have provided encouragement, advice and assistance, both recently and over the years:

Geoffrey Beard, David Beevers, William Braham, Charles Brooking, Emile de Bruijn, Susan Buck, Don Carpentier, Ed Chappell, the Marquess of Cholmondeley, Woody Clark, John Cornforth, Paul Cox, Josephine Darrah, Curt DiCamillo, Andrew Edmunds, Keith Edwards, Peter Farlow, Suzannah Fleming, Jonathan Foyle, Alan Gardner, Ian Gow, Susanne Groom, John and Eileen Harris, Ivan Hall, Michael Hall, Robert Harbord, Michael Harding, Catherine Hassall, Matthew Hollow, Helen Hughes, Paul Humphreys, Richard Ireland, Daniel Jackson, Douglas Kent, John Kenworthy-Browne, Jeff Klee, Robert Leath, Pamela Lewis, Cathy Littlejohn, Alexandra Loske, Sarah Lowengard, Andy Marshall, David Medd, Colin Mitchell-Rose, Kirsten Travers Moffitt, Matthew Mosca, Jeremy Musson, Dominic Myland, Peter Mactaggart, Allyson McDermott, Ken McFarland, John & Mark Nevin, Chris Ohrstrom, Roy Osborne, Ruth Padel, Steven Parissien, Neil Parkinson, James Peill, Morgan Phillips, Margaret Pritchard, Martin Redmond, Una & John Richards, Jacqueline Riding, Bill Rieder, Treve Rosoman, Andrew Saint, Libby Sheldon, Jet Shenkman, Matthew Slocombe, Harriet Standeven, Jamie Stewart, Reid Thomas, Nick Tyson, Jamie Vans, David Walker, Frank Welsh, Jen Westcott, John Wilton-Ely and Charles B. Wood. I am quite sure I shall be squirming with embarrassment at having forgotten someone, but whoever you may be, I am most grateful for any help that you may have given.

Willie Graham should be singled out for very generously providing me with many of the photographs of American houses. Indeed, my American friends have been generous beyond hope and neither my early work in the field nor this book would have been possible without them. I am grateful to the Colonial Williamsburg Foundation; the Mount Vernon Ladies' Association; the Museum of Early Southern Decorative Arts and the Historic Charleston Foundation for recent and earlier help. I am also indebted to my great friend Tom Savage, of the Winterthur Museum, Garden and Library, who has taught me so much about English houses over the years and been a generous and constant supporter.

Other organizations who have been helpful include the Worshipful Company of Painter-Stainers; the Georgian Group; the Handel House Museum; the Colour Reference Library; the National Trust; the Society for the Protection of Ancient Buildings; Spencer House and the Stowe House Preservation Trust.

Thanks too, to my many clients over the years who have given me the opportunity to learn more by working on their buildings.

Charlie Mounter is owed a very special debt of thanks, for it was she who originally contacted me to write a book and who was not going to be deterred by my initial lack of enthusiasm for such an idea. Indeed, she really ought to be added to the three leading lights.

The team at Thames & Hudson have been magnificent. Doubtless there were more than I met, but I am particularly grateful for the ideas, energy and guidance of Tristan de Lancey, Jane Laing, Susanna Ingram and Rose Blackett-Ord. All have worked tirelessly to produce what you see.